HOSPICE SOCIAL WORK

END-OF-LIFE CARE: A SERIES

End-of-Life Care: A Series
Series editor: Virginia E. Richardson

We all confront end-of-life issues. As people live longer and suffer from more chronic illnesses, all of us face difficult decisions about death, dying, and terminal care. This series aspires to articulate the issues surrounding end-of-life care in the twenty-first century. It will be a resource for practitioners and scholars who seek information about advance directives, hospice, palliative care, bereavement, and other death-related topics. The interdisciplinary approach makes the series invaluable for social workers, physicians, nurses, attorneys, and pastoral counselors.

The press seeks manuscripts that reflect the interdisciplinary, biopsychosocial essence of end-of-life care. We welcome manuscripts that address specific topics on ethical dilemmas in end-of-life care, death, and dying among marginalized groups, palliative care, spirituality, and end-of-life care in special medical areas, such as oncology, AIDS, diabetes, and transplantation. While writers should integrate theory and practice, the series is open to diverse methodologies and perspectives.

Joan Berzoff and Phyllis R. Silverman, *Living with Dying: A Handbook for End-of-Life Healthcare Practitioners*

Virginia E. Richardson and Amanda S. Barusch, *Gerontological Practice for the Twenty-first Century: A Social Work Perspective*

Ruth Ray, *Endnotes: An Intimate Look at the End of Life*

Terry Wolfer and Vicki Runnion, eds., *Dying, Death, and Bereavement in Social Work Practice: Decision Cases for Advanced Practice*

Mercedes Bern-Klug, ed., *Transforming End-of-Life Care in the Nursing Home: The Social Work Role*

HOSPICE SOCIAL WORK

DONA J. REESE

COLUMBIA UNIVERSITY PRESS   NEW YORK

COLUMBIA UNIVERSITY PRESS
Publishers Since 1893
New York   Chichester, West Sussex
cup.columbia.edu

Copyright © 2013 Columbia University Press
All rights reserved

Library of Congress Cataloging-in-Publication Data
Reese, Dona J.
  Hospice social work / Dona J. Reese
    p.   cm. — (End-of-life care)
  Includes bibliographical references and index.

  ISBN 978-0-231-13434-7 (cloth : alk. paper) — ISBN 978-0-231-13435-4 (pbk. : alk. paper) —
ISBN 978-0-231-50873-5 (e-book)

I. Social work with the terminally ill — United States. 2. Hospice care — United States.
3. Medical social work — United States. I. Title.

HV3001.A4R44 2013
362.17'560973 — dc23

This book is dedicated to
my son Christopher, who has brought immeasurable meaning
    to my life
my husband Henry, who makes us a family
my parents Donald and Joy Reese, of whom I am a combination
my students and colleagues in the field of hospice social work—
    oh, what a journey we have had!
and mostly to *my clients* at Coastal Hospice in Salisbury,
    Maryland, who taught me more than I ever taught them

CONTENTS

Acknowledgments ix

1. End-of-Life Care in the United States   1
   From Dying at Home to Dying in the Hospital   1
   Rise of the Hospice Movement   3
   Professional Standards for End-of-Life Medical Care   6
   Hospice Model of Care   7
   Hospice Outcomes   8
   Euthanasia and Assisted Suicide   9
   Advance Directives   12
   Current Status of End-of-Life Care in the U.S.   15

2. Current Status of Social Work in Hospice   30
   Lack of Full Utilization of Social Workers on the Interdisciplinary Team   30
   Documentation of Social Work Outcomes   32
   End-of-Life Care Content in Social Work Education   40
   Impact of Efforts to Develop the Field   46

3. A Model for Psychosocial and Spiritual Care in Hospice   54
   Overview of Theory   54
   A Model for Practice   55

4. Hospice Social Work Practice on the Micro Level   76
   Biopsychosocial/Spiritual Assessment and Intervention   76
   Spirituality in Hospice Social Work   119

5. Mezzo Context of Hospice Social Work: Work with Families,
   Groups, and Interdisciplinary Teams   170
   Families   170

Group Intervention in Hospice Social Work   189
Working with Interdisciplinary Teams   193

6. Macro Context of Hospice Social Work: Organization, Community, and Larger Society   221
Deep Ecology   221
Hospice Social Work Intervention at the Organizational Level   223
Hospice Social Work Intervention at the Community Level   230
Emerging Global Issues in End-of-Life Care   235
Policy Practice   235

7. Cultural Competence in Hospice   241
Hospice Philosophy and Diverse Cultural Beliefs — Many Differing
World Views   242
Barriers Within the Hospice Itself   254
Barriers Within the Health Care System   265
Attempts to Address Health Care System Barriers   270
Personal Preparation for Culturally Competent Practice   273
Cultural Competence Training   274
Culturally Competent Micro-Level Practice in Hospice   277

8. Personal Preparation and Social Worker Self-Care   289
Need for Personal Preparation   289
Approach to Personal Preparation   291

9. Future Challenges in the Field of Hospice Social Work:
Looking Ahead   301
Further Needs for Research   302
Further Clarification of Social Work Roles   304
Responsibility for Macro Advocacy   306
Social Work Education Needs   308
Future Vision for the Role of Hospice Within Palliative Care   310

Appendix A. Social Work Assessment Tool   315
Appendix B. Standards for Palliative and End-of-Life Care:
National Association of Social Workers   333
Appendix C. Team Functioning Scale   335
Index   337

ACKNOWLEDGMENTS

I would like to thank the students, colleagues, collaborators, and community leaders who were with me on this journey of learning, and contributed to now precious memories of the development of the work that is woven together in this book. These include my Southern Illinois University students Sarah Cox, Andrea Curtis, Jessica Davis, Paula Ford, Claudette Henderson, and Eugene Kepner; my University of Arkansas students Charlotte Butler, Karen Ciaravino, Elizabeth Melton, Jolanda Nally, Michelle Smith, and Michele Wise-Wright; my University of Illinois students Robin Ahern, Dean Brown, Shankar Nair, Joleen O'Faire, and Claudia Warren; and my University of North Dakota students Chris Rosaasen, Jennifer Schlinger, and Diane Wiersgalla.

Thank you to my Hong Kong collaborators Cecilia Chan and Wallace Chan, and to my predecessor as Leader of the Social Worker Section at the National Hospice and Palliative Care Organization, Mary Raymer. There, with national hospice social work leaders Samira Beckwith, Susan Gerbino, Ruth Huber, Stacy Orloff, Joan Richardson, and Mary-Ann Sontag, we made great strides. Also I was privileged to work with national hospice leaders Stephen Connor, Kathy Egan, Donna Kwilosz, and Dale Larson, with whom I explored ways to develop a high functioning interdisciplinary team.

Thanks to Larry Braden, the visionary hospice medical director of a hospice in Camden, Arkansas, and to the leaders of culturally diverse community groups in Champaign, Illinois; Fayetteville, Arkansas; and Carbondale, Illinois, who partnered with me and have created greater hospice access for African Americans and Latino/as in their communities. And thanks to my academic colleagues at Southern Illinois University—Connie Baker, Sarah Buila, Elaine Jurkowski, and Judy McFadden; my colleague Mark Kaplan at Portland State University, and David Perry at University of North Dakota. Thanks to Virginia Richardson, the editor of the End-of-life series at Columbia University Press, who invited me on this journey, and provided constant encouragement and kept believing in me. And finally, thanks to my graduate assistant Liz Garrett, who helped put the whole thing together. The wonderful adventure of working with all of you has brought great meaning to my life.

HOSPICE SOCIAL WORK

1

END-OF-LIFE CARE IN THE UNITED STATES

This chapter discusses the history of our approach to death and dying in the United States of America. We will discuss the trend toward life-sustaining treatment in the U.S., then the development in the 1970s of the hospice philosophy, which encouraged palliative rather than curative care in terminal illness. We will discuss implications for health care costs, Medicare and Medicaid coverage of hospice, with resulting advantages and disadvantages in policy issues and barriers for utilization, including by some ethnic and racial communities. We will discuss the development of the field of palliative care and ethical issues surrounding passive and active euthanasia or physician-assisted suicide. We will discuss advance directives as a way to clarify patient wishes and uphold patient self-determination. We will conclude with a discussion of policy that covers some recommendations for policy change in the field of hospice and end-of-life care.

FROM DYING AT HOME TO DYING IN THE HOSPITAL

During the first half of the twentieth century in the United States, people typically died at home, cared for by family members. The death of loved ones was a familiar experience, not one to be kept out of sight and awareness. Death was expected as a natural part of life, and religious beliefs about the nature of the afterlife helped many cope with their own deaths or those of loved ones. End-of-life care decisions were made by physicians who had a long-standing and close relationship with their patients (Harper 2011).

Medical advances in the second half of the century, however, made us think life could be prolonged indefinitely. The major infectious diseases could be controlled through medication, and surgical techniques were developed to control other life-threatening illnesses. Patients whose hearts stopped beating could be resuscitated. The well-loved family doctor gave way to doctors unknown to the patient providing aggressive end-of-life care in the hospital (Reith and Payne 2009; Silverman 2004).

The result of these advances was to increase the lifespan from forty-seven years in 1900 to seventy-four years for men and seventy-nine for women in 2004 (Social Security Online 2004). Religious beliefs gave way within the dominant cultural group to the belief that doctors held the key to life and death. At the same time, families felt morally obligated to access all available medical treatments, regardless of the likelihood of effectiveness (Blacker 2004; Buckey and Abell 2010; Forbes, Bern-Klug, and Gessert 2000) and regardless of the cost (Arons 2004).

Thus, today, only 38 percent of deaths occur in hospice (Jennings et al. 2003), with many others occurring in hospitals and nursing homes rather than at home (*Quality of Life Matters* 2004; Silverman 2004), and with the patient surrounded by technology instead of by loved ones. Regardless of the likelihood that patients will recover from life-threatening conditions, physicians attempt to save and prolong their lives through full use of technology or *life-sustaining treatment*. Even with a *terminal prognosis* (a prediction that the patient will not recover from the illness, but will die from it within six months), they often do not provide *palliative care* (treatment with the goal of comfort and control of symptoms rather than cure) until death is imminent (Blacker 2004; Silverman 2004).

QUALITY OF LIFE IN END-OF-LIFE CARE

This prolonged life has not necessarily been experienced as a good quality of life, however, but has resulted in increased numbers of people living in a serious, debilitated state. Many of these are without adequate pain control, wish for but do not receive physician contact, and do not receive adequate emotional support (Peres 2011; Silverman 2004). In addition, patients may be treated with a lack of respect (*Quality of Life Matters* 2004). Loss of dignity during the dying process has been linked with psychological and symptom distress, heightened dependency needs, and loss of the will to live (Chochinov et al. 2002).

Patients who are resuscitated may have to live on life support, including ventilators to allow them to breathe and artificial nutrition and hydration to allow them to gain nourishment. The continued life may be spent undergo-ing surgery and painful treatments that have little chance of improving the patient's condition. At the same time, patients who do not improve may be regarded as failures and avoided by health care professionals (Silverman 2004). In addition, physicians may fail to inform patients of their prognosis and all options for curative and palliative care (Arons 2004). Without knowl-edge of one's prognosis and treatment options, a patient is unable to exercise informed consent. This in turn compromises patient self-determination. For these reasons, a number of authors consider end-of-life care in the U.S. to-day to be inadequate (Kramer, Hovland-Scafe, and Pacourek 2003).

Health care costs have also been a major social problem in the U.S. for decades. The next section will focus on the implications of end-of-life care for the cost of health care in America.

IMPLICATIONS FOR HEALTH CARE COSTS

Costs of this futile treatment have detrimental affects on individuals, families, and our nation (Baily 2011). During the dying process, many families lose most or all of their savings (Reith and Payne 2009). One-third of all health care dollars in the United States are spent on medical care in the last two years of life (Goldberg and Scharlin 2011). Skyrocket-ing costs have made it difficult for U.S. companies to compete on the world market, due to translation of employee health insurance expenses into product prices. The impact on our nation has led some authors to argue that patient self-determination, in terms of choosing the option of curative care, is overemphasized to the detriment of the common good (Baily 2011). Managed care health insurance companies have changed the face of medicine when physicians could not, increasingly refusing to cover "futile care." The next section discusses an alternative perspective, the hospice philosophy.

RISE OF THE HOSPICE MOVEMENT

DEVELOPMENT OF THE HOSPICE PHILOSOPHY

A movement founded in the 1960s in England by Dame Cicely Saunders, and continuing in the 1970s in the United States through the work of

Elisabeth Kubler-Ross, began to advance a new set of values. Saunders founded St. Christopher's Hospice in London in 1967 (www.stchristophers.org.uk). Trained as a social worker, nurse, and physician, she promoted a holistic model of care provided by an interdisciplinary team.

This treatment was focused not on *curative treatment*, with the goal of curing the patient's disease, but on *palliative care*, aimed at promoting quality of life during death and dying: "You matter to the last moment of your life, and we will do all we can, not only to help you die peacefully, but to live until you die" (Dame Cicely Saunders, quoted by AScribe Newswire 2005). The focus was on *palliative care*, the treatment of symptoms rather than the disease.

Death with dignity and patient self-determination are cornerstones of this new perspective. In the face of terminal illness, the patient chooses comfort rather than cure, palliative care or palliation of symptoms rather than curative care aimed at eradication of the disease. The goal is to focus on enjoying one's remaining days and to make legal, emotional, and spiritual preparations for death. Death is accepted as a natural part of life. In the U.S., hospice philosophy is oriented toward death in the home, surrounded by loved ones and an environment arranged according to the patient's wishes. The interdisciplinary hospice team provides holistic care that addresses the physical, psychological, social, and spiritual needs of the patient and significant others (Black 2007). The focus is on advocating for the patient's individual preferences, despite family or physician opinions to the contrary. The patient has rights to information about her prognosis and to make decisions about end-of-life care based on this information. Until her death at St. Christopher's Hospice in 2005, Saunders promoted these values, which came to be known as the hospice philosophy, a new perspective that led to significant changes in end-of-life care around the world.

DEFINITIONS   The National Association of Social Workers (NASW 2011) has provided some definitions that are helpful in distinguishing between several types of care in terminal illness. *End-of-life care* is defined by NASW as "multidimensional assessment and interventions provided to assist individuals and their families as they approach end of life" (p. 4). End-of-life care decisions vary greatly and can include curative care or palliative care, with or without advance directives. Decisions may be made by patients or left to family members and are influenced by psychosocial, spiritual, and cultural factors. End-of-life care may include hospice or palliative care.

Palliative care is defined by NASW (2011) as an approach that focuses on quality of life through prevention and relief of suffering on physical, psychosocial, and spiritual levels. Palliative care offers relief of symptoms when no cure is possible. It may be offered in chronic illness as well as in terminal illness. *Hospice* is a form of palliative care that is offered specifically in terminal illness (Reith and Payne 2009).

DEVELOPMENT OF HOSPICE IN THE UNITED STATES

Shortly after the founding of St. Christopher's, Elisabeth Kubler-Ross, a physician critical of the inhumane treatment of dying patients, became a leader of the hospice movement in the U.S. Her groundbreaking book, *On Death and Dying* (1970), became a best seller and influenced public opinion in the U.S. and globally.

The first U.S. hospice was established in 1971, in Branford, Connecticut, by a team from Yale University consisting of a nurse, two pediatricians, and a chaplain. In 1972 Kubler-Ross testified in front of the Senate, the first of a series of efforts to promote the hospice concept.

Also in 1972, the American Hospital Association developed the "Patient Bill of Rights." This statement provided for the patient's right to make choices relating to types of treatment received, including the right to refuse treatment, to refuse life-sustaining measures, and to terminate treatment. It also provided for the patient's right to all comfort measures. Finally, the patient had the right to know the truth of his condition.

Because of this model, hospice proponents were able to show that home care was less expensive than institutional care, leading to Medicare reimbursement for hospice under the Tax Equity and Fiscal Responsibility Act in 1982 (Harper 2011). Medicare coverage has had a major influence on the care of the dying, as 85 percent of people who die in the U.S. each year are covered by Medicare (Werth and Blevins 2002).

The Medicare Hospice Benefit transformed hospice philosophy into federal regulation, requiring an interdisciplinary approach that includes physician, nursing, home health aide, social work, and spiritual care. The benefit covers prescription medication, medical supplies and equipment, short-term care in an inpatient setting (e.g., for pain and symptom control or caregiver respite), and bereavement counseling for significant others after the patient's death. For each day the patient is enrolled under the Medicare Hospice Benefit, the hospice receives a per diem amount.

In order to receive the benefit, a patient has to be terminally ill, with a physician certifying a prognosis of six months or less. A patient can cancel enrollment in hospice any time and then reenter if she still has a six-month prognosis. A patient can remain in hospice longer than six months if the certifying physician still believes that she has a prognosis of less than six months. Any diagnosis is eligible, although cancer has been the primary diagnosis of patients served, due to the greater ability to predict the course of illness of a cancer diagnosis.

The focus of the Medicare Hospice Benefit was to save money, and thus eligibility limitations are imposed. While enrolled in hospice, the patient must agree to forego curative or life-sustaining treatments and be cared for at home by a significant other.

In 1986 states were given the option to include a hospice benefit within Medicaid programs. Thus hospice care was now available for nursing home residents. This had a major impact, since 35 percent of older adults use nursing home care in the last year of life (Werth and Blevins 2002). Medicaid provides health and long-term care to individuals with low incomes (including those who have been impoverished by health care costs). Not all states cover hospice under Medicaid though. In 1995 the military began to offer hospice benefits to family members.

The hospice movement has continued to grow, with the National Hospice and Palliative Care Organization (NHPCO) reporting a yearly increase in the number of operating hospices nationwide. In 2008 there were more than 4,850 hospices in the U.S. that served 1.45 million people. It is estimated that 38.5 percent of deaths occur within hospice care (NHPCO 2009). The next section will discuss standards for end-of-life care.

PROFESSIONAL STANDARDS FOR END-OF-LIFE MEDICAL CARE

Care that addresses quality of life is now increasingly recognized as an ethical obligation of health care providers, and several expert-developed descriptions of such care exist. In 2001 the Institute of Medicine described quality end-of-life care in terms that reflected the hospice philosophy. These parameters for a good death include a death that is free from avoidable distress and suffering for patients, families, and caregivers, in general accord with patients' and families' wishes and reasonably consistent with clinical, cultural, and ethical standards (Roff 2001). Similarly, in 2003 Robert Wood Johnson developed quality indicators for end-of-life care that reflected a hospice perspective, including emotional, spiritual, and practical support and adequate symptom control.

Singer and colleagues (Singer, Martin, and Kelner 1999) have also contributed in this area by developing a framework based on the perspectives of patients and families. They have identified five domains important to "quality end-of-life care": receiving adequate pain and symptom management, avoiding inappropriate prolongation of dying, achieving a sense of control, relieving burden, and strengthening relationships with loved ones. Farber, Egnew, and Farber (2004) add to this discussion the alternative term *respectful death*, in which a caregiver's perception of what constitutes a "good death" is not imposed upon the patient, but rather the patient's agenda and individual experience is respected. This perspective on care is reflected in the hospice model of care, discussed in the following section.

HOSPICE MODEL OF CARE

Patients are admitted to a hospice program when medical science can offer no cure to them and, in all likelihood, they are expected to die within six months. The patient is aware of the prognosis at admission and agrees to a program of palliative care aimed toward comfort rather than cure. The goal of patient comfort is taken seriously, and hospice staff is highly skilled in symptom control. Enrollment in a hospice program does not mean that the patient will not receive treatment needed for comfort; chemotherapy and radiation may even be used to control pain, and many other treatments are available to control the symptoms of terminally ill patients. However, treatment is not aimed at curing the terminal illness, since it has already been determined that the illness cannot be cured through medical science.

In the United States most hospice care can be, and is, provided in the patient's home. In addition, some hospices have inpatient units or contract for facilities that serve patients who have no primary caregiver who can care for them at home. Hospice services are increasingly provided in nursing homes as well (Reith and Payne 2009), but are underutilized (Chapin et al. 2007). The hospice program provides medical, psychosocial, and spiritual care for the patient through an interdisciplinary, holistic approach. Members who serve on the interdisciplinary team and develop treatment plans for patients include social workers, nurses, home health aides, clergy, physicians, volunteers, administrators, and other professionals as needed. Although each member has an area of expertise, all members address all aspects of care in contacts with the patient and family.

The origins of hospice in a volunteer grassroots movement are still felt today. Hospices provide volunteers who assist in many aspects of hospice care and administration. Volunteers sit with patients while family caregivers take a break or attend other responsibilities, volunteers run errands, provide transportation, bereavement counseling, or clerical duties at the hospice, among many other contributions. The tradition of serving patients without charge is still honored as well; many hospices will serve patients regardless of ability to pay.

In this section we have described the way hospice care is delivered. The next section will discuss evidence regarding the outcomes of patients and families who receive these services.

HOSPICE OUTCOMES

Research has indicated that terminally ill patients served by hospice experience more positive outcomes than those receiving other types of care at the end of life. In comparisons with patients being actively treated for cancer (Harper 2011), hospice patients had a lower incidence of anxiety and grief. It may be theorized that the psychosocial care these patients received helped to allay these feelings. In another study Teno and colleagues (2004) found that family members of patients receiving home hospice services were more satisfied than those dying in an institutional setting or with home health services. Nonhospice patients had high levels of unmet needs for symptom control, physician communication, emotional support, and being treated with respect by health care professionals (Teno et al. 2004). Similar findings were obtained in a comparison of terminally ill African American patients who did or did not receive hospice services (Reese et al. 2004). Other studies have found that in nursing homes hospice patients received better pain control than nonhospice patients and often live longer than those with the same diagnosis who did not choose hospice (Reith and Payne 2009). The next section provides an overview of passive euthanasia, active euthanasia, and assisted suicide.

EUTHANASIA AND ASSISTED SUICIDE

PASSIVE EUTHANASIA

Passive euthanasia, which characterizes hospice care in states in which assisted suicide is illegal, involves *withholding* curative or life-sustaining treatment in the case of terminal illness. In passive euthanasia health care providers allow death to occur naturally, without providing life-sustaining treatment or "heroic efforts" to prolong the patient's life.

Passive euthanasia also includes *withdrawing* care, in the case of a patient receiving life support but without hope of improved quality of life. Courts and philosophers don't distinguish between withholding or withdrawing life-sustaining treatment, but withdrawing care is far more controversial, as landmark court cases indicate. Withdrawal from treatment, such as removal of life support, is considered by many citizens as more aggressive than the withholding of treatment, on a par with assisted suicide (Altilio 2011).

The cases of twenty-one-year-old Karen Ann Quinlan in 1975 and Nancy Cruzan in 1983 promoted public acceptance of passive euthanasia. Ms. Quinlan lost consciousness after overdosing on alcohol and tranquilizers. Physicians resuscitated her, but she suffered brain damage and lapsed into a "persistent vegetative state." Her family fought a legal battle, and finally won, for the right to remove her from life support.

Nancy Cruzan entered a persistent vegetative state after an auto accident and was kept alive only by a feeding tube. For the right to remove that feeding tube, Ms. Cruzan's family took their case all the way to the U.S. Supreme Court, which ruled that the Cruzans had not provided "clear and convincing evidence" that Nancy Cruzan did not wish to have her life artificially preserved. The family later presented evidence of Ms. Cruzan's wishes to the Missouri courts, which allowed them to remove the feeding tube in 1990.

ACTIVE EUTHANASIA AND ASSISTED SUICIDE

Active euthanasia involves deliberately administering medical treatment that causes the death of the patient. In assisted suicide the patient, upon her own request and after an assessment to determine her competence to make this decision, is provided with a lethal dose of medication. The patient self-administers this medication, thereby committing suicide. According to a 1997 Gallup Poll, most Americans by that point supported the legalization of assisted suicide.

Some consider assisted suicide to represent active euthanasia, in which deliberate medical treatment is provided, which leads to death. Proponents of assisted suicide disagree, however. They point out that in assisted suicide a lethal dose of medication is self-administered. This makes assisted suicide different from active euthanasia, in which a physician provides the fatal treatment (Reith and Payne 2009).

Patients' requests for assisted suicide are often motivated by physical symptoms and functional losses related to illness, loss of sense of self, and fears about the future (Reith and Payne 2009). There is some evidence, however, that somatic pain is not as strong a factor in a patient's request for assisted suicide as is emotional pain and loneliness (Schroepfer 2008; van Baarsen 2008). Depression, lack of social support, and lack of hope are determining factors; other findings have indicated, though, that depression was not a factor and that the main motivator for a request for assisted suicide was control and autonomy (Reith and Payne 2009). There is evidence and argument, however, that requests for assisted suicide may be withdrawn when patient concerns are identified and addressed (van Baarsen 2008).

In 1997 the U.S. Supreme Court ruled that mentally competent terminally ill people do not have a constitutional right to physician-assisted suicide, leaving the issue up to the states. Assisted suicide of patients within hospice programs was legalized through Oregon's Death with Dignity Act in 1995 and then again in 1997. In response to Oregon's law, Attorney General John Ashcroft issued a directive criminalizing physician-assisted suicide. This ruling was overturned by federal court in 2004, however. Passage of Oregon's law has led to similar efforts in other states, and Montana and Washington legalized physician-assisted suicide in 2008.

In contrast, some states have passed laws criminalizing assisted suicide. In 1996 the U.S. Circuit Court of Appeals overruled such a law in New York State. In addition, Congress passed legislation barring taxpayer dollars from financing physician-assisted suicide. Roff (2001) suggested that the establishment of federal standards, rather than allowing states authority in this matter, may help to resolve the debate. Unsurprisingly, in addition to the legal debates occurring around these issues, ethical dilemmas occur for clients and health care providers. This will be discussed in the next section.

ETHICAL DILEMMAS

Ethical dilemmas occur when there are conflicts between value constellations. Professional codes of ethics, societal conventions, religious beliefs, laws, and family traditions, among others, may conflict with each other. Conflicting values may also be contained within one value constellation.

Several ethical dilemmas arise within passive or active euthanasia. Client self-determination is an important value in both hospice philosophy and the Code of Ethics of the National Association of Social Workers. It is a value also contained within the Patient Bill of Rights and the Patient Self-Determination Act. In a case where a patient refuses life-sustaining treatment or requests assisted suicide, however, the value of client self-determination conflicts with the medical profession's value of professional beneficence and nonmalificence. The Hippocratic Oath commits physicians to do no harm and to make decisions for the benefit of his patients. The physician may invoke "therapeutic privilege" and make decisions without discussion with the patient, if, in the judgment of the doctor, the patient would become worse if informed of the prognosis. In the same situation, the value of quality of life, as well as law about informed consent, conflicts with the religious value of sanctity of life. These are ethical principles that we all agree to, but how do we translate them into practice?

There are two major perspectives regarding how to rank these values and decide what is most important in a given situation. The *deontological principle* relies on duty, law, rules, based on an a priori agreement on essential facts. Proponents have a perspective about what is right to do, about the intrinsic morality of an act. This perspective is not concerned with consequences of the act. From this perspective, a terminally ill person would be resuscitated and placed on life support, because saving life is the right thing to do, regardless of the suffering of the patient or the financial impact on society.

An alternative perspective is the *utilitarian principle*. The focus of this perspective is the consequences of an action. Concern is for society as a whole rather than the individual; proponents aim toward the greatest good for the greatest number of people. From this perspective, it would be considered better not to resuscitate the patient, based on concern for quality of life and cost of a treatment that is considered futile. The money saved by withholding futile treatment can be used instead to provide a basic level of care for all Americans. The treatment may even be withheld for patients who request it—insurance companies may not cover the cost of futile treatment, and some physicians do not believe it is appropriate to provide futile care. A drawback of this approach is a lack of agreement about what is best for society, necessitating choosing the majority opinion. This approach may thus fail to honor minority opinions.

Some ethicists have tried to find a middle ground between the two poles, arguing that one must consider both the ultimate ends and the intrinsic morality of the action. Ethics committees established in hospitals struggle to resolve these value conflicts. As discussed earlier, these decisions have been the subject of court battles and news headlines as our culture struggles to come to terms with end-of-life care in an age in which life can be sustained in the absence of quality of life. One approach to resolving these questions has been in the effort to establish advance directives.

ADVANCE DIRECTIVES

A situation in which ethical decisions become particularly difficult is when the patient is incapacitated and unable to make his wishes known. In 1990 the federal government addressed this issue through the Patient Self-Determination Act. Under this law, hospitals, skilled nursing facilities, home health agencies, hospice programs, and health maintenance organizations that participated in the Medicare or Medicaid programs were required to develop policies and procedures, keep chart documentation, and inform and educate patients, family members, and staff about the patient's rights under state law to prepare *advance directives*.

Advance directives include *living wills, medical powers of attorney*, and *do not resuscitate* orders. A living will is a legal document prepared by the patient which specifies the patient's wishes regarding life-sustaining treatment. A medical power of attorney establishes a legal right for a designated surrogate to make health care decisions for the patient if the patient is physically or mentally unable to do so. A do not resuscitate (DNR) order expresses the patient's wish not to receive cardiopulmonary resuscitation at the point of death. Under the Patient Self-Determination Act, providers must ask patients whether they have executed an advance directive and document the existence or nonexistence of patients' preferences in their medical records.

ADVANCE DIRECTIVES POLICY CONSIDERATIONS

Despite the Patient Self-Determination Act, in practice many people die without self-determination in end-of-life care preferences. This law has been controversial, and its enforcement is questionable (Arons 2004; Werth and Blevins 2002). In general, fewer than 25 percent of Americans have established advance directives (Arons 2004). This is especially true among younger individuals, men, and individuals representing diverse cultural and economic groups (Galambos 1998).

Providers struggle to resolve how to comply with this law, and compliance may be limited to inquiry about established advance directives and provision of a pamphlet by an admissions clerk. Questions asked at admission have not resulted in many advance directives being established, even when the admissions interview is with a social worker (Happ et al. 2002). Health care providers are compliant with providing information and developing policies, but not in documenting patients' preferences in their charts or in complying with these preferences (Galambos 1998).

BARRIERS TO ESTABLISHING ADVANCE DIRECTIVES

In the absence of an advance directive, physicians may fear liability (Reith and Payne 2009) and feel obligated to provide life-sustaining treatment. States may have requirements for resuscitation outside the hospital unless an advance directive is produced (Keigher 1994). Barriers to establishing advance directives include ineffective methods of promoting advance directives and lack of communication between patients and their physicians and family members (Bomba, Morrissey, and Leven 2011).

INEFFECTIVE METHODS OF PROMOTING ADVANCE DIRECTIVES   Questioning by an admissions clerk has not proven to be effective in promoting the use of advance directives. An approach that was extremely successful in a home health agency, in contrast, involved a social work visit in the home to discuss end-of-life issues. In this project eighty-three of ninety-four participants were willing to complete an advance care planning process in their homes, and many enrolled in hospice after this process (Ratner, Norlander, and McSteen 2001). Multiple social work sessions with clients should be held, geared toward the individual's values (Reith and Payne 2009). Galambos (1998) recommends that public education about advance directives needs to begin when individuals are still young and healthy, and Arons (2004) advocates for social workers to become involved in policy practice in this area. Bomba, Morrissey, and Leven (2011) have developed and tested a Community Conversations on Compassionate Care Program that they found to be successful in encouraging individuals to complete advance directives.

LACK OF PATIENT-PHYSICIAN COMMUNICATION   Physicians fail to inform patients and families about the natural progression of a disease and the quality of life that likely will accompany it (Zilberfein and Hurwitz 2004); thus the patient is unable to give "informed" consent. The inequality of the patient-physician relationship creates an atmosphere in which patient preferences are not sought by the physician (Arons 2004). Physicians place orders to limit therapy in the patient's chart without discussion with the patient (Levin et al. 1999); perhaps this partially reflects a value on physician authority rather than patient self-determination.

LACK OF PATIENT-FAMILY COMMUNICATION   There is also a lack of communication between patients and family members and friends about end-of-life care wishes (Bomba, Morrissey, and Leven 2011). End-of-life care decisions tend to be collaborative (Keigher 1994), made at the time of the illness rather than in advance, and patients tend to leave decisions up to loved ones rather than communicating preferences. Providers have expressed doubt that this surrogate decision making accurately reflects patient wishes (Neuman and Wade 1999). Sutton and Liechty (2004) suggest that support groups may be helpful in allowing patients and loved ones to develop the ability to communicate about these issues.

BARRIERS TO IMPLEMENTING ADVANCE DIRECTIVES

Even when advance directives are completed, they may not be upheld by health care providers or significant others (Reith and Payne 2009). Barriers to implementation of advance directives include lack of communication between patients and providers, value conflicts between patients and providers, and conflicting patient and family preferences.

LACK OF COMMUNICATION BETWEEN PATIENTS AND PROVIDERS   A majority of individuals with advance directives have not made their physicians aware of them (Galambos 1998). Bomba, Morrissey, and Leven (2011) have developed programs to promote physician awareness as well as implementation of advance directives.

VALUE CONFLICTS BETWEEN PATIENTS AND PROVIDERS   This author and colleagues (Reese et al. 2005) found that medical students were less favorable toward palliative care than were citizens in their community. Physicians and social workers have contrasting training and values, which may lead to conflict (Nadicksbernd, Thornberry, and von Gunten 2011). Violation of patient wishes may occur in either direction, however, with life-sustaining treatment being removed without patient or family consent or treatment being continued despite patient and family wishes to the contrary (Galambos 1998).

CONFLICTING PATIENT AND FAMILY PREFERENCES   A study by this author (Reese 2000) found that the most important factor in placement of hospice patients in the hospital by family members, rather than honoring the wish to die at home without life-sustaining treatment, was denial of their terminality. If family members' preferences conflict with patient preferences, physicians may prefer to cooperate with the family member's preferences (Galambos 1998). It is important to communicate to patients and families the consequences of a 911 call or aggressive treatment, particularly when the patient has signed a DNR order (Gerbino and Henderson 2004).

Clearly, these legal and ethical issues are still unresolved. Policy problems and practice problems result. The remainder of the chapter will review the current status of end-of-life care in the U.S. and make recommendations for changes that may help to develop the field.

CURRENT STATUS OF END-OF-LIFE CARE IN THE U.S.

Although active debate is still ongoing about end-of-life care, and opinions differ by geographic region and by ethnic, cultural, or religious group, hospice philosophy has taken hold within the dominant culture of the U.S. The majority of Americans want to die at home and would want palliative rather than curative care in terminal illness (National Hospice and Palliative Care Organization 2002). Intensive care patients from the dominant culture say that they are prepared to shorten healthy life for better care at the end of life (Bryce et al. 2004). An Oregon study found that most individuals who died in 2000–2002 had advance directives and were enrolled in hospice (Tilden et al. 2004).

Nationally, though, despite American orientation toward the major tenets of hospice philosophy, almost 50 percent of Americans still die in the hospital. This varies across the country, with 73 percent dying in the hospital in Washington, DC, and 32 percent in Oregon (Hansen, Tolle, and Martin 2002). An average of only 38.5 percent of Americans died under the care of a hospice in 2008 (National Hospice and Palliative Care Organization 2009).

In addition, patients are referred to hospice shortly before death; the median length of stay was nineteen days in 1998 (General Accounting Office 2000) and is currently reported by the Centers for Medicare and Medicaid Services (2008) as being approximately fourteen days. Entering hospice at this late stage makes pain and symptom management the main objective, leaving little time for psychosocial or spiritual intervention (Kovacs, Bellin, and Fauri 2006).

FACTORS LIMITING USE OF HOSPICE

Factors limiting hospice use include the same ones that limit the use of advance directives: ineffective methods of promoting hospice and lack of communication and value conflicts between patients, physicians, and family members. The Medicare requirement for a prognosis of six months or less acts as a barrier as well. Factors that particularly act to limit access for diverse cultural groups include financial concerns of health care providers and Medicare regulations including referral by a physician, the requirement for a *primary caregiver* (a significant other, living in the home, who agrees to take primary responsibility for the care of the patient), and lack of reimbursement for inpatient and curative care. Finally, one factor that limits use of hospice is a philosophy differing across cultural and religious beliefs. Those with strong religious faith, among many diverse cultural groups, want to extend their lives through terminal illness and oppose physician-assisted suicide.

Medicare coverage of hospice, though a great benefit to the field, initiated a move away from the holistic, volunteer-oriented origins of hospice. Professionalism of hospice and socialization into the health care system culture eventually resulted in an overemphasis on physician and nursing care and a concomitant lack of emphasis on psychosocial and spiritual needs (Parker Oliver et al. 2009). Thus a major reason for inability to consider hospice is not routinely addressed—the denial of terminality experienced by patients, family members, and physicians themselves.

Medicare requires that a patient be certified as terminally ill by a physician to be eligible for insurance coverage under the Medicare Hospice Benefit. This requirement acts as a major barrier to hospice access for diverse cultural groups, as diverse groups are less likely to have health insurance than the dominant culture (Reese et al. 1999). In addition, preparation for end-of-life care is still not routinely provided in medical training; thus physicians may not even be familiar with the option of hospice. As with advance directives, physicians may have values that are more oriented toward curative care than are their patients' values; this may prevent them from providing the option of palliative care (Reese et al. 2005).

In addition, physicians are uncomfortable giving bad news and tend to be overoptimistic in the prognosis given to patients and significant others (Werth and Blevins 2002). Physicians lack skills in communicating the prognosis and treatment options to patients; thus conversations about terminality between patients and health care personnel are frequently inadequate or even nonexistent (Reith and Payne 2009).

This lack of physician communication skills, paired with an absence of interdisciplinary care, makes it unlikely that clients are presented with the option of hospice by their health care providers. Those who are referred to hospice are likely to be referred very late (Teno et al. 2007), when the fact of terminality is obvious and curative care options have been exercised up until the last weeks before death. A study by this author (Reese 1995) found that a number of home health care patients that were considered terminally ill by their nurses did not have a terminal prognosis according to their physicians. Most of the physicians referred these patients to hospice soon after, however, where they died shortly thereafter.

Despite this, due to a lack of public education by hospices, referral by physicians remains the major way that patients learn about hospice. Misinformation abounds, particularly among diverse cultural groups, including the idea of hospice as lack of care or even as a form of active euthanasia for all patients. Even more frequently, patients have never heard of hospice. This explains the findings that although most Americans are oriented toward hospice philosophy, few die under the care of a hospice (National Hospice and Palliative Care Organization 2002).

The Medicare requirement limiting care to persons with a prognosis of six months or less also creates a barrier to hospice access. Physicians have difficulty making this determination (Center for Bioethics, University of Minnesota 2005), which may be appropriate for cancer but not for other diagnoses which are not as predictable or are characterized by a lengthy dying process. In 1998 the percentage of hospice noncancer admissions decreased dramatically, reflecting the problems associated with determining a six-month prognosis for these patients.

A history of investigation by the Health Care Financing Administration (HCFA, now Centers for Medicare and Medicaid Services) has exacerbated this problem. In 1994 HCFA published a memo about problems with questionable physician certification of hospice patients. They conducted an investigation of doctors who had referred patients to hospice who did not die within six months. Afterward physicians were fearful of being punished if an enrollee lived longer than six months and for this reason hesitated to refer terminally ill patients to hospice (Werth and Blevins 2002). Medicare has since developed a policy that allows recertification of hospice patients who live longer than six months; it is important to educate providers about this policy.

Financial concerns of health care providers also act as barriers to hospice referral. In the early days of hospice, when services were provided on a volunteer basis, services were offered free of charge to those who could not pay. This tradition has continued until today in many hospices. In some, however, lack of insurance acts as a barrier, particularly for those from diverse cultural groups. In addition, some authors assert that a patient choice of solely palliative care may go against a provider emphasis on full use of technology regardless of associated cost (Finn 2002).

Several other Medicare policies act as barriers to hospice access for diverse cultural groups. Medicare requires that a primary caregiver be available in the home. Research has indicated, though, that, for many culturally diverse individuals, family members must work and are not able to stay at home with the patient (Werth and Blevins 2002). Also, the Medicare requirement for an informed consent that acknowledges terminality and foregoes life-sustaining treatment, as well as lack of Medicare Hospice Benefit coverage for hospice stays or curative care, act as barriers for cultural groups that believe that accepting death is a lack of faith (Reese et al. 1999).

Those with a strong religious faith, including many from diverse cultural groups, want to extend their life in terminal illness (Reese et al. 1999). The rise of the Republican right, with its emphasis on conservative Christian principles, has recently promoted an orientation toward life-sustaining treatment in terminal illness. An absolutist perspective that assumes adherence to these principals should be enforced through law regardless of individual differences in philosophy and values has lent even more force to this trend.

An example is the 2005 case of Terri Schiavo, a brain-damaged woman who was being served by a hospice in Florida. Her husband had consented to palliative care for her, claiming that she had communicated to him her wish not to be kept alive artificially if in a persistent vegetative state. Ms. Schiavo had received artificial nutrition for fifteen years after her heart had stopped in 1990. Her feeding tube had been removed by court order in March of 2005, but her parents fought a lengthy court battle to have the tube reinserted. Politicians intervened in the case, passing emergency legislation to order doctors to reinsert the tube or calling for federal courts to review the case—including the state governor, U.S. House and Senate, and even President Bush, who signed a bill into law in the middle of the night. A series of court rulings, progressing up to the U.S. Supreme Court level, upheld Ms. Schiavo's right to die, however. Public sentiment reflected and may have influenced the actions of the politicians (Branford 2005). Citizens conducted demonstrations, and a California businessman offered Terri Schiavo's husband one million dollars to keep his wife alive (he refused).

RISE OF PALLIATIVE CARE AS A SEPARATE FIELD OF PRACTICE

Hospice is a form of palliative care, in which the goal is palliation of symptoms rather than cure of an incurable disease. Hospice provides treatment specifically for terminally ill patients. Palliative care is also provided outside the hospice setting to patients who are chronically ill. For example, HIV cannot be cured, but current treatments relieve symptoms and delay the course of the disease for a number of years. Thus patients with this illness, who are not considered to be terminally ill in the sense that they are expected to die within six months, may be seen on an outpatient basis in a nonhospice program referred to as "palliative care."

Terminally ill patients who have not chosen hospice may also receive care for their symptoms from a palliative care program, however. Partially due to a lack of hospice outreach, and partially in response to the barriers to hospice referrals already described, palliative care for terminally ill patients has risen in the past couple decades to be a separate service from hospice care.

Palliative care as it is provided in the United States addresses many of the barriers to hospice referral. Medicare regulations relevant to hospice do not pertain to palliative care. Denial of terminality does not have to be addressed, since patients do not have to sign an informed consent recognizing terminality, and physicians do not have to have a conversation about the prognosis. Patients can receive curative care as well as palliative care, thus value conflicts with providers and family members are less likely. The Medicare requirement for a six-month prognosis does not apply, physicians do not have to certify that the patient is terminally ill, and there is no requirement for a primary caregiver. Lack of service to those without health insurance is still a concern and presents a barrier to access for diverse cultural groups.

The field of palliative care has been developed in competition with hospice and has not used the lessons hospice has learned. Palliative care programs don't always provide interdisciplinary care; thus they may not adequately address psychosocial and spiritual issues with clients.

RECOMMENDATIONS FOR ADDRESSING THE BARRIERS TO HOSPICE ACCESS

Recommendations for addressing the barriers to hospice access include an interdisciplinary approach to care within physicians' offices in which social workers provide the counseling to patients and families. Hospice care and philosophy should be integrated into other services; the hospice team should provide consultation to staff and intervention with clients from the first diagnosis until death. Care should be a continuum — moving from diagnosis to palliative/curative care, then to hospice. Medicare coverage of these consultation services should be provided, and the hospice social worker should play a major role in consultation.

In addition, general education of consumers must be provided by the hospice field, and Medicare reimbursement is needed for preadmission informational visits by hospice staff. Public education efforts should be cognizant of the relevance of their message to diverse cultural groups. Those without access to health care may not be able to relate to public education about the right to die and refuse treatment (Keigher 1994). In addition, particular emphasis should be placed on dispelling myths among diverse cultural groups about services provided (Werth and Blevins 2002).

Medicare eligibility requirements should also be made more flexible, redefining end-of-life by severity of illness as opposed to prognosis (Werth and Blevins 2002). Access would also be increased, particularly for diverse cultural groups, by allowing patients to continue to receive disease-modifying treatment along with hospice care.

RECOMMENDATIONS FOR THE PALLIATIVE CARE FIELD

According to the hospice philosophy, patient awareness of terminality is necessary for a good quality of life in death and dying. This awareness is necessary for informed choices within self-determination, including making decisions about end-of-life care consistent with one's cultural and religious beliefs and communicating preferences about one's environment. Awareness is also necessary to address psychosocial issues such as suicidal ideation, death anxiety, social support, financial arrangements, safety and comfort issues, anticipatory grief, and denial itself. Awareness must also be present to address major spiritual issues including meaning of life and suffering, unfinished business, clarification of religious beliefs, relationship with the Ultimate, isolation, and transpersonal experiences.

Denial of terminality can be a positive coping skill. In most cases patients move in and out of awareness of terminality according to their emotional resources at the time. When they are in an emotional state in which they can handle this awareness, they need someone to talk with in order to address psychosocial and spiritual issues. Thus we recommend that palliative care programs develop a collaborative relationship with hospice teams to take advantage of their skills in addressing these issues. In particular, social workers and spiritual caregivers should be called upon to provide services to clients in these areas. The time to begin this collaborative approach is at the time of diagnosis, long before the patient has to address terminality.

The ability of patients within palliative care programs to move back and forth between curative and palliative care is beneficial; this can create access for those whose religious beliefs prevent them from resigning themselves to terminality. Lack of service to those without health insurance needs to be addressed, however, perhaps by setting up a foundation for such care.

ADDITIONAL HOSPICE POLICY ISSUES

Many problems abound with inadequate Medicare reimbursement of hospices. This is a major factor for hospice financial well-being, since most hospice patients are covered by Medicare. The Medicare Hospice Benefit provides a per diem rate to hospices, and if the expense of the treatment is more than the reimbursement, the hospice must absorb the loss (Werth and Blevins 2002). The first and last weeks of hospice enrollment tend to involve the most expensive treatment, so the short hospice stay so often seen today intensifies these financial difficulties. These financial issues may make it difficult for hospices to provide the most effective (and most expensive) pain medications. Recommendations include increasing per diem rates, adjusting reimbursement for patients with expensive treatments, making a minimum payment of fourteen days, allowing reimbursement to nurse practitioners and physicians' assistants, placing a ceiling on potential expenditures, and allowing social workers to bill separately for services (Goldberg and Scharlin 2011).

Rural hospices may have particular difficulty making ends meet. The Medicare reimbursement rate for rural hospices is lower, even though they may incur additional expenses associated with travel. A proposal has been made to Congress for demonstration projects to allow individuals in rural areas to receive inpatient hospice care and respite care longer than is allowed in the hospice legislation. Recommendations have also been made for a 10 percent increase in rural reimbursement rates and adjusting for travel expenses for rural hospices (Werth and Blevins 2002).

Another policy issue concerns the services provided by for-profit hospices. The number of for-profit hospices quadrupled from 1994–2004, and research has indicated that patients of for-profit hospices received a significantly narrower range of services than patients of nonprofit hospices (Carlson, Gallo, and Bradley 2004).

Another question concerns encouragement of hospice enrollment by Health Maintenance Organizations (HMOs). Some authors suggest that HMOs may be encouraging enrollment in hospice because of the cost savings. This raises a question about patient self-determination in end-of-life care treatment choice.

Finally, the domination of the hospice field by physicians and nurses is also a concern due to the current overemphasis on a biomedical model of care. The holistic model first developed by Dame Cicely Saunders has been neglected, with nonmedical staff referred to as "ancillary staff." Chapter 2 will discuss the current status of social work in the hospice field.

CONTINUUM OF CARE

The National Hospice and Palliative Care Organization advocates for "continuum of care" in order to address barriers to hospice referral, utilization, and financing. At present, the Centers for Medicare and Medicaid Services (CMS) restricts Medicare reimbursement for hospice services to patients who have been certified by a physician as having six months or less to live. If so certified, CMS will pay for palliative care, but not curative care. In order to receive hospice services, the patient must sign an informed consent statement recognizing the terminal prognosis. These regulations present barriers for patients with chronic illnesses in which a terminal prognosis cannot easily be made (such as congestive heart failure) as well as for patients and families who are not willing or psychologically or spiritually ready to give up all curative measures.

Palliative care programs in the U.S. are free of these restrictions, but often do not utilize the knowledge developed within the hospice field. For example, they may not provide holistic care through an interdisciplinary team that includes a social worker and a spiritual caregiver (although this is becoming more common). Thus, they may not fully address psychosocial and spiritual issues pertaining to terminal illness.

The idea of continuity of care includes two approaches: 1. supplementing existing hospice services with palliative care integrated into nonhospice care settings to form a continuum of care, of which hospice is a part, and 2. expanding the scope and mission of hospices to serve populations of patients who have longer to live and who are in various health care settings (Jennings et al. 2003). These approaches can help meet the psychosocial and spiritual needs of patients and families who need intervention to help them prepare for end-of-life care decisions consistent with acceptance of a terminal prognosis. Clients need this intervention through an interdisciplinary team, beginning at first diagnosis of a life-threatening illness and continuing through curative, palliative, and end-of-life care (Schumacher 2003).

This chapter discussed the history of our approach to death and dying in the United States of America. From a tradition of dying at home surrounded by loved ones, we transitioned to a majority of deaths occurring in the hospital. Often these deaths occur during the administration of life-sustaining treatments. The hospice philosophy, developed first in England and promoted in the U.S. by Elisabeth Kubler-Ross, encouraged palliative rather than curative care in terminal illness, with patient quality of life and self-determination among its highest values. Hospice care in the U.S. has usually been provided in the home, although inpatient hospices have been developed as well.

Health care costs have been a major social problem in our country for decades, and since hospice care was found to be less expensive than life-sustaining treatment, Medicare and Medicaid developed coverage of all hospice expenses including medication and equipment, making it an extremely beneficial service for dying patients and their families. Health insurance coverage of this approach to end-of-life care led to standards of practice, including the requirement for social work services and evaluation techniques, and has greatly helped to expand and develop the hospice field.

Health insurance coverage has also led to some policy problems, though, which include the requirement for a physician to make a terminal prognosis—in other words, that the patient will die within six months. In addition, the patient must sign a statement recognizing the terminal illness and foregoing curative care. Making an accurate prognosis is extremely difficult, even impossible, for a physician to do, and being ready to sign an informed consent for only palliative care is very difficult for a patient to be ready for without preparation through social work intervention. This is especially difficult for some ethnic and racial communities with a history of mistreatment by the health care system and/or who rely on the family and their elders to make such decisions rather than the patient. These problems have served as barriers to hospice utilization and in part have led to the development of the field of palliative care, which, in addition to treating chronically ill patients who are not necessarily terminally ill, may treat terminally ill patients who are not ready or aware enough of their prognosis to go through the process required for hospice admission.

Alternatively, in contrast to the barriers preventing patients from taking advantage of hospice care in terminal illness, there has been a movement toward physician-assisted suicide. The main motivation for this appears to be patients' desire for control of their illness and dying process, although there is a need for differential diagnosis to make sure depression and untreated symptoms are not the problem. In this chapter we discussed ethical issues having to do with end-of-life care including physician-assisted suicide.

We also discussed advance directives as a tool for upholding patient self-determination to help them communicate their wishes in end-of-life decisions. We concluded this chapter with a discussion of policy issues in the field and some recommendations for policy change, including developing a continuum of care between life-sustaining and palliative care options. Chapter 2 will focus in specifically on the field of social work within hospice care; we will review the history, efforts toward development, and current status of the profession of social work on the hospice interdisciplinary team.

REFERENCES

Altilio, T. 2011. "Palliative Sedation: A View Through the Kaleidoscope." In Terry Altilio and Shirley Otis-Green, eds., *Oxford Textbook of Palliative Social Work*, pp. 661–669. New York: Oxford University Press.

Arons, S. 2004. "Current Legal Issues in End-of-Life Care." In J. Berzoff and P. Silverman, eds., *Living with Dying: A Handbook for End-of-Life Practitioners*, pp. 730–760. New York: Columbia University Press.

AScribe Newswire. 2005. "Hospice Community Mourns Death of Dame Cicely Saunders: Pioneer in Field of Hospice Changed End-of-Life Care." Online news article, retrieved July 20, 2005, from http://www. ascribe.org/cgi-bin/behold.pl?a scribeid=20050714.122258andtime=14%2043%20PDTandyear=2005andpublic=1.

Baily, M. 2011. "Futility, Autonomy, and Cost in End-of-Life Care." *Journal of Law, Medicine and Ethics* 39, no. 2: 172–182.

Black, K. 2007. "Advance Care Planning Throughout the End-of-Life: Focusing the Lens for Social Work Practice." *Journal of Social Work in End-of-Life and Palliative Care* 3, no. 2: 39–58.

Blacker, S. 2004. "Palliative Care and Social Work." In Joan Berzoff and Phyllis Silverman, eds., *Living with Dying: A Handbook for End-of-Life Healthcare Practitioners*, pp. 409–423. New York: Columbia University Press.

Bomba, P. A., M. Morrissey, and D. C. Leven. 2011. "Key Role of Social Work in Effective Communication and Conflict Resolution Process: Medical Orders for Life-Sustaining Treatment (MOLST) Program in New York and Shared Medical Decision Making at the End of Life." *Journal of Social Work in End-of-Life and Palliative Care* 7, no. 1: 56–82.

Branford, B. 2005. "U.S. Courts and Politicians Collide." *BBC News: UK Edition.* March 31, 2005. Retrieved July 20, 2005 from http://news.bbc.co.uk/1/hi/world/americas/4368055.stm.

Bryce, C. L., G. Loewenstein, R. M. Arnold, J. Schooler, R. S. Wax, and D. C. Angus. 2004. "Quality of Death: Assessing the Importance Placed on End-of-Life Treatment in the Intensive-Care Unit." *Medical Care* 42, no. 5: 423–31.

Buckey, J. W., and N. Abell. 2010. Life-sustaining Treatment Decisions: A Social Work Response to Meet Needs of Health Care Surrogates." *Journal of Social Work in End-of-Life and Palliative Care* 6:27–50.

Carlson, M. D., W. T. Gallo, and E. H. Bradley. 2004. "Ownership Status and Patterns of Care in Hospice: Results from the National Home and Hospice Care Survey." *Medical Care* 42, no. 5: 432–438.

Center for Bioethics, University of Minnesota. 2005. *End of Life Care: An Ethical Overview.* Center for Bioethics, University of Minnesota. Retrieved from: http://www.ahc.umn.edu/bioethics/prod/groups/ahc/@pub/@ahc/documents/asset/ahc_75179.pdf.

Centers for Medicare and Medicaid Services. 2008. "Conditions of Participations." Retrieved from https://www.cms.gov/CFCsAndCoPs/05_Hospice.asp#TopOfPage.

Chapin, R., T. Gordon, S. Landry, and R. Rachlin. 2007. "Hospice Use by Older Adults Knocking on the Door of the Nursing Facility: Implications for Social Work." *Journal of Social Work in End-of-Life and Palliative Care* 3, no. 2: 19–38.

Chochinov, H. M., T. Hack, T. Hassard, L. J. Kristjanson, S. McClement, and M. Harlos. 2002. "Dignity in the Terminally Ill: A Cross-sectional, Cohort Study." *Lancet* 360 (December 21/28): 2026–2030.

Farber, S., T. Egnew, and A. Farber. 2004. "What Is Respectful Death?" In J. Berzoff and P. Silverman, eds., *Living with Dying: A Handbook for End-of-Life Healthcare Practitioners,* pp. 102–127. New York: Columbia University Press.

Finn, W. 2002. "The Evolution of the Hospice Movement in America." *Revija za Socijalnu Politiku* 9, nos. 3/4: 271–279.

Forbes, S., M. Bern-Klug, and C. Gessert. 2000. "End-of-Life Decision Making on Behalf of Nursing Home Residents with Dementia." *Image: Journal of Nursing Scholarship* 20:251–258.

Galambos, C. 1998. "Preserving End-of-Life Autonomy: The Patient Self-Determination Act and the Uniform Health Care Decisions Act." *Health and Social Work* 23, no. 4: 275–281.

General Accounting Office (GAO). 2000. "Medicare: More Beneficiaries Use Hospice, but for Fewer Days of Care." GAO/HEHS Publication no. 00–182. Washington, DC: General Accounting Office.

Gerbino, S., and S. Henderson. 2004. "End-of-Life Bioethics in Clinical Social Work Practice." In Joan Berzoff and Phyllis R. Silverman, eds., *Living with Dy-*

ing: *A Handbook for End-of-Life Healthcare Practitioners,* pp. 593–608. New York: Columbia University Press.

Goldberg, J., and M. Scharlin. 2011. "Financial Considerations for the Palliative Social Worker." In Terry Altilio and Shirley Otis-Green, eds., *Oxford Textbook of Palliative Social Work,* pp. 709–718. New York: Oxford University Press.

Hansen, S. M., S. W. Tolle, and D. P. Martin. 2002. "Factors Associated with Lower Rates of In-hospital Death." *Journal of Palliative Medicine* 5, no. 5: 677–685.

Happ, M. B., E. Capezuti, N. E. Strumpf, L. Wagner, S. Cunningham, L. Evans, and G. Maislin. 2002. *Journal of the American Geriatrics Society* 50, no. 5: 829–835.

Harper, B. C. 2011. "Palliative Social Work: An Historical Perspective." In Terry Altilio and Shirley Otis-Green, eds., *Oxford Textbook of Palliative Social Work,* pp. 11–20. New York: Oxford University Press.

Jennings, B., T. Ryndes, C. D'Onofrio, and M. A. Baily. 2003. "Access to Hospice Care: Expanding Boundaries, Overcoming Barriers. *Hastings Center Report Special Supplement* 33, no. 2: S3–S59.

Keigher, S. 1994. "Patient Rights and Dying: Policy Restraint and the States." *Health and Social Work* 19, no. 4: 298–303.

Kovacs, P. J., M. H. Bellin, and D. P. Fauri. 2006. "Family-Centered Care: A Resource for Social Work in End-of-Life and Palliative Care." *Journal of Social Work in End-of-Life and Palliative Care* 2, no. 1: 13–27.

Kramer, B., C. Hovland-Scafe, and L. Pacourek. 2003. "Analysis of End-of-Life Content in Social Work Textbooks." *Journal of Social Work Education* 39, no. 2: 299–320.

Kubler-Ross, E. 1970. *On Death and Dying.* New York: Macmillan.

Levin, J. R., N. S. Wenger, J. G. Ouslander, G. Zellman, J. F. Schnelle, J. L. Buchanan, S. H. Hirsch, and D. B. Reuben. 1999. "Life-Sustaining Treatment Decisions for Nursing Home Residents: Who Discusses, Who Decides and What Is Decided?" *Journal of the American Geriatrics Society* 47, no. 1: 82–87.

Nadicksbernd, J. J., K. Thornberry, and C. F. von Gunten. 2011. "Social Work and Physician Collaboration in Palliative Care." In Terry Altilio and Shirley Otis-Green, eds., *Oxford Textbook of Palliative Social Work,* pp. 471–476. New York: Oxford University Press.

National Association of Social Workers. 2011. NASW *Standards for Social Work Practice in Palliative and End of Life Care.* Washington, DC: National Association of Social Workers.

National Hospice and Palliative Care Organization. 2002. *Delivering Quality Care and Cost-Effectiveness at the End of life: Building on the Twenty-Year Success of the Medicare Hospice Benefit.* National Hospice and Palliative Care Organization. Retrieved from: http://nhpco.org/files/public/delivering_quality_care.pdf.

——. 2009. "NHPCO Facts and Figures: Hospice Care in America." Retrieved from www.nhpco.org/files/public/Statistics_Research/NHPCO_facts_and_figures.pdf.

Neuman, K., and L. Wade. 1999. "Advance Directives: The Experience of Health Care Professionals Across the Continuum of Care." *Social Work in Health Care* 28, no. 3: 39–54.

Parker Oliver, D., E. Wittenberg-Lyles, K. T. Washington, and S. Sehrawat. 2009. "Social Work Role in Hospice Pain Management: A National Survey." *Journal of Social Work in End-of-Life and Palliative Care* 5:61–74.

Peres, J. R. 2011. "Public Policy in Palliative and End-of-Life Care." In Terry Altilio and Shirley Otis-Green, eds., *Oxford Textbook of Palliative Social Work*, pp. 753–769. New York: Oxford University Press.

Quality of Life Matters. 2004. "Home Hospice Care Receives Highest Family Rating Among End-of-Life Care Sites." *Quality of Life Matters* 6, no. 1: 1–2.

Ratner, E., L. Norlander, and K. McSteen. 2001. "Death at Home Following a Targeted Advance-Care Planning Process at Home: The Kitchen Table Discussion." *Journal of the American Geriatrics Society* 49, no. 6: 778–781.

Reese, D. 1995. "Physician Failure to Predict Terminality in Home Health Care Patients." Unpublished MS.

——. 2000. "The Role of Primary Caregiver Denial in Inpatient Placement During Home Hospice Care." *Hospice Journal* 15, no. 1: 15–33.

Reese, D., R. Ahern, S. Nair, J. O'Faire, and C. Warren. 1999. "Hospice Access and Utilization by African Americans: Addressing Cultural and Institutional Barriers Through Participatory Action Research." *Social Work* 44, no. 6: 549–559.

Reese, D., L. Braden, C. Butler, and M. Smith. 2004. "African American Access to Hospice: An Interdisciplinary Participatory Action Research Project." Paper presented at the Clinical Team Conference, National Hospice and Palliative Care Organization, March, Las Vegas, Nevada.

Reese, D., C. L. W. Chan, D. Perry, D. Wiersgalla, and J. Schlinger. 2005. "Beliefs, Death Anxiety, Denial, and Treatment Preferences in End-of-Life Care: A Comparison of Social Work Students, Community Residents, and Medical Students." *Journal of Social Work in End-of-Life and Palliative Care* 1, no. 1: 23–47.

Reith, M., and M. Payne. 2009. *Social Work in End-of-Life and Palliative Care.* Chicago: Lyceum.

Roff, S. 2001. "Analyzing End-of-Life Care Legislation: A Social Work Perspective." *Social Work in Health Care* 33, no. 1: 51–68.

Schroepfer, T. 2008. "Social Relationships and Their Role in the Consideration to Hasten Death." *Gerontologist* 48, no. 5: 612–621.

Schumacher, J. D. 2003. "The Future of Hospice Leadership—How Do We Go from Good to Great?" Opening plenary of the Eighteenth Management and Leadership Conference, National Hospice and Palliative Care Organization, Phoenix.

Silverman, P. R. 2004. "Dying and Bereavement in Historical Perspective." In Joan Berzoff and Phyllis Silverman, eds., *Living with Dying: A Handbook for End-of-Life Healthcare Practitioners*, pp. 128–149. New York: Columbia University Press.

Singer, P. A., D. K. Martin, and M. Kelner. 1999. "Quality End-of-Life Care: Patient's Perspectives." *Journal of the American Medical Association* 281:163–168.

Social Security Online. 2004. Retrieved October 11, http://www.ssa.gov/OACT/STATS/table4c6.html.

Sutton, A. L., and D. Liechty. 2004. "Clinical Practice with Groups in End-of-Life Care." In Joan Berzoff and Phyllis Silverman, eds., *Living with Dying: A Handbook for End-of-Life Healthcare Practitioners*. New York: Columbia University Press.

Teno, J., B. Clarridge, V. Casey, L. Welch, T. Wetle, R. Shield, and V. Mor. 2004. "Family Perspectives on End-of-Life Care at the Last Place of Care." *Journal of the American Medical Association* 291:88–93.

Teno, J. M., J. E. Shu, D. Casarett, C. Spence, R. Rhodes, and S. Connor. 2007. "Timing of Referral to Hospice and Quality of Care: Length of Stay and Bereaved Family Members' Perceptions of the Timing of Hospice Referral." *Journal of Pain and Symptom Management* 34, no. 2: 120–125.

Tilden, V. P., S. W. Tolle, L. L. Drach, and N. A. Perrin. 2004. "Out-of-Hospital Death: Advance Care Planning, Decedent Symptoms, and Caregiver Burden." *Journal of the American Geriatric Society* 52, no. 4: 532–539.

van Baarsen, B. 2008. "Suffering, Loneliness, and the Euthanasia Choice: An Explorative Study." *Journal of Social Work in End-of-Life and Palliative Care* 4, no. 3: 189–213.

Werth, J., and D. Blevins. 2002. "Public Policy and End-of-Life Care." *American Behavioral Scientist* 46, no. 3: 401–417.

Zilberfein, F., and E. Hurwitz. 2004. "Clinical Social Work Practice at the End of Life." In Joan Berzoff and Phyllis R. Silverman, eds., *Living with Dying: A Handbook for End-of-Life Healthcare Practitioners*, pp. 297–317. New York: Columbia University Press.

2

CURRENT STATUS OF SOCIAL WORK IN HOSPICE

In this chapter, we will review the history and current status of the profession of social work on the hospice interdisciplinary team, reviewing barriers and successes in its development, including difficulties in working across interdisciplinary barriers, the challenge and progress of documentation of outcomes, and major efforts within the field of social work to develop social work curricula, certification for hospice social workers, standards for practice, among a number of other efforts. Finally, we will present research evidence that these major and remarkable efforts have had a significant impact on the field of social work in hospice.

LACK OF FULL UTILIZATION OF SOCIAL WORKERS ON THE INTERDISCIPLINARY TEAM

Social work services have been integral to the provision of hospice care from the beginning of the hospice movement in the U.S. and are required for Medicare certification of hospices. Moreover, research has indicated that psychosocial and spiritual issues are primary determinants of quality of life and decision making in end-of-life care (Reese 2011b; Soltura and Piotrowski 2011). A classic study by Kulys and Davis (1986) found, however, that social workers were not seen by hospice directors as uniquely qualified to deliver psychosocial services. Social workers played no unique role in the hospices other than providing financial assistance. They were more active than nurses in providing only two services: financial counseling and civic legal assistance. They were considered more qualified than nurses to provide only three services: using community resources, making referrals to community resources, and providing financial information. Nurses, in contrast, were considered most qualified, and were providing, most of the psychosocial care.

Studies over the years have continued to reveal that social workers' expertise has not been fully utilized on the hospice team (Reese and Raymer 2004; Reith and Payne 2009; Sontag 1996b). Social workers in many areas of the country have seen their caseloads rise as colleagues were laid off or positions were simply not replaced (Parker Oliver and Peck 2006). Hospices employ almost four times as many nurses as social workers (National Hospice and Palliative Care Organization 2002; Reith and Payne 2009). Today nursing caseloads are much lower than social work caseloads; nurses have an average of 13.3 cases, and social workers have an average of 24.2 (National Hospice and Palliative Care Organization 2009). Not surprisingly, patients receive many more nursing visits than social work visits (Parker Oliver and Peck 2006). In fact, the median number of visits to a hospice patient for a social worker has been documented at two, whereas for a nurse it was ten (Reese and Raymer 2004).

Many social workers see patients only on an "as needed" basis determined by a nurse. This is problematic especially since research indicates that social service needs are often not accurately identified by the nurse (Dyeson and Hebert 2004; Reith and Payne 2009). Non–social workers regularly provide psychosocial care, while social workers are involved primarily in assessment activities. Social workers may have difficulty in gaining access to patients and families (Dyeson and Hebert 2004), and hospices may be reluctant to acknowledge a family's need for social work intervention until a problem has reached crisis proportions. Social workers often feel a lack of support from administrators (Parker Oliver and Peck 2006; Reith and Payne 2009). Social workers are often assigned duties outside the social work position; many social workers serve as bereavement coordinator in addition to social worker (Reese and Raymer 2004). The undervaluing of social work services may be reflected in their salaries—hospice social workers are paid less than nurses with a similar education (Goldberg and Scharlin 2011; Reese and Raymer 2004).

REASONS FOR LACK OF FULL UTILIZATION

One reason for the failure to fully utilize social work services on the team is the contemporary focus on medical care in the hospice field, as discussed in chapter 1 (National Association of Social Workers, Social Work Policy Institute 2010). Service provision as well as federal policy has focused primarily on the physical aspects of dying. This shift away from the holistic philosophy of hospice has been furthered by the context of health care financing, which is based primarily on a medical model of care (Reith and Payne 2009; Sontag 1996a). In addition, inadequate health insurance reimbursement rates have forced hospice administrators to eliminate or greatly reduce budget items considered nonessential (Goldberg and Scharlin 2011). The minimal utilization of social work services on the hospice team implies that hospice administrators have considered the contribution of social workers to be less important than the nursing contribution or even nonessential.

Why have administrators viewed social work services as nonessential? A number of reasons have been proposed. One is that most hospice administrators are nurses (Goldberg and Scharlin 2011; Reese and Beckwith 2005), and competition has existed between nurses and social workers in the hospice field (Corless and Nicholas 2004; Forrest and Derrick 2010; Stark 2011). Secondly, nurses may view themselves as equally qualified to provide psychosocial care (Corless and Nicholas 2004) and consider social workers as unqualified to provide therapy (Hodgson et al. 2004). Another reason for a lack of recognition of the importance of social work services in hospice is the lack of documentation of social work outcomes (Goldberg and Scharlin 2011). Finally, a factor that exacerbates these problems is the lack of end-of-life care content in social work education, which creates a social work force that is unprepared to explain its role or in fact to achieve a level of excellence in the services provided. Hospice social workers have made little progress until recent years in developing standards for practice and certifying or credentialing workers. These factors and the end-of-life care social work field's progress in addressing them are discussed in the following section.

DOCUMENTATION OF SOCIAL WORK OUTCOMES

Data collection and outcomes measurement have historically received little attention in the field of hospice social work. This dearth of knowledge became particularly apparent in 1996 after a roundtable discussion in Chicago of the Social Worker Section of the National Council of Hospice and Palliative Professionals (NCHPP), part of the NHPCO. At this meeting numerous social workers reported drastically increasing caseloads as well as significant reductions of social work staff. A follow-up review of the literature after the meeting yielded little if any evidence that social work intervention made a difference. It was also around this time that the federal CMS issued a proposed revision of the Medicare guidelines. It was recommended that the definition of a hospice social worker be changed from someone with an undergraduate social work degree from a school accredited by the Council on Social Work Education to an individual with essentially any degree in a human services field. This proposed revision was not accepted at that time (although in recent years it finally passed). It was clear that the profession of social work was under siege and the cost of poor data collection and outcomes measurement was a lack of recognition of the contributions of social workers on the hospice team.

In response to this void, the Social Worker Section of NCHPP planned three projects. First, the National Hospice Social Work Survey sought to document the impact of social work services on hospice outcomes as well as the role of the social worker on the team (Reese and Raymer 2004). Second, the Social Work Outcomes Task Force designed the Social Work Assessment Tool to measure the effectiveness of social work intervention (Reese et al. 2006). The hope was that this assessment could be completed as part of the ongoing performance improvement activities of a hospice or palliative care program as well as ultimately contributing to a national database on hospice and palliative care social work outcomes. Third, Csikai and Raymer (2005) developed a continuing education project under a Project on Death in America grant aimed at professional development among practicing hospice social workers. These projects will be discussed further on in the chapter.

PIONEERING STUDIES

In 1997 three pioneering studies had already demonstrated that early and frequent social work involvement in hospice (Mahar, Eickman, and Bushfield 1997; Paquette 1997) and a prehospice program (Cherin et al. 2000) was related to reduced costs. All implemented new programs in which social work involvement was increased, including involvement in the intake interview (Cherin et al. 2000; Mahar, Eickman, and Bushfield 1997; Paquette 1997). All found beneficial differences between pre- and post-test measures, including fewer hospitalizations, on-call visits, and hours for nursing visits (Mahar, Eickman, and Bushfield 1997; Paquette 1997). Increased social work involvement was also associated with lower pain medication costs (Cherin et al. 2000; Mahar, Eickman, and Bushfield 1997), less frequent use of IVs (Paquette 1997), higher quality of life for patients (Cherin et al. 2000), improved nurse, client, and physician satisfaction (Paquette 1997), and decreased staff turnover (Paquette 1997).

Later studies confirmed these results and contributed new information. In 1999 Archer conducted a study of caregiver satisfaction with hospice social work services. She found that most primary caregivers were very satisfied; she recommended, though, that social work services should have been brought in earlier in some cases and that better communication between staff was needed. Doherty and DeWeaver (2004) also found evidence of client and caregiver satisfaction.

The results of these early studies consistently indicated that early and continuing social work involvement was associated with beneficial hospice outcomes. The studies used small, nonrandom samples, though, and each was conducted within only one agency. The studies did not document relationships between specific social work involvement measures and specific hospice outcome measures. Although the results showed that increased social work services improved outcomes, the studies did not specifically identify these services. In addition, these results, despite their importance, were not widely disseminated in the field. Thus lack of awareness of the importance of hospice social work services continued.

NATIONAL HOSPICE SOCIAL WORK SURVEY The National Hospice Social Work Survey (Reese and Raymer 2004) sought to build on this knowledge with a survey of a national stratified random sample of 330 patient cases within 66 hospices. Results indicated that 1. social work involvement was significantly associated with hospice processes, 2. hospice processes were significantly associated with hospice outcomes, and 3. social work involvement was significantly associated with hospice outcomes. Specific aspects of social work involvement, hospice processes, and hospice outcomes were identified.

Measures Indicators of social work involvement that predicted hospice processes and hospice outcomes included 1. service delivery (participation in intake, more client contacts), 2. qualifications of the social worker (holding an MSW, more experience since the social work degree), 3. qualifications of the social work supervisor (the supervisor is a social worker), 4. hospice spending for social work services (higher BSW and MSW starting salaries, larger overall budget for social work services), and 5. staffing (higher full-time equivalent of social workers, no additional duties outside of the social worker position, higher social worker to patient ratio).

The coinvestigators, building upon existing NHPCO guidelines for hospice social work services, and upon input from experts in the field, developed most of the measures for the survey. In addition, they measured team functioning with the Team Functioning Scale (Sontag 1995, alpha = .86) and severity of case with a revised version of the Social Work Acuity Scale for Hospice (SWASH, Huber and Runnion 1996, alpha = .70),

Service Delivery   Social worker participation in the intake interview, as shown in previous studies, had important implications—it was associated with more issues being addressed by the social worker on the hospice team, lower home health aide costs, lower labor costs, and lower overall hospice costs. If the social worker addressed more issues on the team, fewer home health aide visits were needed. More contacts between social workers and clients meant better client satisfaction. Unfortunately, the social worker participated in the intake interview in only 38 percent of the hospices.

Qualifications of the Social Worker   If the social worker had a MSW, she addressed more issues on the team, fewer nights of continuous care were needed for patients, and there was better team functioning. Better team functioning was measured by Sontag's Team Functioning Scale (1995), which was based on how fully each discipline was respected and utilized on the team. Team functioning, in terms of full utilization of social work services, was important—it was associated with fewer patient hospitalizations, lower home health aide costs, lower nursing costs, lower labor costs, and lower overall hospice costs. If the social worker had more experience since the social work degree, there were fewer nights of continuous care of the patient, there was a lower average cost per patient, lower home health aide costs, and better client satisfaction.

Qualifications of the Social Work Supervisor   If the supervisor of the social workers was a social worker himself, more issues were addressed by the social worker on the team. As noted, addressing more issues on the team was important since this had further implications for hospice outcomes. Unfortunately, only 18 percent of the social workers were supervised by a social worker.

Hospice Spending for Social Work Services and Staffing   Higher BSW and MSW starting salaries, along with more social workers in the hospice and a larger social work budget in general, were associated with more issues addressed on the team, lower pain control costs, and better client satisfaction. Having more social workers in the hospice was associated with fewer patient hospitalizations. If the social worker was assigned only to the social worker position, with no additional duties, there was better team functioning, more issues addressed on the team, fewer nights of continuous care provided, and lower patient pain costs. Finally, a higher social worker to patient ratio was associated with better team functioning, more issues addressed on the team, lower home health aide costs, lower nursing costs, lower labor costs, lower overall hospice costs, and a lower severity rating of the hospice case.

The remarkable results of this study were that with two visits to a client, social work services predicted many important outcomes for both individual clients and the hospice. New information was found about the relationships between social work involvement and hospice processes, including social work input to the team and team functioning. The implications of these hospice processes to hospice outcomes facilitates a beginning understanding of the mechanism by which social work services predict hospice outcomes.

This study was only a developmental step in documenting social work outcomes, though, and further work was needed. Causal relationships could not be assumed due to the cross-sectional survey design of this study. A true experimental design with random assignment to experimental and control groups is needed to allow us to claim that social work services were the *cause* of the beneficial outcomes. Finally, a limitation of the study was that few individual client outcomes were identified. The next step was to document social work outcomes by measuring these specific client outcomes. The Social Work Assessment Tool project accomplished that goal.

SOCIAL WORK ASSESSMENT TOOL   Hospice administrators routinely conduct performance improvement activities in order to evaluate the success of the program. Assessment of hospice social work services, however, has been largely limited to process evaluations conducted by non–social workers. For example, a nurse may review a patient chart and document whether the social worker conducted a psychosocial assessment within the time frame required by Medicare. This process evaluation focus is different from an outcomes focus, which would assess whether a client *benefited* from the service provided—e.g., did the client's death anxiety decrease after receiving social work intervention?

Based on this situation, social workers from around the nation had contacted the NCHPP Social Worker Section and described the need for a tool to measure social work outcomes. In response to this need, the Social Worker Section of NCHPP formed a committee of experienced hospice researchers and practitioners known as the Social Work Outcomes Task Force.[1] This task force developed the Social Work Assessment Tool (SWAT, Reese et al. 2006, see appendix A), the first measure of social work outcomes in hospice. This tool was based on a conceptual model developed by Reese (1995–96), along with items from the National Hospice Organization's pathways document (National Hospice and Palliative Care Organization 1997) and practice wisdom of the task force.[2] It included items measuring the major psychosocial and spiritual variables known to predict hospice outcomes for clients (Reese 1995–96). These variables included cultural and religious beliefs, suicidal ideation, desire to hasten death, death anxiety, preferences about environment, social support, financial resources, safety issues, comfort issues, complicated anticipatory grief, denial, and spirituality.

The thinking of the task force was that the SWAT would serve as a reminder of important issues to address, leading to improved practice and client outcomes. Use of the SWAT would also facilitate social worker documentation, and the data collected by the SWAT could be used for routine performance improvement activities. A standardized assessment tool such as the SWAT would allow for development of a national database, which might be used to document social work outcomes nationally. Data could be used to develop national benchmarks and standardization of practice with patients and families.

Spirituality in Social Work   It is generally agreed that social workers are responsible for addressing psychosocial issues (National Association of Social Workers 2011). A number of authors have argued that this role should include a focus on spiritual issues as well (Nakashima 2003; National Association of Social Workers 2011; Reith and Payne 2009). Spirituality has often been found to be a source of struggle, growth, and an important source of coping and psychological adjustment in terminal illness (Reith and Payne 2009). Results of the National Hospice Social Work Survey showed that 58 percent of hospice social workers addressed spiritual issues in case discussions with their interdisciplinary teams, and 62 percent addressed spiritual issues in

---

1. Mary Raymer, Dona Reese, Stacy Orloff, Susan Gerbino, and Ruth Huber.
2. The National Hospice Organization changed its name to the National Hospice and Palliative Care Organization in 2000.

counseling sessions with clients (Reese 2001). Social work approaches in spiritual intervention will be discussed further in another chapter.

Development of the SWAT The task force conducted two pilot studies before using the SWAT in a national model performance improvement project (Reese et al. 2006). During the course of this work, the task force received many requests for the SWAT from all over the world, attesting to the need for such a measure in the field. Along with this enthusiasm, however, difficulties were experienced with the lack of orientation of some social workers toward quantitative evaluation of outcomes. Some lacked awareness of the relevance of SWAT issues in hospice outcomes and expressed discomfort in addressing the issues with clients. The task force experienced difficulties in recruiting participants for the studies, obtaining data from some who did volunteer, social workers' resistance to completing a tool longer than one page, and lack of willingness to invite clients to participate. These difficulties, commonly experienced in hospice social work research, reflect the caution toward and even aversion of social workers toward outcomes assessment.

These barriers, though making it impossible to thoroughly test the tool and satisfy certain research requirements, gave the task force an understanding of the practical realities of the field. They developed a one-page tool that would really be used by hospice social workers—it was designed to be completed by the social worker after each social work visit. The patient and primary caregiver were both rated on their progress on the major issues. Scores at the first visit served as a pretest, and could be compared to scores at the last visit (the post-test), to document whether the patient and primary caregiver had made progress on these major issues.

National Model Performance Improvement Project After development, the SWAT was used in a national model performance improvement project with a convenience sample of 19 social workers from 14 hospice programs. Participating social workers used the SWAT with 101 patients and 81 primary caregivers. Length of participation in the study varied because of continual recruitment of new volunteers and ranged from 1 to 215 days, with a median of 44 days. The task force also collected feedback about the use of the SWAT in qualitative telephone interviews with participants.

Results showed that SWAT scores for patients improved significantly between the first and second social work visit. Although there was a trend for scores to improve for primary caregivers, the difference was not statistically significant.

Participants reported a number of benefits of using the SWAT, saying that it was quick and easy to use, a comprehensive reminder of important issues to address, and helps the social worker identify needed resources and potential problems. Some thought it was helpful to quantify progress and were in favor of national use for performance improvement efforts. They thought the SWAT was relevant for use with economically or culturally diverse clients.

Some participant responses reflected lack of readiness of the field for quantitative social work outcomes measurement—for example, concern about the time required to complete the SWAT and preference for qualitative rather than quantitative assessment and for process rather than outcomes evaluation. Helpful suggestions included the need for training to build skills in assessing the factors included in the SWAT and the need for additional tools that 1. assess outcomes for patients who are unresponsive or have dementia and 2. that assess mezzo and macro level outcomes. The authors expressed concern about some participants' hesitation to assess or intervene with the SWAT issues.

Participants also provided information on how social work outcomes were being assessed in their hospice at that time. Some reported no social work performance improvement efforts being conducted or process rather than outcomes evaluation. Some were based on social workers' performance goals. A few programs did assess client outcomes, measuring whether clients had attained goals they had set themselves during the initial visit. Some of these client outcomes assessments were qualitative in nature and some assessed the mezzo and macro levels in addition to micro level outcomes.

Importance of the SWAT   The few existing measures of psychosocial outcomes have been developed by non–social workers, and do not reflect social work research about the major psychosocial and spiritual variables predicting hospice outcomes. During the course of the project, requests came from all over the world for a copy of the SWAT. Widespread use of the tool even before it was disseminated is evidence of the need for it. Lack of full utilization of social workers on the team may be partially due to lack of documentation of social work outcomes; from this point of view the SWAT is key to development of the field.

Strengths and Limitations of the Study   The SWAT project was again just a developmental step in social work outcomes measurement. As such, there are strengths as well as weaknesses in this project. The study improved upon the National Hospice Social Work Survey in its nonexperimental design—the use of pretests and post-tests provides more evidence that social work services were the *cause* of the change in SWAT scores. However, the study still did not use a true experimental design because of the ethical and Medicare regulation–based impossibility of randomly assigning clients to groups that would receive or not receive social work services, thus it is impossible to know whether the clients would have resolved issues on their own without services. Also, the participating clients were receiving hospice services from other team members as well as social workers; it is impossible to know whether the social work services alone led to the improved outcomes. The authors' assumption is that if clients are improving in areas that social workers are responsible for addressing, much or most of that improvement is due to social work intervention.

Due to difficulty in obtaining data, the task force was unable to conduct planned reliability and validity testing and to document a relationship between use of the SWAT and social work documentation and outcomes. In addition, although the SWAT project documented client improvement after social work services, it still did not document the effectiveness of specific intervention approaches. Finally, as mentioned by participants, the SWAT is most relevant on a micro level of practice; group practice and community intervention efforts need to be evaluated as well.

The task force plans to continue testing of the SWAT to address these issues and to work toward development of a national database. Further work needs to be done to explore the lack of improvement in primary caregiver scores and to work with social workers toward awareness of the importance of quantitative outcomes assessment and addressing the SWAT issues with clients. This awareness can be promoted through social work education.

END-OF-LIFE CARE CONTENT IN SOCIAL WORK EDUCATION

Social workers have reported a lack of end-of-life care training in their professional education, (Csikai and Raymer 2005; Raymer and Reese 2004) and research indicates that textbooks frequently used in social work education include very little content on end-of-life care (Berzoff and Silverman 2004a). Many schools have no coverage at all of death, dying, or bereavement, and, when covered, this content is usually presented as a minor part of another course or in an elective that few students take (Kramer, Hovland-Scafe, and Pacourek 2003). Christ and Sormanti (1999) reported that curriculum content is not well-integrated with theory and research.

Only 25 percent of faculty surveyed believed that students who took existing social work courses were adequately prepared for providing end-of-life care to clients (Christ and Sormanti 1999). In other research, second-year MSW students agreed with this assessment, with most students responding that they felt "a little" or "somewhat" prepared to help clients and families who were grieving or dying (Kramer 1998). In the practice world, oncology social work supervisors have reported serious gaps in the social work curricula in the areas of terminal illness and bereavement (Sormanti 1994). In addition, practicing social workers have not considered themselves well-trained for hospice social work, have not been clear about their role on the team, and have not felt that adequate continuing education resources were available (Christ and Sormanti 1999; Csikai and Raymer 2005; Kovacs and Bronstein 1999; Kramer 1998). Subsequent research has provided evidence of the difficulty on the part of social workers in identifying spiritual issues in work with clients (Reese 2001) or in addressing psychosocial and spiritual issues even if identified (Reese et al. 2006).

EFFORTS MADE TO IMPROVE END-OF-LIFE CARE SOCIAL WORK

In response to this situation, a number of efforts have been made by end-of-life care social workers to advance the field. In 1999 Grace Christ from Columbia University obtained a grant from the Soros Foundation and created the Social Work Leadership Development Awards within the Project on Death in America (Christ and Sormanti 1999). This project funded forty-two social work scholars and mentored their development into national leaders in end-of-life care. Since that time the Hartford Foundation developed the Geriatric Social Work Faculty Scholars Program aimed at developing leaders in the field of aging. A number of these scholars developed social work curricula and continuing education programs in end-of-life care, and networking among these scholars has led to development of a national research agenda, standards for practice in the field, and collaboration on development of social work education. The National Social Work Summit on End-of-Life and Palliative Care, held at Duke University in the spring of 2002, urged social work education content as one of the top priorities (Kramer, Hovland-Scafe, and Pacourek 2003).

SOCIAL WORK CURRICULA   In 1998 Kramer had demonstrated the effectiveness of a course on grief, death, and loss on increasing perceived competence and sense of preparation, including personal preparation. In 2003 Kramer, Hovland-Scafe, and Pacourek identified ten critical areas of end-of-life content for use in social work education: 1. the social work perspective on end-of-life care, 2. culture-, gender-, and age-relevant psychosocial assessment of clients at the end of life, 3. social work assessment and intervention with diverse family forms and informal caregivers facing end of life, 4. differential diagnosis and treatment in the end-of-life context, 5. communication with patients, families, and other care providers, 6. symptoms along the continuum of illness and near the time of death, 7. pain, distress, and suffering management, 8. loss, grief, and bereavement, 9. ethical and legal issues, and 10. healthcare systems, policy, and advocacy (appendix, 317–320). Kovacs and Bronstein (1999) surveyed 108 hospice social workers and identified a need for electives in medical social work, family treatment, and crisis intervention. Gaps in education they identified included content on loss and grief and preparation for interdisciplinary collaboration. On-the-job training that was needed included medical terminology and integration of personal experiences with professional work.

Ellen Csikai and Mary Raymer (2005) conducted focus groups with end-of-life care social work experts, and a survey of 391 health care social workers. They asked what educational content and skills were needed for competence in end-of-life care social work practice. Their results indicated that the most needed content included assessment skills, psychosocial needs of patients and families and interventions to address these needs, and communication with the interdisciplinary team. Csikai and Raymer used the results of their research to develop a continuing education workshop which has been delivered nationally on a regular basis. They also recommended that this content be included in social work program curricula. As a result of these efforts, the field has greatly developed, with more curricula in development but with many new resources available (Walsh-Burke and Csikai 2005).

In addition, the Association of Oncology Social Work has developed two online end-of-life care courses, and the NCHPP Social Work Section's Competency-Based Education Task Force developed a Web-based training module to distinguish between grief and depression. The National Association of Social Work has established a health specialty practice section, the Council on Social Work Education has a Health Symposium, and the Society for Social Work and Research has an End-of-Life Care Researchers' Interest Group—all of which serve as important forums for dissemination of information to the field.

CERTIFICATION FOR HOSPICE SOCIAL WORKERS New York University and Smith College both have postmaster's certificate programs in end-of-life care. In addition, the National Association of Social Workers has collaborated with the National Hospice and Palliative Care Organization to develop BSW and MSW level credentials for social workers who meet national standards of excellence. These are the certified hospice and palliative social worker (CHP-SW) and the advanced certified hospice and palliative social worker (ACHP-SW). This is an important step in the field, as other disciplines on the hospice team have had certification for quite some time. Social workers should encourage their colleagues to pursue this certification and advocate with their hospice organizations to require it when hiring social workers. This development in the field will communicate to the Centers for Medicare and Medicaid Services, which has just lowered the required qualifications for hospice social workers to a bachelor's degree in a related field, the expected standards for hospice social work practice.

STANDARDS FOR PRACTICE Several professional organizations have developed standards for end-of-life care social work practice. For example, the Society for Social Work Leadership in Health Care developed standards for social workers in end-of-life care in 2000. In 2004, NASW, under the leadership of PDIA scholar Elizabeth Clark, made end-of-life care one of its top priorities and developed Standards for Palliative and End-of-Life Care based on the findings of the 2002 Duke Summit (National Association of Social Workers, 2004). The Social Worker Section of NCHPP also provides Guidelines for Social Work in Hospice (National Hospice and Palliative Care Organization, 2008).

LITERATURE In 2004 Joan Berzoff and Phyllis Silverman edited the first textbook on end-of-life care social work. In 2005 the *Journal of Social Work in End-of-Life and Palliative Care* published its first issue; this first and only journal in end-of-life care social work serves as an important forum for disseminating new knowledge created in the field. In 2011 the *Oxford Textbook* of *Palliative Social Work*, edited by Terry Altilio and Shirley Otis-Green, was published, creating this important addition of social work to the edited volumes existing for other disciplines.

IMPLICATIONS OF RESEARCH FINDINGS FOR SOCIAL WORK EDUCATION

Much work has been done to establish a framework for social work education in end-of-life care. Still, there is a lot of work left for us to do. Social work education is key to continuing our progress in advancing the field of end-of-life care social work. Social work education should use a holistic approach, including bio/psycho/social/spiritual aspects of end-of-life care and addressing the micro, mezzo, and macro levels of practice. It should provide theoretical frameworks and tested practice models that incorporate all of these aspects. It should incorporate current literature, research, and standards for practice (Christ and Sormanti 1999).

One of the highest priorities is teaching research skills and a value orientation toward documenting social work outcomes on all system levels. Personal preparation is key, including addressing student death anxiety and awareness of beliefs about end-of-life care and how they may differ from clients served (Reese et al. 2010). Much of this recommended content can be taught within hospice field placements.

MICRO LEVEL EDUCATIONAL CONTENT Research has identified major micro level psychosocial and spiritual issues that predict hospice outcomes (Reese 1995–96; Reese et al. 2006). Social workers need theoretical frameworks, assessment skills, and tested intervention models to address these issues. Micro level issues, included in the Social Work Assessment Tool (Reese et al. 2006), are the following: spirituality, death anxiety, denial of terminality, suicidal ideation, assisted suicide, end-of life care decisions including advance directives, patient preferences about environment, safety, and comfort issues, and complicated anticipatory grief (e.g., guilt, depression, etc.). Crisis intervention skills are crucial for hospice social work practice (Kovacs and Bronstein 1999), but social workers should understand that early and frequent social work involvement in a case can prevent crisis (Reese and Raymer 2004).

MEZZO LEVEL EDUCATIONAL CONTENT Social workers must be prepared to work with families on the mezzo level; hospice social workers have reported the importance of social work courses in family treatment (Kovacs and Bronstein 1999). The Social Work Assessment Tool (Reese et al. 2006) includes the mezzo level variables of social support and financial resources. Ability to serve families is key; research with the SWAT indicated less effectiveness of social work intervention with primary caregivers (Reese et al. 2006). Research has also shown that primary caregivers in denial are more likely to place patients in the hospital when dying, in opposition to their wish to die at home (Reese 2000). Finally, social workers play an important role in bereavement; most supervisors of bereavement programs in hospice are social workers (Reese and Raymer 1999).

It is also of great importance to prepare social workers for work on a high functioning interdisciplinary team (Stark 2011). Social work input has been found to predict team functioning (Reese and Raymer 2004). It is important to prepare social workers to provide staff support and advocate with the team for client self-determination. It is critical to educate social workers about their role in hospice so they can articulate that role to other disciplines. Evidence about the crucial need for early and frequent social work intervention makes it essential for social workers to understand that they must be involved throughout the course of a client case, including carrying on-call responsibilities (Reese and Raymer 2004). It is necessary to include content about how to promote high-functioning interdisciplinary teams. This content is very effectively taught in an interdisciplinary class setting.

MACRO LEVEL   Little awareness seems to exist in the hospice field of the responsibility of social workers for macro practice. Social workers are more highly trained than the other health care disciplines in intervention with organizations and communities; thus they should provide leadership in these areas.

Organizational Practice   Social workers should be involved in administration of the hospice agency. They should provide supervision of social workers, as this is key to hospice outcomes (Reese and Raymer 2004) and is a responsibility included in the National Association of Social Workers's *NASW Standards for Palliative and End-of-Life Care* (2011). They should provide leadership in the development of organizational cultural and linguistic competence, including increasing the diversity of staff and providing cultural competence training (del Rio 2004).

Community Practice   Social workers should be prepared for outreach to the community through skills in general public education, collaboration with the broader health care system, and cultivating relationships with leaders of diverse cultural groups in order to increase access for these communities. They should develop skills in needs assessment studies to identify populations that are not being served by hospice or unmet needs for services. Social workers should possess skills in collaboration with other health care providers.

IMPACT OF EFFORTS TO DEVELOP THE FIELD

Considering the tremendous efforts to advance our field, one might ask whether the perception of the social work role has changed since the Kulys and Davis study in 1986. The answer to this question appears to be yes. Reese (2011a) conducted a survey of forty-three hospice directors in thirty-four states as well as Washington, DC, replicating the classic Kulys and Davis study. She developed a questionnaire listing a number of services considered by social workers to pertain to their role. This list included the original services articulated in the Kulys and Davis study as well as additional services based on the above-described current social work literature, curricula, and standards for practice. She asked the directors to identify which professional discipline on the team 1. spends the most time providing the service and 2. is most qualified to provide the service.

As expected, 70 percent of the directors were nurses and only 7 percent were social workers. Directors' responses were in close agreement, and the discipline considered most qualified also spent the most time providing the service. Social workers were considered by directors to be most qualified to provide twelve out of twenty-three of the services (as opposed to three in the Kulys and Davis study). They were still considered most qualified to provide financial counseling (98 percent checked social work as most qualified to provide this service) and referrals to resources (83 percent). But, in addition to those roles attributed to social workers in the Kulys and Davis study, they were also considered most qualified to provide ten other services—these are listed in table 2.1. They included assessment and counseling for a variety of psychosocial issues, promoting cultural competence, community outreach, and bereavement counseling. Clearly, the role of social work has expanded in the eyes of hospice directors since 1986.

TABLE 2.1. Social Work Roles: Hospice Directors' Views of Which Discipline Is Most Qualified

ACTIVITY	DISCIPLINE MOST QUALIFIED IN ACTIVITY SOCIAL WORKERS CONSIDERED MOST QUALIFIED				
	NURSE	SOCIAL WORKER	SPIRITUAL CAREGIVER	ALL	MULTIPLE DISCIPLINES MOST QUALIFIED
Financial counseling	0%	98%	0%	0%	2%
Referrals	7%	83%	0%	7%	2%
Assessment of emotional and social problems	12%	79%	2%	2%	5%
Counseling about suicide	0%	67%	12%	5%	16%
Facilitating social support	0%	66%	7%	0%	27%
Counseling about denial	20%	54%	2%	10%	15%
Promoting cultural competence	8%	54%	5%	14%	19%
Community outreach	3%	50%	8%	13%	26%
Counseling re. anticipatory grief	5%	46%	27%	7%	15%
Crisis intervention	32%	45%	0%	12%	10%
Bereavement counseling	0%	42%	28%	0%	30% (sw, scg, ber, and/or vol)
Counseling about death	21%	28%	27%	16%	9%

ACTIVITY	DISCIPLINE MOST QUALIFIED IN ACTIVITY NURSE AND SOCIAL WORKERS CONSIDERED MOST QUALIFIED				
	NURSE	SOCIAL WORKER	SPIRITUAL CAREGIVER	ALL	NURSE AND SOCIAL WORKER MOST QUALIFIED
Intake interview	18%	2%	0%	0%	75%

ACTIVITY	DISCIPLINE MOST QUALIFIED IN ACTIVITY NURSE CONSIDERED MOST QUALIFIED				
	NURSE	SOCIAL WORKER	SPIRITUAL CAREGIVER	ALL	MULTIPLE DISCIPLINES MOST QUALIFIED
Civil and legal assistance	95%	0%	0%	0%	5%

TABLE 2.1. Social Work Roles: Hospice Directors' Views of Which Discipline Is Most Qualified *(continued)*

On-call	90%	0%	0%	5%	5%
Counseling about safety issues	77%	7%	0%	5%	12%
Supervising hospice workers	71%	7%	2%	5%	14%
Directing the hospice	71%	7%	2%	2%	16%
Discharge planning	63%	28%	0%	0%	9%
Upholding preferences about the environment	45%	33%	0%	10%	12%
Advocacy	42%	24%	0%	22%	12%

ACTIVITY	DISCIPLINE MOST QUALIFIED IN ACTIVITY SPIRITUAL CAREGIVER CONSIDERED MOST QUALIFIED				
	NURSE	SOCIAL WORKER	SPIRITUAL CAREGIVER	ALL	MULTIPLE DISCIPLINES QUALIFIED
Supporting direct spiritual experience	0%	0%	88%	5%	7%
Discussing meaning of life	2.3%	19%	58%	12%	9%
Ensuring culturally competent end-of-life care decisions	5%	14%	52%	17%	11%

Nevertheless, nurses were still considered most qualified to perform eight social work functions (see table 2.1). Notably, these do not include any counseling about mental health issues. Of concern, however, is the directors' opinion that nurses are most qualified to direct the hospice and supervise staff.

Spiritual caregivers were considered most qualified to provide three services (see table 2.1). Two—supporting direct spiritual experience and discussing meaning of life—were based on the two dimensions within Reese's definition of spirituality (2001). The third, surprisingly, was ensuring culturally competent end-of-life decisions. More research is needed to provide information about the relative qualifications of spiritual caregivers and social workers in providing these services. It seems clear, though, due to the importance of spirituality in terminal illness (Reith and Payne 2009), with spiritual issues being the most frequently discussed issues on hospice home visits, even by social workers (Reese and Brown 1997), that social workers must consider addressing them as part of their role in hospice (Reith and Payne 2009).

Seventy-five percent of directors also reported that both social workers and nurses are most qualified to conduct the intake interview. This is an advance in the field, since several authors have found that social work participation in the intake interview predicts beneficial hospice outcomes (Cherin et al. 2000; Mahar, Eickman, and Bushfield 1997; Paquette 1997; Reese and Raymer 2004).

The field of hospice care has changed over the years in response to health care reimbursement and professionalism of hospice. The conception of Dame Cicely Saunders, who was trained as a physician, nurse, and social worker, hospice began in the U.S. in the early 1970s with a vision of holistic care that addressed biopsychosocial and spiritual needs of clients. This changed in the 1980s with Medicare reimbursement and a new focus based on a medical model of care. During the late 1980s and early 1990s the role of social workers was minimized and nonmedical staff was considered "ancillary." Tremendous efforts by social workers in the areas of research and development of curricula, certification, credentialing, practice standards, and development of literature, however, have had a clear impact on the current status of social work in hospice. Much work is left to do, however. Social workers must educate the interdisciplinary team about their role in hospice. They must continue to document social work outcomes to demonstrate their importance to the field. Finally, social work education is key to continuing our progress in advancing the field of hospice social work. We must prepare students to become aware of personal issues, provide biopsychosocial/spiritual care, and address micro, mezzo, as well as macro levels of practice. In this way client needs can be met consistent with the holistic vision of early hospice care.

Another area for work is the development and evaluation of specific models of practice for hospice social work. When social workers were asked in the National Hospice Social Work Survey (Reese and Raymer 2004) what models of practice they used with clients, it was difficult for them to articulate theoretical frameworks or practice models. They mentioned many specific techniques, as will be discussed in later chapters, but not often specifying a certain treatment model. Chapter 3 will present a model of variables that is based on social work research about client outcomes in the field of hospice. This model has been used as the basis for the Social Work Assessment Tool. Chapter 3 reviews research documenting the relationships between the variables in the models and their role in hospice patient outcomes. In addition, chapter 3 presents theoretical frameworks for understanding these relationships. This model will be used as a framework for the rest of the book, in terms of understanding and organizing issues to address in hospice social work intervention.

REFERENCES

Altilio, T., and S. Otis-Green. 2011. *Oxford Textbook of Palliative Social Work*. New York: Oxford University Press.

Archer, K. 1999. "Toward a Measure of Caregiver Satisfaction with Hospice Social Services." *Hospice Journal* 14, no. 2: 1–15.

Berzoff, J., and P. Silverman. 2004a. "Introduction." In Joan Berzoff and Phyllis R. Silverman, eds., *Living with Dying: A Handbook for End-of-Life Healthcare Practitioners*, pp. 1–17. New York: Columbia University Press.

——. 2004b. *Living with Dying: A Handbook for End-of-Life Healthcare Practitioners*. New York: Columbia University Press.

Cherin, D. A., G. J. Huba, L. A. Melchior, S. Enguidanos, W. J. Simmons, and D. E. Brief. 2000. "Issues in Implementing and Evaluating a Managed Care Home Health Care System for HIV/AIDS: Visiting Nurse Association Foundation of Los Angeles." *Drugs and Society* 16, nos. 1–2: 203–222.

Christ, G., and M. Sormanti. 1999. "Advancing Social Work Practice in End-of-Life Care." *Social Work in Health Care* 30, no. 2: 81–99.

Corless, I. B., and P. K. Nicholas. 2004. "The Interdisciplinary Team: An Oxymoron?" In Joan Berzoff and Phyllis R. Silverman, eds., *Living with Dying: A Handbook for End-of-Life Healthcare Practitioners*, pp. 161–170. New York: Columbia University Press.

Csikai, E. 2002. "The State of Hospice Ethics Committees and the Social Work Role." *Omega: Journal of Death and Dying* 45, no. 3: 261–275.

Csikai, E, and M. Raymer. 2005. "Social Workers' Educational Needs in End-of-Life Care." *Social Work in Health Care* 41, no. 1: 53.

del Rio, N. 2004. "A Framework for Multicultural End-of-Life Care: Enhancing Social Work Practice." In Joan Berzoff and Phyllis R. Silverman, eds., *Living with Dying: A Handbook for End-of-Life Healthcare Practitioners*, pp. 439–461. New York: Columbia University Press.

Doherty, J. B., and K. L. DeWeaver. 2004. "A Survey of Evaluation Practices for Hospice Social Workers." *Home Health Care Services Quarterly* 23, no. 4: 1–13.

Dyeson, T., and C. Hebert. 2004. "Discrepant Perceptions of Home Health Care Professionals Regarding Psychosocial Issues of Older Patients." *Gerontologist* 44, no. 1: 409.

Forrest, C., and C. Derrick. 2010. "Interdisciplinary Education in End-of-Life Care: Creating New Opportunities for Social Work, Nursing, and Clinical Pastoral Education Students." *Journal of Social Work in End-of-Life and Palliative Care* 6, nos. 1–2: 91–116.

Goldberg, J., and M. Scharlin. 2011. "Financial Considerations for the Palliative Social Worker." In Terry Altilio and Shirley Otis-Green, *Oxford Textbook of Palliative Social Work*, pp. 709–718. New York: Oxford University Press.

Hodgson, H., S. Segal, M. Weidinger, and M. B. Linde. 2004. "Being There: Contributions of the Nurse, Social Worker, and Chaplain During and After a Death." *Generations* 28, no. 2: 47–52.

Huber, R., and V. Runnion. 1996. "Social Work Acuity Scale for Hospice." Unpublished MS.

Kovacs, P., and L. Bronstein. 1999. "Preparation for Oncology Settings: What Hospice Workers Say They Need." *Health and Social Work* 24, no. 1: 57–64.

Kramer, B. 1998. "Preparing Social Workers for the Inevitable: A Preliminary Investigation of a Course on Grief, Death, and Loss." *Journal of Social Work Education* 34, no. 2: 1–17.

Kramer, B., C. Hovland-Scafe, and L. Pacourek. 2003. "Analysis of End-of-Life Content in Social Work Textbooks." *Journal of Social Work Education* 39, no. 2: 299–320).

Kulys, R., and M. Davis. 1986. "An Analysis of Social Services in Hospice." *Social Work* 11, no. 6: 448–454.

Mahar, T., L. Eickman, and S. Bushfield. 1997. "Efficacy of Early Social Work Intervention." Paper presented at the National Hospice and Palliative Care Organization's Eleventh Management and Leadership Conference.

Nakashima, M. 2003. "Beyond Coping and Adaptation: Promoting a Holistic Perspective on Dying." *Families in Society: The Journal of Contemporary Human Services* 84, no. 3: 367–376.

National Association of Social Workers. 2004. NASW *Standards for Social Work Practice in Palliative and End of Life Care*. Washington, DC: National Association of Social Workers. Retrieved from: http://www.socialworkers.org/practice/bereavement/standards/standards0504New.pdf.

——, Social Work Policy Institute. 2010. *Hospice Social Work: Linking Policy, Practice, and Research*. Washington, DC: National Association of Social Workers.

National Hospice and Palliative Care Organization (formerly National Hospice Organization). 1997. *A Pathway for Patients and Families Facing Terminal Illness.* Arlington, VA: NHO.

——. 2002. "The 2001 Data Set Survey: Building a National Hospice Database." *Newsline* 12, no. 1: 1, 8.

———. 2008. *Guidelines for Social Work in Hospice.* Arlington, VA: NHPCO.

——. 2009. "NHPCO Facts and Figures: Hospice Care in America." Retrieved from www. nhpco.org/files/public/Statistics_Research/NHPCO_facts_and_figures. pdf.

Paquette, S. 1997. "Social Work Intervention and Program Cost Reduction Outcomes." Paper presented at the National Hospice and Palliative Care Organization's Eleventh Management and Leadership Conference.

Parker Oliver, D., and M. Peck. 2006. "Inside the Interdisciplinary Team Experiences of Hospice Social Workers." *Journal of Social Work in End-of-Life and Palliative Care* 2, no. 3: 7–21.

Raymer, M., and D. Reese. 2004. "The History of Social Work in Hospice." In Joan Berzoff and Phyllis R. Silverman, eds., *Living with Dying: A Handbook for End-of-Life Healthcare Practitioners*, pp. 150–160. New York: Columbia University Press.

Reese, D. (formerly Ita, D.) 1995–96. "Testing of a Causal Model: Acceptance of Death in Hospice Patients." *Omega: Journal of Death and Dying* 32, no. 2: 81–92.

——. 2000. "The Role of Primary Caregiver Denial in Inpatient Placement During Home Hospice Care." *Hospice Journal* 15, no. 1: 15–33.

——. 2001. "Addressing Spirituality in Hospice: Current Practices and a Proposed Role for Transpersonal Social Work. *Social Thought: Journal of Religion in the Social Services* 20, nos. 1–2: 135–161.

——. 2011a. "Interdisciplinary Perceptions of the Social Work Role in Hospice: Building Upon the Classic Kulys and Davis Study." *Journal of Social Work in End-of-Life and Palliative Care* 7, no. 4: 383–406.

——. 2011b. "Spirituality and Social Work Practice in Palliative Care." In Terry Altilio and Shirley Otis-Green, eds., *Oxford Textbook of Palliative Social Work*, pp. 201–213. New York: Oxford University Press.

Reese, D., and S. Beckwith. 2005. "Organizational Barriers to Cultural Competence in Hospice." Paper presented at the National Hospice and Palliative Care Association, Opening Doors, Building Bridges: Access and Diversity Conference, August, St. Louis.

Reese, D., and D. Brown. 1997. "Psychosocial and Spiritual Care in Hospice: Differences Between Nursing, Social Work, and Clergy." *Hospice Journal* 12, no. 1: 29–41.

Reese, D., C. L. W. Chan, W. C. H. Chan, and D. Wiersgalla. 2010. "A Cross-National Comparison of Hong Kong and U.S. Student Beliefs and Preferences in End-of-Life Care: Implications for Social Work Education and Hospice Practice." *Journal of Social Work in End-of-Life and Palliative Care* 6, nos. 3–4: 1–31.

Reese, D., and M. Raymer. 1999. "National Hospice Organization Social Work Survey and Bereavement Follow-up Study: Final Results." Paper presented at the National Hospice Organization, Twenty-first Annual Symposium and Exposition, October, Long Beach, CA.

——. 2004. "Relationships Between Social Work Services and Hospice Outcomes: Results of the National Hospice Social Work Survey." *Social Work* 49, no. 3.

Reese, D., M. Raymer, S. Orloff, S. Gerbino, R. Valade, S. Dawson, C. Butler, M. Wise-Wright, and R. Huber. 2006. "The Social Work Assessment Tool (SWAT): Developed by the Social Worker Section of the National Council of Hospice and Palliative Professionals, National Hospice and Palliative Care Organization." *Journal of Social Work in End-of-Life and Palliative Care* 2, no. 2: 65–95.

Reith, M., and M. Payne. 2009. *Social Work in End-of-Life and Palliative Care.* Chicago: Lyceum.

Soltura, D. L., and L. F. Piotrowski. 2011. In Terry Altilio and Shirley Otis-Green, eds., *Oxford Textbook of Palliative Social Work*, pp. 495–501. New York: Oxford University Press.

Sontag, M. 1995. "Team Functioning Scale." Unpublished MS.

——. 1996a. "A Comparison of Hospice Programs Based on Medicare Certification Status." *American Journal of Hospice and Palliative Care* 13, no. 2: 32–41.

——. 1996b. "Hospices as Providers of Total Care in One Western State." *The Hospice Journal*, 11(3), 71–94.

Sormanti, M. 1994. "Fieldwork Instruction in Oncology Social Work: Supervisory Issues." *Journal of Psychosocial Oncology* 12, no. 3: 73–87.

Stark, D. 2011. "Teamwork in Palliative Care: An Integrative Approach." In Terry Altilio and Shirley Otis-Green, eds., *Oxford Textbook of Palliative Social Work*, pp. 415–424. New York: Oxford University Press.

Walsh-Burke, K., and E. L. Csikai. 2005. "Professional Social Work Education in End-of-Life Care: Contributions of the Project on Death in America's Social Work Leadership Development Program." *Journal of Social Work in End-of-Life and Palliative Care* 1, no. 2: 11–26.

3

A MODEL FOR PSYCHOSOCIAL AND
SPIRITUAL CARE IN HOSPICE

This chapter presents our model of variables, which we use as a basis for hospice social work intervention. It is based on social work research about the psychosocial and spiritual issues that influence hospice patient and family outcomes. Research also indicates that social workers address these variables and clients improve on these issues after social work intervention. This model is the framework for the Social Work Assessment Tool (Reese et al. 2006), which can be used as both a reminder of the important issues to address and as a way to document social work outcomes in hospice and palliative care. This chapter discusses the relationships in the model (shown in figure 3.1), provides an overview of theory explaining these relationships as well as research evidence of their place in the model. We start with a theoretical perspective that provides a basic framework for the model.

OVERVIEW OF THEORY

In Erik Erikson's psychosocial theory (1950), human development simultaneously progresses in several different systems—the biological, psychological, and societal systems. To this model some authors have added the spiritual system, which they propose develops along with the other systems (Canda and Furman 2010; Jacobs 2004; Wilber 1993). In a national survey of hospice social workers and review of patient charts, 58 percent of hospice social workers addressed spiritual issues in case discussions with their interdisciplinary teams and 62 percent addressed spiritual issues in counseling sessions with clients (Reese 2001). In a chart review conducted in one hospice, the most frequently addressed issue was spirituality. Not surprisingly, spirituality was addressed most often by the chaplain, but social workers provided intervention with spiritual issues more often than nurses (Reese and Brown 1997).

These biopsychosocial and spiritual systems influence and are influenced by all the others in the course of development through a series of life stages. Each life stage has psychosocial tasks that must be completed in order to resolve the psychosocial crisis of that stage. Successfully completed tasks over the course of a lifetime contribute to ego integrity, which provides the ability to face death without great fear. Dying can be seen as an additional life stage with psychosocial tasks of its own (Simmers, Simmers-Nartker, and Simmers-Kobelak 2008), with spiritual issues playing a central role in these psychosocial tasks. Thus, despite spiritual development through life, enhanced spiritual growth may be seen among those confronted with mortality (Doka 2011; Nakashima 2003; Reith and Payne 2009).

A MODEL FOR PRACTICE

Figure 3.1 illustrates a path model of variables that social work research indicates are most important in predicting hospice social work outcomes. The research methods used do not allow us to claim that one variable *causes* another, but we know that one is related to another or *predicts* the level of the other. For example, we know that spirituality and social support are related; those with high levels of spirituality also have high levels of social support. We don't know which causes the other, however, because we don't know whether spirituality or social support developed first. In this discussion we will discuss research results as well as theory that proposes which variable may have come first. This model is relevant to the experience of patients as well as their significant others. The experience of families and significant others will be discussed at length in chapter 5.

Few studies have been conducted directly with hospice clients. Evidence exists, though, to support most of the paths in the model. In this model one's level of spirituality is predicted by one's level of development, confrontation with mortality, and cultural group. How much social support one perceives is predicted by one's cultural group along with one's spirituality. Death anxiety, grief, depression, and a sense of control are predicted by spirituality along with perceived social support. Cultural group impacts the need for control a client may feel. Denial of terminality, despite being informed of

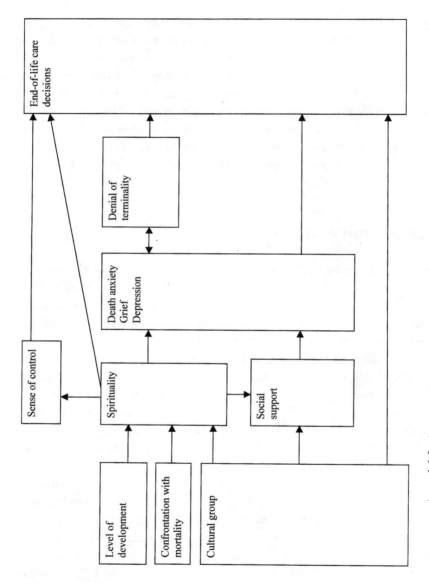

FIG. 3.1. A model for intervention

one's prognosis, is thought to be a way to cope with death anxiety, grief, depression, and loss of control. End-of-life decisions are in turn predicted by spirituality, denial, social support, and cultural group. We will discuss the predictors of each variable below.

PREDICTORS OF SPIRITUALITY

The author defines spirituality as a two-dimensional construct that includes transcendence in terms of philosophy of life and transcendence in terms of unity consciousness. Both religious and nonreligious beliefs, philosophies, and world views fit into the philosophy of life dimension.

Three factors in figure 3.1 predict the level of spirituality an individual experiences—one's level of development, confrontation with mortality, and the cultural group one affiliates with.

LEVEL OF DEVELOPMENT AND SPIRITUALITY   A number of theories describe human capabilities as advancing through predictable levels of development as life progresses. According to Eriksonian psychosocial theory, ego integrity is defined as the ability to accept one's life as is and to face death without great fear (Erikson 1950). Achievement of ego integrity is the positive outcome of the psychosocial crisis of the life stage of later adulthood.

In the author's view, accepting one's life as it is, the positive experiences along with the negative, is a result of finding a sense of meaning in one's life through developing a philosophy of life. A sense that one's life has been complete and fulfilling can lead to well-being during the final months (Cadell, Shermak, and Johnston 2011; Reith and Payne 2009). These concepts are relevant to the philosophy of life dimension of spirituality, and research indicates that older adults are indeed more highly spiritual (Harrawood 2009; Hooyman and Kramer 2006; Turesky and Schultz 2010). Younger adults, in contrast, have been found to have a sense of unfinished business, which has been found to predict death anxiety (Bell, Ziner, and Champion 2009).

Transpersonal theory is also consistent with this point of view. Transpersonal theory is based on the perspective that human development is a process of evolution in which each person, and the human species as a whole, will eventually attain unitary consciousness (Canda and Furman 2010). Levels of consciousness as proposed by Wilber (1993) include 1. the pre-egoic, in infancy and early childhood, in which the child has not yet achieved an awareness of ego separate from the world around him, 2. the egoic, from older childhood on, in which the individual achieves a clear sense of autonomous ego, ability for rational thought, and mature social relationships, and 3. the transegoic stage, which is normally not achieved until adulthood, and possibly not at all. In this stage the sense of self is not limited to ordinary space, time, or ego boundaries, and the identity encompasses the totality of the universe. Separations and distinctions no longer exist, and the individual develops the perspective that everything, including oneself, is one with all. This expansion of one's identity from a separate and distinct ego to inclusion of an interconnected web of existence is known as ego disidentification and is relevant to the unity consciousness dimension of spirituality. From this perspective, ordinary life is infused with a sense of the sacred (Jacobs 2004). Heightened empathy and compassion, and thus highly developed moral standards, naturally arise as the individual experiences a profound connection with others (Canda and Furman 2010; Jacobs 2004). Transpersonal experiences are also thought to be common in this stage.

Transpersonal theory, then, views spirituality as developing through life with higher levels of spirituality being more likely in later adulthood. This theory, along with psychosocial theory, predicts that older adults will be more highly spiritual. Spirituality is a primary way of coping with terminality (Crunkilton and Rubins 2009), which will be discussed further in the following section.

CONFRONTATION WITH MORTALITY AND SPIRITUALITY   This explanation of elderly individuals' ability to cope with death through high levels of spirituality does not explain the ability of younger people to cope with death, however. Young people, even children, although presenting issues unique to their developmental stages, appear to go through a process during terminality that is quite similar to the elderly. It seems useful to note that dying may be an additional life stage with its own opportunities for growth or distress. Evidence exists that confrontation with mortality spurs a period of spiritual growth in terminally ill patients (Harris 2008; Nakashima 2003), their loved ones (Sand, Olsson, and Strang 2010) and even in staff who work with them (Callahan 2009; Otis-Green 2011; Derezotes and Evans 1995; Sinclair 2011). The life stage of dying is thought by Reed (1987) to have associated psychosocial tasks, which include maintaining a meaningful quality of life, coping with disfigurement and loss of function, confronting spiritual and existential questions, and planning for survivors. Spirituality is seen as integral to the achievement of these psychosocial tasks.

Kubler-Ross's stage theory (1970) may provide additional illumination regarding the dynamics of this stage of terminality. Reed proposes that transpersonal perspectives accrued over the lifespan may help the individual maintain a sense of well-being when faced with death, but found that terminality, not age, influences spiritual growth (Reed 1987). This may in part explain the transpersonal experiences, common in the highest levels of spirituality according to transpersonal theory, that are often documented among hospice patients (Gardner 2011; Gibbs and Achterberg-Lawlis 1978; Kuhl 2011; Pflaum and Kelley 1986).

CULTURAL GROUP AND SPIRITUALITY Several authors have found a relationship between cultural group and spirituality. The transcendence in terms of philosophy of life dimension of spirituality may include religious beliefs. Cultural groups vary in the strength of religious beliefs, strength of belief in life after death, and extent of reliance on religious beliefs in coping (Cohen and Hall 2009; Hooyman and Kramer 2006).

For example, the church is very important in traditional African American culture (Allen, Davey, and Davey 2010; Hooyman and Kramer 2006). Christianity was forced upon African American slaves and was used to justify slavery. But the new Christian religious beliefs, practices, and traditions formed a new basis of social cohesion, creating solidarity and a sense of union between these strangers from a variety of African nationalities. Despite prohibition of any assembly of slaves without the presence of European Americans, the "invisible institution" of the African-American church took root through secret meetings in secluded places (Raboteau 1978). The church became the most important social institution in African American culture and has remained a source of social stability through the disruptive effects of emancipation and migration to northern urban areas. The pastor, as the leader of this institution, has played a significant leadership role in African American culture (Frazier and Lincoln 1974). As a result, African Americans traditionally seek advice about end-of-life care decisions from their pastors.

In contrast, AIDS patients from a variety of cultural groups may be alienated from religious communities. This may be based on lifestyles that include risk factors for AIDS, including IV drug use and homosexuality. Especially conservative religious communities may disapprove of individuals with these lifestyles and expect them to change or discourage their affiliation. As a result, there may be a general trend for AIDS patients to hold a negative view of religion. We should keep in mind that these patients still express that spirituality (perhaps rather than formal religion) is their primary way of coping, bringing them comfort, and mental health and possible physical health benefits (Sunil and McGehee 2007). Battle and Idler (2003) found that, especially for African Americans, religious participation reduced depression in patients faced with serious illness or bereavement.

PREDICTORS OF SOCIAL SUPPORT

Terminally ill patients and families have emphasized that meaningful relationships with loved ones is a key component of end-of-life care and of well-being at the end of life (Gassman 2010; Munn and Zimmerman 2006). Figure 3.1 illustrates the factors that predict a client's level of social support. Research indicates that social support is related to both cultural group and spirituality. In this model we use the concept of *perceived* social support rather than the number of social relationships or interactions that can be counted by an outside observer. Relationships and interactions may be viewed as positive or negative by an individual and may be valued to a different extent than would be judged by an outside observer. For example, the demands of social obligations or demands of caring for others may outweigh the benefits of these social ties. Thus measuring social support as the amount of social support that an individual perceives herself to possess may provide a more accurate result (Gardner 2011).

CULTURAL GROUP AND SOCIAL SUPPORT   Cultural groups vary in the level of cohesion they experience. Traditional African American culture is characterized by a high level of social support through kinship networks and churches (Bullock 2011). A participant in a study with African American ministers related that "hospice is all white people have. African-Americans take care of their own" (data from Reese et al. 1999). This is not the case, though, with African Americans who are not involved with the church—for example, HIV patients (Reese 1995–96). Hispanic cancer patients have also been found to have lower social support (Ell and Nishimoto 1989).

SPIRITUALITY AND SOCIAL SUPPORT   There is a relationship between spirituality and social support that can be explained through transpersonal theory. When faced with a terminal prognosis, an individual may become aware of his true nature separate from ego, identity, or role in society, facilitating transition into a transegoic perspective (Smith 1995). This has implications for the nature of social relationships. As an individual experiences deep connection with others in the transegoic stage, compassion and heightened empathy (Canda and Furman 2010) naturally arise. Personal gain ceases to be a prime objective; relationships are characterized by concern about the welfare of all. It is reasonable to expect that conflicts and competition would be reduced and relationships would improve. Thus transpersonal theory helps to explain a proposed impact of spirituality on social support. Crunkilton and Rubins (2009) discuss findings by Breitbart and Heller (2003) that when spiritual well-being was addressed, along with physical and psychological needs, patients showed psychological well-being and improved social support. These findings support the model in figure 3.1, which shows an impact of spirituality on social support.

PREDICTORS OF DEATH ANXIETY

Death anxiety, grief, depression, and a loss of control are major emotional issues during terminal illness. Death anxiety is defined as fear regarding one's own death. Dimensions of death anxiety discovered by Conte, Weiner, and Plutchik (1982) include fear of the unknown, fear of suffering, fear of loneliness, and fear of personal extinction. Similarly, Beresford and colleagues describe death anxiety as "thoughts of losing control over their mind, worries about leaving loved ones behind, worries about painful death and worries about prolonged illness" (Beresford, Adshead, and Croft 2007:169). Not surprisingly, many terminally ill patients suffer from anxiety (Berzoff 2004). A study by Reese and Kaplan (2000) found that high levels of both spirituality and perceived social support predicted lower levels of anxiety about one's health in HIV positive women. Of these two variables, though, spirituality was the strongest predictor.

SPIRITUALITY AND DEATH ANXIETY   There is a substantial amount of research evidence that spirituality predicts lower death anxiety (Doka 2011; Harrawood 2009). Younger individuals, for example, have more unfinished business than older adults. Unfinished business is a spiritual conflict contained within the philosophy of life dimension of spirituality. This spiritual conflict predicts higher death anxiety (Mutran et al. 1997); logically, then, it seems that resolving this conflict would reduce death anxiety.

Conte, Weiner, and Plutchik's (1982) conceptualization of death anxiety helps us to understand the impact of spirituality on death anxiety. As mentioned earlier, these authors found death anxiety to be composed of four factors—fear of the unknown, fear of suffering, fear of loneliness, and fear of personal extinction. It seems logical to think that religious beliefs about the afterlife, an issue falling under the philosophy of life dimension of spirituality, could reduce fear of the unknown, of loneliness, and of personal extinction after death. It should be noted, though, that one study found the opposite to be true—gay men with AIDS who still followed the religion of their childhood suffered more death anxiety than those who were nonreligious (Franks, Templer, and Cappelletty 1990–91). Thus, depending on the content of the religious belief, one's beliefs may reduce or increase death anxiety (Doka 2011). Most studies have found religious beliefs to comfort, though, rather than increase anxiety.

Transpersonal theory helps to explain how spirituality may reduce death anxiety. In the transegoic stage of development, as an individual's identity expands from a separate and distinct ego to ego disidentification, a sense of interconnectedness with all, it makes sense that fear of loneliness and personal extinction would subside (Smith 1995). In a study of sixty-nine hospice patients by this author, those with higher spirituality, according to this author's definition, had lower death anxiety (Reese 1995–96).

SOCIAL SUPPORT AND DEATH ANXIETY   There is also evidence that a higher level of perceived social support is associated with a lower level of death anxiety in terminally ill patients (Azaiza et al. 2010). Perceived social support is considered a coping resource that can be drawn upon in times of stress and is known to buffer the mental health impacts of major life events (Puterman, DeLongis, and Pomak 2010). It has been theorized that those close to an individual may enhance coping through reinterpreting one's situation, enhance self-esteem through reassurance, and enhance a sense of mastery through encouragement (Thoits 1995). Those who perceive high levels of social support may also be more likely to seek and receive help during a life crisis (Cutrona 1986), although the literature is conflicting regarding this point. Finally, current research has found physiological components to the impact of social support—social support increases the production in the body of the neuropeptide oxytocin (Carter et al. 2007), which in turn suppresses subjective responses to psychosocial stress (Emiliano et al. 2007).

PREDICTORS OF GRIEF AND DEPRESSION

Two additional major emotional issues during terminal illness are grief and depression. One of Kubler-Ross's (1970) original stages of grief was depression, but today we consider it important to distinguish between *anticipatory grief, complicated grief,* and *depression.* A natural and healthy response to a terminal prognosis is *anticipatory grief,* the patient and significant others' feelings of sadness about the life to be lost. Anticipatory grief has many of the same characteristics as those experienced during bereavement, which is grief experienced by a loved one after a death occurs (National Cancer Institute 2011). Terminally ill patients and significant others commonly experience anticipatory grief, but complicated grief and depression are far less common. Rates of major depression in cancer patients have been reported as 8 percent to 26 percent (BrintzenhofeSzoc 2011). It is important for social workers to develop skills in differential diagnosis in this area. While treating anticipatory grief as depression is inappropriate, depression is a risk factor for suicide and should be ruled out (Walsh-Burke 2004).

Grief is considered *complicated* when it is not resolved within a reasonable period of time (conventionally thought of as approximately six months after a loss). Underlying the complicated grief may be feelings of guilt, anger, or other forms of unfinished business that must be addressed before the grief can be resolved. Symptoms of complicated grief may include depression, anxiety, or post-traumatic stress disorder or, in contrast, a complete absence of grief and mourning (National Cancer Institute 2011).

According to the World Health Organization (2011), *depression* is a common mental disorder. Symptoms include "depressed mood, loss of interest or pleasure, feelings of guilt or low self-worth, disturbed sleep or appetite, low energy, and poor concentration." Depression can become chronic and interfere with functioning. Severe depression can lead to suicide (Walsh-Burke 2004).

Kubler-Ross's (1970) classic theory describes common "stages" that terminally ill individuals experience when grieving the loss of their own lives. These stages are not necessarily sequential and may reoccur a number of times. They include the stages of denial and isolation, anger, bargaining, depression, and acceptance. Later in life, Kubler-Ross and Kessler (2001) added the stages of forgiveness and surrender.

Kubler-Ross's stage theory has fallen into disfavor because the stages do not appear to be consecutive, and the theoretical reasons why such stages should exist are not explained. Also, as already discussed, depression is a separate concept from grief. However, Kubler-Ross accurately describes what grieving persons experience, and her theory can help to fill in the outlines of the model presented here.

Commonly used assessment and intervention models for depression and suicide are not relevant for those rationally choosing the option of suicide in the absence of depression (Csikai 2004). In Oregon, where assisted suicide is legal, physicians conduct assessments of the patients, and, if depression is detected, the physician may possibly withhold approval for assisted suicide. However, there is no legal requirement to assess the patient for depression. Research has indicated that a major motivation for assisted suicide is the need for a sense of control over the circumstances of death (Moody 2010).

In Oregon, hospices care for patients selecting the option of assisted suicide. In other states where assisted suicide is not legal, patients nevertheless quite often consider the option of suicide (Goy and Ganzini 2011), sometimes request the help of hospice staff, and sometimes independently carry out suicide while under hospice care. Some research has indicated that the desire for a hastened death is much more common among those with severe depression (Levene and Parker 2011; Reith and Payne 2009). This situation highlights the importance of correct assessment of complicated grief and depression and the ability to distinguish these from patients experiencing anticipated grief or making a rational choice of assisted suicide.

These emotional issues are similarly affected by spirituality and social support. The following discussion outlines the research evidence and further theoretical explanations about the relationships between these variables.

SPIRITUALITY, GRIEF, AND DEPRESSION   Research documents psychological benefits from spiritual beliefs and practices, including a general sense of well-being in terminal illness, comforting emotions and feelings and easing the emotional burden of the illness, and reduced grief and depression (Crunkilton and Rubins 2009; Hooyman and Kramer 2006; Nakashima 2003). Sullivan (2003) discusses intervention with hopelessness at the end of life and suggests that a form of hope at this time may be based on religious beliefs about comfort in the afterlife. These feelings of well-being, comforting emotions, and hope indicate a lower level of depression. Also, spirituality helps patients develop a sense of acceptance of the illness relevant to resolving anticipatory grief. Another effect, a reduced sense of self-blame, is relevant to complicated grief (Siegel and Schrimshaw 2002).

SOCIAL SUPPORT, GRIEF, AND DEPRESSION   Gard (2000) writes about the effectiveness of the social support received in a teen bereavement group in helping teenagers resolve grief. Without the opportunity to talk with supportive friends and family, people may not express their grief and, as a result, never resolve it. Patients themselves need the opportunity to perform emotional tasks such as saying good-bye that require a network of supportive family and friends (Doka 2011).

PREDICTOR OF A SENSE OF CONTROL: SPIRITUALITY

Spiritual beliefs and practices also impart a sense of empowerment and control (Doka 2011; Siegel and Schrimshaw 2002), or positive intentionality (Daaleman, Cobb, and Frey 2001). This relationship can be explained as resulting from an active stance toward death. Death is not something that one passively waits for, but a process that one actively plans and engages in. From this point of view, one has a sense of control over the quality of the dying process. Since the major motivation for assisted suicide is the desire for a sense of control, intervention into this issue could influence some patients to decide against assisted suicide.

PREDICTOR OF DENIAL: DEATH ANXIETY AND DENIAL

During the past half-century, rapid advances in medical technology have resulted in life-sustaining techniques used in cases where there was no hope of improved quality of life for terminally ill patients. The belief that the medical profession can prolong life indefinitely has encouraged a denial of our own mortality and an absence of tools with which to face death.

Denial of terminality, which is a lack of awareness of one's terminal prognosis despite being informed of it, is a coping mechanism that lowers death anxiety by allowing only as much awareness of the facts into current thoughts as the individual can manage (Bregman 2001). Denial is a normal reaction to grief (Blacker and Jordan 2004; Reith and Payne 2009), but can become dysfunctional if it interferes with communication or realistic treatment decisions.

Avery Weisman (cited by Connor 1986) proposed three degrees of denial in the terminally ill patient, which include the following:

1. *First Order Denial*—the patient's denial of the primary facts of illness
2. *Second Order Denial*—denial of the significance of an illness
3. *Third Order Denial*—the patient's inability to believe that the disease will result in death, even after fully accepting the diagnosis and its significance

There is some disagreement in the literature regarding the influence of denial on patient outcomes. Some authors and practitioners maintain that denial is a positive coping mechanism, which helps terminally ill patients adjust to their situation (Blacker and Jordan 2004). Some authors maintain that it is not always in the best interest of the patient to reveal the terminal diagnosis (Adler 1989). Some people believe that anticipatory grief is rare. To accept a loved one's death while she is still alive may leave the mourner feeling that the dying patient has been abandoned. Expecting the loss often makes the attachment to the dying person stronger. Although anticipatory grief may help the family, the dying person may experience too much grief, causing the patient to become withdrawn.

Connor's (1986) position is that conscious levels of denial may serve to control anxiety in a positive coping strategy, but unconscious levels of denial, associated with psychopathology, can result in detrimental impacts on the patient and those who care for him (Reith and Payne 2009). An example is placement in the hospital for life-sustaining treatment when a patient has expressed the wish for palliative care.

From this perspective, an individual with death anxiety may develop denial as a way to cope. Then the denial may in turn reduce the individual's death anxiety (Parry 2001); thus the two-way connection between death anxiety and denial in figure 3.1.

Sullivan (2003) discusses the idea of hope, which is not necessarily only for cure or survival but can be hope for comfort, dignity, intimacy, or salvation. Kubler-Ross (1970) views denial as one of the beginning stages of adjustment to terminal illness. Hospice social work intervention can help patients navigate past denial and into a sense of hope that fortifies their quality of life in terminal illness.

PREDICTORS OF END-OF-LIFE CARE DECISIONS

Hospice philosophy is consistent with attitudes toward *passive euthanasia,* which, as discussed in chapter 1, includes either withholding or withdrawing life-sustaining treatment in the case of a terminally ill patient without hope of improved quality of life. In Oregon, the only state in which *active euthanasia* is legal, hospice also plays a role in supporting patients' wishes for assisted suicide. Several variables in the model have been found to predict end-of-life care decisions consistent with hospice philosophy: spirituality, denial, social support, and cultural group. The model of variables as a whole has also been found to predict end-of-life care decisions (Reese 1995–96).

SPIRITUALITY AND END-OF-LIFE CARE DECISIONS

Philosophy of Life Dimension   Spirituality has been found to predict whether a patient is oriented toward euthanasia in terminal illness (Doka 2011). Those with more traditional religious beliefs are less oriented toward palliative care (Gallup 1997). Religious commitment, as discussed, can be thought of as being contained within the philosophy of life dimension of spirituality. Foster and McLellan (2002) discuss the importance of spiritual issues in making end-of-life decisions. Family members may insist on curative care and life support until they have been able to find a sense of meaning in the death of a loved one and an acceptance of the loved one's life. Thus, resolution of spiritual issues is key in the ability to make end-of-life care decisions (Doka 2011). We must be careful not to mislabel this process as denial.

Unity Consciousness Dimension   Crunkilton and Rubins (2009:82) report that "a strong sense of spiritual well-being may protect individuals from depression and a desire for hastened death." This refers more to the unity consciousness dimension of spirituality.

DENIAL AND END-OF-LIFE CARE DECISIONS   Although denial can be a helpful way of coping with the anxiety inherent in a terminal prognosis, it can interfere with decisions about end-of-life care. Kulys (1983) found that elderly individuals in denial were less likely to plan for health crises. A study conducted by the author (Reese 2000) with a sample of sixty-eight home hospice patients revealed that primary caregivers in denial of the patient's terminality were more likely to place hospice patients in inpatient treatment. Moreover, patients placed in inpatient settings were more likely to die there, rather than at home as planned by the patient. These findings suggest an impact of primary caregiver denial upon patient self-determination and indicate the importance of addressing denial in counseling with primary caregivers of terminally ill patients.

SOCIAL SUPPORT AND END-OF-LIFE CARE DECISIONS   There is indication that Caucasian patients who have good social support are more likely to have end-of-life care wishes that are consistent with hospice philosophy (Reese 1995–96). It makes sense, if an individual has significant others willing to provide care for her in the home, that hospice care would be a more realistic plan. This is not the case with the African American population, however. African Americans who have more frequent contact with family members have been found to have a greater desire to prolong life (Reith and Payne 2009). Additional reasons for African Americans to prefer life-sustaining treatment are discussed below.

CULTURAL GROUP AND END-OF-LIFE CARE DECISIONS   Various cultural groups have been observed to differ regarding preferences about end-of-life care. These differences may be partly due to religious beliefs, history of discrimination, as well as cultural values. For example, African Americans with traditional beliefs tend to prefer life-sustaining treatment. Reasons for this preference may include a mistrust of the white health care system as well as a belief that God will perform a miracle if given time (Stark 2011). Traditional Asian clients, as another example, may not want to die in the home due to a belief that the patient's ghost may negatively influence the survivors. Catholics may also hold values opposed to euthanasia (Reese, Chan, Chan, and Wiersgalla 2010). Hospice philosophy has tended to be more consistent with Caucasian Protestant values, which is a great concern to the hospice field. General U.S. public perspectives have, nevertheless, over time started to become more oriented toward palliative care in terminal illness (Gallup International Institute 1997).

SENSE OF CONTROL AND END-OF-LIFE CARE DECISIONS   Lack of a sense of control or helplessness is a vulnerability variable that predicts increased suicide risk for cancer patients (Breitbart 1989). As we have discussed earlier in this chapter, a major motivation for assisted suicide is a desire for a sense of control. Thus a patient's sense of control may influence decisions for active rather than passive euthanasia.

PREDICTION OF HOSPICE SOCIAL WORK OUTCOMES

The previous discussion outlines the ways in which the variables in figure 3.1 are related. The model has been shown to influence several hospice social work outcomes.

ABILITY TO SUSTAIN HOME HOSPICE CARE   Despite expressing the wish to die in the home, a number of home hospice patients are rushed to the hospital at the last minute and either die there or are resuscitated, their lives are extended. The extended life is most likely to be lived on life support rather than at the previous quality of life. Research has indicated that denial on the part of family members is the most important reason for this provision of life-sustaining treatment and hospital placement when death is imminent (Reese 2000).

PLANNING FOR DEATH   Path analysis of an earlier version of the model (Reese 1995) revealed an overall significant effect of the model, explaining 23 percent of the variance in the end-of-life decisions. End-of-life care decisions in this case was operationalized as decision regarding a do not resuscitate order, presence of a will, and funeral plans. In addition to the effects of the model as a whole, cultural and religious beliefs about end-of-life care was found to have a significant direct effect upon planning for death. Additional research also found that end-of-life decisions (such as the choice of curative care and whether to enroll in hospice) were influenced by cultural and religious beliefs (Reese et al. 1999).

This model includes the major psychosocial and spiritual factors demonstrated by social work research to predict hospice outcomes. Research has indicated that these are the major issues that need to be addressed by social workers (Reese et al. 2006), that social workers do address these issues with clients, and usually to a greater degree than other disciplines on the team (Reese and Brown 1997), and that hospice directors in general believe that social workers are most qualified to address these issues (Reese 2011). The

Social Work Assessment Tool (Reese et al. 2006) has shown that hospice social work intervention predicts improvement in these issues.

What does this mean for practice? How do we intervene with these variables? The next chapter will discuss micro level intervention techniques in hospice social work.

REFERENCES

Adler, S. S. 1989. "Truth Telling to the Terminally Ill: Neglected Role of the Social Worker." *Social Work* 34:158–160.

Allen, A. J., M. P. Davey, and A. Davey. 2010. "Being Examples to the Flock: The Role of Church Leaders and African American Families Seeking Mental Health Care Services." *Contemporary Family Therapy: An International Journal* 32, no. 2: 117–134.

Azaiza, F., P. Ron, M. Shoham, and I. Gigini. 2010. "Death and Dying Anxiety Among Elderly Arab Muslims in Israel." *Death Studies* 34, no. 4: 351–364.

Battle, V. D. and E. L. Idler. 2003. "Meaning and Effects of Congregational Religious Participation." In M. A. Kimble and S. H. McFadden, eds., *Aging, Spirituality, and Religion: A Handbook*, 2:121–133. Minneapolis: Fortress Press.

Bell, C. J., K. Ziner, and V. L. Champion. 2009. "Death Worries and Quality of Life in Younger Breast Cancer Survivors." *Western Journal of Nursing Research* 31, no. 8: 1076–1077.

Beresford, P., L. Adshead, and S. Croft. 2007. *Palliative Care, Social Work, and Service Users: Making Life Possible*. Philadelphia: Kingsley.

Berzoff, J. 2004. "Psychodynamic Theories in Grief and Bereavement." In Joan Berzoff and Phyllis R. Silverman, eds., *Living with Dying: A Handbook for End-of-Life Healthcare Practitioners*, pp. 242–262. New York: Columbia University Press.

Blacker, S., and A. R. Jordan. 2004. "Working with Families Facing Life-Threatening Illness in the Medical Setting." In Joan Berzoff and Phyllis Silverman, eds., *Living with Dying: A Handbook for End-of-Life Healthcare Practitioners*, pp. 548–570. New York: Columbia University Press.

Bregman, L. 2001. "Death and Dying." *Christian Century* 118, no. 17: 33–37.

Breitbart, W. 1989. "Suicide." In J. C. Holland and J. H. Rowland, eds., *Handbook of Psychooncology: Psychological Care of the Patient with Cancer*, pp. 291–299. New York: Oxford University Press.

Breitbart, W., and K. S. Heller. 2003. "Reframing Hope: Meaning Centered Care for Patients Near the End of Life." *Journal of Palliative Medicine* 6:979–988.

BrintzenhofeSzoc, K. 2011. "Clinical Trials and the Role of Social Work." In Terry Altilio and Shirley Otis-Green, eds., *Oxford Textbook of Palliative Social Work*, pp. 141–152. New York: Oxford University Press.

Bullock, K. 2011. "The Influence of Culture on End-of-Life Decision Making." *Journal of Social Work in End-of-Life and Palliative Care* 7, no. 1: 83–98.

Cadell, S., S. Shermak, and M. Johnston. 2011. "Discovering Strengths and Growth in Palliative Care." In Terry Altilio and Shirley Otis-Green, eds., *Oxford Textbook of Palliative Social Work*, pp. 215–222. New York: Oxford University Press.

Callahan, A. M. 2009. "Spiritually-Sensitive Care in Hospice Social Work." *Journal of Social Work in End-of-Life and Palliative Care* 5, nos. 3–4: 169–185.

Canda, E., and L. Furman. 2010. *Spiritual Diversity in Social Work Practice: The Heart of Helping*. New York: Oxford University Press.

Carter, C. S., H. Pournajafi-Nazarloo, K. M. Kramer, T. E. Ziegler, R. White-Traut, D. Bello, and D. Schwertz. 2007. "Oxytocin: Behavioral Associations and Potential as a Salivary Biomarker." *Annals of the New York Academy of Sciences* 1098 (March): 312–322.

Cohen, A. B., and D. E. Hall. 2009. "Existential Beliefs, Social Satisfaction, and Well-being Among Catholic, Jewish, and Protestant Older Adults." *International Journal for the Psychology of Religion* 19, no. 1: 39–54.

Connor, S. 1986. "Measurement of Denial in the Terminally Ill: A Critical Review." *Hospice Journal* 2, no. 4: 51–68.

Conte, H., M. Weiner, and R. Plutchik. 1982. "Measuring Death Anxiety: Conceptual, Psychometric, and Factor-Analytic Aspects." *Journal of Personality and Social Psychology* 43, no. 4: 775–785.

Crunkilton, D., and V. Rubins. 2009. "Psychological Distress in End-of-Life Care: A Review of Issues in Assessment and Treatment." *Journal of Social Work in End-of-Life and Palliative Care* 5, nos. 1–2: 75–93.

Csikai, E. 2004. "Advanced Directives and Assisted Suicide: Policy Implications for Social Work Practice." In Joan Berzoff and Phyllis R. Silverman, eds., *Living with Dying: A Handbook for End-of-Life Healthcare Practitioners*, pp. 761–777. New York: Columbia University Press.

Cutrona, C. 1986. "Behavioral Manifestations of Social Support: A Microanalytic investigation. *Journal of Personality and Social Psychology* 51, no. 1: 201–208.

Daaleman, T. P., A. K. Cobb, and B. B. Frey. 2001. "Spirituality and Well-being: An Exploratory Study of the Patient Perspective." *Social Science and Medicine* 53, no. 11: 1503–1511.

Derezotes, D., and K. Evans. 1995. "Spirituality and Religiosity in Practice: In-depth Interviews of Social Work Practitioners." *Social Thought* 18, no. 1: 39–56.

Doka, K. J. 2011. "Religion and Spirituality: Assessment and intervention. *Journal of Social Work in End-of-Life and Palliative Care* 7, no. 1: 99–109.

Ell, K., and R. Nishimoto. 1989. "Coping Resources in Adaptation to Cancer: Socioeconomic and Racial Differences." *Social Service Review* 63:433–446.

Emiliano, A. B., T. Cruz, V. Pannoni, and J. L. Fudge. 2007. "The Interface of Oxytocin-Labeled Cells and Serotonin Transporter-Containing Fibers in the Primate Hypothalamus: A Substrate for SSRIs Therapeutic Effects?" *Neuropsychopharmacology* 32, no. 5: 977–988.

Erikson, E. H. 1950. *Childhood and Society*. Philadelphia: Norton.

Foster, L., and L. McLellan. 2002. "Translating Psychosocial Insight Into Ethical Discussions Supportive of Families in End-of-Life Decision-Making." *Social Work in Health Care* 35, no. 3: 37–51.

Franks, K., D. I. Templer, and G. Cappelletty. 1990–91. "Exploration of Death Anxiety as a Function of Religious Variables in Gay Men with and Without AIDS." *Omega: Journal of Death and Dying* 22, no. 1: 43–50.

Frazier, E. F., and C. E. Lincoln. 1974. *The Negro Church in America: The Black Church Since Frazier*. New York: Schocken.

Gallup International Institute. 1997. *Spiritual Beliefs and the Dying Process*. Princeton: Nathan Cummings Foundation.

Gard, C. J. 2000. "Coping with Loss." *Current Health* 26, no. 7: 26–28.

Gardner, D. S. 2011. "Palliative Social Work with Older Adults and Their Families." In Terry Altilio and Shirley Otis-Green, eds., *Oxford Textbook of Palliative Social Work*, pp. 397–411. New York: Oxford University Press.

Gassman, J. 2010. "The Chronically Ill and End-of-Life Care." In J. D. Atwood, and C. Gallo, eds., *Family Therapy and Chronic Illness*, pp. 179–205. New Brunswick, NJ: Aldine Transaction.

Gibbs, H., and J. Achterberg-Lawlis. 1978. "Spiritual Values and Death Anxiety: Implications for Counseling with Terminal Cancer Patients." *Journal of Counseling Psychology* 25:563–569.

Goy, E., and L. Ganzini. 2011. "Prevalence and Natural History of Neuropsychiatric Syndromes in Veteran Hospice Patients." *Journal of Pain and Symptom Management* 41, no. 2: 394–401.

Harrawood, L. K. 2009. Measuring Spirituality, Religiosity, and Denial in Individuals Working in Funeral Service to Predict Death Anxiety." *Omega: Journal of Death and Dying* 60, no. 2: 129–142.

Harris, H. 2008. Growing While Going: Spiritual Formation at the End of Life." *Journal of Religion, Spirituality and Aging* 20, no. 3: 227–245.

Hooyman, N. R., and B. J. Kramer. 2006. *Living Through Loss: Interventions Across the Life Span*. New York: Columbia University Press.

Jacobs, C. 2004. Spirituality and End-of-Life Care Practice for Social Workers." In Joan Berzoff and Phyllis R. Silverman, eds., *Living with Dying: A Handbook for End-of-Life Healthcare Practitioners*, pp. 188–205. New York: Columbia University Press.

Kubler-Ross, E. 1970. *On Death and Dying*. New York: Macmillan.

Kubler-Ross, E., and D. Kessler. 2001. *Life Lessons*. Llandeilo, Carmarthenshire: Cygnus.

Kuhl, D. 2011. "Exploring the Lived Experience of Having a Terminal Illness. *Journal of Palliative Care* 27, no. 1: 43–52.

Kulys, R. 1983. Readiness Among the Very Old to Face Future Crises." *Journal of Gerontological Social Work* 5, no. 4: 3–26.

Levene, I., and M. Parker. 2011. "Prevalence of Depression in Granted and Refused Requests for Euthanasia and Assisted Suicide: A Systematic Review." *Journal of Medical Ethics* 37, no. 4: 205–211.

Moody, H. R. 2010. *Aging: Concepts and Controversies*. Thousand Oaks, CA: Pine Forge.

Munn, J., and S. Zimmerman. 2006. "A Good Death for Residents of Long-Term Care: Family Members Speak." *Journal of Social Work in End-of-Life and Palliative Care* 2:45–59.

Mutran, E. J., M. Danis, K. A. Bratton, S. Sudha, and L. Hanson. 1997. "Attitudes of the Critically Ill Toward Prolonging Life: The Role of Social Support." *Gerontologist* 37, no. 2: 192–199.

Nakashima, M. 2003. "Beyond Coping and Adaptation: Promoting a Holistic Perspective on Dying." *Families in Society: The Journal of Contemporary Human Services* 84, no. 3: 367–376.

National Cancer Institute. 2011. *Loss, Grief, and Bereavement*. Retrieved from http://www.cancer.gov/cancerinfo/pdq/supportivecare/bereavement.

Otis-Green, S. 2011. "Legacy Building: Implications for Reflective Practice." In Terry Altilio and Shirley Otis-Green, eds., *Oxford Textbook of Palliative Social Work*, pp. 779–783. New York: Oxford University Press.

Parry, J. K. 2001. *Social Work Theory and Practice with the Terminally Ill*. 2d ed. New York: Haworth Social Work Practice Press.

Pflaum, M., and P. Kelley. 1986. "Understanding the Final Messages of the Dying." *Nursing86* 16, no. 60: 26–29.

Puterman, E., A. DeLongis, and G. Pomak. 2010. "Protecting Us from Ourselves: Social Support as a Buffer of Trait and State Rumination." *Journal of Social and Clinical Psychology* 29, no. 7: 797–820.

Raboteau, A. 1978. *Slave Religion: The "Invisible Institution" in the Antebellum South*. New York: Oxford University Press.

Reed, P. 1987. "Spirituality and Wellbeing in Terminally Ill Hospitalized Adults." *Research in Nursing and Health* 10, no. 5: 335–44.

Reese, D. (formerly Ita, D.). 1995. "Predictors of Patient and Primary Caregiver Ability to Sustain a Planned Program of Home Hospice Care." Ph.D. diss., University of Maryland, 1994. *Dissertation Abstracts International.* University Microfilms No. 9526600.

Reese, D. (formerly Ita, D.). 1995–96. "Testing of a Causal Model: Acceptance of Death in Hospice Patients." *Omega: Journal of Death and Dying* 32, no. 2: 81–92.

——. 2000. "The Role of Primary Caregiver Denial in Inpatient Placement During Home Hospice Care." *Hospice Journal* 15, no. 1: 15–33.

——. 2001. "Addressing Spirituality in Hospice: Current Practices and a Proposed Role for Transpersonal Social Work." *Social Thought: Journal of Religion in the Social Services* 20, no. 1–2: 135–161.

——. 2011. "Interdisciplinary Perceptions of the Social Work Role in Hospice: Building Upon the Classic Kulys and Davis Study." *Journal of Social Work in End-of-Life and Palliative Care* 7, no. 4: 383–406.

Reese, D., R. Ahern, S. Nair, J. O'Faire, and C. Warren. 1999. "Hospice Access and Utilization by African Americans: Addressing Cultural and Institutional Barriers Through Participatory Action Research." *Social Work* 44, no. 6: 549–559.

Reese, D., and D. Brown. 1997. "Psychosocial and Spiritual Care in Hospice: Differences Between Nursing, Social Work, and Clergy." *Hospice Journal* 12, no. 1: 29–41.

Reese, D., C. L. W. Chan, W. C. H. Chan, and D. Wiersgalla. 2010. A Cross-national Comparison of Hong Kong and U.S. Student Beliefs and Preferences in End-of-Life Care: Implications for Social Work Education and Hospice Practice." *Journal of Social Work in End-of-Life and Palliative Care* 6, nos. 3–4: 1–31.

Reese, D., and M. Kaplan. 2000. "Spirituality, Social Support, and Worry About Health: Relationships in a Sample of HIV+ Women." *Social Thought: Journal of Religion in the Social Services* 19, no. 4: 37–52.

Reese, D., M. Raymer, S. Orloff, S. Gerbino, R. Valade, S. Dawson, C. Butler, M. Wise-Wright, and R. Huber. 2006. "The Social Work Assessment Tool (SWAT): Developed by the Social Worker Section of the National Council of Hospice and Palliative Professionals, National Hospice and Palliative Care Organization." *Journal of Social Work in End-of-Life and Palliative Care* 2, no .2: 65–95.

Reith, M., and M. Payne. 2009. *Social Work in End-of-Life and Palliative Care.* Chicago: Lyceum.

Sand, L., M. Olsson, and P. Strang. 2010. "What Are Motives of Family Members Who Take Responsibility in Palliative Cancer Care?" *Mortality* 15, no. 1: 64–80.

Siegel, K., and E. W. Schrimshaw. 2002. "The Perceived Benefits of Religious and Spiritual Coping Among Older Adults Living with HIV/AIDS." *Journal for the Scientific Study of Religion* 41, no. 1: 91–102.

Simmers, L., K. Simmers-Nartker, and S. Simmers-Kobelak. 2008. *Introduction to Health Science Technology.* New York: Cengage Learning.

Sinclair, S. 2011. "Impact of Death and Dying on the Personal Lives and Practices of Palliative and Hospice Care Professionals." *Canadian Medical Association Journal* 183, no. 2: 180–187.

Smith, E. 1995. "Addressing the Psychospiritual Distress of Death as Reality: A Transpersonal Approach." *Social Work* 40, no. 3: 402–412.

Stark, D. 2011. "Teamwork in Palliative Care: An Integrative Approach." In Terry Altilio and Shirley Otis-Green, eds., *Oxford Textbook of Palliative Social Work,* pp. 415–424. New York: Oxford University Press.

Sullivan, M. 2003. "Hope and Hopelessness at the End of Life." *American Journal of Geriatric Psychiatry* 11, no. 4: 393–405.

Sunil, T. S., and M. McGehee. 2007. "Social and Religious Support on Treatment Adherence Among HIV/AIDS Patients by Race/Ethnicity." *Journal of HIV/AIDS and Social Services* 6, nos. 1, 2: 83–99.

Thoits, P. A. 1995. "Stress, Coping, and Social Support Processes: Where Are We? What Next?" *Journal of Health and Social Behavior* 35:53–79. (Special issue: *Forty Years of Medical Sociology: The State of the Art and Directions for the Future*).

Turesky, D. G., and J. M. Schultz. 2010. "Spirituality Among Older Adults: An Exploration of the Developmental Context, Impact on Mental and Physical Health, and Integration Into Counseling." *Journal of Religion, Spirituality and Aging* 22, no. 3: 162–179.

Walsh-Burke, K. 2004. "Assessing Mental Health Risk in End-of-Life Care." In Joan Berzoff and Phyllis R. Silverman, eds., *Living with Dying: A Handbook for End-of-Life Healthcare Practitioners,* pp. 360–379. New York: Columbia University Press.

Wilber, K. 1993. 2d ed. *The Spectrum of Consciousness.* Wheaton, IL: Quest.

World Health Organization. 2011. *Depression.* Retrieved from http: //www.who.int/mental_health/management/depression/definition/en/.

4

HOSPICE SOCIAL WORK PRACTICE ON THE MICRO LEVEL

This chapter will cover assessment and intervention on the micro level, in other words, with individuals. In the first section of the chapter, I will discuss micro level intervention based on the model discussed in chapter 3. The second section of the chapter will focus more in depth on spirituality and spiritual intervention in hospice social work practice.

BIOPSYCHOSOCIAL/SPIRITUAL ASSESSMENT AND INTERVENTION

It is no surprise that terminally ill patients have many threats to their psychological well-being. What is surprising, though, is that in comparison to patients being actively treated for cancer, hospice patients have less incidence of worrying, feeling sad, and feeling nervous (Addington-Hall and O'Callaghan 2009). This may be partly attributable to the impact on development of confrontation with mortality, partly attributable to a unique perspective on the part of hospice patients, and partly attributable to social work intervention with these issues (Reese and Raymer 2004). This section will discuss intervention techniques for enhancing well-being in hospice patients and their significant others. While using these techniques, the social worker should always be open to the possibility that some clients will be unable to accomplish these steps. Hospice philosophy's perspective is that, in this case, the worker simply offers his presence.

QUALITY OF LIFE IN DYING

Hospice philosophy envisions care for patients and families that enhances the quality of life in dying. *Quality of life* is a multidimensional construct that includes biological, psychological, social, and spiritual aspects of well-being (Henoch, Axelsson, and Bergman 2010). These dimensions are not independent, but influence each other — so intervention in one area has an impact in another. For example, there is evidence that social support and spirituality predict reduced psychological suffering in terminal illness and that spirituality predicts high levels of social support (Reese 1995–96). Furthermore, there is some indication that psychosocial intervention improves physical comfort (Reese and Raymer 2004). We will discuss these aspects further on in this chapter.

Two common concerns of hospice patients are the need for adequate pain and symptom management and the desire to avoid prolonging life when life-sustaining measures further suffering (Raymer and Reese 2004). Safety and comfort in dying are key priorities included in the Pathway Document of the National Hospice and Palliative Care Organization (1997). Social workers see assessment of and counseling about safety as a classic aspect of the social work role; however, a recent national survey of hospice directors found that directors see this as the nurse's role (Reese 2011a).

Other common physical concerns of terminally ill patients, thought to be brought on in part by emotional suffering, are difficulty sleeping and concentrating (Noppe 2004). Pain amplifies emotional issues and leads to a loss of dignity while dying (Walsh-Burke 2004). There is some evidence that social work intervention reduces pain — the National Hospice Social Work Survey found hospices that provided higher levels of social work intervention had lower pain costs (Reese and Raymer 2004). Psychosocial approaches have been developed, such as relaxation exercises that can have an impact on physical symptoms. Other research indicates that high levels of social support and spirituality predict improved health status (Lavretsky 2010).

In order to address all dimensions, hospice care is delivered through an interdisciplinary team. Because hospice recognizes the relatedness of these dimensions, all disciplines on the team address all aspects of the client experience. At the same time, each discipline has special expertise in certain areas, and referrals should be made to the appropriate team member when needed. In reality, blurring of professional roles along with turf battles between disciplines sometimes makes it difficult to know when to refer a client and to which team member. These issues are discussed further in the section on team functioning in chapter 5.

HOSPICE PHILOSOPHY AND A STRENGTHS PERSPECTIVE FOR HOSPICE SOCIAL WORK

Probably the most important value within hospice philosophy is patient self-determination. This along with other hospice perspectives is inherently consistent with the values and strengths perspective of the social work profession.

Social workers remind team members of this perspective in their advocacy for client end-of-life care preferences. This includes fostering the patient's active participation in making decisions, advocating for the family's perspective with the team, as well as advocacy with organizational policy (Bern-Klug, Gessert, and Forbes 2001; Raymer and Gardia 2011). Many times the patient and family need help communicating their wishes to each other and coming to a resolution of differences in perspectives. The social worker can help facilitate this communication. Establishing advance directives may be useful in resolving these differences (Berzoff and Silverman 2004).

The solution-focused approach lends itself to use in hospice (Simon 2010) because of its strengths perspective as well as because it can be used as a brief model, providing a powerful impact even in one session. The miracle question can be tailored to the end-of-life care situation, perhaps asking, "Imagine having a sense of peace, feeling relaxed and calm about this situation. How do you imagine you want to spend your time? What would you like to be doing?" Every day becomes precious for hospice patients, and it is worthwhile to discuss what entails quality of life. In this way clients can be supported in focusing on solutions rather than problems, in developing quality of life for their final days. This approach also follows the lead of clients rather than directing them, both consistent with hospice philosophy and social work values.

In turn, social workers can learn from the hospice perspective in its acceptance of some clients' inability to resolve end-of-life issues. We must not expect too much of our clients. Sometimes "a good death" is not possible, and pressure to resolve issues may cause clients increased anxiety. Active listening skills may be helpful here, if clients are able to discuss their feelings. Sometimes they are unable to do even this, and sometimes the best approach is the traditional hospice solution of "just offering one's presence" (Bern-Klug, Gessert, and Forbes 2001). The following section will discuss psychosocial assessment and its relevance for evaluation in hospice.

SOCIAL WORK ASSESSMENT TOOL

For Medicare certification, hospices are required to include a social worker on the interdisciplinary team, and the social worker is required to provide a psychosocial assessment. The information gathered in the assessment is the foundation of a care plan that should be formulated with the
interdisciplinary team (Weisenfluh 2011). In an effort to reduce costs, hospice directors may restrict the number of social workers in the agency and
increase the caseload. The National Hospice Social Work Survey (Reese
and Raymer 2004) found that 1. social workers participated in the intake
interview in only 38 percent of hospices, 2. social worker caseloads were
on average three times the size of nurse caseloads (sw: seventeen, nurse:
six) and 3. while nurses visited each patient an average of ten times, the average number of social work visits to a patient was only two. Thus in effect
social work intervention was restricted mainly to psychosocial assessment
and crisis intervention. Outcomes are better, though, with social work participation in the intake interview and with early and frequent social work
intervention. Social workers can prevent crisis, leading to better quality
of life for the patient and family and lower costs for the hospice due to
lower pain costs, fewer visits by other disciplines, fewer nights of continuous care, and fewer hospitalizations.

The Social Work Assessment Tool (SWAT, Reese et al. 2006, see chapter 2 for a discussion of its development and see appendix A for the SWAT
itself and a handbook for its use—Reese et al. 2007) includes major factors,
based on social work research, that are affected by social work intervention
in hospice and palliative care.[1] It includes aspects of the clinical model in
chapter 3, along with factors from the Pathway Document (National Hospice
and Palliative Care Organization 1997). These issues should be included in
the psychosocial assessment conducted by the social worker. A number of
hospices nationally have included the SWAT in their computerized psychosocial assessment form. If not, the social worker can still independently assess

---

1. The Social Work Assessment Tool (SWAT), along with its handbook, was developed and is main-
tained by the Social Worker Section, National Hospice and Palliative Care Organization on their Web
site, in the members only section. This is an important resource—professionals refer to www.nhpco.
org and consumers refer to www.caringinfo.org. The SWAT instrument is also included in an article
published by the *Journal of Social Work in End-of-Life and Palliative Care*: D. Reese, M. Raymer, S.
Orloff, S. Gerbino, R. Valade, S. Dawson, C. Butler, M. Wise-Wright, and R. Huber, "The Social Work
Assessment Tool (SWAT)." *Journal of Social Work in End-of-Life and Palliative Care* 2, no. 2 (2006):
65–95. See appendix A, this volume.

these factors. The SWAT should be completed by the social worker after the first visit, then after each subsequent visit in order to document social work outcomes. The SWAT Handbook in appendix A summarizes how to address each issue.

The reason for the use of the SWAT at every visit is that we are usually unable to know which visit will be the last for a terminally ill patient. The assessment at the first visit serves as a pretest; any assessment after the first visit may serve as the post-test. By comparing the pretest and post-test scores, we can document social work effectiveness. Statistical analysis consists of a simple paired samples t-test, which can be done through Microsoft Excel. But it is also useful just to compare the scores for improvement, even without statistics. Areas that improve can be used to show the importance of social work intervention to hospice administrators. If there are areas that do not show improvement, this may be a helpful indicator of areas in which social workers need continuing education or need to put more focus. As always, sometimes clients do not have the ability to transform in a certain area, and all we can do in this type of situation is to offer our presence.

Use of the SWAT to do continual assessment along the way is also useful as a reminder of the factors that are important in hospice social work intervention. The SWAT is a one-page checklist that the social worker can complete after leaving the patient's home to note, in her clinical judgment, how the patient and primary caregiver are doing on each included issue.

During the first session we conduct the psychosocial assessment as required by our hospice agency as well as the CMS. This is often computerized and conducted through a laptop. If the SWAT is not included in the hospice's computer program, the social worker can advocate for this inclusion and meanwhile rate the items in the SWAT after the session is over.

Another assessment tool is the Psychosocial Pain Assessment Form developed by Shirley Otis-Green (2006). Developed for use in the palliative care field, this tool nevertheless has helpful strategies for assessing hospice patient quality of life using a holistic approach. In addition, the National Association of Social Workers includes, in its NASW *Standards for Social Work Practice in Palliative and End of Life Care* (2011; see appendix B), these additional areas for assessment:

- Relevant past and current health situation (including the impact of problems such as pain, depression, anxiety, delirium, decreased mobility)
- Family structure and roles

- Patterns/style of communication and decision making in the family
- Stage in the life cycle, relevant developmental issues
- Spirituality/faith
- Cultural values and beliefs
- Client's/family's language preference and available translation services
- Client's/family's goals in palliative and end of life treatment
- Social supports, including support systems, informal and formal care givers involved, resources available, and barriers to access
- Past experience with illness, disability, death, and loss
- Mental health functioning including history, coping style, crisis management skills, and risk of suicide/homicide
- Unique needs and issues relevant to special populations such as refugees and immigrants, children, individuals with severe and persistent mental illness, and homeless people
- Communicating the client's/family's psychosocial needs to the interdisciplinary team.

These issues are all implied in the items contained in the SWAT; we limited the length of the SWAT in response to social worker feedback in pilot studies (Reese et al. 2006). Thus social workers should use their own clinical training and study of assessment to inform their understanding of implications of SWAT items, since they are not spelled out in the instrument itself. In this chapter we will focus on the use of the SWAT for assessment.

Issues included in the Social Work Assessment Tool are the following: end-of-life care decisions consistent with client cultural and religious norms including advance directives, patient thoughts of suicide or wanting to hasten death, death anxiety, patient preferences about environment, social support, financial resources, safety, comfort, complicated anticipatory grief (e.g., guilt, depression, etc.), denial of terminality, and spirituality.

The SWAT is designed for quickness of use; only one item is included to assess each of these areas, and the social worker uses the SWAT as a checklist, personally rating each issue after the visit without necessarily asking the client questions. Some of the items can be assessed and rated without directly questioning the client. It should be noted that the SWAT measures only micro level outcomes with individual patients and primary caregivers; other measures are needed to evaluate mezzo and macro social work outcomes.

The following will discuss intervention with these issues. As mentioned earlier, the author will organize the discussion based on the model of variables presented in chapter 3.

HOSPICE SOCIAL WORK INTERVENTION

GENERAL CONSIDERATIONS   Table 4.1 shows a list of issues addressed and interventions used by hospice social workers with their patients, based on unpublished data from the National Hospice Social Work Survey (Reese and Raymer 2004). This table, developed from a national mixed methods study of 65 hospice social workers and 325 patient charts, gives a realistic sense of the day-to-day experience of hospice social workers. We can be proud of them for their obvious integration of a strengths perspective and advocacy for their clients. Social support was a major aspect of the services provided—including fostering informal support systems, connecting to formal supports, and personally providing social support to their clients.

The social workers addressed spirituality in depth, even though they weren't aware of it. When asked, only 23 percent said they addressed spirituality with their clients. When we reviewed their charts, however, we learned that 62 percent actually did explore spiritual issues with their clients! But a general lack of training—73 percent said their training to address spirituality was inadequate or very much inadequate—left them unable to identify issues addressed with clients as spiritual in nature (Reese 2011b).

Despite many strengths found in this summary of their interventions, you won't see all areas addressed by this group of social workers. In addition, there were some references to educating clients on the hospice philosophy. The author deleted these because of ethical concerns—in a profession and medical service devoted to client self-determination, we don't educate clients in a certain value system. Finally, they didn't work with family members to the same degree as patients. This is a concern in the hospice field—in the study using the Social Work Assessment Tool (Reese et al. 2006), post-test scores indicated significant improvement on the part of patients, but not with primary caregivers. Thus it is important that we focus more on work with families.

Social work services provided to clients included psychosocial assessment, education, resource and referral services, crisis intervention, description to client of scope of social work services, development of mutually agreed upon goals, development of a therapeutic relationship, risk assessment, and evaluation of progress toward goals. The Social Work Policy Institute (2010) also includes symptom relief for pain, discharge planning, assistance in securing legal documents, advocacy, identification of abuse and neglect, and bereavement as social work clinical responsibilities. Clinical models used by social workers in the National

TABLE 4.1 Issues Addressed and Interventions Documented with Patients in the National Hospice Social Work Survey

ASSESSMENT

ISSUES		ASSESSMENT TECHNIQUES
SPIRITUALITY		ASSESSING SPIRITUAL NEEDS
		Identifying spiritual strengths
	Philosophy of life dimension	Identifying patient beliefs
SOCIAL SUPPORT	Assessment of needs	Facilitated discussion on patient/family needs
		Financial issues/assessment
	Assessment of support system	Identify support system
DEATH ANXIETY	Assessment of fears	Explored patient fears and death anxiety
DEPRESSION	Assessment of risk of suicide	Education on risk of suicide
		Discussion of suicide
END-OF-LIFE CARE DECISIONS	Assessment of preferences	Values clarification
		Identify/discuss patient's thoughts//feelings about dying at home
		Discussed wishes for care/goals
		Patient's desire to try experimental treatment
		Caregiver options/goals for in-home care
		Patient's preference for future care
		Need for placement
		Need for increased patient care
	Assessment of values	Discussion of hospice philosophy
	Addressing pain	Scaling of pain level

Factors in model not reported as being assessed by social workers: level of development, cultural group, sense of control, grief, denial.

INTERVENTION

ISSUES		INTERVENTION TECHNIQUES
DEVELOPMENTAL LEVEL	Clients with disability	Patient's developmental disability/ how to help him understand his physical decline
CULTURAL GROUP	Comfort level with health care workers of a different race	Increasing trust for patient/family with nurse and social worker
SENSE OF CONTROL	Education	Educate on the right to patient self-determination
	Patient grieving loss of control and independence	Normalizing this issue, offering support
		Exploring ways to retain independence/modify lifestyle
	Advocacy	Encourage patient to make own decisions
		Supported patient in taking control, making own decisions
		Validation for patient's decisions and wishes
		Advocated for patient wishes
SPIRITUALITY	Liaison with spiritual caregiver	Liaison with personal spiritual caregiver for visit
		Referral to hospice spiritual caregiver
		Referral to client's church
Philosophy of life dimension	Unfinished business	Explore with patient wishes/ desires for use of time left
		Discussing saying good-bye to loved ones
		Discussion on forgiveness
		Coordinated out-of-state trip for patient/care-giver
	Meaning of life and suffering	Reminiscing

		Discussing meaning of life
		Finding meaning in suffering, decline, death
	Belief system	Discussing life cycle
	Belief in life after death	Willingness to support their beliefs
	Philosophy of living until you die	
Unity consciousness dimension	Isolation	Body image issues—"you are not your body"
		Patient trust issues with both hospice staff and family members
	Transpersonal experiences	Discussion/validation with caregiver on the therapeutic use of prayer
		Prayer at bedside with patient/caregiver
		Discussion of near death experiences
SOCIAL SUPPORT	Connection with support system	Encouraged use of support system
		Encourage use of church support
		Address patient's worry about being a burden to family
	Patient behavioral issues	Setting limits with patient
	Business issues	Handling business matters
	Referral to services	
	Financial concerns/assistance	Contacted Department of Human Services for assistance
	Government benefits	Accessing social security benefits
		Advocated for Medicare/Medicaid hospice benefits
	Paid caregiver	Referral for hired caregiver
	Assisting with paperwork	Paperwork/forms
	Volunteers	Referral to hospice/volunteers

		Coordination of paid caregiving
	Transportation	Referral for transportation assistance
		Referral for legal services
	Referral for placement	Arrange nursing home placement
	Medical care	Set up medical alert system
		Referral for medical equipment
	Referral for other hospice support	Encouraged use of bereavement services
		Provided resource material/ information
		Education on support services
		Education on role of MSW in hospice
		Information about hospice care and services
	Staff providing support	Provided emotional support
		Celebration of patient's 100th birthday
	Support regarding funeral	Connection to financial assistance for funeral expenses
		Funeral arrangements
	Setting up care plans	Coordination of services to enable patient to go home
	Advocacy	Assistance dealing with insurance company
		Advocated for patient benefits
		Intervened with apartment manager
		Mediate between nursing home administrator and family
		Met with pharmacist
		Advocated re. problem with medical bill

DEATH ANXIETY	Anxiety about dying in sleep	Encouraged verbalization of fears
		Taught relaxation techniques
		Options for decreasing anxiety
GRIEF	Education	Education on anticipatory grief
		Effects of alcoholism on grief process
	Patient's anticipatory grief	Facilitated grief process
	Prior losses of patient	Discussed patient's losses
	Current loss of boyfriend, patient grieving change in relationship	Encouraged expression of grief, offered support
DEPRESSION	Patient's depression	Discussion of suicide with patient
DENIAL	Patient denial of terminality	Discussion on patient's insight about illness
		Particularizing issues into manageable parts
		Realities of prognosis/terminal illness/preparing patient
GENERAL COPING WITH EMOTIONAL DISTRESS	Coping strategies	Patient validated for his humor
		Reviewed past coping techniques/strengths
		Education on coping
	Normalization and validation	Normalization and validation of feelings
	Encourage expression	Encouraged patient to verbalize feelings openly
	Cognitive-behavioral intervention	Cognitive behavioral issues
		Addressed false beliefs
		Cognitive techniques to alter self-talk
		Arranged time for patient and caregiver to express feelings
	Self-medication through substance abuse	Crisis intervention with alcoholic patient

END-OF-LIFE CARE DECISIONS	Legal assistance	Patient/family writing will together
		Living will
		Assisted patient in completing DNR
	Advocacy	Mediate between patient needs and attorney needs
		Advocated for family with funeral home
		Support for patient's right to die with dignity
		Support action to keep patient at home
		Empowerment of patient/spouse/caregiver to be active member of team/decision maker
		Schedule family conference with hospice team
		Modeled advocacy for family
	Decisions about funeral	Education/referral for cremation service
	Medical information	Meeting with family and physician to discuss pros/cons of life support
		Education on prognosis
		Discussion of disease process
		Education on what happens at time of death
		Medical issues related to type of death
		Teaching signs/symptoms/death
		Education/information on medications
		Education on comfort/quality of life
		Education on needs of the dying

TABLE 4.1 Issues Addressed and Interventions Documented with Patients in the National Hospice Social Work Survey *(continued)*

		Education on pain control
		Education on DNR order
		Education on advance directives
		Hand-outs/literature/information
	Education about resources	Education on out of home placements
		Options of care for patient's spouse with dementia
	Adjustment to changes in care	Patient's adjustment to nursing home
		Patient's adjustment to live-in caregiver
		Accepting volunteers/respite care
	Facilitating decision-making	Advance directives
		DNR order
		Discussion of nursing home placement
		Discussion on private hire caregiver vs. use of family members
		Discussed differences in dying at home vs. dying at hospital
	Supporting planning	Discussion/development of care plan
		Discharge planning
	Addressing pain	Visualization/pain management technique
		Recognizing confusion caused by pain medication
		Talked with hospice nurse about medication for patient

Analysis of unpublished data, National Hospice Social Work Survey (Reese and Raymer, 2004).

Hospice Social Work Survey included an insight-oriented, cognitive, problem-solving approach, family systems therapy, and solution-focused, behavioral, and task-centered approaches.

Most social work interviewing and counseling skills are relevant to hospice social work intervention. We will briefly touch on just a few points here. When working with hospice patients, our goal is not to address all mental health, substance abuse, marriage and family dynamics issues, etc. The last months of a patient's life is not the time to challenge clients to make major changes in areas not directly related to experiencing "a good death." A useful intervention that may be used to address a variety of issues is journaling, with patients who have the physical ability.

Models used must be short-term or adapted for short-term use. The first session with a hospice patient or family may very well be the last, in these days of last-minute referrals and underutilized social work services. The average number of visits by a social worker to a hospice patient is two (Reese and Raymer 2004)—it is possible the first visit may be only opportunity for intervention with the patient and family. Thus intervention must be provided immediately, starting with the intake and assessment interview.

GENDER   Just a note about gender; there are some common differences in the experience of women and men when facing mortality. Women express more distress than men (Noppe 2004), but this appears to be because they are more willing to discuss issues or are more aware of them. Husband caregivers underestimate patient depression, while daughter and other female caregivers are more accurate (Bassett, Magaziner, and Hebel 1990; Magaziner 1992). Women use an emotion-focused coping style, while men use a problem-focused coping style (Noppe 2004; Reith and Payne 2009). It tends to be easier for social workers to engage females in work on issues; working with males takes different skills. Women may respond better to interventions providing social support, including peer support groups, while men may be more likely to respond to a more problem-focused approach. Noppe (2004) gives the example of a man who may need to work in the garage as a way of expressing his grief. Still, she notes that men who do participate in more support-based approaches will respond as positively as women do.

ON-CALL RESPONSIBILITIES   On-call responsibilities are seen as the nurse's role in a recent survey of hospice directors (Reese 2011a). However, increased social work services result in fewer requests for on-call visits (Reese and Raymer 2004). This fact implies that on-call visits often have a psycho-

social nature and reflects the effect on pain control of social work intervention (Reese and Raymer 2004).

Social workers are often relieved if they are not expected to serve on call.
This relays the message, though, that social work intervention is not as important as nursing intervention in hospice. It is important for the full use of
social workers on the team that social workers advocate for being included
in on-call responsibilities!

BEREAVEMENT COUNSELING   Eighty percent of bereavement coordinators
are social workers (Reese and Raymer 2004). It is beyond the scope of this
book to address this service in hospice. One question to ponder though is
continuity of care—should the same social worker providing services before
death offer support after death? One problem is that, although Medicare
requires bereavement services for a year after the death, there is no reimbursement for these services. Thus in many hospices bereavement services
may involve little more than a letter of condolence. The National Hospice
Social Work Survey did not document improvement in a bereavement scale
score after one year of receiving bereavement services. This is an area that
needs further development.

BRIEF TREATMENT MODELS   Due to current problems with late referral of
clients, along with restricted access of clients to social work services resulting from lack of full utilization of social workers on the interdisciplinary
team, a social worker sees an individual client an average of two times (Reese
and Raymer 2004). Because of these problems, along with the difficulty of
predicting when death will occur, a social worker must use brief treatment
models with hospice clients. The mental health care system has also seen
a restricted number of sessions due to the influence of managed care; thus
many traditional intervention models have been revised so that they can be
used successfully within a single session to a few sessions. Doka (1995/96)
tailored a task-centered model for coping with terminal illness. Person-centered models have been recommended for use in hospice work and systems
theory-based approaches. Elements from a number of theories need to be applied flexibly when working with clients for only one or two meetings. Crisis
intervention is a model often used by hospice social workers.

CRISIS INTERVENTION   Crisis intervention is a key social work function in
hospice. All too often, though, social work services are limited, social workers have a large caseload that only allows for psychosocial assessment and

intervention when needed as determined by a nurse. So there is a tendency for social workers to be called in mainly in times of crisis. Social workers can indeed help to resolve a crisis, but evidence exists of much better patient outcomes if social workers participate in the intake interview and regularly thereafter—we assume this is because social work intervention can prevent crisis.

That being said, crisis intervention skills are crucial for hospice social work practice (Kovacs and Bronstein 1999). Gary Gardia (2010) has developed a rapid response team that responds to the needs of short-stay patients. He points out that in 2008 the median length of stay of patients in hospice care was 21.3 days. This means that patients are being referred to hospice only during the last few days or weeks of life. This limits the scope of team intervention, and short-term models are key.

In the Rapid Response Program (Gardia 2010), separate social workers are scheduled to be available at all times, in order to provide patients expected to live one week or less with the same quality of care provided to longer-stay patients. For example, a patient admitted on Friday and expected to die during the weekend could still receive the same quality of care since social workers were available during the weekend. The social workers assigned to the Rapid Response Program were qualified with MSWs and clinical licenses in order to provide this quality of care.

Chung (1993) discusses integrating a crisis intervention approach with Carl Rogers's client-centered principles in hospice social work practice. She advocates for the expression of feeling by the client as therapeutic. She notes that crisis intervention capitalizes on a client's willingness to make changes during a crisis due to vulnerability. This feeling of vulnerability may engender feelings of dependence on the hospice social worker, which creates conflict with the client-centered approach as well as with social work values. Chung suggests upholding social work ethics by countering temporary dependency with assurances of self-worth and coping capacity and upholding Rogerian client-centered approach principles of honoring client experience, subjective reality, and belief in human potential.

However, Chung notes that in the brief time available for hospice social work intervention a social worker cannot be nondirective. Thus the social worker cannot wait until the client's human potential is realized, for example, through the client overcoming guilt about not calling the hospice sooner and arriving at a sense of self-worth. The social worker needs to normalize the client's guilt and point out the reasonableness of not wanting to impose an unfamiliar situation on the patient during the end of life. This intervention is more directive than a client-centered approach but is necessary because of the brief time frame.

Regardless of the condensed time, the three Rogerian conditions for facilitating a therapeutic environment can be upheld: congruence, unconditional positive regard, and empathy. It is critical to establish a relationship quickly, communicating that the client's personal feelings will be understood, respected, and taken seriously. Chung reminds us that professional jargon should be avoided and the client's personal way of communicating should be respected so as to create a more informal rather than clinical environment.

Chung also makes the point that the nature of crisis is that old coping methods are not working, and the client may need suggestions for new ones—an intervention that would also be seen as too directive and behavioral for client-centered therapy. She notes that we also need to incorporate family systems theory into our assessment of client situations. Finally, she recommends that, although there is no time for a lengthy family history, past losses should be explored since they impact on current grief. The client's personal exposure in such a short time should be taken into consideration when sensitively terminating the session, with the realization that this session may possibly be the only or the last social work session provided to the client. Finally, Chung reminds us that all hospice interventions are client led and tempered by the pace at which the client is able to work.

In a short-term model, immediate needs must be prioritized and met quickly. Needs must be conceptualized in a holistic way, including biopsychosocial and spiritual needs. Maslow's hierarchy of needs may lend guidance for prioritizing needs (Maslow 1971). According to Maslow, physiological and safety needs come first; then, when these are satisfied, the client can focus on belongingness and love, esteem. These needs, lower in the hierarchy, are referred to as basic needs. Metaneeds, being needs, or growth needs, which are further on in the hierarchy, include cognitive needs, aesthetic needs, self-actualization, and, finally, self-transcendence (Maslow 1970).

The model of variables underlying our conceptualization of clinical work with clients fits with this perspective. Addressing pain and physical suffering must take priority. Addressing denial (only if necessary) to ensure a safe environment, patient self-determination, and to come to terms with realities about available medical treatment. Allowing the patient to have a sense of control over these decisions is very important. Anxiety about death is greatly impacted by physical needs. Then social support, which influences death anxiety, might be seen as a concept related to belongingness and love. We might see the self-actualization stage as similar to the philosophy of life dimension of spirituality, and Maslow described self-transcendence as having to do with unity consciousness—our second dimension of spirituality. Thus, the priority of issues included in our model moves from right to left. We can't converse with a patient about the meaning of her life when she is in severe pain. Then again, we must keep in mind that the factors on the left of the model influence the factors on the right—so an optimal resolution of the basic needs requires attention to the metaneeds as well.

Interventions pertaining to symptom relief include assessment and monitoring of pain relief, counseling on misconceptions about pain medication (such as a fear of addiction). It is not necessary to worry about addiction in a terminally ill patient because of the short duration of their treatment and the lack of necessity for normal functioning. The patient may also need financial assistance to pay for pain medication, which may be accessed from some pharmaceutical companies. The social worker may address patient confusion caused by the pain medication, referring the patient to the nurse for further symptom relief. Allied therapists as well as social workers may also participate in alternative care for symptom relief, including relaxation and meditation techniques, Reiki, aromatherapy, massage, therapeutic touch, and visualization techniques to manage pain, among many others.

DOCUMENTATION   The Social Work Policy Institute (2010) argues for the importance of documentation of social work intervention with clients. They note that electronic case files may not have space for full social work documentation. Also, some social workers may leave this responsibility up to other disciplines to make notes about the patient's plan of care. A final point is that much of social work intervention is provided over the telephone, either with clients directly or with community resources. Unless this is documented, we have no basis to continue to advocate for the recognition of this work.

Without social work documentation of interventions and outcomes, there is no evidence of the value of social work services. Lack of such evidence was the reason given for the Centers for Medicare and Medicaid Services' recent decision to degrade the qualifications for a hospice social worker to a related degree, not necessarily social work. Thus the importance of social work documentation cannot be overstated. Social workers should advocate with hospice administrators for electronic or paper formats to document social work assessment, plan of care, and interventions. Some social workers have successfully advocated for the Social Work Assessment Tool (SWAT) to be included in the electronic assessment forms they complete with clients.

EVIDENCE-BASED PRACTICE   Evaluation of hospice social work intervention is in its infancy. Very few studies have been conducted that document social work outcomes with hospice clients, and even fewer that evaluate specific intervention models. Evidence-based practice, in which the social worker evaluates models being used and then uses those models that have been found to be effective with hospice clients, is needed (Waldrop 2008).

ADDRESSING FACTORS IN THE MODEL OF VARIABLES

LEVEL OF DEVELOPMENT   Erikson's psychosocial theory (1950) describes psychosocial issues according to level of development. Most hospice patients are sixty-five or older—in Erikson's later adulthood stage, the developmental task is acceptance of one's life as it is, the psychosocial crisis is ego integrity versus despair, and the central process for achieving a positive outcome is introspection. A social worker can help the client achieve ego integrity through reminiscence, in which many older adults are able to view their life experiences, even negative ones, as having meaning. Meaning is often found by realizing the positive outcomes of negative experiences, even terminal illness. For example, clients may realize that their dying process has brought their family closer together and helped them appreciate life more. Clients may also experience a spiritual crisis—for example, when wondering "Why would God do this to me?"—and may need to examine their belief system to find an answer. Another spiritual issue that may arise is unfinished business, when there is a need to resolve a conflict, seek forgiveness or reconciliation, arranging for a last experience that may help them accept their lives as they are. Clients pondering these issues are developing within the philosophy of life dimension of spirituality. The Psychosocial Inventory of Ego Strength (Markstrom et al. 1997), based on Erikson's psychosocial theory, has certain questions relevant to the later adulthood stage that could be useful in assessment:

I feel okay with the way I've handled my life so far
I can accept the fact that I've made mistakes in my life
I can't seem to forgive myself for a lot of things I've done in the past
When I reflect on the past, I feel sadness and regret
I may have difficult times ahead, but I'll try to face them with courage
I'm not afraid of what the future has in store for me

I'm afraid of what might happen to me in the future
I don't look forward to the future

A former soldier, now a terminally ill hospice patient, had strong regret about men he had killed on the battlefield in World War I. He talked to the social worker about it, and she helped him through the process of forgiveness. Since he was religious, he was able to ask God for forgiveness. Also in prayer he asked for the forgiveness of the men he had killed in battle. Finally, he worked to forgive himself for his actions.

Psychosocial development proceeds along with spiritual development, and resolution of these issues reflects development in the philosophy of life dimension. The ability to accept one's life the way it is makes it possible to have a sense that one's life has been meaningful. This may explain why a higher age is related to higher spirituality scores (Harrawood 2009) and higher quality of life scores in terminal illness (McMillan and Small 2002). We will discuss this further later in the chapter.

WORK WITH YOUNG ADULTS Different issues arise in work with young adults. It is more difficult to accept one's life as it is when you have not lived as long as expected, when you are just establishing an identity, or are working on establishing intimacy or raising children. Research indicates that younger adults have greater death distress than older adults (Harrawood 2009). Younger adults have much unfinished business—they have not yet accomplished or experienced what they hoped for in life and may feel that such an untimely death is unfair (Mutran et al. 1997). They also have higher death anxiety and register lower spirituality in comparison to older adults (Harrawood 2009; Reese 1995–96).

WORK WITH ADOLESCENTS Jones (2006) found that the first priority in the needs of adolescents at the end of life (ages fifteen to twenty-one) was personal control—including education about their disease, medical information, structured conversations, spiritual support, and assistance with funeral arrangements. Their second priority was to continue normal activities—including school interventions, normal childhood activities, and assistance with talking to friends. The third priority was communication and expression, including the ability to talk freely about their fears and feelings, assistance with sharing concerns with parents and siblings, and creative expression. Fourth, they needed consistent caregivers and companionship, with consistent communication between caregivers. Finally, they needed control over medical and treatment decisions, including pain control and symptom management and the choice of where to die (summarized by Orloff 2011:83–84).

WORK WITH CHILDREN In this author's experience, a small child may accept death more readily than an adult. This may be due to children's accustomed lack of control over their circumstances, to unquestioning religious beliefs, or a spiritual awareness with which adults may have lost touch. According to their level of development, children may not understand the finality of death (Cincotta 2004). At the same time, for a child to cope with one's own terminality, she needs strong family support (Cincotta 2004).

Jones's (2006, summarized by Orloff 2011:83) study documented the priorities of younger children (up to age fourteen), finding that their first priority was communication and expression—including assistance with sharing concerns with parents and siblings, the choice of where to die, and the ability to talk freely about their fears and feelings. Their second priority was disease information and medical control—including medical information, education about the disease, and control over treatment decisions. Third was participating in normal activities—including school interventions, normal childhood activities, and assistance with talking with friends. Fourth was counseling and support—including supportive counseling, companionship, and structured conversations—and last was the need for consistent caregivers. Work with terminally ill children will be discussed more in the following chapter, on families.

This author had a case of a child who was given an explanation by her mother for why she was dying—the child said, "you have a certain amount of time on this earth, and that's it. Once your time is up, you die." This child was able to just accept this fact without great distress. Part of the positive outcome of this case was the result of the mother's modeling of a matter-of-fact way of accepting death as a natural part of life.

CONFRONTATION WITH MORTALITY Some conceptualize dying as a separate life stage with a growth process and tasks of its own (Reed 1987; Byock

1996; cited by Browning 2004). During this stage an individual may enter the transegoic stage much more readily. Attaining a high level of transpersonal development would explain the transpersonal experiences reported by many terminally ill patients (Berzoff 2004; Gibbs and Achterberg-Lawlis 1978; Pflaum and Kelley 1986; Reese 2011b). It would also explain the ability of many dying patients to accept death without great fear.

Psychosocial tasks within the life stage of dying include maintaining a meaningful quality of life, coping with disfigurement and loss of function, confronting spiritual and existential questions, and planning for survivors. Spirituality is seen as integral to the achievement of these psychosocial tasks (Reed 1987; Reith and Payne 2009). Byock (1996:251, cited by Browning 2004:27) adds to these a sense of completion with worldly affairs, a sense of completion in relationships with community, a sense of meaning about one's individual life, an experienced love of self, and experienced love of other, a sense of completion in relationships with family and friends, an acceptance of the finality of life — of one's existence as an individual — a sense of a new self beyond personal loss, a sense of meaning about life in general, and a surrender to the transcendent, to the unknown: "letting go."

Elizabeth Smith (2001) uses transpersonal theory to explain growth within this stage, which includes four dimensions:

a) normalization of death
b) divine intention, i.e., a belief in a supernatural force or higher power that creates cosmic order
c) surrender, i.e., the ability to let go of control of the outcome of events and accept the unknown
d) transpersonal existence, i.e., a belief in a continued existence beyond the known mortal self

She suggests that the social worker develop an understanding of patients' worldviews and how their emotions flow from their core beliefs. This approach, similar to cognitive therapy in its explanation of emotions flowing from beliefs, can be used to reduce patients' grief about the loss of physical identity. Smith's transegoic model will be discussed later in this chapter.

CULTURAL GROUP   One's cultural group may directly impact one's spirituality, need for control, level of social support, and end-of-life care decisions (see figure 4.1). Through the intermediary variables in the model, cultural group indirectly affects one's emotional response to terminality. Understanding of cultural norms and perspectives is key to work with clients that differ in cultural background from the social worker. One must learn about traditional norms of diverse cultural groups (while not stereotyping or making assumptions about individual clients), participate in cultural competence training, and conduct outreach to diverse community leaders and their people. Social workers have a responsibility to provide leadership in their hospice in developing cultural competence.

Tasks for the social worker pertaining to cultural group include exploring a patient and family's connection to their ethnic background—again, one must not assume that a client conforms to a traditional ethnic perspective. Another aspect to gain understanding of is a client's comfort level with hospice workers of a different race or ethnicity. A history of oppression has left many people very anxious about medical treatment within the mainstream white health care system. Thus the social worker may need to work to strengthen the client connection and sense of trust with the hospice staff. We will discuss these points in more detail in the chapter 7, on cultural competence.

SEXUAL ORIENTATION—GAY, LESBIAN, BISEXUAL AND TRANSGENDERED CLIENTS
An erroneous assumption that may be made by social workers who are not sensitive to differing paradigms is that their clients are heterosexual and not transgendered. The lesbian, gay, bisexual, and transgendered (LGBT) population may have special concerns caused by insensitivity to their needs or discrimination on the part of health care providers (Smolinski and Colon 2011), lack of health insurance coverage for a LGBT partner, lack of legal protections, lack of access to resources, and physician refusal to communicate with the patient's partner despite a power of attorney (Reese and Melton 2003). Partners may not be allowed to visit the patient while in care, may be left out of medical decision making, and do not have rights to social security or Medicaid benefits or inheritance of property because of the illegalization of marriage between LGBT partners.

Although advance directives may address some of these issues, few people establish these. Wills, advance directives, health care proxy, durable power of attorney, and living wills are particularly important, then, for LGBT couples without the right to marriage or civil union. These legal documents must also be clear about plans for minor children (Smolinski and Colon 2011).

Patients may not share their sexual orientations because of perceived risk of judgment (Smolinski and Colon 2011). Nondisclosure decreases well-being because it decreases potential avenues for social support (McGregor et al. 2001). This will depend, though, on the clients' developmental stage and possible affiliation with a new rights-affirming LGBT culture (Smolinski and Colon 2011).Several authors suggest that health care providers need training and special skills in order to address the needs of the LGBT community, including addressing one's own homophobia and discomfort about sexuality, policies requiring nondiscrimination, inclusive language on forms (Smolinski and Colon 2011), preparation to answer questions about services provided to LGBT couples (Saulnier 2002), education about special issues facing this population as well as resources available (Connolly 1996), and development of skills in communicating with LGBT clients (Smolinski and Colon 2011).

SPIRITUALITY   As is apparent in the discussion so far, spirituality is inherent in work with hospice patients no matter where one begins to address needs. Referring again to figure 4.1, level of development, confrontation with mortality, and cultural group predict spirituality, and then spirituality has a direct or indirect effect on anything else. Spiritual intervention cannot be left to spiritual caregivers unless there is a specific client request or need for response to a specific religious concern. Despite a lack of training and inability to identify issues as spiritual, social workers in the National Hospice Social Work Survey (Reese and Raymer 2004) addressed spirituality in quite some depth with their patients according to a chart review (see table 4.1). Considering this, social workers must seek continuing education in spirituality in social work practice so they are qualified to provide intervention in this area. We will discuss spirituality further in a chapter specifically devoted to this topic.

SENSE OF CONTROL   Mainstream U.S. culture is characterized by a well-developed internal locus of control. Individualism, belief in a right to autonomy and empowerment are inherent in our worldview. From the Declaration of Independence to the 2010 Supreme Court upholding of the constitutional right to bear arms, we have declared our intention to march to the beat of a different drummer.

Patient self-determination is a cornerstone of hospice philosophy and of key importance to many patients. The Patient Self-Determination Act reflects this value (Ivanko 2011). For patients with a mainstream U.S. cultural heritage, maintaining a sense of control, including involvement in treatment decisions and having preferences honored about arrangements in their environment, may be a vital aspect of psychological well-being (Levine and Karger 2004; Reith and Payne 2009; Zilberfein and Hurwitz 2004). Research has found, in fact, that fear of losing autonomy and control is the most common reason given for the decision to opt for assisted suicide in Oregon (Schroepfer, Linder, and Miller 2011). This underscores the importance of attention to this issue; hospice social workers have indicated that, even in hospice, unmet needs included fear of losing independence and being a burden on loved ones (Arnold et al. 2006). The social workers surveyed felt that these needs can be met through intervention and referrals.

Most people still do not die within hospice, however, and may be subjected to circumstances during terminal illness in which health professionals do not understand their end-of-life care preferences. Most people say they want to die at home, but in 2009 75 percent died in a hospital or nursing home (Byock 2009).

Hospice care can be of great value to the majority of terminally ill patients with the need for a sense of control over their circumstances (Chibnall at al. 2002). Just the fact of being empowered by hospice may negate the need for seeking control through suicide. A sense of control may also reduce the level of death anxiety, grief, and depression (see figure 4.1). Thus sense of control is an important aspect for hospice social work intervention. One aspect of this intervention, though, may be help working through grief over the realities of loss of independence and physical abilities.

In cultural groups that value individual self-determination, and with patients who retain that right, a place to begin is informing clients about the legal right to informed consent before any treatment can be performed. The social worker can invite the patient to make his own treatment decisions and support and validate him in taking control, making his own decisions and expressing wishes. After patients are able to clarify and articulate their wishes, the task of the social worker is to advocate for the patient's wishes with the team, social agencies, physicians, etc. In cases where the patient prefers palliative care, the social worker may need to help family members understand that they are not morally obligated to provide all possible curative care (Bern-Klug, Gessert, and Forbes 2001).

At the same time, we must attend to differences in perspectives about sense of control according to culture. Chinese and Asian cultures are more communal than those in the U.S., and decisions about end-of-life care are made by the elders in the family rather than the individual patient. Thus forgetting to consult these respected family members would be an affront.

African American culture is also more communal, and on end-of-life care traditional African Americans seek the advice of their community leaders, their Christian ministers. At the same time, there is a need for control over intervention by white hospice workers, based on fears resulting from a long history of mistreatment by the white health care system. Hospice staffs across the nation are almost entirely white (Reese and Beckwith 2005), partly explaining the lack of African American patients who opt for hospice. Other oppressed groups may have the same fears; thus the hospice focus on patient self-determination is particularly important to such clients (Reese et al. 2004). We must further keep in mind though, that based on this same mistrust of the white health care system, along with traditional religious belief in prayer for a miracle, the patient's preference may be for life-sustaining treatment. A number of diverse cultural group patient preferences may be out of line with hospice philosophy; we will discuss this further in chapter 7. A final thought is that a sense of helplessness can be compounded for people who are socially vulnerable—through poverty, bias, oppression, or prejudice. It is the responsibility of social workers to advocate for change in the factors in the social environment that contribute to these burdens at the end of life.

SOCIAL SUPPORT A key aspect of a "good death" for patients and families is support and caring (Gardner 2011), and social support plays an important role in our model of variables (see figure 4.1). Cultural group predicts social support. Some cultural groups are quite communal, and responsibility for each other is expected. In such groups, as with Asian and Chinese people, elderly parents are cared for by their children, and lack of social support is not as common. Spirituality also predicts social support. High levels of spiritual development come with a capacity for deep compassion, an interest in the well-being of all rather than only of oneself. It follows that highly spiritual people would have more positive relationships.

A Gallup poll (1997) found that some major concerns of the general public when thinking about dying included worrying that their care would be a burden to others, worrying about not having the chance to say good-bye to loved ones, and worrying about how their loved ones would be cared for after their deaths. Additional social concerns may have to do with financial needs connected with the illness and death. Social support helps to allay these sources of death anxiety (Glajchen 2011; Walsh and Hedlund 2011).

Social support also reduces grief and depression (Panzarella, Alloy, and Whitehouse 2006). A major factor in teenagers' well-being is peer support, and teen bereavement support groups have been found to be effective in resolving grief (Gard 2000). Clients in general also need the opportunity to express their grief as part of the process of resolving it. Patient anticipatory grief is also helped through the opportunity to say goodbye to a network of supportive family and friends (Pessin, Rosenfeld, and Breitbart 2002).

In addition, social support predicts end-of-life care decisions. Those with more social support are more likely to make end-of-life care decisions consistent with hospice philosophy (Reese 1995–95); perhaps this is because they have significant others available to serve as primary caregivers and help them through the dying process. Schroepfer (2008) found that social support predicted a lower likelihood of desiring a hastened death.

The social worker's assessment involves exploration of the biopsychosocial and spiritual needs of the patient and family. Identification of needs leads to a plan for meeting those needs, either through accessing informal supports, connecting the clients to formal supports in the environment, or creating supports like a support group for patients or family members.

Intervention with social support by the social workers in the National Hospice Social Work Survey was extensive (see table 4.1). We will briefly discuss some of these interventions here.

Social workers encourage clients to use their existing informal support systems. They foster closeness and intimacy, engage in family counseling if directly pertaining to client adjustment to terminality. They help promote open discussions and provide insight into family strength, needs, and adjustment. They help resolve conflicts between the patient and loved ones, encouraging the patient to ask for forgiveness or forgive others. In one of the most profound responsibilities of hospice social work, they help patients and loved ones say good-bye. Social workers also encourage clients to use many formal supports. They educate clients about existing resources, including hospice services, and help them make a plan for accessing them. They explain the Medicare Hospice Benefit, which includes all services, equipment, and medication. They may well have to explain the hospice social worker's role to clients who often hold a stereotyped view of social workers as welfare or protective service workers. When clients are interested, they help them access support from their churches or from support groups. They may have to advocate for client needs with managed care systems.

A classic social work role is referral for financial assistance; in fact, this was the only unique role hospice social workers were considered to have in the opinion of hospice directors in the classic Kulys and Davis study (1986). Social workers most certainly still do this, and they refer their clients to a wide variety of services to meet their needs and enhance their well-being.

They access public sources of financial assistance, access federal government benefits such as social security and Medicare or Medicaid. They arrange for hired caregivers, private duty nursing services, and hospice volunteers, arrange for transportation. They help patients and families to access legal assistance, and help them write wills, perhaps through patient and family collaboration.

If significant others are not able to care for the patient at home, social workers arrange for alternatives of inpatient hospice care, a hospice bed within a hospital, or hospice care within a nursing home when the patient is not able to safely stay alone. The social worker may help the patient plan to resolve business matters, may make referrals for needed medical equipment or a medical alert system. Social workers provide case management, coordinating services to which they have referred the patient. They help in planning of trips for the patient and the caregiver.

Social workers also provide social support themselves, providing assistance with completing paperwork, offering emotional support and hope, and attending birthday celebrations. Going a step further, they provide advocacy for their clients—in accessing all resources, working to make the environment more supportive toward the client needs. This might include intervening with the client's apartment manager or nursing home administrator, advocacy with Medicare, mediating between patient needs and attorney needs, meeting with the pharmacist about the patient's medication needs, resolving a problem with a medical bill, and advocating for the family with the funeral home. In short, there is no better friend to a hospice client than a social worker!

Social workers help patients process concerns about being a burden to their loved ones and the difficulty adjusting to changes in care—whether a nursing home, a live-in caregiver, volunteers, or respite care. After the death of the patient, social workers encourage loved ones to use the hospice bereavement services. They help make connections for financial assistance for funeral expenses, help families make funeral arrangements, and, finally, attend the funeral and annual hospice memorial service.

DEATH ANXIETY Seeing the fear in my patient's eyes was an inspiration for me to return to school to learn how to address death anxiety. Anxiety about one's terminal illness is only a natural response. Addressing death anxiety is important in promoting a good quality of life during terminal illness. Spirituality (Reese 2011b) along with social support (Walsh and Hedlund 2011) can reduce death anxiety. Denial is also a natural coping mechanism that can help if it remains on a conscious level (Blacker and Jordan 2004; Connor 1986).

Death anxiety should only be assessed after pain is adequately controlled. Symptoms of anxiety can be the result of illness or the side effects of medication: sweating, shortness of breath, gastrointestinal distress, heart palpitations (Payne and Massie 2000). In addition, physical symptoms contribute greatly to anxiety in the patient as well as her loved ones. Many interventions addressing pain and symptoms were noted under the category of death anxiety by social workers in the National Hospice Social Work Survey (Reese and Raymer 2004).

Most patients who are depressed also report anxiety, although the opposite is not true (Pessin, Rosenfeld, and Breitbart 2002). A helpful scale for assessing the level of anxiety and depression is the Hospice Anxiety and Depression Scale (HADS, Zigmond and Snaith 1983). This scale does not try to distinguish between depression and anxiety, since depressed patients report anxiety as well. Also, it only measures cognitive as opposed to physical symptoms because it is difficult to distinguish whether physical symptoms are brought on by emotional distress or by illness and medication. It is a brief, fourteen-item instrument that is convenient to use with severely ill patients. Differential diagnosis, using the DSM-IV, is also recommended by Walsh and Hedlund (2011).

Factor analysis by Conte, Weiner, and Plutchik (1982) identified four dimensions of death anxiety, including fear of the unknown, fear of suffering, fear of loneliness, and fear of personal extinction. All these can be thought of as relevant to spirituality, partly explaining how spirituality decreases death anxiety. Interventions include helping the patient to clarify beliefs—this addresses questions about the afterlife and may reduce most dimensions of death anxiety. This, of course, does not mean that the social worker will suggest beliefs, but rather help the client to identify and develop his own beliefs.

In addition, coming to a sense that one's own life has been valuable as it is and developing a sense of oneness may decrease a fear of personal extinction. Smith's (1995) transegoic model is powerful in promoting this perspective. Her techniques foster an awareness of an identity that is not restricted to the physical body, but rather a transpersonal identity reflective of unity consciousness: "you are not your body." Other transpersonal techniques include teaching relaxation and meditation.

As previously mentioned, social support can decrease death anxiety. Those close to an individual may enhance coping through reinterpreting one's situation, reassurance, and encouragement (Thoits 1995). Those who perceive high levels of social support may also be more likely to seek and receive help during a life crisis (Cutrona 1986).

Two contrasting examples show how various factors affect the level of a patient's death anxiety versus an ability to accept death. In the first example, a young white police officer was sent to hospice by his doctor, saying that medical science couldn't help him any more, but if they came up with an experimental treatment, the doctor would call him. The man was unwilling to talk of his feelings about dying or process what was happening to him. He never prepared himself and was very anxious about his terminality. He had no spiritual beliefs or concerns to process in that area. He had very few visitors and very little social support. He was married, but did not seem close to his wife. As time went by, if a hospice staff member came to visit him, he asked very anxiously, "Do you have bad news for me?" As he approached death, he became confused and began punching any hospice staff member who came near his bed. He died yelling "Code 13! Code 13!" which referred to "Officer in Distress."

A second example could not be more different. An elderly African American woman was dying of cancer. Several family members lived with her, and she was able to comfort her family through her own acceptance of her death. She spoke of God frequently, and the social worker once asked her, "Do you feel the presence of God?" And the client replied, "Oh, yes, all the time!" One day when the social worker visited, the client's church choir, of which she was a member, was standing in a circle around her bedroom, singing and clapping their hands very quietly. The woman died very peacefully, with a sense of acceptance of her death, bringing her family great comfort.

What factors explain the difference between these two cases? We can reference the model of variables in figure 4.1 for an explanation. The first difference is age. The young man was not ready for death, was just forming his identity as a police officer, had much unfinished business to attend to. The second factor is confrontation with mortality. The young man did not appear to allow himself to think about the meaning of his life and his death and go through the development that can occur while facing mortality. The third factor is cultural group. African American people connected with a church community experience a great deal of social support. This could be seen by the woman's church choir visiting and singing softly around her bed. The young man, in contrast, had very few visitors or family members and did not seem to have a close relationship with his wife. The fourth factor is sense of control. The young man wanted more treatment, he was not fully in approval of being in hospice, but his doctor had told him there was just no more treatment that would be effective for his illness. The woman, in contrast, appeared to be in full acceptance of her terminality. Spirituality is the next difference. The man did not express any spiritual questions or comments; this was not an issue of concern to him. A minister did come to visit him one day, but he did not seem to be fully interested in the conversation. The woman was fully living in unity consciousness at all times, with a sense of peace and joy clearly exuding from her. As we've mentioned, social support was lacking for the man, but in abundance for the woman. Death anxiety was evident for the man, as he fearfully asked, "Do you have bad news for me?" and punched the hospice staff who came near his bed. No death anxiety was evident for the woman, who said she felt the presence of God "all the time." The man was fighting for his life and didn't seem to get past death anxiety or denial, to the point that he experienced grief and depression. The woman didn't go through any of these difficult emotions. The man was waiting for his doctor to call with an experimental treatment, which was his end-of-life decision. The woman had made peace with her situation and had freely chosen hospice.

GRIEF, COMPLICATED ANTICIPATORY GRIEF, DEPRESSION, AND SUICIDE All clients obviously experience anticipatory grief during terminal illness and need support in managing their feelings (Walsh and Hedlund 2011). Kubler-Ross's (1970) classic work described normal stages of grief that, although criticized by recent theorists, underlie much of our thinking today (Bregman 2001). These stages include denial, anger, bargaining, depression, and acceptance. Kubler-Ross and Kessler (2001) later added the additional stages of forgiveness and surrender (Reith and Payne 2009). These normal feelings of grief should not be pathologized and viewed as mental health problems.

Complicated anticipatory grief, as opposed to the normal grieving process, involves some unresolved issues such as guilt and anger or failure to express the feelings of grief (Hooyman and Kramer 2006). It is important for social workers to develop skills in differential diagnosis in this area. While treating anticipatory grief as depression is inappropriate, depression is a risk factor for suicide and should be ruled out (Walsh and Hedlund 2011).

It is common for hospice patients to express a desire for assisted suicide (Linder 2004). A 1996 study in Washington State found that 26 percent of physician respondents reported that at least one patient had made such a request during the previous year (Back et al. 1996). A study by Csikai (2004) found that 32 percent of social workers in states where assisted suicide is illegal had received a request from a patient, and 17 percent had received a request from a family member, to discuss assisted suicide. It should be noted that attitudes toward assisted suicide vary by cultural groups; for example African Americans, Arab Americans, and Mexican Americans may have a more negative attitude toward assisted suicide than non-Hispanic whites (Duffy et al. 2006).

The desire for suicide may stem from the desire of many hospice patients to control the circumstances of death (Schroepfer, Linder, and Miller 2011). A sense of personal control both acts as a stress buffer and also directly influences mental health (Thoits 1995). Moreover, occasional thoughts of suicide may serve as a coping mechanism, allowing patients to express the magnitude of their distress, and may not be a serious desire for a hastened death (Rosenfeld et al. 2000). Another desire for suicide may be based on the fear of being a burden to loved ones as medical costs and caregiving needs increase. The increased social acceptance of assisted suicide may make this option more acceptable to patients, even admirable (Goelitz 2005).

In this author's practice experience in a state that did not allow assisted suicide, requests for assisted suicide were nevertheless not rare. They often came in the form of a request to the nurse for a lethal dose of morphine. When the nurse in one case refused to provide the lethal dose, her patient committed suicide by shooting himself with a gun. This event caused profound grief on the part of the nurse and the family. It is important in cases where there is suicidal ideation to refer the patient for assessment by the social worker. The social worker can assess whether the patient is requesting suicide based on rational reasons or depression. In case of depression, a suicide assessment is appropriate. Csikai and Manetta (2002) point out that social workers can play a role in preventing suicide resulting from depression.

A rational desire to hasten death based on a desire for control is different from suicidal ideation resulting from complicated anticipatory grief or depression. Social workers have a critical role in providing information about assisted suicide along with all possible end-of-life care decisions (Schroepfer, Linder, and Miller 2011), and must be prepared. Even in states where assisted suicide is legal, social workers addressing this issue experience dilemmas and conflicts based on hospice philosophy, social work values, and personal values (Miller, Mesler, and Eggman 2002).

Hospice philosophy in states that have not legalized assisted suicide holds the preference for allowing death to occur naturally—hospices in these states do not prolong life or unnaturally hasten death. When the patient's desire for death is rational and not based on depression, but suicide is not legal in the state, the social worker faces additional ethical dilemmas

(Csikai 2004; Schroepfer, Linder, and Miller 2011). An important procedure for a social worker in such a case would be to advise the patient of relevant laws and policies, about which she should be knowledgeable. In preparation social workers should examine their own perspectives about this issue. A study by Csikai (1999) found that values, educational level, and religious beliefs were important factors in predicting social worker's perspectives about euthanasia and assisted suicide. The most important predictor for social workers' attitudes was respect for self-determination, a key social work and hospice value (Schroepfer, Linder, and Miller 2011).

Suicidal ideation may, however, stem from depression (Reith and Payne 2009). A study of terminally ill palliative care patients found that the desire for hastened death was predicted by depression and hopelessness and was reduced by social support and physical functioning (Breitbart et al. 2000; Linder 2004). Unmet physical symptoms and other biopsychosocial/ spiritual needs may result in feelings of sadness and hopelessness that affect the will to live (Linder 2004; Walsh-Burke 2004). It is possible that when these needs are met the client will experience good quality of life in dying and will no longer desire to hasten death (Bern-Klug, Gessert, and Forbes 2001; Linder 2004). In addition, relief of depression may be a key factor in documented cost savings of hospices that have a higher level of social work intervention because of reduced use of medical resources (Reese and Raymer 2004).

DIFFERENTIATING BETWEEN A NORMAL RESPONSE AND AN EXCESSIVE REACTION Death depression is defined as death-related feelings of sadness, dread, meaninglessness, and lethargy (Triplett et al. 1995). Several depression symptoms are physical—weight loss, diminished appetite, fatigue, sleep disturbance, and poor concentration. These are difficult to distinguish from symptoms of illness, however. It may be more effective in hospice patients to assess only the emotional symptoms of depression, including loss of interest or pleasure—such as lack of interest in visits from loved ones—feelings of hopelessness, worthlessness, and guilt. A helpful question might be, "have you been feeling depressed most of the time for the past two weeks?" (Pessin, Rosenfeld, and Breitbart 2002). Since it is difficult to distinguish between anxiety and depression in hospice patients, the HADS (Zigmond and Snaith 1983) may be helpful for assessment. This scale detects both depression and anxiety and focuses only on cognitive rather than physical symptoms. An alternative might be the Beck Depression Inventory Short Form (Walsh-Burke 2004). Van Loon (1999) recommends that all patients desiring to die be assessed for depression and suicide risk, which will then lead to the appropriate intervention or response.

Goelitz (2005) provides guidelines for the assessment of suicidal ideation or desire to hasten death among terminally ill clients. She notes the importance of assessing depression and suggests using the criteria in the *Diagnostic and Statistical Manual of Mental Disorders IV-TR* (American Psychiatric Association 2000). But Goelitz (2005:1) writes that even if a patient does not meet the *DSM IV-TR* criteria for depression, they may be at risk for suicide if they experience the following:

- social isolation
- prior psychiatric histories
- substance abuse
- poor family supports
- family history of suicide
- inadequate symptom control
- feelings of helplessness or loss of control
- hopelessness
- suffering

Goelitz recommends taking these factors into consideration, exploring biopsychosocial/spiritual issues, perhaps brought up in the assessment session, including clients' understanding of the disease process, symptom control, desire for control over the dying process, and biopsychosocial and spiritual needs.

If a patient appears to be at risk, it is time to ask direct questions about thoughts of suicide. An assessment of suicide risk includes asking whether a patient has thought of hastening their death, how often they think about this, how long they have had these thoughts, whether they have a plan for carrying it out, whether they have the means to do it (for example, if their plan involves a gun, do they have a gun), and whether they believe they will really do it. The desire for death may fluctuate with suicidal patients and may cease if needs are met. Goelitz (2005) thus recommends conducting this assessment repeatedly with patients who have been identified as a risk for suicide.

INTERVENTION WITH GRIEF AND DEPRESSION Cognitive and behavioral interventions may be helpful in addressing grief and depression. Social support addresses grief and depression (Schroepfer 2008); thus work to enhance social support may help. We also know that spirituality reduces depression; social workers should provide opportunities to resolve conflicts or ask for forgiveness, and refer patients to religious leaders for specifically religious questions. Smith's transegoic model (1995) also helps clients move into the transegoic stage of transpersonal development and disidentify with the body; through this developmental process the client's grief over loss of physical function is lessened. Smith's stages of growth will be discussed later on in this chapter.

INTERVENTION WITH SUICIDE Meeting unmet needs may address suicidal ideation. The first priority is uncontrolled physical symptoms (Walsh-Burke 2004). Next is unrecognized delirium and untreated depression. These symptoms, left unrelieved, can lead to desperation, hopelessness, and desire for hastened death. Interventions may include pain and symptom control, psychiatric medication, counseling regarding complicated anticipatory grief, obtaining resources to support the family in caregiving, addressing financial needs, advocating for patient self-determination, and addressing needs for social support and spiritual concerns. Patients may need help with feelings of hopelessness and spiritual distress such as lack of meaning. Patients may have medical concerns, such as questions related to illness and symptom management. Some patients may feel more comfortable if their original attending physicians stay involved. Discussion and expression of needs and desire for a hastened death, normalization and validation of concerns, may help patients cope. The team's attention to a patient's needs and advocacy for his wishes may help a patient feel in control (Varghese and Kelly 2001). The entire interdisciplinary team is needed to address the entire spectrum of needs—biopsychosocial/spiritual.

When hospice social workers in states where assisted suicide is illegal were asked by patients and family members to discuss the option of assisted suicide, 23 percent suggested inclusion of the family in the discussion, 17 percent discussed all options available to relieve suffering including assisted suicide, 16 percent discussed all options excluding assisted suicide, 10 percent suggested that the patient discuss it with her physician, 6 percent requested a psychiatric evaluation, and 1 percent changed the subject (Csikai 2004).

DENIAL OF TERMINALITY A difficult issue to handle, one that influences end-of-life decisions and one that is heavily influenced by family dynamics, is denial of terminality. Denial is a controversial topic that is difficult to distinguish from religious beliefs and the concept of hope. *Denial* can be defined as lack of awareness of a terminal prognosis despite being told of it. Weisman (cited by Connor 1986) proposed three degrees of denial in the terminally ill patient, which include the following:

1. *First Order Denial*—the patient's denial of the primary facts of illness
2. *Second Order Denial*—denial of the significance of an illness
3. *Third Order Denial*—the patient's inability to believe that the disease will result in death, even after fully accepting the diagnosis and its significance

Denial is one of Kubler-Ross's stages of grief, and a common, and often considered healthy, way of coping for both patients and those who love them (Blacker and Jordan 2004; Parry 2001). The anxiety triggered by threatening information such as a terminal prognosis leads to denial as a way of coping (see figure 4.1). Denial then helps to reduce death anxiety to a manageable level—thus the influence between death anxiety and denial works both ways, reflected by the arrow between death anxiety and denial in figure 4.1. In most cases hospice professionals see no need to intervene with denial. Even if there is no intervention to reduce the denial, though, the social worker must still offer a silent opportunity to discuss feelings, and a challenge arises to not promote denial. Parry (2001) discusses the need for the social worker to be with a patient who is experiencing denial without actually participating in the denial.

In some cases, however, patients or family members may exhibit a dysfunctional level of denial (Connor 1993) that interferes with safety or self-determination when decisions are made that reflect an assumption of recovery.

This author had a case of a man with heart disease who had signed a do not resuscitate order and was accepting of his terminal prognosis. This client actually died six times, and each time a family member called 911 and had the patient resuscitated against his wishes. The social worker and all the hospice team members kept working with the family, helping the patient to communicate his wishes, until they finally let him die without calling 911.

Family members in denial can also leave patients alone without the proper care. Communication constraints in a family, in other words—lack of open communication about end-of-life issues—is a significant predictor of family conflict in families with terminally ill patients (Kramer et al. 2010).

It is important, therefore, for the social worker to develop skills in distinguishing between these aspects of the client experience, to avoid pathologizing normal grief experiences or rational decisions about hastening death, but to provide clinical intervention when needed. It is also important to develop skills in helping patients and families engage in honest communication about terminal illness so that advance directives and decisions about end-of-life care can be made (Roff 2001).

Denial is included in the SWAT, but it is not something you can directly ask the patient. A client in denial can't report that this is the case. This is something the social worker can observe in the patient and family members during the course of the assessment. Questions could be asked about the patient's condition and whether the clients believe it will be cured. Questions also need to be asked that determine the safety of the client and loved ones, and whether safety is being interfered with due to an inability to recognize the seriousness of the illness and prognosis.

Again, it is important to distinguish between denial—a lack of awareness of the prognosis as a coping mechanism—and religious belief in a miracle or hope that the body will somehow heal itself. Physicians are in reality unable to provide an exact prediction of the course of the disease; there are some patients who recover or live longer than expected. This may result in hope in patients for a better outcome (Finucane 1999). In addition, a key factor in spiritually and culturally competent practice is to honor the spiritual beliefs of the client. This may include a belief in spiritual healing or a belief that God will perform a miracle. These beliefs are different from a lack of awareness of the prognosis and must be honored and respected by the hospice staff. For example, a belief that God will perform a miracle may be common among African American people with traditional beliefs. These beliefs can change over time if the miracle does not occur, changing from "We thank you God for performing a miracle" to "Lord, we don't understand your will, but if it be Thy will to take Sister Frances, we pray that you take her without pain." Respecting client beliefs and allowing their expression is key to promoting utilization of hospice by diverse cultural groups.

In intervention with denial, the social worker must avoid confronting the patient and stripping them of denial in order to protect psychological well-being. A little bit of denial is considered positive, clients will develop the ability to face a terminal prognosis at their own rates or sometimes not at all. Hospice staff accept the individual experience of a client and don't confront or use any strong intervention techniques. The hospice perspective is that sometimes all one can do is offer one's presence. Thus it is only necessary to intervene when harmful situations develop. In this case safety is key, and a hospice value is to advocate for patient self-determination. Even in such a case the question of the prognosis does not need to be argued, but just the facts—the care and environmental conditions necessary to keep the patient or loved ones safe—and that of the patient's stated wishes. Patients go in and out of denial and will bring up questions about their terminality during periods when they are ready to address it. That being said, to some extent patients may follow the lead of medical personnel in discussing death (Chibnall et al. 2002).

Another difficult element to respond to is the difficulty patients and family members have in speaking to each other openly about terminality. It is possible that each side realizes the truth but does not want the other to realize it. Or, it is possible that one side is in denial while the other is not. Often patients desire to talk with their loved ones about the fact they are dying, but the loved ones are unwilling to have this conversation. It may be helpful for the social worker to meet separately with the patient and then with family members in order for them to feel comfortable speaking openly. When clients are ready, and if they desire support with this, a social worker can then hold a joint meeting to help them speak with each other about the topic.

Another important issue is that end-of-life care decisions are very difficult to make without a realistic understanding of the current and future expected condition of the patient. Thus low-key realistic facts may be needed in order to help in the decision-making process—for example, resuscitation is likely to leave the patient in a comatose state, living on life support, although there is some chance of recovery back to the current condition. It is helpful to have a nurse's assistance in communicating medical facts while assisting patients and family members in making end-of-life care decisions.

Finally, Sullivan (2003) discusses the idea of hope, which is not necessarily only for cure or survival, but can be hope for comfort, dignity, intimacy, or salvation. Parker-Oliver (2002) defines hope as the positive expectation for meaning attached to life events with the emphasis on meaning instead of life events. This definition reflects the spiritual issue of meaning discussed earlier. Hope may be for time to finish important projects or goals, travel, make peace with loved ones or God, experience a peaceful death. Cure may not always be possible, but healing—restoration of wholeness—may be possible to the very end of life (Coffey 2004; Puchalski 2002). Hospice social work intervention can help patients navigate past denial and into a sense of hope that fortifies their quality of life in terminal illness.

END-OF-LIFE CARE DECISIONS   Making end-of-life care decisions has many psychosocial, spiritual, and cultural implications, and the presence of a social worker in this discussion has been found to be helpful (Bern-Klug, Gessert, and Forbes 2001; Csikai 2004). Their interventions include clarifying advance directives, advocating for the patient's right to choose, supportive counseling, acting as liaison to the team, and encouraging family involvement and the exploration of end-of-life options and resources (National Association of Social Workers 2011). All the variables in figure 4.1 directly or indirectly influence end-of-life decisions. Intervention with these issues may lead clients to change their preferences and decisions over time. Desire for a sense of control is a major factor leading to the decision for assisted suicide. Spirituality and social support can reduce death anxiety, which then results in a reduced need to cope through denial. The level of denial influences one's willingness to opt for palliative care. Influences on spirituality, shown in figure 4.1, indirectly influence end-of-life care decisions. Cultural group and spirituality may enhance social support, which has a beneficial effect on grief and depression. If grief becomes complicated or develops into depression, suicidal ideation could occur.

Many ethical dilemmas occur when addressing end-of-life care decisions with patients and families. These dilemmas often have to do with communication between patients, families, and health care providers. Social workers have expressed ethical concerns with cases in the areas of self-determination, access to services, implementing advance directives, and assessment of mental competence (Egan and Kadushin 1999) as well. Social work skills are helpful in all these areas.

Sometimes hospices or health care providers have ethics committees that can discuss a difficult case and make recommendations to team members for how to handle the difficult ethical issues that may arise. Hospice social workers have expressed the need for such a committee. But often decisions have to be made quickly, and there is no time to defer to an ethics committee. Interdisciplinary teams meet more frequently and should also be a forum for discussion of ethical dilemmas. If issues cannot be resolved through team discussion, social workers often discuss them with the hospice director. (Csikai 2004).

Social workers will be required to independently resolve many ethical dilemmas though, because of the immediate action often required in hospice cases. The National Association of Social Workers has developed a policy to guide social workers in addressing end-of-life care decisions. However, many social workers may not be aware of this policy; continuing education is needed in this area (Csikai 2004).

The majority of individuals in the U.S., particularly if they are enrolled in hospice of course, emphasize quality of life over length of life in making end-of-life care decisions (Rosenfeld, Wenger, and Kagawa-Singer 2000). This is less so with individuals subscribing to a traditional religion as well as with many diverse cultural groups. Patients and families may struggle with decisions about advance directives, durable power of attorney, health care proxies, guardians, withholding and withdrawing of treatment, out-of-hospital do not resuscitate orders, pain management, questions about assisted suicide, and funeral and burial/cremation options. An *advance directive* is the patient's written preferences for end-of-life medical treatment, established by the patient in case he should become mentally incompetent to make his own decisions at the end-of-life. A *living will* documents the patient's preference that no life-sustaining medical treatments should be used. A *power of attorney* is an individual who is legally authorized to make decisions for the patient. A *durable power of attorney* remains in effect if the individual becomes incompetent. If the patient has not established any of these, state laws allow loved ones to make medical decisions for the patient (Nicholson and Matross 1989). For some states, this means only blood relatives or legal spouses; this is a problem for same-sex couples if they are not allowed to marry in that state.

The social worker advises clients on all options and helps them become aware of the cultural, religious, ethical, and emotional values that may influence decisions. The worker helps the clients to clarify values and assesses whether there are conflicts or concerns. Clients also may need much information about local laws and practices regarding these decisions along with policies regarding family medical leave, referrals to attorneys, and procurement of legal forms. The social worker must be knowledgeable about law and policy and can provide information about advance directives and their role in promoting patient self-determination. Finally, the social worker acts as an advocate for the patient and family with the hospice team and medical professionals.

It is important to include families in discussion of these issues as well as patients. Patients often prefer to leave such decisions to family members

(Csikai 2004). They may need a social worker's help to approach family members for such a discussion. Alternatively, sometimes patients and significant others will disagree about treatment decisions. Social workers may find themselves helping to resolve those differences and advocating with the family to uphold the patient's wishes.

Elderly clients, along with Hispanic and Chinese clients, may prefer family input. In some cultural traditions, such as Chinese, the patient may defer to the elders of the family to make decisions. In the absence of advance directives and other legal documents in a case in which the patient is physically or cognitively unable to express preferences, the social worker can help the family identify the patient's wishes. These discussions require social workers' special understanding and skills with family dynamics as well as their skills in culturally competent practice. In all cases the social worker should be aware of one's own biases and avoid their influence on interventions (Galambos 1998).

The Center for Practical Bioethics has developed a *Caring Conversations* workbook (available online) that helps families have discussions about end-of-life decisions. Patients and families are guided through the steps of reflect, talk, appoint, and act. The workbook contains questions to help patients reflect on their end-of-life preferences, guides them in talking with their loved ones about these preferences, assists them in appointing a surrogate decision maker in case they are unable to make their own decisions, and helps them to act by preparing an advance directive. The practical approach in this workbook is nonthreatening, informative, and very helpful. In addition, a number of other workbooks and value histories have been developed to support clients in the advance directive process.

African American clients and a number of other cultural groups may want their personal religious leaders to be involved in making end-of-life treatment decisions. Client preferences and beliefs must be honored even if different from hospice philosophy.

Discussion of end-of-life care decisions is an important part of the initial assessment; but it is not enough to have the patient sign an informed consent at admission to the hospice program, however. There is a need to occasionally check back about preferences. Despite having a DNR order on file, when patients were asked whether they wanted to be resuscitated, some said yes (Reese 1995). It is important to make sure that clients are actively involved, that patients' preferences are accurately documented, and to "create a climate in which informed choice and consent are genuine" (Mizrahi 1992:250).

In addition, end-of-life care decision making includes expressing preferences about one's living environment. Preferences should be elicited and explored, such as whether one wants pets close by, wants to sleep in one's own bed, where one wants the bed to be placed, where one wants to live, etc. If clients are emotionally ready, the social worker can help them plan for where and how they would like the death to take place.

In order to help clients make these decisions, the social worker should obtain and provide any information needed—such as the natural course of the illness, what to expect at the time of death, and treatment decisions that may be necessary. It is helpful to point out when palliative care is most comfortable as opposed to curative care or resuscitation. These topics are very difficult for clients to face, and social workers should provide emotional support and help clients identify ways of coping. They should support the patient in identifying preferences and feeling comfortable in making a request of their loved ones to honor these preferences. At times patients will prefer curative care; social workers, while providing information about the lack of benefit of curative care, should honor and advocate for these wishes as well.

A frequent problem is family members feeling responsible to provide curative care and feeling guilty for agreeing to palliative care. Social workers can help the patient discuss their wishes with loved ones and help families understand they are not responsible for the death.

In addition to working with patients and families to make end-of-life treatment decisions, a role of the social worker is advocating for patient preferences with the hospice team. Finally, the social worker is an advocate for agency policies that allow for differing beliefs and preferences, leading the way in developing cultural competence. For example, policies that do not require the patient to sign a do not resuscitate order or to die at home may help to remove barriers to access for African Americans.

MENTORING AND SUPERVISING OTHER SOCIAL WORKERS   A final consideration for discussion is our ethical responsibility to contribute to the next generation of hospice social workers (Zilberfein and Hurwitz 2004; Bradsen 2005). The hospice social worker, after gaining several years of experience, and ideally LCSW licensure, is ready to supervise social work students in a field placement. The social worker should develop a relationship with the local school of social work to make this possible. Active efforts to recruit diverse students should be made with the hope that some will be hired after graduation to increase the diversity of the hospice staff. These students can be assigned some macro practice responsibilities that may not be in the social worker's job description, such as outreach to diverse communities and policy practice. In addition, after gaining enough experience, the social worker is ready to take on a supervisory and perhaps hospice director role, working toward the ideals expressed in chapter 6, on macro intervention.

This section has given an overview of clinical work with individuals in hospice, based on the theoretical framework discussed in chapter 3. Clinical work with hospice patients is likely to result in benefits for the social worker as well as the client; we have evidence of spiritual development, as well as a great sense of reward, for both. A typical conclusion is that the social worker has learned and received much more from her clients than she ever provided to them. Self-care is quite important, and skills in advocacy and collaboration with an interdisciplinary team are also required—these topics will be discussed in chapter 5. The next section will focus more in depth on spirituality in hospice social work.

SPIRITUALITY IN HOSPICE SOCIAL WORK

This section will expand on addressing spirituality in hospice social work practice. We will discuss the status of spiritual intervention in the hospice social work field, personal preparation for such practice, assessment and intervention techniques based on the theoretical model presented in chapter 3, ethical considerations, and macro interventions and theory relevant to spirituality. We will begin with a discussion of the definition of spirituality.

This author defines spirituality as a two-dimensional construct, including transcendence in terms of philosophy of life and transcendence in terms of unity consciousness. The first dimension, transcendence in terms of philosophy of life, is intellectual in nature and has to do with perspectives, values, and belief systems about cosmology, the purpose of life, the nature of the universe, and one's place in it. Both religious and nonreligious beliefs fit into this dimension. Philosophy of life becomes transcendent when it is focused on the welfare of all rather than one's own self-interest.

The second dimension, transcendence in terms of unity consciousness, is transrational and has to do with direct spiritual experience. The term *unity consciousness* was coined by Maslow in his later work (1971), in which he added a new human need to his hierarchy of needs, above self-actualization.

This new need was self-transcendence; in transcending the individual self we become aware of the unity of all. This dimension may be described as a feeling of unity with the totality of the universe, a sense of oneness with God, others, nature, etc., communication with the spiritual dimension, peace of mind, a sense of compassion, or a sense of awareness of one's higher or spiritual self.

CURRENT SOCIAL WORK PRACTICE IN INTERVENTION WITH SPIRITUALITY IN HOSPICE

Dame Cicely Saunders, in her beginning articulation of hospice philosophy, taught that "spiritual work is of paramount importance . . . [and] goes hand in hand all the time with our medical work" (Saunders, cited by Driscoll 2001). Medicare policy also requires holistic care that includes attention to spiritual needs. Moreover, the fourth edition of the *Diagnostic and Statistical Manual of Mental Disorders* (*DSM-IV-TR*, American Psychiatric Association 2000) has included a V-code diagnosis of "Religious or Spiritual Problem," implying that social workers are ethically bound to prepare ourselves to identify and address such problems.

Social work is inherently a spiritual activity if defined as a separate concept from religion, and spirituality is generally defined in the social work literature as a distinct concept from religion. Religion is defined by Joseph (1988) as an external expression of faith comprised of worship practices within a moral community. Persons may seek spiritual growth within or outside of a religious community. Spirituality and religion are highly correlated (Reese 1995–96), but members of an organized religion may not necessarily be highly spiritual based on the dimensions already described. Also, individuals who do not affiliate with an organized religion may be highly spiritual, and spirituality need not be theistic. Existentialist and Buddhist perspectives, for example, may be atheistic.

Separating religion from spirituality is helpful in counseling, since it allows professionals to acknowledge the positive effects of spirituality despite awareness of dysfunctional uses of religion. It also allows nonclerical professionals to address spirituality without training in theology and leads to practice techniques that are relevant to any client, regardless of religious perspective.

Entry into the social work profession is founded on transcendence in philosophy of life when it entails a desire to help others and to contribute positively to society. The individual is transcending or rising above self-centered goals to concern him/herself with the welfare of all. Graham, Kaiser, and Garrett (1998) propose that the core of the helping relationship is spiritual, but that social workers do not recognize and name it as such.

Furthermore, social work operates from a strengths perspective; according to this perspective, social workers seek to assess and build on a client's resources and positives rather than concentrate on pathology, and, for many, their spiritual nature is a tremendous strength from which to draw. Spirituality has been found to be a factor in resiliency in many clients.

The Council on Social Work Education has required inclusion of spirituality in the social work curriculum since 1995. Evidence exists, however, that social workers still consider their training in spirituality as inadequate (Dane 2004) and that spiritual *assessment* in hospice is conducted by social workers in a minority of cases, is not incorporated into the psychosocial treatment plan, and focuses mainly on religion and clergy involvement with the patient (Reese 2011).

Most hospice social workers do discuss spirituality with their *interdisciplinary teams* (Reese 2001). The National Hospice Social Work Survey found that 3 percent of the social workers actually had an official role in addressing spirituality in the hospice—for example, were responsible for conducting the spiritual assessment. Six percent, however, stated they only address spirituality if a chaplain is unavailable (Reese 2001).

In addition, social workers address spirituality in *intervention* with terminally ill patients (Derezotes and Evans 1995; Reese 2001). In fact, a chart review in one Midwestern hospice found that the majority of issues discussed by clients with social workers were spiritual issues. In this hospice, and typically in the hospice field, chaplains visit clients less frequently than social workers, and social workers address spirituality more frequently than nurses (Reese and Brown 1997). Thus social workers play a major role, perhaps the primary role on the team, in addressing spirituality with hospice clients.

Some concerns are noted here, however—medical social workers address spirituality less often than mental health social workers (Russel, Bowen, and Nickolaison 2000), hospice social workers are often unaware that they are addressing spirituality since they have had inadequate social work training in this area and are unable to identify issues as spiritual in nature, and, although most social workers address spirituality at some point with some cases, all cases do not receive spiritual intervention. The more frequently a social worker visits a client, the greater likelihood of addressing spirituality.

Social workers also address spirituality more frequently in a case if the family has a lower income and if the significant other of the patient is more highly spiritual. A surprising result is that, despite the lack of training in spiritual intervention and the lack of knowledge that they are addressing spirituality, social workers who do address spiritual issues with hospice clients achieve better client outcomes on several different measures. This indicates the importance of addressing such issues in hospice social work (Reese 2001).

Several case studies have described successful social work intervention addressing spirituality in terminal illness (Dane 2004; Early 1998; Smith 1995). In addition, use of the Social Work Assessment Tool, which includes two items measuring spirituality, has found significant results overall between pre- and post-tests in social work outcomes studies (Reese et al. 2006). Few other evaluation studies specifically of social work intervention with spirituality exist, however. Although some excellent practice models have been developed (see for example, Smith's transegoic model, 1995, and Foster and McLellan's discussion of family work with spiritual issues, 2002), and Canda and Furman (2010) have contributed a foundation for spirituality in social work with the development of their textbook, the development of a theoretical base for hospice social work interventions with spirituality is in its infancy.

The lack of training and preparation, lack of competency, along with organizational barriers to addressing spirituality in hospice social work practice, coupled with the documented importance of addressing spirituality, leaves us with some ethical concerns. It is impossible to conduct an adequate spiritual assessment unless the social worker is able to identify and elicit discussion of major spiritual issues. Ethical questions arise, such as whether social workers are imposing their own belief systems on clients. Proselytization is clearly in violation of social work ethics and, when Christian in nature, is perceived as a form of discrimination by diverse religious groups since Christianity is the religion of the dominant culture in our society (Joshi 2002). Another ethical concern is that without training it is not possible to practice within the accepted social work body of knowledge regarding spirituality in practice.

Inclusion of spiritual content in social work curricula needs to be enforced, further development of models of practice is needed and publication of models that are being used in practice but have not been disseminated to the profession as a whole. Further research is needed, subsequently, to test these practice models for effectiveness. Social work education should address the importance of spirituality to low income and diverse populations, values about whether social workers should address spirituality, personal issues of the social worker that inhibit intervention in this area, clinical issues for clients that pose barriers, and proper documentation of spiritual interventions in patient charts. Regardless of the lack of training and lack of models for practice, the absence of deliberate and explicit efforts to address spirituality, and the low frequency of addressing it, results surprisingly still show an impact on client outcomes from social work intervention with spiritual concerns. One would expect even better client outcomes with specific training in this area.

Some barriers to the development of spiritual intervention in the hospice social work field were noted by hospice social workers in the National Hospice Social Work Survey (Reese 2001). First, there may be a lack of documentation of spiritual intervention by social workers who do address spirituality. Second, although participants believed it is appropriate for social workers to address spirituality, one participant stated that it's not until one gets into hospice that a social worker finds out it's OK and that this belief may be unique to hospice. Third, social workers must engage in personal preparation, including addressing their own spirituality, before addressing it with clients (Jacobs 2004). They may be fearful of doing this, especially with issues of mortality, but one participant made the point that the emotional impact of hospice work is what gives it its meaning. Fourth, there may be turf issues between chaplains and social workers, or chaplains may define spirituality differently from social workers, or social workers may feel that the chaplains are well qualified to address such issues and leave this responsibility up to them. Fifth, budgeting for increased social work and chaplain services increases intervention with spiritual issues; this problem needs to be addressed to provide adequate spiritual care. Finally, the short length of stay in hospice needs to be addressed at a programmatic and national level; Medicare regulations need to be reviewed for barriers to referral, and transitional programs including both palliative care and hospice need to be developed.

In summary, social workers address spirituality with terminally ill patients, but are unlikely to conduct a spiritual assessment, have little training in this area, and have produced few or no evaluation studies of the effectiveness of their spiritual interventions. In addition, few practice models exist; thus the interventions being used may lack a theoretical orientation. The inadequacy of training, lack of demonstration of effectiveness, and the lack of models for practice indicates a need for further work in this area. This chapter addresses this need by presenting a theoretical base and related techniques for social work intervention with spirituality in terminal illness.

TEAM ISSUES IN ADDRESSING SPIRITUALITY

A point has been made, and is well taken, that board-certified chaplains have specific training to offer spiritual care to all patients regardless of religious tradition (Driscoll 2001). Hospice social workers are unable to leave this work in the hands of spiritual caregivers, however, because the bulk of what hospice clients want to talk with their social workers about is spiritual in nature.

When this author first practiced hospice social work, a client asked, "Why would God do this to me?" I was totally taken aback, having never received any training in addressing spiritual issues. I said, "Let me refer you to our hospice chaplain." The patient died before the chaplain could arrive, never having had her question resolved. This experience taught me the point already expressed—hospice social workers must know how to confront spiritual issues with their clients.

We have noted that the training issues that need to be addressed before social workers can claim expertise in this area. Turf issues on the interdisciplinary team need to be addressed as well. Team barriers include lack of knowledge of the expertise of other professions, role blurring, conflicts arising from differences between professions in values and theoretical base, negative team norms, client stereotyping, and administrative barriers. (Reese and Sontag 2001). Chaplains may view social workers as encroaching on their professional turf (Soltura and Piotrowski 2011). At the same time, chaplains provide psychosocial care, which may be viewed by social workers as better left to social work (Furman and Bushfield 2000).

The Social Worker Section and the Spiritual Caregiver Section of the National Council of Hospice and Palliative Professionals, part of the National Hospice and Palliative Care Organization, addressed these dilemmas and suggested solutions in a collaborative paper presented at the NHPCO conference in 2005: "The Social Work of Spiritual Care and the Spiritual Care of Social Work: The Meanings of Hope and Love." They pointed out the language differences between the two fields, but noted that the commonalities—a focus on hope and love—and noted our common ultimate purpose: to serve hospice clients (DeFord and Bushfield 2005). They went on to present other papers together and coauthor a book (Bushfield and DeFord 2009).

Possible solutions to team conflict issues include informing other team members of the social work role, values, theory, and areas of training and expertise; learning about theirs and respecting them; asking their advice in addressing their areas of expertise; making treatment plans within team meetings that clarify which team member will address which issues in the case; obtaining training in areas in which you need more skills; and supporting the spiritual caregiver in being accepted as a full member of the team.

Egan and Labyak (2001) developed the concept of the *transdisciplinary* team, in which the team transcends turf issues by providing core training for all disciplines regarding primary biopsychosocial-spiritual needs, with patient and family values guiding all interventions. Similarly, the Consensus Conference (Puchalski et al. 2009) recommends that all health care professionals develop core skills to enable a culturally sensitive spiritual screening to identify spiritual distress.

GUIDELINES FOR REFERRAL TO A SPIRITUAL CAREGIVER

If social workers possess this knowledge and skill based on the recognized body of knowledge of their profession, this author's view is that they address the patient and family's needs when they arise to the degree they are responsibly capable. All professionals need to be mindful of the limits of their training and scope of practice, however, so that they can make timely and appropriate referrals to spiritual care specialists such as a board certified chaplain on the hospice team.

Another point to keep in mind is that for some diverse cultural groups, such as African Americans, the patient's own pastor is traditionally the one sought out for guidance in life-threatening illness and end-of-life care (Bullock 2006). In the Jewish faith it may be the community rabbi who is the trusted spiritual provider with whom profound questions are explored. Collaboration within a high-functioning team requires coordinated intervention to ensure that needs and concerns are approached in a consistent way, without repeating interventions and with the inclusion of the patient and family's personal spiritual caregiver, or a caregiver of their religion, to explore specific religious questions. A relationship with a spiritual caregiver and a supportive spiritual community may be seen as a spiritual strength, and the client should be encouraged to connect with these resources (Doka 2011). The social worker should become knowledgeable about diverse religious and nonreligious spiritual support systems in the community either to supplement work with the client or to make a referral in the event that client and practitioner are unable to work together around these issues.

PERSONAL PREPARATION TO ADDRESS SPIRITUALITY

If we define spirituality as a separate concept from religion, in which one dimension is philosophy of life that may or may not include religious beliefs, then our work is focused not on promoting a certain religion but on helping clients clarify their own worldviews. This is called a spiritually sensitive helping relationship, where we relate across belief systems (Jacobs 2004).

Social workers must take care to remain nonjudgmental of clients' spiritual beliefs and practices. Preparation for this work requires that we distinguish our own spirituality from that of our clients (Dane 2004). Failure to do this, instead imposing our own perspectives on our clients, increases the risk of failure to help the client, harming the client–social worker relationship (Driscoll 2001).

An example from this author's hospice social work experience is a young Catholic patient who believed she was dying because God was punishing her for an abortion she had had in the past. Having had no training in how to address spiritual questions, I expressed my own belief to my patient, saying, "God wouldn't punish you for an abortion." The patient ignored me and was not helped in the slightest by this contribution. Finally I referred her to the Catholic priest on our interdisciplinary team, who resolved this painful issue for her by performing a Catholic ritual of reconciliation. Referral to a spiritual caregiver was helpful in this case, since specific religious beliefs were the focus, and the religious ritual was able to resolve the client's spiritual conflict.

Given the individual nature of spiritual beliefs, it is likely that a social worker might possess a spiritual orientation different from that of the client. In these situations one should deal with this difference as any other, by acknowledging the difference and taking a one-down position, inviting the client to explain his beliefs to you. In no instance is it ever appropriate to impose one's spiritual values on a client.

To avoid imposing one's values, self-knowledge is essential (Dane 2004; Nakashima 2003; Sheridan et al. 1992). Often one's own worldview is unconscious, and it does not become a focus of awareness until the individual is faced with a differing worldview. At this point the contrasting worldview may seem offensive. Until we bring our own worldview into consciousness and become aware of how we came to adopt it (Nakashima 2003), and of the fact that it is just one of many, we will inadvertently impose it on others. A social worker must clarify her own belief system and examine any unresolved spiritual issues of her own along with any personal biases. As in any area of intervention, self-awareness helps prevent a social worker from projecting personal issues and concerns onto a client. Finally, the worker must assess her ability to respect the client's right to self-determination. Recognition of the right to self-determination is a hallmark of the profession, and, if this matter is in jeopardy, practitioners should consider referring the client to another professional.

AREAS OF IMPORTANCE IN SOCIAL WORK PRACTICE

Areas of importance for addressing spirituality in social work practice are the following: philosophy, assessment, developing a spiritually sensitive helping relationship, addressing spiritual issues, and utilizing the spiritual dimension therapeutically. Developing a spiritually sensitive helping relationship has previously been discussed; we will address the rest of these areas in the following sections.

PHILOSOPHY AND WAY OF BEING   Integrating spirituality into our philosophy and way of being with clients means that we view clients as sacred beings. Mother Teresa, a Catholic nun who worked with impoverished people in India, is quoted as having said, "It is Jesus that I met in the black holes of the slums, Jesus, the naked man on the cross" (Siemaszko 1997). When we view clients as sacred beings, we see them as having unconditional worth, with unlimited possibilities for growth. We start wherever the client's goals and needs are and encourage the potential for growth while incorporating the client's own practices and beliefs. From this perspective, crises are seen as opportunities for growth. This is a mutual process; the social worker grows as well through this relationship.

An elderly white male hospice patient initially refused to allow an African American certified nursing assistant into his home. The hospice told him that in order to receive hospice services he would be required to accept the staff assigned to him. By the time of his death, the patient had totally transformed, seeing the African American nursing assistant as an angel of mercy who attended him in his hour of greatest need.

Joleen Benedict, a private practitioner in New Jersey, has developed a method for "creating a sacred space" just before seeing a client, for the purpose of evoking this philosophy. It includes a brief meditation in which the social worker relaxes and centers and becomes present in the moment, then makes a brief statement: "I intend to perceive this client as a unique sacred being" (Joleen Benedict, personal communication 1996).

Dignity and worth of the person is a core social work value, according to the National Association of Social Workers' *Code of Ethics* (1999). Our code of ethics enjoins us to respect the inherent dignity and worth of the person, treat each person in a caring and respectful fashion, mindful of individual differences and cultural and ethnic diversity. It may become difficult to do this in reality, after a social worker has been in practice for some time and is prey to compassion fatigue. Clients are not necessarily pleased you're there and may not appear to have the potential for change or the desire for change. Holding a spiritual perspective in our work makes it much more possible to uphold this ethical principle.

ASSESSMENT OF SPIRITUALITY   Important aspects to address in a spiritual assessment include the belief system of the client, spiritual issues and concerns, functional and dysfunctional use of religion, and spiritual development. As we explore each area, we can identify spiritual strengths and needs.

Several frameworks for assessment of spirituality have been developed that explore one or more of these areas (Hooyman and Kramer 2006). *Domains of Spirituality* (Nelson-Becker, Nakashima, and Canda 2006), contains four preliminary questions:

1. What helps you to experience a deep sense of meaning, purpose, and moral perspective in your life?
2. Is spirituality, religion, or faith important in your life? If so, please give examples. If not, please explain why they are not important.

3. If important to you, what terms do you prefer?

4. Would you like to incorporate spirituality, religion or faith in our work together? Please explain.

In addition, Hodge (2003) has developed a Framework for Spiritual Assessment that uses interview questions to explore 1. an initial narrative framework focusing on spiritual experiences throughout life and 2. an interpretive anthropological framework discussing with the client the relationship between spirituality and affect, spiritual behavior, cognition (religious/ spiritual beliefs), communion (relationship to the Ultimate), conscience (values, guilt, and forgiveness), and intuition.

Another way of gathering information about spirituality is to use a genogram. A genogram can serve as a helpful way to stimulate discussion about spirituality and client goals (Bullis 1996). Questions about spirituality can be incorporated into the construction of a routine family genogram, or a spiritual genogram can be constructed. It may be helpful to begin with a discussion of the definition of spirituality for the clients and offer our own definition in order to give a broader picture than just asking about religious affiliation. A spiritual genogram addresses the client's previous spiritual experiences, such as the practices, beliefs, and influence of the family of origin (Bullis 1996; Hooyman and Kramer 2006). Current spiritual orientation and practices, as well as particular spiritual conflicts (such as conversion to another faith) that the client has experienced are also examined. It explores the influence of current significant others on spiritual functioning (Bullis 1996) and spiritual practices that are important to the client, such as reading spiritual or inspirational literature, prayer, and meditation (Sheridan et al. 1992). It assesses the client's perspective as to the quality of her or his spiritual existence. It is useful to inquire about the nature and strength of various family members' spirituality and whether it helped them cope with major life events. The role of spirituality in family dynamics and functioning can be assessed across individual members and generations in this way.

BELIEF SYSTEM OF THE CLIENT Understanding the client's belief system allows the social worker to gear interventions toward the client's point of view. Spiritual beliefs and practices may be important sources of strength for the client (Doka 2011). A belief system may be based on a religion or on the client's individual worldview or philosophy of life. The social worker will want to inquire about religious background and current affiliation with organized religion, any rituals or practices that the client or family members want integrated into the care plan, and any religious leaders or supports that the client would like to be involved. This is necessary in order to respond in a manner that is appropriate to the client's needs and may be an important source of comfort. Clients that don't have traditional rituals may be encouraged to create them for the same reason. The role and nature of spiritual intervention is defined by the client, not by the social worker; one has to know the client perspective to accomplish this (Doka 2011).

For example, traditional African American views are oriented toward "giving God time to perform a miracle" (Bullock 2011; Reese et al. 1999). Some cultural perspectives include a taboo about discussing death — such as African American (Bullock 2011; Reese et al. 1999) and Chinese (Reese et al. 2010), making it difficult to legally document end-of-life care decisions. In this case, it may be possible to postpone or avoid making some decisions. Some decisions may be required, though, such as the Medicare requirement of acknowledgment of terminality. The social worker can recognize the difficulty of such discussions, but explain why the discussion is required and provide emotional support and also understanding if the client decides not to participate in hospice as a result. It should be noted that social workers should advocate for changing such policies so as to develop more culturally competent services.

Suggestions for areas to explore with regard to the client belief system include the religious tradition of the client's parents, the client's own spiritual beliefs and practices, and the extent to which the client is connected to a religious community (Hooyman and Kramer 2006). The social worker must understand the importance of the family's faith tradition to the client throughout their development as well as experiences of baptism, confirmation, bat or bar mitzvah, rites of passage, membership, and any deviation from the family's religious orientation (Bullock 2011; Hodge 2003; Jacobs 2004).

SPIRITUAL ISSUES AND CONCERNS Major issues within the philosophy of life dimension of spirituality include meaning of life and suffering, unfinished business, and belief systems. Issues within the unity consciousness dimension include relationship with the Ultimate, sense of connectedness, and transpersonal experiences (Reese 2011). How one defines and experiences the Ultimate is a highly personal matter and depends upon one's belief system. This concept might refer to God for some, the divine self (Bullis

1996), or the general experience of union with all described by transpersonal or deep ecology theorists. Connectedness refers to human relationships entailing a sense of support and closeness as well as a sense of connectedness with a spiritual dimension. The client can be asked about conversions, spiritual awakenings, transpersonal communion, and peak experiences, along with the current existential experience of the transcendent (Hodge 2003). These issues may be raised spontaneously or revealed through metaphors or dreams. It is helpful, though, as much as possible, to come to an understanding of these areas during assessment.

FUNCTIONAL AND DYSFUNCTIONAL USE OF RELIGION At times clients use religious beliefs in the service of psychosocial problems, which can be considered dysfunctional use of religion. A social worker must be very careful in making this determination, because it could be a result of a judgmental attitude on the part of the social worker toward the client's belief system. This determination depends on whether the use of a religious belief results in harm to the client or another. An example of this may be when a client excuses child abuse through the Bible verse "Spare the rod and spoil the child." Others who hold this belief do not injure their children: an individual who abuses his child does not do it in order to adhere to this belief—he does it because of a personal psychosocial problem. Other examples may include a passive dependence on God when that entails denial to a pathological degree or domestic violence excused by the biblical directive for wives to submit to their husbands.

A hospice case example from this author's practice experience is of a thirty-year-old son struggling to find meaning in his fifty-year-old mother's premature death due to breast cancer. He could not believe that God would allow his mother to die; he explained her terminality to himself by concluding that his mother was dying because she did not have enough faith in a miracle. He was from a traditional African American culture, which made this problem even more difficult to assess—this cultural belief system does include an expectation that God will perform a miracle and heal the patient. Cultural competence might dictate that the social worker honor this belief. But this perspective, when held too long, began to cause the mother distress. She tossed back and forth on her bed, in emotional pain and agitation. She could not die in peace as long as her son suffered with this perspective. The son was in great pain as well from this religious dilemma. This is the point at which we could consider his use of this belief as dysfunctional, because it was causing great distress for his mother as well as himself. In this case the social worker helped the son clarify his belief by asking the question, "Is it the patient's fault if she is dying?" The son, in thinking more about his belief, was able to release his perspective and come to a different conclusion about the meaning of his mother's death, also based on his belief system—"we loved you, but God loved you more." He said to his mother, "It's OK, Mom, you can go," and she died twenty minutes later.

SPIRITUAL DEVELOPMENT A powerful technique for assessing spiritual development is Bullis's spiritual genogram or timeline (1996). The client can draw it like a "spiritual" genogram, making a "spiritual family tree" that includes "spiritual ancestors and influences." These might include significant books, experiences, lectures, events, relatives, and friends that have shaped the client's spiritual orientation or outlook. The time line records information similar to the spiritual genogram, such as significant events, persons, and experiences that have had a formative effect on the client's spirituality; but draws them along a chronological continuum (Doka 2011). This technique, while used for assessment, is therapeutic in itself, because it helps the client to understand the contribution of important life experiences. Use of this technique as an intervention will be discussed further in the next section.

ADDRESSING MAJOR SPIRITUAL ISSUES IN HOSPICE

The two dimensions of spirituality, which represent respectively an intellectual perspective and an experiential awareness, call for therapeutic techniques addressing both levels—in other words, both discussions on a rational level and experiential exercises. Rational discussions can help clients to develop new perspectives, and the use of guided imagery and symbolism can facilitate changes beyond the rational level, with a revised intellectual perspective resulting from these experiences as well. Experiential techniques can be quite powerful, effecting dramatic changes and major therapeutic breakthroughs over a short period of time.

Due to the possible intensity of the experience, however, many authors note cautions when using experiential techniques. Canda and Furman (2010) advise social workers not to "try out" new techniques on clients that they have never used before. The social worker should be competent in the approach, through specific training if possible, and definitely through significant personal experience with the technique. In addition, social workers should exercise caution if the client is fragile psychologically or physically and gear the techniques accordingly. Adults should have a well-established ego before it is safe to transcend it. In particular, psychotic patients may have difficulty in practicing techniques that foster an altered state of consciousness. If the technique requires a physical capacity the client doesn't have, for example, a breathing technique when the client is using oxygen and has difficulty breathing, a more appropriate technique should be chosen for that client. But often simple exercises are helpful in reducing the symptoms of mental or physical disorders (Canda and Furman 2010).

Finally, interventions to address spirituality should only be used with the client's permission and after explaining the purpose of the technique. Assessments should gather information about the client's belief system, and contracting should determine the issues the client is interested in exploring. Interventions should reflect the client's belief system and the agreed upon treatment plan.

PHILOSOPHY OF LIFE DIMENSION

MEANING IN LIFE AND SUFFERING A key task in facing mortality is arriving at a sense of the meaning of one's life and suffering (Doka 2011; Jacobs 2004). Family members also need to find a sense of meaning in the death of their loved one and an acceptance of their loved one's life, and Foster and McLellan (2002) argue that this is key in the ability to make end-of-life care decisions that do not prolong life.

In the National Hospice Social Work Survey only 5 percent of social workers reported addressing meaning in life and suffering with clients. In a chart review of their cases, though, researchers found that 43 percent of the social workers actually did address this issue. This is a disturbing reminder of the need for social work training in addressing spiritual issues. Interventions used by these social workers included helping clients to reminisce, conducting a life review, discussing the meaning of their lives and the meaning of their decline and death, holding a family discussion of the value of the patient's life, and following up with a family request to contribute to research efforts related to the patient's illness.

Reminiscing or life review is often used to help clients formulate a sense of meaning in one's life, see crisis as an opportunity for transpersonal growth, discover one's transpersonal mission, and develop ego integrity as conceptualized in Erikson's (1950) psychosocial theory (Doka 2011; Smith and Gray 1995). A powerful approach to life review is Bullis's (1996) spiritual genogram exercise, which charts a client's spiritual family tree. The client draws her conceptualization of spiritual ancestors, including significant books, experiences, lectures, events, relatives, and friends, which have shaped her spiritual orientation or outlook. Alternatively, the genogram may be in the form of a time line that represents the map of the client's life.

After completion of the genogram, the client can see more clearly the impact that peak events, nadir experiences, and plateau experiences (Maslow 1970) have had on his transpersonal development. Evidence of the growth resulting from adversity helps the client to accept past trauma, find meaning in suffering, and develop a belief system that includes a personal death perspective. A hospice patient is often able to perceive positive outcomes resulting from negative past events, and even from terminality, for example in the resolution of conflicts with others, reconnection with family, etc. This exercise could help a client to answer the common question "Why would God do this to me?" In formulating an individual answer to this question, a client develops a personal death perspective, which promotes transpersonal growth in the philosophy of life dimension of spirituality.

Leichtentritt and Rettig (2001) have developed a dramaturgy approach, used with Israelis, to establish new meanings of dying and its aftermath, that aims at promoting continuity with one's identity, heritage, and legacy. It uses eight meaning-making strategies to construct the "good death":

1. Using story in the form of drama
2. Describing multiple scenarios
3. Assuming the director and playwright roles in varying degrees
4. Explaining what a good death is not
5. Comparing previous experiences with death
6. Using questions, similes, and metaphors
7. Commenting with sarcastic remarks and black humor
8. Describing dreams

Other ways of finding meaning include meditation (Canda and Furman 2010), journaling (Vaughn and Swanson 2006), discussion of dreams and drawings (Goelitz 2001a, 2001b), and meaning-based group psychotherapy (Breitbart and Heller 2003). Dignity therapy enhances a sense of meaning and purpose by recording and transcribing patients' discussion of aspects of their lives that have been most meaningful (Chochinov et al. 2002). Patients and families may also find meaning by using their own situation as an opportunity for helping others (Trombetti 2006). Peay (1997) describes a dying woman who was bitter over life events and helped by a hospice priest to dedicate her dying to alleviating the suffering of a young bereaved mother. The patient was transformed, her whole being "infused with radiant love," her thoughts focused on praying for and helping the young mother.

Canda and Furman (2010) discuss the healing impact that rituals may have, whether religious or developed to symbolize the issue at hand, in resolving the emotional impact of traumatic experiences. Finally, Besthorn's (Besthorn and McMillen 2002) deep ecology perspective provides social workers with a framework by which they can assist their clients in finding expression for the pain and loss due to alienation from nature. Experiences with nature can heal this split, helping clients find a new sense of purpose, meaning, and connection in their lives. This approach encourages clients to utilize the transpersonal properties of nature to realize a deeper sense of self.

UNFINISHED BUSINESS   Social workers can explore with clients their desires for the use of remaining time, with the aim of completing unfinished business (Early 1998). Unfinished business may include saying good-bye to loved ones, resolution of prior grief (Smith and Gray 1995), accomplishing final goals, dreams never fulfilled, or last experiences desired (Smith and Gray 1995), reconciliation with estranged loved ones, or resolving concerns regarding sin, guilt, and the need for forgiveness of self and others (Canda and Furman 2010; Doka 2011; Puchalski et al. 2009). Social work interventions with unfinished business in the National Hospice Social Work Survey (Reese 2001) included work on forgiveness, discussion of use of remaining time, and coordinating an out-of-state trip for the patient and significant other.

ACCOMPLISHING FINAL GOALS   In some cases it will not be possible for clients to meet final goals, and the goal of social work intervention may be to help the client accept this (Goelitz 2001b). In some cases, though, it is possible to plan for final activities or counseling sessions that will resolve these issues (Early 1998). Early (1998) describes asking a dying adolescent if there were things he would like to do before he died and helping the client to address these issues with his family. Terminally ill clients have planned for a cruise they have always dreamed of, finished a book they wanted to write. This is the goal of the Make-A-Wish Foundation, which assists terminally ill people in fulfilling dreams in the time they have remaining.

RECONCILIATION WITH ESTRANGED LOVED ONES Reconciliation with estranged loved ones becomes quite important to some patients on their death beds, thus social work skills in this area are needed (Bern-Klug, Gessert, and Forbes 2001).

RESOLVING CONCERNS REGARDING SIN AND GUILT Another social work responsibility is helping patients to resolve feelings of guilt due to past or current actions. As mentioned in earlier examples in this book, one hospice patient in this author's experience asked for help resolving guilt over killing enemy soldiers in wartime. In another example a Catholic patient agonized with a past abortion, which she viewed as sin, and questioned whether God had stricken her with cancer as a punishment. In another case a man had continuing nightmares about flames leaping all around him. They appeared to the social worker to be images of hell. Unfortunately, the client would not discuss them other than mentioning the recurring dreams once to the social worker. He also would not agree to talk with a religious leader. In a case like this the hospice social worker just offers his presence and hopes that the support provided will be of comfort and perhaps even help the client silently resolve the issue.

If clients have strong regrets over investing their lives in secular pursuits, one last noble act such as donating an organ, changing one negative pattern, or making a donation may help to alleviate these regrets (Peay 1997). In some cases religious ritual may help the client to resolve guilt; if the client is interested, the social worker should make a referral to the appropriate religious leader. Referral to a clergy member may allow resolution of issues falling under the auspices of the religious institution, such as marriage, reconciliation of the client with the institution, or resolution of issues specific to religious beliefs.

A hospice patient had been living with his partner for a number of years, and according to his belief system, he felt he should make her "an honest woman" by marrying her. He dressed in a suit, stood up beside his bed, and the hospice chaplain was called to the bedside to perform the ceremony, helping the patient to conclude unfinished business and die in peace.

Loewenberg (1988) outlines assessment of whether there is an objective reason for the guilt, or whether it is based on imagined transgressions. If the guilt is real, he suggests helping the client to transform guilt-producing behavior into more moral and satisfying behavior. Acceptance of the individual while not condoning unethical behaviors can be an important support in resolving this issue. Loewenberg (1988) also suggests helping the client refocus on strengths. Alternatively, if the guilt is not based on actual misdeeds, the social worker can help the client to understand the irrational basis for his feelings. The determination of whether or not an act is unethical should be based on the client's own belief system and not the worker's beliefs.

THE NEED FOR FORGIVENESS OF SELF AND OTHERS The client may have a need to ask for forgiveness from others or may need to forgive someone else for a past hurt. Forgiveness releases pain, guilt, shame, and anger toward the self or other. Forgiving does not mean that the person "forgives and forgets," but that she learns from her mistakes and moves on. Clients can let others go their own way without being trapped in an adversarial mentality. They let go of the need for vengeance and release bitterness and resentment.

Swett (personal communication 1990) has developed a powerful guided imagery technique for assisting clients in forgiving past hurts, even in situations where face-to-face contact between the client and the one she needs to forgive is impossible. In this exercise the client imagines an umbilical cord connecting her to the person she needs to forgive. The client imagines a filter on this connection so that only positive energy may flow through. Next the client imagines positive spiritual energy flowing through her, through the umbilical cord, and through the other person, so that all are washed clean of negative energy. If necessary, the connection may be cut altogether and the other person allowed to go on a separate path.

In cases where the client has guilt over past actions, it may be possible to set up a meeting with the person offended to ask for forgiveness. Or, alternatively, to set up a meeting with a person that the client needs to forgive. Marshall Rosenberg (2011) has developed a model for conflict resolution, "Non-Violent Communication," in which each party expresses feelings and needs: "When you did ___, I felt ___, Because I need ___." The goal is for each party to have his needs met without judging the other. Worthington and DiBlasio (1990) outline techniques for promoting mutual forgiveness within troubled relationships. These include owning one's hurtful actions, eschewing future hurtfulness, forgiving the partner for past hurts, atonement for hurting the partner, and sacrifice for each partner.

BELIEF SYSTEM The crisis inherent in terminal illness may challenge some clients' belief systems (Jacobs 2004). Some may feel abandoned by God, angry at God, or unable to engage in usual coping mechanisms such as prayer or rituals. The social worker may invite the client to discuss beliefs and clarify values; development of a belief system may help to lessen death anxiety. Peay (1997) suggests reading passages and examining various belief systems. Keeping a spiritual journal, in which the client writes down any thoughts or feelings about God, the afterlife, religion, or spirituality (Smith 1993; Vaughn and Swanson 2006) may also be helpful. There may be a need for liaison with a personal or hospice spiritual caregiver.

Several models, including Assagioli's psychosynthesis (1977), specifically focus on helping the client to develop a transpersonal belief system. The exercise in disidentification (Assagioli) asks the client to affirm with conviction and become aware of the facts that "I have a body, but I am not my body. I have an emotional life, but I am not my emotions or my feelings. I have an intellect, but I am not that intellect. I am I, a center of pure consciousness." The "I" can observe and control these other aspects of the self. Through developing this perspective, the individual gains the ability to disidentify with these parts of the self and become aware of the transpersonal essence of her being. This new perspective helps to reduce death anxiety.

Assagioli (1977) developed an additional exercise asking the client to answer the question "Who am I?" The client will usually reply from the perspective of his societal roles. After this reply, ask him again to respond to the question "Who am I?" Each successive time, the client will respond with a deeper answer, more reflective of a transpersonal perspective on the nature of the self.

Smith's (1995) transegoic model also facilitates transpersonal development into the transegoic stage. Another approach to helping the client disidentify with her ego and social roles includes visualizing letting go of roles that have defined her (Peay 1997). Social workers in the National Hospice Social Work Survey addressed client belief systems by exploring beliefs about the afterlife and discussing the reasons for the patient's death anxiety (Reese 2001).

UNITY CONSCIOUSNESS DIMENSION OF SPIRITUALITY

RELATIONSHIP WITH THE ULTIMATE   Unity consciousness, or sense of connection with all, is often reflected in the U.S. culture in concerns about one's relationship with God (Doka 2011). It should be kept in mind that this issue is culturally and perhaps developmentally related. Professionals in Hong Kong did not notice this issue with patients (Reese et al. 2010), and a study of spiritual issues with bereaved children did not document this issue (Reese and Rosaasen 1999).

Nevertheless, relationship with God was the most frequently addressed issue regardless of profession in one chart review of spiritual and psychosocial issues addressed with patients by hospice staff (Reese and Brown 1997). One of the first questions patients may have in terminal illness is "Why would God do this to me?" Anger at God may result (Jacobs 2004), and possibly a sense of being punished by God for some infraction. There may be fears about the afterlife and of being unacceptable to God. In such cases it may be helpful to assure the client of the normalcy of anger toward God during terminal illness or life crises. The social worker can provide an opportunity to ventilate the anger and make peace with it. The worker can ask the client questions regarding his concerns about a relationship with God and his ideas of ways to resolve his situation. If desired by the client, the social worker can assist in prayer; ethical guidelines for prayer with clients will be discussed further on. Also, if desired by the client, this may be the time to refer to a spiritual caregiver for specific religious rituals for reconciliation with God.

Joseph (1988) found that one's relationship with God may be affected by unresolved issues from developmental stages. The client's relationship with her father in childhood may be reflected in her view of God, especially if the nature of God is seen as masculine. If the client had a conflicted relationship with her father as a child, she may not trust or feel close to God, may be afraid of what God might require of her, may see God as authoritarian, judgmental, unforgiving. Conceptualization of God as a father or male figure may create barriers for those who have experienced abuse by men. An example is a woman who had been abused by her father. She was unable to feel she had a relationship with God until she conceptualized God as a female mother figure. It is helpful in cases where relationship with God is affected by developmental issues to help the patient separate feelings about God from significant others, assist the patient in clarifying her own view of

God, and focus on unresolved developmental issues in counseling as a way to address problems in the client's relationship with God (Joseph 1988).

Another technique that can be used to promote a sense of connection to the Ultimate is the Spiritual Shower (Swett, see box), in which the client is asked to visualize white spiritual light, in the form of a shower over him, entering through the top of the head and flowing out of the hands and feet. At first the light washes out any darkness, areas of sickness, or negative energy or emotion. The client is next asked to visualize that the holes in the hands and feet are closed, and the light then fills the client, entering any empty spaces, and finally spilling out the pores of the body to take up an impenetrable bubble of light. Other approaches to this issue include discussions of worthiness to God (Early 1998), work on developmental issues that affect the client's concept of God (Joseph 1988), referral to a clergy member to discuss specific religious beliefs (Early 1998), and art depicting one's conceptualization of God (Smith 1993).

SENSE OF CONNECTION   A number of issues can interfere with the client's sense of connection and unity (Doka 2011). One of the things social workers do best is helping to restore close relationships and resolve conflicts with others. Helpful approaches include helping clients and families explore ways to maintain intimacy, stressing the importance of sharing feelings as a way to cope, helping a family reassure the client that it is acceptable to talk to them about illness and death, and arranging meetings between clients and those with whom they want to be reconciled. The social worker can request that the children contact the patient, help the family say good-bye to the patient, let go, and give permission for the patient to die. The client's faith community may be an important source of support (Doka 2011). Hospice itself may serve as a cohesive community that promotes a sense of belonging for the client, and the relationship between the social worker and client can in itself lead to an increased awareness of one's commonality with the rest of humanity (Graham, Kaiser, and Garrett 1998). The social worker can be helpful to the patient in establishing trust in the hospice staff and family members. Finally, Canda and Furman (2010) note the impact of mutually beneficial human-nature relationships in experiencing a profound sense of connection.

TRANSPERSONAL EXPERIENCES   Terminal illness is known to spur a period of spiritual growth (Jacobs 2004; Nakashima 2003), and, according to Wilber (1993), transpersonal experiences occur within the highest stages of transpersonal development. Gibbs and Achterberg-Lawlis (1978) reported

THE SPIRITUAL SHOWER

PURPOSE: TO CLEANSE AND RELEASE ONE FROM EMOTIONAL BURDENS

1. *Relax physically.* Go apart to a quiet place. Sit comfortably. Relax each part of your body, one area at a time. Imagine yourself sitting in peaceful surroundings.

2. *Think of a troubling situation, relationship, or emotional burden.* Do not get emotionally involved with the problem, but acknowledge it.

3. *Visualize a box in your mind's eye*—one that is open, with a lid lying nearby. Place the emotions, the hurt, the doubt, confusion, the worry—put all of that into the box and put the lid on it. Your love for the person(s) involved remains with you, but all other emotional debris goes into the box.

4. *Visualize a brilliant light* coming toward you, from above. Give the closed box into the light. Let go of the box, and see it be absorbed into the light. Feel warmth and love coming from the light. Lift up other burdens, if necessary.

5. After lifting all of your burdens into the light, *you will need to be washed clean* of the residue of your problems. Imagine it as a kind of powdery dirt, like coal dust, on you and in you. Visualize a warm light flowing from the top of your head (like water from a showerhead) and washing down through all of your body. See the light rinsing out all of the dark dirt and debris. Feel the light flowing down your body to your hands and feet—washing, cleansing, healing. Visualize openings in your hand and feet. See the darkness (your burdens) running out of your hands and feet and being carried away into the light, surrounded with light. Keep draining out the darkness, until there is none left.

6. Close the openings in your hands and feet. Continue to visualize the warm light flowing down through the top of your head. But, instead of flowing out, now *see your body being filled with this light,* beginning with your feet, and continuing upward to the top of your head.

7. *Allow the light to heal any damage* and fill any empty places within you. Visualize the image of being filled with light for a time, until you feel relaxed, comforted, and whole.

(L. Swett)

that half their sample of hospitalized terminally ill patients volunteered visions of God or other religious figures or deceased family members. These experiences were comforting, and the patients expressed relief in being able to discuss them without fear of rejection. Pflaum and Kelley (1986) found five commonly recurring themes in the experience of dying patients: 1. being in the presence of the dead, 2. preparing to travel or change, 3. seeing a place, 4. choosing when to die, and 5. knowing the time of death.

This author (2001) conducted a survey of sixty-six terminally ill home hospice patients in one Northeastern state and asked, "We have found that hospice patients often have spiritual experiences. Have you had any experiences that you would say are spiritual?" Nine patients declined to answer this question, some stating, "I don't want to talk about it." Of the remaining fifty-seven patients, 44 percent responded in the affirmative.

Transpersonal experiences are characterized by an awareness beyond the physical senses, often having to do with unity consciousness, oa sense of communication, awareness, or connection with a nonphysical dimension, or a loss of a sense of separate identity that is replaced with a sense of union with all or merging with a higher power (Nakashima 2003). Singh (1998) proposes that this potential for transformation is strong for every dying individual. It is partly through these experiences that dying individuals experience great spiritual growth; they are a comfort to patients and bring them a sense of peace (Nakashima 2003).

In this author's survey (2001), patient responses most often described an experience in which deceased loved ones appeared to them—usually spouses or family members. For example, the experiences might include a vision of a deceased spouse or family member coming to escort the patient, sometimes saying, "Come on" or telling the patient everything was going to be all right. Three patients saw religious figures (Jesus or angels). One patient and his wife both saw a ray of light come through the yard and into the window, entering the patient's heart. One patient had an experience with precognition, in which he had a vision of his niece talking to his brother, just before the actual event that mirrored the vision. Only one patient described an experience, concerning clairvoyance, from his earlier life rather than during the dying process.

The wife of a patient relayed the following story to the author, according to what the patient had told her. The patient died of a heart attack and went through a black tunnel with a tiny light at the end. He saw Jesus Christ in the tunnel, handing him a note. The patient felt he had not lived a very moral life and was afraid to look because he was afraid the note would say he was going to hell. He finally read the note, which said, "I will show you the way." The note was signed, "Jesus Christ." At this point the patient spontaneously resuscitated and related that he was filled with the "holy spirit." The bed was shaking, the patient was shouting, the patient was "saved" and "born again" after that day. The Lord gave him Scriptures that he should read in church; in other words, he believed he was channeling messages from God rather than developing his own sermons. He was a different person; he prayed for everybody. He saw Jesus at the foot of the bed again that night and knew everything would be OK. He kept saying to his wife, "Can't you see him?"

How do social workers respond to a client or family member who communicates such an experience? In the National Hospice Social Work Survey (Reese and Raymer 2004), only 5 percent of social workers reported addressing direct spiritual experiences with clients, and the chart review revealed only 6 percent. Interventions used included validation of the family's beliefs in a miracle, validation of the caregiver's prayer for a miracle, validation of the use of prayer, and discussion of near-death experiences; some social workers prayed at the bedside with the patient and caregiver.

We suggest it is important to distinguish between the psychosocial and spiritual dimensions (Graham, Kaiser, and Garrett 1998; Robbins, Canda, and Chatterjee 1998) and not to interpret the client's experience in a materialistic way (Grof and Grof 1989). "To give only psychological or sociological answers to spiritual questions represents a failure to fully hear the client and be 'where the client is'" (Graham, Kaiser, and Garrett 1998:53). The social worker should normalize those experiences as common during death and dying and relate the perspective that such experiences are an outcome of the spiritual growth that occurs when facing mortality. The social worker can help the client understand the meaning and symbolism of their experiences if this is appropriate. If the experience symbolizes a dilemma or unfinished business, the client may be assisted to resolve the issue. For example, a client who insists she must pack her bags and get ready to board a train may be concerned about preparation for death. The client may be assisted in making arrangements for a funeral, preparing a will. When the issue of concern to the client is resolved, Pflaum and Kelley (1986) note that the clients' agitation is reduced.

Grof (1988) describes the role of the therapist in response to transpersonal experiences as supporting the experiential process with full trust in its healing nature, without trying to change it, even without full understanding of its meaning. Gibbs and Achterberg-Lawlis explain that "as living becomes less real and death imagery becomes the patient's closer contact, patients' divulging of most meaningful thoughts is not likely to occur in an intellectualizing atmosphere" (1978:568). Nakashima (2003) argues that the field of social work's common interventions, based on ego psychology and cognitive-oriented counseling, are not relevant to dying persons. Cognitive abilities may be compromised in dying; these traditional approaches lack an explanation for the dying patient's "extraordinary experiences that seem to operate beyond ego functioning" (Nakashima 2003:371).

As noted earlier, these experiences are usually not disturbing to patients, but are, rather, comforting and have been found to reduce death anxiety. Such experiences may be more challenging for the patient's family, though, who may need help in accepting and supporting the patient's experiences (Pflaum and Kelley 1986). In dominant U.S. culture, we may have no context in which to understand such experiences other than psychiatric illness. Also, differing cultures will have different interpretations, according to cultural and religious beliefs. Among families with traditional Chinese beliefs, a vision of a deceased family member may be frightening and interpreted as a "hungry ghost" that cannot reincarnate until it seeks revenge for wrongs or an early death (Reese et al. 2010). These beliefs must be honored, and the social worker should follow the patient and family's lead on how to respond to such experiences, for example whether a religious ritual or support from a spiritual caregiver may be helpful. At the same time, it may help for the social worker to relate that such experiences are common among terminally ill patients, and that they are frequently a comfort to the patient.

UTILIZING THE SPIRITUAL DIMENSION THERAPEUTICALLY

Smith (1995) describes two death perspectives present in U.S. society today:

1. a perspective in which the inevitability of death is denied and death is regarded as a failure, as a meaningless end, or as the enemy to be hated and feared, and
2. a perspective that recognizes the continuity of living and dying, sees death as a natural process—the final stage in the life cycle—and often includes philosophical interpretations on the meaning of death.

Smith (1995) and Nakashima (2003) note that Western psychology has traditionally reflected the first stance, having been concerned with the individual or the self; and that Eastern psychology has reflected the second, having been concerned with being part of something larger or the transcendence of self. Tibetan Buddhists engage in mindfulness—a focus on fully experiencing, and only in the present moment. Nakashima (2003) points out that this practice helps an individual develop an awareness of mortality, as he experiences each moment passing, and that this leads to a sense of peace. Buddhist traditions include contemplation of death, and the *Tibetan Book of the Dead* gives instructions for dying. Elderly individuals in this culture practice the skills of dying and preparing for death.

This is a proactive approach to death and helps to transcend the ego (Nakashima 2003; Smith 1995). Nakashima notes that "the growth experiences of dying individuals often come from this transpersonal or transego realm" (2003:371). Smith (1995) argues that those who hold the second perspective and who reflect deeply on their mortality can be expected to adopt more meaningful goals and commitments in life.

Smith (1995) states that the quest to integrate these two aspects of human nature, the self and the transcendence of self, might be considered one's spiritual striving. She teaches that if these two aspects are not integrated the person experiences spiritual distress. Smith (1991) developed a scale to measure transpersonal development and found that, indeed, the scores on this scale were related to emotional well-being. She asserts that if we can help a client to begin to integrate these two aspects of the self and find some meaning in death, a sense of spiritual well-being is experienced.

Transpersonal social work practice views problems in light of the existence of a higher level of consciousness and supports clients in their development toward that level. According to our theoretical framework, transpersonal development can address death anxiety and depression, enhance social support, provide a sense of control, and enable clients to make end-of-life care decisions. A number of transpersonal interventions are shown in table 4.2. These techniques are thought to be a source of resilience and healing, and the effects are more immediate and can be more powerful than talk therapy that remains on a more cognitive level. The techniques have to be used repeatedly to maintain the effects, like physical exercise or good nutrition.

Canda (1990) uses the term *prayer activities*, which encompasses not only verbal prayer, but meditation, contemplation, and ritual, and many of the techniques listed in table 4.2. This broad definition of prayer refers generally to spiritual practice, which serves as "a means of communicating and communing with God, a transcendent reality, or the divine self" (Bullis 1996:62). Prayer can be defined as communication with the universe, the one mind, or the Absolute. From Canda's perspective, prayer can be understood as the spiritually sensitive relationship as a whole, whether it includes spoken prayers or not. He points out that the process of living itself may become a prayer—that holistic prayer becomes a way of being, not limited to specific acts of verbal praying. Prayer can be conscious or subconscious, and "as life becomes prayer, one's spiritual growth leads one beyond the ego-center toward the God-center, in oneself, all people, and all creation" (Canda 1990). Prayers can be used with clients according to the client's spiritual perspective as well as privately by the social worker outside the client session.

TABLE 4.2 Transpersonal Interventions

Meditation from all traditions
Movement meditation
Yoga
Disciplined breathing techniques
Guided visualization
Healing imagery
Holistic therapies integrating body and mind
Therapeutic use of symbolism and ritual
Biofeedback
Self-reflecting journaling
Art and music therapies
Deep relaxation exercises
Use of intuition in practice
Spiritual practice of all types
Prayer from all traditions
Ritual
Scripture reading
Therapeutic rites of passage
Group chanting
Working with dreams
Jungian active imagination
Fritz Perls's Gestalt practice
Acupuncture
Grof's holotropic breathwork
Contemplation

ETHICAL CONSIDERATIONS Canda (1990) discusses the ethical considerations that must be adhered to when integrating spiritual practice into social work intervention. He notes that prayer should be used only after a client has indicated a readiness and interest, only at the client's request and need as ascertained during the spiritual assessment. Spiritual intervention should be used only in support of client self-determination, building on client strengths with regard to her own religious and spiritual commitments and religious community participation. It is used to enhance the client's spiritual growth rather than to impose the worker's own biases for how that growth should proceed. It is inappropriate for the social worker to use verbal prayers with clients who do not share the worker's beliefs. Spiritual interventions are used to support the plan and process of professional helping in accordance with professional social work standards for practice and should complement rather than replace professional knowledge and skill. In order to engage in such practices, the relationship between the social worker and client must include mutual trust and respect, with open discussion of the spiritual views of both. The social worker must be qualified through training and personal preparation to conduct such practices and should be spiritually developed herself. Otherwise, if there is a need for spiritual intervention and these conditions are not met, the social worker should refer the client elsewhere. Canda (1990) notes that consultation with clergy or pastoral counselors should be available to help the practitioner with any difficulties that may be encountered.

An additional consideration involves the use of spiritual practice with psychotic clients. This is generally avoided since a psychotic client may not have the ability to return to a regular level of consciousness after entering an altered state during spiritual practice. It should be noted, though, that qigong practitioners have personally related to this author the claim that psychosis can be improved through qigong practice since it teaches the client control over these states (Yan Xin Qigong Health and Fitness Center, personal communication 1997).

Additional considerations include state licensing board regulations about social work intervention with spirituality and the use of spiritual practices by a social worker without specific training in such practices. Also, it should be noted that using sacred practices from a religious tradition without authorization from this tradition's spiritual leaders can be considered disrespectful and offensive. For example, during a conference of the Society for Spirituality and Social Work, attendees demonstrated the use of a traditional Native

American spiritual healing ritual. According to the beliefs of the tribe in which this ritual originated, the ritual may only be performed by an authorized spiritual leader. The attendees performing this ritual were not members of any Native American tribe, let alone spiritual leaders. Although their intent was to honor and value this spiritual tradition, these attendees caused great offense to Native Americans in the audience.

One might think that, considering the controversial nature of spiritual practice with clients, especially prayer, and the potential for ethical concerns, it might be simpler to just avoid spiritual intervention with clients. Clients commonly ask social workers for spiritual intervention, however, especially prayer. In matters of life and death, when it is clear how important this request is to the client, basic human compassion dictates that one complies.

The father of a family died, and the family was standing all around his bed. The social worker asked the family, "What has helped you to deal with problems in the past?" A family member said, "We always prayed." The social worker said, "Would you like to pray now?" The family member said, "Yes, please." The social worker asked, "Would you like to say the prayer?" The client asked, "Would you do it please?" In this case the social worker felt she could not refuse this family's request at this crucial time. She asked a few questions about the family's religious beliefs and then said a generic prayer she felt would fit their belief system: "God we ask that you bless this family's loved one and comfort them in their loss."

The following discussion addresses several therapeutic approaches for utilizing the spiritual dimension.

MEDITATION Teaching traditional meditation practice and practicing with the client can be very valuable in promoting spiritual growth (Bullis 1996; Grof and Grof 1989) as well as stress relief. Meditation can take many forms; Canda and Furman (2010) describe basic meditation techniques, which include 1. *paying attention*—helps patients to develop mindfulness and awareness of the true essence of being: for example, savor a shower, each moment with a loved one, realize that each moment is precious; 2. *intentional breathing*—relieves stress, helps to further paying attention: one can add a mantra, either religious, or one's own thought—for example, "peace" on the inbreath, "for all" on the outbreath. In addition, Bullis (1996) has developed an approach to meditation that includes relaxation, visualization, affirmation, confirmation, appreciation, and conclusion.

> The client visualizes the development of a rose from a bud, which symbolizes his own spiritual development. The visualization involves looking at a rosebush, visualizing one stem with leaves and a rosebud. The bud begins to separate very slowly, until a fully open rose is visualized. Visualize smelling the perfume, expanding the vision to include the whole rosebush. Imagine the life force that arises from the roots to the flower and originates the process of opening. Identify with the rose—symbolically we are this rose—the same life that animates the universe and has created the miracle of the rose is producing in us a like, even greater miracle—the awakening and development of our spiritual being and that which radiates from it.

GUIDED IMAGERY Assagioli (1977) developed the Exercise of the Blossoming of the Rose to promote transpersonal development. This is a visualization technique that could be used with hospice patients even if weak and bedridden. It could promote awareness of spiritual wellness, even in the presence of severe physical debility. This exercise is provided in the following box based on Assagioli's description:

SMITH'S TRANSEGOIC MODEL Elizabeth Smith (1995) developed the transegoic model, the name of which refers to the transegoic stage of spiritual development in Wilber's (1993) transpersonal theory. The purpose of the transegoic model is to "move a person from a fearful reactive stance to a proactive conscious awareness that allows for optimal growth in the confrontation of one's personal mortality" (Smith 1995). It can be used to address anxiety about any kind of loss (Smith has also used it for divorce) as well as death anxiety with anticipatory grief. It is based on the perspective that dying has the potential for great growth and transformation and aims to foster this process. Smith's transegoic model is shown in box 4.2. It is composed of four stages, with two phases within each stage.

Stage 1: Normalization of Death

1. *Phase 1: Recognizing role captivity.* After a client works through denial, an awareness of the reality of terminality begins to develop. An objective of this phase is helping the client to define himself in this new role of terminally ill patient.

2. *Phase 2: Resolving prior grief and fear.* A technique that can be used in this phase is a "death rehearsal" where the client plans the circumstances of death, in-

---

TRANSEGOIC MODEL

STAGE 1: NORMALIZATION OF DEATH

> *Phase 1:* Recognizing role captivity.
> *Phase 2:* Resolving prior grief and fears.

STAGE 2: FAITH IN THE EXISTENTIAL SELF

> *Phase 1:* Discovering one's meaning in life.
> *Phase 2:* Identifying the will or the "I".

STAGE 3: EGO "DISATTACHMENT"

> *Phase 1:* Discovering one's meaning in death.
> *Phase 2:* Disidentification.

STAGE 4: SELF-TRANSCENDENCE

> *Phase 1:* Acknowledging the transpersonal self.
> *Phase 2:* Discovering one's transpersonal mission

(Smith 1995)

---

cluding whom she wants to be present. This may lead to a discussion of whom the client does *not* want to be present, which could create an opportunity to explore unresolved hurt, anger, and unfinished business from the past, with the possibility that the social worker can help to address these.

Stage 2: Faith in the Existential Self

1. *Phase 1: Discovering one's meaning in life.* This phase uses Frankl's logotherapy (1984) to help the patient discover the meaning of his life. Frankl states that the will to meaning is fundamental to hope. One of the most distressing thoughts of individuals in the process of confronting their mortality is the sense that they are about to be cut off from all that has been meaningful to them. The objective of this phase is to review one's life and in the process identify one's significant others and objects and incorporate them into the self. The social worker explores the meaning of these relationships and helps the client discover that the meaning

she has assigned them resides within the client—the client will never be separated from that meaning. A case example given by Smith describes a patient whose ability to play the piano was an important part of her identity. The social worker explored the idea with the patient that the talent she had remained with her; the fact that she was too ill to play and would not be able to play the piano after death did not remove the talent from her.

2. *Phase 2: Identifying the will or the "I."* This phase is based on Assagioli's psychosynthesis (1977), along with symbolic interactionism (Mead et al. 1990). The client is helped to differentiate the subjective "me" (the self who acts in a relationship) and the "I" (the self who acts independently). Assagioli developed the perspective that the I is in part the "will," and that this will can be used to empower the true self. This empowering of the self enables one to restore control over death by reframing it and moving from a reactive stance to a proactive stance.

Stage 3: Ego "Disattachment"

1. *Phase 1: Discovering one's meaning in death.* This is again discovery of meaning, but the focus changes from finding meaning in life to finding meaning in death and dying. It incorporates Maslow's (1985) concept of "being cognition"— a feeling of oneness with the universe—unifying, complete, self-sufficient. It resolves dichotomies, polarities, and conflicts. In other words, one can experience meaning in suffering by experiencing being cognition—as opposed to the idea that death is senseless. One may feel totally out of control and disempowered, but can change this by finding meaning in one's death. A technique is to identify a time when the client had a mystical experience during which this feeling of oneness was present. The client should explore the context of the experience that held meaning and relate it to the present possibility of death. How are these experiences alike? How are they different?

2. *Phase 2: Disidentification.* Assagioli's (1977) psychosynthesis includes the concept of "disidentification." The "Who Am I?" exercise helps an individual to identify the symbolic interactionist "I" (Mead et al. 1990) within. The therapist asks the client, "Who are you?" The client will respond with social roles (the symbolic interactionist "me")—a lawyer, a bachelor, a Catholic. The therapist continues to ask, "Who are you?" When this question is asked repeatedly, the client will run out of social roles, and what is left is the I. Confronting one's mortality naturally requires the stripping away of these roles. The client experiences a kind of ego death. What is left is the I that simply is.

The client can consider that she need not act but can simply be—this is a free-ing concept. One is not one's body, one's thoughts, or one's emotions. Learning to come from that empowered place is the exercising of the will and the realization of the transcendent self (Nakashima 2003; Smith 1995).

In Smith's (1995) case example, the client was lying in bed looking out the win-dow. She had lost her physical ability to dance, but saw the wind blowing through the leaves, she felt the wind was dancing through the leaves, she felt that she *was* that wind. She felt a connection with all, or unity consciousness.

Smith (1995) also discusses disidentification from other aspects of the cli-ent identity. For example, the client was distressed over the loss of her hair—the social worker asked, "are you your hair?" She helped the client identify the meaning of the hair—the client has these qualities, not the hair. She helped the client disidentify from the hair and redefine herself with no hair. Similar tech-niques can be used to address the loss of a breast, limb, or other disfigurement, assign new meaning to the image of the self, and experience the self as complete and whole.

Stage 4: Self-Transcendence

1. *Phase 1: Acknowledging the transpersonal self.* The goal of this phase is to achieve liberation by defining the transpersonal self through incorporation of the idealized self-image. Experiences of being cognition help to identify and define the higher self or transpersonal self. The transpersonal self is described as the de-tached observer of one's psychological processes. This phase involves self-redefini-tion from a place of love rather than fear. As fear reasserts itself, the social worker can help the client recycle through some of the previous stages of the model. Smith says the client provides content and the worker provides the context.

2. *Phase 2: Discovering one's transpersonal mission.* The goal of this phase is discovering one's transpersonal mission, in other words, one's meaning for life after death. This is based on the client's own personal theology, spirituality, or conscious awareness. If the client believes in an afterlife, this may have to do with a mission the client will fulfill during the afterlife. If not, it could be a mis-sion in the next life or something the client will leave behind that has meaning to those still living. To do this, the client projects the self into the transpersonal realm and defines the purpose of the transpersonal self as the client perceives it to be—the reason for being of the higher self. Smith describes a technique for achieving this goal:

SOCIAL WORKER: "How do you see yourself as a dead person? What will you be doing?"

CLIENT: "I will be at the right hand of Jesus." "I will be working with animals in heaven." "I will be a memory to my husband and children."

Smith gives an example of how to follow up with the client who said she will be a memory. She worked with the client in the present to become the best memory she could be. The client became active making audiotapes and videotapes, writing cards into the future, and planned one last vacation together with her family. Projecting herself into the future as a memory restored her sense of hope and meaning in the present.

SPIRITUALITY OF CHILDREN

Reese and Rosaasen (1999) studied children's spiritual needs in bereavement. There is some indication that child bereavement can interfere with development, and loss of a parent in childhood correlates with problems as an adult. Does the resolution of spiritual issues impact child development along with the biopsychosocial dimensions? Our experience with adults would indicate that this is so. According to the Smith transegoic model (1995), transpersonal or spiritual development occurs through the dimensions of spiritual awareness and development of a personal death perspective, and this development reduces psychosocial distress in facing mortality. Adults are thought to face psychospiritual crises, in which spiritual issues must be confronted in order to resolve the crisis and move on to further development.

Development has an impact on this process. Older adults are more highly spiritual and less anxious about death, while adolescents and young adults are particularly anxious about death and less spiritual. This is explained by the idea of adolescents and young adults, based on their developmental level, being involved in creating their own identity and separate sense of ego. Thus they are not ready to lose this separate identity.

Joseph (1988) described how religious and spiritual dimensions engage dynamically with various personality dimensions and can be examined within a developmental context. She used open-ended questions to practitioners designed to identify stage-specific, life-cycle-related religious and spiritual issues—from the preschool stage to the frail elderly stage.

Preschool—religion was source of interest and curiosity to the preschool child. God was viewed as magical and all-powerful. Children at this age confuse God with problems they experience with their parents.

School-age—religion sets guidelines for behavior for the child (even if parents are not religious).

Adolescent issues—youth begin to question the literal acceptance of beliefs—searching faith, expanding beyond family teachings, and may reject institutional religion. Alternately, depending on parents' and peers' views—they may become highly involved in a religious movement. The idealism of youth plays a part.

Reese and Rosaasen's study (1999) used qualitative methods to elicit issues raised by bereaved children. We interviewed parents of ten bereaved children, ages two to thirteen. In analyzing the data through the Glaser and Strauss constant comparative method (1967), we assessed whether the children's needs paralleled Reese's taxonomy of spiritual issues in terminal illness, detailed earlier in this chapter. All participants mentioned a religious connection, and all the children referred to religious or spiritual ideology.

All the participants reported that their children were adjusting well at the time of the interview. We asked about any needs of the children; most turned out to be spiritual needs according to our taxonomy.

PHILOSOPHY OF LIFE DIMENSION

MEANING IN LIFE AND SUFFERING Children wonder why this is happening to them. A child was angry and wanted to scream at a friend because she asked why her father had died. Another child had a need for information—she wanted to read her father's suicide note, wondering why Daddy didn't get better, wondering what his last day was like.

UNFINISHED BUSINESS All but two families expressed this issue; the youngest children didn't seem to express it. One son didn't get a chance for a promised weekend with his father—he felt cheated and refused to attend the funeral. Other children felt cheated out of the rest of their lives with their fathers. In the case of the suicide of a grandfather, the family felt that he had left much unfinished—plans for going to the lake, celebrating his birthday.

BELIEF SYSTEM All the children believed that their loved one was in heaven. A child wanted to know that the loved one was OK in the afterlife. A child drew pictures of his father with wings, halo, and a white gown.

UNITY CONSCIOUSNESS DIMENSION OF SPIRITUALITY

RELATIONSHIP WITH THE ULTIMATE There was no mention among the children of their relationship with a supreme being or consciousness of unity with a spiritual dimension. This was the only issue in the taxonomy of spiritual issues that did not come up in the interviews.

This was surprising to us because of other indicators of the importance of this issue—relationship with God was the most frequently discussed issue in a chart review of visits to adult hospice patients (Reese and Brown 1997). Joseph (1988) wrote about how the relationship with parents in childhood may affect the relationship with God—perhaps a child's relationship with his parent is more important than his relationship with God (in the case that the child believes in God). In an unpublished study conducted by Theresa Porter (1999) of teenagers that adhere to Satanism, disruption of the relationship with the father, including by death, appeared to be a factor in attraction to Satanism. This is one indication that bereavement could disrupt spiritual development and lends support to Joseph's finding (1988) that children may confuse God with problems they experience with their parents.

SENSE OF CONNECTION There was much need expressed for connection. The children needed connection with the surviving parent. The children asked for more time with their surviving father—to see him, talk on the phone—expressed concern for the welfare of the surviving parent, wanted the surviving parent to take on the role of the deceased parent (for example, the mother teaching the son to shave). Children became closer to the surviving parent, children asked to sleep with the surviving parent, expressed an increased desire to have more affection from the parent, and eventually began to trust that the surviving parent would not leave them also. There was a need expressed for connection with the deceased loved one—one child asked to send a balloon up to his sister. One child wrote a letter to his deceased father; a child said he wished he could be with his sister—wishing he was dead too so he could be with her. All the children believed that their loved one was with them in spirit. A sense of isolation was expressed—they were reluctant to share their experience with their friends and teachers; it seemed they thought they were each different and unique.

TRANSPERSONAL EXPERIENCES One child told a story about feeling that his deceased father sat beside him on the couch and talked with him. Another child mentioned a visit with an angel. Another saw his deceased parent in the hallway. A number of stories like this indicated that children were having experiences of communication with their loved ones after death.

SUMMARY

Participants stated that the level of spirituality of the child determines their adjustment to their bereavement. One teenager without a strong sense of spirituality had more difficulty adjusting—he had severe panic attacks and vomited in stressful situations. We concluded that children's spiritual issues in death and dying seem to be similar to adults. The issues appear to remain constant regardless of developmental level, except relationship with the ultimate. We conclude that spirituality predicts bereavement risk. This may make sense based on findings that almost all needs identified by this study were spiritual needs according to the taxonomy of spiritual issues we used. Higher levels of spirituality in terms of resolution of these spiritual issues would indicate a better adjustment during bereavement. And we know through many studies that spirituality reduces adults' psychosocial distress and death anxiety when facing death.

Children's spirituality and practice addressing spirituality with children is an area not thoroughly addressed in social work education. We need to develop practice techniques to intervene in this area. We also need further research on the impact of bereavement and relationship with the father on spiritual development.

Spirituality is a major aspect of hospice care, and social workers need to focus on skill development in this area. This chapter has reviewed current social work practice in intervention with spirituality in hospice, noting that a major part of social work intervention is focused on spirituality, but social work training in this area is still not adequate. We noted that turf issues between social workers and spiritual caregivers may interfere with hospice intervention in this area and discussed ways of addressing them as well as guidelines regarding when to refer a client to a spiritual caregiver. We discussed personal preparation and its importance in addressing spirituality. We discussed areas of importance in social work practice: philosophy and way of being, assessment of spirituality, clinical intervention with spiritual issues and concerns, functional and dysfunctional use of religion, and spiritual development. We reviewed ways of utilizing the spiritual dimension therapeutically and noted ethical considerations including the qualifications of the social worker and the need to gear interventions toward the worldview and beliefs of the client—only at their request. This chapter is a beginning, a guidepost to many other readings that will enhance intervention in this area. The following chapter will review mezzo level intervention in hospice social work, including work with families, groups, and interdisciplinary teams.

REFERENCES

Addington-Hall, J., and A. O'Callaghan. 2009. "A Comparison of the Quality of Care Provided to Cancer Patients in the UK in the Last Three Months of Life in In-Patient Hospices Compared with Hospitals, from the Perspective of Bereaved Relatives: Results from a Survey Using the VOICES Questionnaire." *Palliative Medicine* 23, no. 3: 190–197.

American Psychiatric Association. 2000. *Diagnostic and Statistical Manual of Mental Disorders IV-TR*. 4th ed. Arlington, VA: American Psychiatric Association.

Arnold, E. M., K. A. Artin, D. Griffith, J. L. Person, and K. G. Graham. 2006. "Unmet Needs at the End of Life: Perceptions of Hospice Social Workers. *Journal of Social Work in End-of-Life and Palliative Care* 2, no. 4: 61–83.

Assagioli, R. 1977. *Psychosynthesis: A Manual of Principles and Techniques*. New York: Penguin.

Back, Anthony L., Jeffrey I. Wallace, Helene E. Starks, and Robert A. Pearlman. 1996. "Physician-Assisted Suicide and Euthanasia in Washington State: Patient Requests and Physician Responses." *Journal of the American Medical Association* 275, no. 12: 919–925.

Bassett, S., J. Magaziner, and J. R. Hebel. 1990. "Reliability of Proxy Response on Mental Health Indices for Aged, Community-Dwelling Women." *Psychology and Aging* 5, no. 1: 127–132.

Bern-Klug, M., C. Gessert, and S. Forbes. 2001. "The Need to Revise Assumptions About the End of Life: Implications for Social Work Practice." *Health and Social Work* 26, no. 1: 38–48.

Berzoff, J. 2004. "Psychodynamic Theories in Grief and Bereavement." In Joan Berzoff and Phyllis R. Silverman, eds., *Living with Dying: A Handbook for End-of-
Life Healthcare Practitioners*, pp. 242–262. New York: Columbia University Press.

Berzoff, J., and P. R. Silverman, eds. 2004. "Introduction: Clinical Practice." In
Joan Berzoff and Phyllis R. Silverman, eds., *Living with Dying: A Handbook for
End-of-Life Healthcare Practitioners*, pp. 265–272. New York: Columbia Univer-
sity Press.

Besthorn, F. H., and D. P. McMillen. 2002. "The Oppression of Women and Nature: Ecofeminism as a Framework for an Expanded Ecological Social Work."
Families in Society 83, no. 3: 221–232.

Blacker, S., and A. R. Jordan. 2004. "Working with Families Facing Life-Threatening Illness in the Medical Setting." In Joan Berzoff and Phyllis Silverman,
eds., *Living with Dying: A Handbook for End-of-Life Healthcare Practitioners*, pp.
548–570. New York: Columbia University Press.

Bradsen, C. K. 2005. "Social Work and End-of-Life Care: Reviewing the Past and
Moving Forward." *Journal of Social Work in End-of-Life and Palliative Care* 1,
no. 2: 45–70.

Bregman, L. 2001. "Death and Dying." *Christian Century* 118, no. 17: 33–37.

Breitbart, W., and K. S. Heller. 2003. "Reframing Hope: Meaning Centered Care for
Patients Near the End of Life." *Journal of Palliative Medicine* 6:979–988.

Breitbart, W., B. Rosenfeld, H. Pessin, M. Kaim, J. Funesti-Esch, M. Galietta et
al. 2000. "Depression, Hopelessness, and Desire for Hastened Death in Terminally Ill Patients with Cancer." *Journal of the American Medical Association* 284:
2907–2911.

Browning, D. 2004. "Fragments of Love: Explorations in the Ethnography of Suffering and Professional Caregiving." In Joan Berzoff and Phyllis R. Silverman,
eds., *Living with Dying: A Handbook for End-of-Life Healthcare Practitioners*, pp.
21–42. New York: Columbia University Press.

Bullis, R. 1996. *Spirituality in Social Work Practice*. Washington, DC: Taylor and
Francis.

Bullock, K. 2006. "Promoting Advance Directives Among African Americans: A
Faith-Based Model." *Journal of Palliative Medicine* 9, no. 1: 183–195.

——. 2011. "The Influence of Culture on End-of-Life Decision Making." *Journal of
Social Work in End-of-Life and Palliative Care* 7, no. 1: 83–98.

Bushfield, S. and B. DeFord. 2009. *End-of-Life Care and Addiction: A Family Systems Approach*. New York: Springer.

Byock, I. 1997. *Dying Well: Peace and Possibilities at the End of Life*. New York:
Riverhead.

Canda, E. 1990. "An Holistic Approach to Prayer for Social Work Practice. *Social Thought* 16, no. 3: 3–13.

Canda, E., and L. Furman. 2010. *Spiritual Diversity in Social Work Practice: The Heart of Helping.* New York: Oxford University Press.

Chibnall, J. T., S. D. Videen, P. N. Duckro, and D. K. Miller. 2002. "Psychosocial-Spiritual Correlates of Death Distress in Patients with Life-Threatening Medical Conditions." *Palliative Medicine* 16:331–338.

Chochinov, H. M., T. Hack, S. McClement, M. Harlos, and L. Kristjanson. 2002. "Dignity in the Terminally Ill: An Empirical Model." *Social Science Medicine* 54:433–443.

Chung, K. 1993. "Brief Social Work Intervention in the Hospice Setting: Person-Centered Work and Crisis Intervention Synthesized and Distilled." *Palliative Medicine* 7, no. 1: 59–62.

Cincotta, N. 2004. "The End of Life at the Beginning of Life: Working with Dying Children and Their Families." In Joan Berzoff and Phyllis R. Silverman, eds., *Living with Dying: A Handbook for End-of-Life Healthcare Practitioners,* pp. 318–347. New York: Columbia University Press.

Coffey, E. P. 2004. The Symptom Is Stillness: Living with and Dying from ALS." In Joan Berzoff and Phyllis R. Silverman, eds., *Living with Dying: A Handbook for End-of-Life Healthcare Practitioners,* pp. 43–56. New York: Columbia University Press.

Connor, S. 1986. "Measurement of Denial in the Terminally Ill: A Critical Review." *Hospice Journal* 2, no. 4: 51–68.

——. 1993. "Denial in Terminal Illness: To Intervene or Not to Intervene." *Hospice Journal* 8, no. 4: 1–15.

Conte, H., M. Weiner, and R. Plutchik. 1982. "Measuring Death Anxiety: Conceptual, Psychometric, and Factor-Analytic Aspects." *Journal of Personality and Social Psychology* 43, no. 4: 775–785.

Csikai, E. L. 1999. "The Role of Values and Experience in Determining Social Workers' Attitudes Toward Euthanasia and Assisted Suicide." *Social Work in Health Care* 30, no. 1: 75–95.

——. 2004. "Advanced Directives and Assisted Suicide: Policy Implications for Social Work Practice." In Joan Berzoff and Phyllis R. Silverman, eds., *Living with Dying: A Handbook for End-of-Life Healthcare Practitioners,* pp. 761–777. New York: Columbia University Press.

Csikai, E. L., and A. A. Manetta. 2002. "Preventing Unnecessary Deaths Among Older Adults: A call to action for social workers. *Journal of Gerontological Social Work* 38, no. 3: 85–97.

Cutrona, C. 1986. "Behavioral Manifestations of Social Support: A Microanalytic Investigation." *Journal of Personality and Social Psychology* 51, no. 1: 201–208.

Dane, B. 2004. Integrating Spirituality and Religion." In Joan Berzoff and Phyllis R. Silverman, eds., *Living with Dying: A Handbook for End-of-Life Healthcare Practitioners*, pp. 424–438. New York: Columbia University Press.

DeFord, B., and S. Bushfield. 2005. "The Social Work of Spiritual Care and the Spiritual Care of Social Work: The Meanings of Hope and Love." Paper presented at the National Hospice and Palliative Care Organization annual clinical conference.

Derezotes, D., and K. Evans. 1995. "Spirituality and Religiosity in Practice: In-depth Interviews of Social Work Practitioners." *Social Thought* 18, no. 1: 39–56.

Doka, K. J. 1995/96. "Coping with Life-Threatening Illness: A Task Model." *Omega* 32, no. 2: 111–113.

——. 2011. "Religion and Spirituality: Assessment and Intervention." *Journal of Social Work in End-of-Life and Palliative Care* 7, no. 1: 99–109.

Driscoll, J. 2001. "Spirituality and Religion in End-of-Life Care." *Journal of Palliative Medicine* 4, no. 3: 333–335.

Duffy, S. A., F. C. Jackson, S. M. Schim, D. L. Ronis, and K. E. Fowler. 2006. "Racial/Ethnic Preferences, Sex Preferences, and Perceived Discrimination Related to End-of-Life Care." *Journal of the American Geriatrics Society* 54, no. 1: 150–157.

Early, B. 1998. "Between Two Worlds: The Psychospiritual Crisis of a Dying Adolescent." *Social Thought: Journal of Religion in the Social Services* 18, no. 2: 67–80.

Egan, M., and G. Kadushin. 1999. "The Social Worker in the Emerging Field of Home Care: Professional Activities and Ethical Concerns." *Health and Social Work* 24, no. 1: 43–55.

Egan, K. A., and M. J. Labyak. 2001. "Hospice Care: A Model for Quality End-of-Life Care." In B. R. Ferrell, and N. Coyle, eds., *Textbook of Palliative Nursing*, pp. 7–26. New York: Oxford University Press.

Erikson, E. H. 1950. *Childhood and Society*. Philadelphia: Norton.

Finucane, T. E. 1999. "How Gravely Ill Becomes Dying: A Key to End-of-Life Care." *Journal of the American Medical Association* 282, no. 17: 1670–1672.

Foster, L., and L. McLellan. 2002. "Translating Psychosocial Insight Into Ethical Discussions Supportive of Families in End-of-Life Decision-Making." *Social Work in Health Care* 35, no. 3: 37–51.

Frankl, Viktor E. 1984. "Logotherapy." In Raymond J. Corsini, ed., *Encyclopedia of Psychology*. Vol. 2. New York: Wiley.

Furman, L., and S. Bushfield (formerly S. Fry). 2000. "Clerics and Social Workers: Collaborators or Competitors?" *ARETE: Journal of University of South Carolina School of Social Work* 24, no. 1: 30–39.

Galambos, C. 1998. "Preserving End-of-Life Autonomy: The Patient Self-Determination Act and the Uniform Health Care Decisions Act." *Health and Social Work* 23, no. 4: 275–281.

Gallup International Institute. 1997. *Spiritual Beliefs and the Dying Process.* Princeton: Nathan Cummings Foundation.

Gard, C. J. 2000. "Coping with Loss." *Current Health* 26, no. 7: 26–28.

Gardia, G. 2010. "Rapid Response: Addressing Suffering When Time Is Very Short." Paper presented at the Eleventh Clinical Team Conference, National Hospice and Palliative Care Organization, September, Atlanta.

Gardner, D. S. 2011. "Palliative Social Work with Older Adults and Their Families." In Terry Altilio and Shirley Otis-Green, eds., *Oxford Textbook of Palliative Social Work*, pp. 397–411. New York: Oxford University Press.

Gibbs, H., and J. Achterberg-Lawlis. 1978. "Spiritual Values and Death Anxiety: Implications for Counseling with Terminal Cancer Patients." *Journal of Counseling Psychology* 25:563–569.

Glajchen, M. 2011. In Terry Altilio and Shirley Otis-Green, eds., *Oxford Textbook of Palliative Social Work*, pp. 223–233. New York: Oxford University Press.

Glaser, B. G., and A. L. Strauss. 1967. *The Discovery of Grounded Theory: Strategies for Qualitative Research.* New York: Aldine.

Goelitz, A. 2001a. "Dreaming Their Way Into Life: A Group Experience with Oncology Patients." *Social Work with Groups* 24, no. 1: 53–67.

———. 2001b. "Nurturing Life with Dreams: Therapeutic Dream Work with Cancer Patients." *Clinical Social Work Journal* 29, no. 4: 375–385.

———. 2005. "Identifying Suicidality at End of Life." *American Academy of Hospice and Palliative Medicine Bulletin* 6, no. 3: 1–2.

Graham, M., T. Kaiser, and K. Garrett. 1998. "Naming the Spiritual: The Hidden Dimension of Helping." *Social Thought* 18, no. 4: 49–61.

Grof, S. 1988. *The Adventure of Self-discovery.* Albany: State University of New York Press.

Grof, S., and C. Grof. 1989. *Spiritual Emergency.* New York: Putnam.

Harrawood, L. K. 2009. Measuring Spirituality, Religiosity, and Denial in Individuals Working in Funeral Service to Predict Death Anxiety." *Omega: Journal of Death and Dying* 60, no. 2: 129–142.

Henoch, I., B. Axelsson, and B. Bergman. 2010. "The Assessment of Quality of Life at the End of Life (AQEL) Questionnaire: A Brief but Comprehensive Instrument for Use in Patients with Cancer in Palliative Care." *Quality of Life Research* 19, no. 5: 739–750.

Hodge, David R. 2003. *Spiritual Assessment: Handbook for Helping Professionals.* Botsford, CT: North American Association of Christians in Social Work.

Hooyman, N. R., and B. J. Kramer. 2006. *Living Through Loss: Interventions Across the Life Span*. New York: Columbia University Press.

Ivanko, B. 2011. "Quality Improvement and Organizational Change." In Terry Altilio and Shirley Otis-Green, eds., *Oxford Textbook of Palliative Social Work*, pp. 745–752. New York: Oxford University Press.

Jacobs, C. 2004. "Spirituality and End-of-Life Care Practice for Social Workers." In Joan Berzoff and Phyllis R. Silverman, eds., *Living with Dying: A Handbook for End-of-Life Healthcare Practitioners*, pp. 188–205. New York: Columbia University Press.

Jones, B. 2006. "Companionship, Control, and Compassion: A Social Work Perspective on the Needs of Children with Cancer and Their Families at the End of Life." *Journal of Palliative Medicine* 9, no. 3: 774–788.

Joseph, M. 1988. "Religion and Social work Practice." *Social Casework* 69:443–452.

Joshi, K.Y. 2002. "Patterns and Paths: Ethnic Identity Development in Second Generation Indian Americans." *Dissertation Abstracts International, A: The Humanities and Social Sciences* 62, no. 10: 3585-A.

Kovacs, P., and L. Bronstein. 1999. "Preparation for Oncology Settings: What Hospice Workers Say They Need." *Health and Social Work* 24, no. 1: 57–64.

Kramer, B. T., M. Kavanaugh, A. Trentham-Dietz, M. Walsh, and J. A. Yonker. 2010. "Predictors of Family Conflict at the End of Life: The Experiences of Spouses and Adult Children of Persons with Lung Cancer." *Gerontologist* 50, no. 2: 215–225.

Kubler-Ross, E. 1970. *On Death and Dying*. New York: Macmillan.

Kubler-Ross, E., and D. Kessler. 2001. *Life Lessons*. Llandeilo, Carmarthenshire: Cygnus.

Kulys, R., and M. Davis. 1986. "An Analysis of Social Services in Hospice." *Social Work* 11, no. 6: 448–454.

Lavretsky, H. 2010. "Spirituality and Aging." *Aging Health* 6, no. 6: 749–769.

Leichtentritt, R. D., and K. D. Rettig. 2001. "The Construction of the Good Death: A Dramaturgy Approach." *Journal of Aging Studies* 15, no. 1: 85–104.

Levine, A., and W. Karger. 2004. "The Trajectory of Illness." In Joan Berzoff and Phyllis R. Silverman, eds., *Living with Dying: A Handbook for End-of-Life Healthcare Practitioners*, pp. 273–296. New York: Columbia University Press.

Linder, J. 2004. "Oncology." In Joan Berzoff and Phyllis R. Silverman, eds., *Living with Dying: A Handbook for End-of-Life Healthcare Practitioners*, pp. 696–722. New York: Columbia University Press.

Loewenberg, F. 1988. *Religion and Social Work Practice in Contemporary American Society*. New York: Columbia University Press.

McGregor, B., C. Carver, M. Antoni, S. Weiss, S. Yount, and G. Ironson. 2001. "Distress and Internalized Homophobia Among Lesbian Women Treated for Early Stage Breast Cancer." *Psychology of Women Quarterly* 25:1–9.

McMillan, S., and B. Small. 2002. "Symptom Distress and Quality of Life in Patients with Cancer Newly Admitted to Hospice Home Care." *Oncology Nursing Forum* 29, no. 10: 1421–1428.

Magaziner, J. 1992. "The Use of Proxy Respondents in Health Studies of the Aged." In R. Wallace and R. Woolson, eds., *The Epidemiologic Study of the Elderly*. New York: Oxford University Press.

Markstrom, C. A., V. M. Sabino, B. J. Turner, and R. C. Berman. 1997. "The Psychosocial Inventory of Ego Strengths: Development and Validation of a New Eriksonian Measure." *Journal of Youth and Adolescence* 26, no. 6: 705–732.

Maslow, A. 1970. *Motivation and Personality*. 2d ed. New York: Harper and Row.

——. 1971. *The Farther Reaches of Human Nature*. New York: McGraw-Hill.

Mead, G., B. N. Melzer, P. L. Berger, T. Luckmann, S. S. Duval, and R. R. Wicklund. 1990. "The Social Context of Consciousness." In J. Pickering, M. Skinner, J. Pickering, M. Skinner, eds., *From Sentience to Symbols: Readings on Consciousness*, pp. 190–215. Toronto: University of Toronto Press.

Miller, P. J., M. A. Mesler, and S. T. Eggman. 2002. "Take Some Time to Look Inside their Hearts: Hospice Social Workers Contemplate Physician Assisted Suicide." *Social Work in Health Care* 35, no. 3: 53–64.

Mizrahi, T. 1992. "The Direction of Patients' Rights in the 1990s: Proceed with Caution." *Health and Social Work* 17:246–252.

Mutran, E. J., M. Danis, K. A. Bratton, S. Sudha, and L. Hanson. 1997. "Attitudes of the Critically Ill Toward Prolonging Life: The Role of Social Support." *Gerontologist* 37, no. 2: 192–199.

Nakashima, M. 2003. "Beyond Coping and Adaptation: Promoting a Holistic Perspective on Dying." *Families in Society: The Journal of Contemporary Human Services* 84, no. 3: 367–376.

National Association of Social Workers. 1999. *Code of Ethics of the National Association of Social Workers*. Retrieved from http://www.socialworkers.org/pubs/code/code.asp.

——. 2011. *NASW Standards for Social Work Practice in Palliative and End of Life Care*. Washington, DC: Author.

National Hospice and Palliative Care Organization (formerly National Hospice Organization). 1997. *A Pathway for Patients and Families Facing Terminal Illness*. Arlington, VA: NHPCO.

Nelson-Becker, H., M. Nakashima, and E. R. Canda. 2006. "Spirituality in Professional Helping Interventions." In B. Berkman, ed., *Handbook of Social Work in Health and Aging*, pp.797–807. New York: Oxford University Press.

Nicholson, B. L., and G. N. Matross. 1989. "Facing Reduced Decision-Making Capacity in Health Care: Methods for Maintaining Client Self-determination." *Social Work* 34: 234–238.

Noppe, I. C. 2004. "Gender and Death: Parallel and Intersecting Pathways." In Joan Berzoff and Phyllis R. Silverman, eds., *Living with Dying: A Handbook for End-of-Life Healthcare Practitioners*, pp. 206–225. New York: Columbia University Press.

Orloff, S. F. 2011. "Pediatric Hospice and Palliative Care: The Invaluable Role of Social Work." In Terry Altilio and Shirley Otis-Green, eds., *Oxford Textbook of Palliative Social Work*, pp. 79–86. New York: Oxford University Press.

Otis-Green, S. 2006. "Psychosocial Pain Assessment Form." In K. Dow, ed., *Nursing Care of Women with Cancer*, pp. 556–561. St. Louis, MO: Elsevier Mosby.

Panzarella, C., L. B. Alloy, and W. G. Whitehouse. 2006. "Expanded Hopelessness Theory of Depression: On the Mechanisms by Which Social Support Protects Against Depression." *Cognitive Therapy and Research* 30, no. 3: 307–333.

Parker Oliver, D. 2002. "Redefining Hope for the Terminally Ill." *American Journal of Hospice and Palliative Care* 19, no. 2: 115–120.

Parry, J. K. 2001. *Social Work Theory and Practice with the Terminally Ill.* 2d ed. New York: Haworth Social Work Practice Press.

Payne, D., and M. J. Massie. 2000. "Anxiety in Palliative Care." In H. M. Chochinov and W. Breitbart, eds., *Handbook of Psychiatry in Palliative Medicine*, pp. 63–74. New York: Oxford University Press.

Peay, P. 1997. "A Good Death." *Common Boundary*, September/October. Retrieved from commonboundary.org.

Pessin, H., B. Rosenfeld, and W. Breitbart. 2002. "Assessing Psychological Distress Near the End of Life." *American Behavioral Scientist* 46, no. 3: 357–372.

Pflaum, M., and P. Kelley. 1986. "Understanding the Final Messages of the Dying." *Nursing86* 16, no .6o: 26–29.

Porter, T. 1999. "Satanism in Youth." Unpublished MS.

Puchalski, C. M. 2002. "Spirituality and End-of-Life Care: A Time for Listening and Caring." *Journal of Palliative Medicine* 5, no. 2: 289–294.

Puchalski C, B. Ferrell, R. Virani, S. Otis-Green, P. Baird, J. Bull, H. Chochinov, G. Handzo, H. Nelson-Becker, M. Prince-Paul, K. Pugliese, and D. Sulmasy. 2009. "Improving the Quality of Spiritual Care as a Dimension of Palliative Care: The Report of the Consensus Conference." *Journal of Palliative Medicine* 12, no. 10: 885–904.

Raymer, M., and G. Gardia. 2011. "Enhancing Professionalism, Leadership, and Advocacy: A Call to Arms." In Terry Altilio and Shirley Otis-Green, eds., *Oxford*

Textbook of Palliative Social Work, pp. 683–687. New York: Oxford University Press.

Raymer, M., and D. Reese. 2004. "The History of Social Work in Hospice." In Joan Berzoff and Phyllis R. Silverman, eds., *Living with Dying: A Handbook for End-of-Life Healthcare Practitioners*, pp. 150–160. New York: Columbia University Press.

Reed, P. 1987. "Spirituality and Wellbeing in Terminally Ill Hospitalized Adults." *Research in Nursing and Health* 10, no. 5: 335–44.

Reese, D. (formerly D. Ita). 1995. "Predictors of Patient and Primary Caregiver Ability to Sustain a Planned Program of Home Hospice Care." Ph.D. diss., University of Maryland, 1994. *Dissertation Abstracts International*. University Microfilms No. 9526600.

——. 1995–96. "Testing of a Causal Model: Acceptance of Death in Hospice Patients." *Omega: Journal of Death and Dying* 32, no. 2: 81–92.

——. 2001. "Addressing Spirituality in Hospice: Current Practices and a Proposed Role for Transpersonal Social Work." *Social Thought: Journal of Religion in the Social Services* 20, nos. 1–2: 135–161.

——. 2011a. "Interdisciplinary Perceptions of the Social Work Role in Hospice: A Replication of the Classic Kulys and Davis Study." *Journal of Social Work in End-of-Life and Palliative Care* 7, no. 4: 383–406.

——. 2011b. "Spirituality and Social Work Practice in Palliative Care." In Terry Altilio and Shirley Otis-Green, eds., *Oxford Textbook of Palliative Social Work*, pp. 201–213. New York: Oxford University Press.

Reese, D., R. Ahern, S. Nair, J. O'Faire, and C. Warren. 1999. "Hospice Access and Utilization by African Americans: Addressing Cultural and Institutional Barriers Through Participatory Action Research." *Social Work* 44, no. 6: 549–559.

Reese, D., and S. Beckwith. 2005. "Organizational Barriers to Cultural Competence in Hospice." Paper presented at the National Hospice and Palliative Care Association, Opening Doors, Building Bridges: Access and Diversity Conference, August, St. Louis.

Reese, D., L. Braden, C. Butler, and M. Smith. 2004. "African American Access to Hospice: An Interdisciplinary Participatory Action Research Project." Paper presented at the Clinical Team Conference, National Hospice and Palliative Care Organization, March, Las Vegas.

Reese, D., and D. Brown. 1997. "Psychosocial and Spiritual Care in Hospice: Differences Between Nursing, Social Work, and Clergy." *Hospice Journal* 12, no. 1: 29–41.

Reese, D., C. Butler, M. Raymer, R. Huber, S. Orloff, and S. Gerbino. 2007. *Social Work Assessment Tool: Information Booklet*. Online publication, accessible to members only. National Hospice and Palliative Care Organization. Retrieved from www.nhpco.org.

Reese, D., C. L. W. Chan, W. C. H. Chan, and D. Wiersgalla. 2010. "A Cross-National Comparison of Hong Kong and U.S. Student Beliefs and Preferences in End-of-Life Care: Implications for Social Work Education and Hospice Practice." *Journal of Social Work in End-of-Life and Palliative Care* 6, nos. 3–4: 1–31.

Reese, D., and E. Melton. 2003. "Needs of Lesbian Women in End-of-Life Care." Unpublished MS.

Reese, D., and M. Raymer. 2004. "Relationships Between Social Work Services and Hospice Outcomes: Results of the National Hospice Social Work Survey." *Social Work* 49, no. 3: 415–422.

Reese, D., M. Raymer, S. Orloff, S. Gerbino, R. Valade, S. Dawson, C. Butler, M. Wise-Wright, and R. Huber. 2006. "The Social Work Assessment Tool (SWAT): Developed by the Social Worker Section of the National Council of Hospice and Palliative Professionals, National Hospice and Palliative Care Organization." *Journal of Social Work in End-of-Life and Palliative Care* 2, no. 2: 65–95.

Reese, D., and C. Rosaasen. 1999. "Spiritual Needs of Bereaved Children." Paper presented at the Society for Spirituality and Social Work National Conference, June, St. Louis.

Reese, D., and M-A. Sontag. 2001. "Barriers and Solutions for Successful Inter-Professional Collaboration on the Hospice Team." *Health and Social Work* 26, no. 3: 167–175.

Reith, M., and M. Payne. 2009. *Social Work in End-of-Life and Palliative Care.* Chicago: Lyceum.

Robbins, S. P., E. R. Canda, and P. Chatterjee. 1998. *Contemporary Human Behavior Theory: A Critical Perspective for Social Work.* Boston: Allyn and Bacon.

Roff, S. 2001. "Analyzing End-of-Life Care Legislation: A Social Work Perspective." *Social Work in Health Care* 33, no. 1: 51–68.

Rosenberg, M. 2011. "Center for Non-Violent Communication." Retrieved from http:www.cnvc.org/.

Rosenfeld, B., W. Breitbart, S. Krivo, and H. M. Chochinov. 2000. "Suicide, Assisted Suicide, and Euthanasian in the Terminally Ill." In H. M. Chochinov and W. Breitbart, eds., *Handbook of Psychiatry in Palliative Medicine*, pp. 51–62. New York: Oxford University Press.

Rosenfeld, K. E., N. S. Wenger, and M. Kagawa-Singer. 2000. "End-of-Life Decision Making: A Qualitative Study of Elderly Individuals." *Journal of General Internal Medicine* 15:620–625.

Russel, R., S. Bowen, and B. Nickolaison. 2000. "Spiritually Derived Interventions in Social Work Practice and Education." Paper presented at the Annual Program Meeting of the Council on Social Work Education, New York.

Saulnier, C. 2002. "Deciding Who to See: Lesbians Discuss their Preferences in Health and Mental Health Care Providers." *Social Work* 47, no. 4: 355–366.

Schroepfer, T. 2008. "Social Relationships and Their Role in the Consideration to Hasten Death." *Gerontologist* 48, no. 5: 612–621.

Schroepfer, T. A., J. F. Linder, and P. J. Miller. 2011. "Social Work's Ethical Challenge: Supporting the Terminally Ill Who Consider a Hastened Death." In Terry Altilio and Shirley Otis-Green, eds., *Oxford Textbook of Palliative Social Work*, pp. 651–659. New York: Oxford University Press.

Sheridan, M., R. Bullis, C. Adcock, S. Berlin, and P. Miller. 1992. "Practitioners' Personal and Professional Attitudes and Behaviors Toward Religion and Spirituality: Issues for Education and Practice." *Journal of Social Work Education* 28, no. 2: 190–203.

Siemaszko, C. 1997. "Angel of the Poor." *Daily News*, September 6. Retrieved from http://articles.nydailynews.com/1997–09–06/news/18043708_1_mother-teresa-calcutta-irish-sisters.

Simon, J. 2010. *Solution-Focused Practice in End-of-Life and Grief Counseling.* New York: Springer.

Singh, K. 1998. *The Grace in Dying.* San Francisco: Harper.

Smith, D. 1993. "Exploring the Religious-Spiritual Needs of the Dying." *Counseling and Values* 37:71–77.

Smith, E. D. 1991. "The Relationship of Transpersonal Development to the Psychosocial Distress of Cancer Patients." *Dissertation Abstracts International* 51 (January).

——. 1995. "Addressing the Psychospiritual Distress of Death as Reality: A Transpersonal Approach." *Social Work* 40, no. 3: 402–412.

——. 2001. "Alleviating Suffering in the Face of Death: Insights from Constructivism and a Transpersonal Narrative Approach." *Social Thought: Journal of Religion in the Social Services* 20, nos. 1–2: 45–62.

Smith, E., and C. Gray. 1995. "Integrating and Transcending Divorce: A Transpersonal Model." *Social Thought* 18, no. 1: 57–74.

Smolinski, K. M., and Y. Colon. 2011. "Palliative Care with Lesbian, Gay, Bisexual, and Transgender Persons." In Terry Altilio and Shirley Otis-Green, eds., *Oxford Textbook of Palliative Social Work*, pp. 379–386. New York: Oxford University Press.

Social Work Policy Institute. 2010. *Hospice Social Work: Linking Policy, Practice, and Research.* Washington, DC: National Association of Social Workers.

Soltura, D. L., and L. F. Piotrowski. 2011. In Terry Altilio and Shirley Otis-Green, eds., *Oxford Textbook of Palliative Social Work*, pp. 495–501. New York: Oxford University Press.

Sullivan, M. 2003. "Hope and Hopelessness at the End of Life." *American Journal of Geriatric Psychiatry* 11, no. 4: 393–405.

Swett, L. N.d. "Spiritual Shower." Unpublished manuscript.

Thoits, P.A. 1995. "Stress, Coping, and Social Support Processes: Where Are We? What Next?" *Journal of Health and Social Behavior* 35:53–79. Special issue, *Forty Years of Medical Sociology: The State of the Art and Directions for the Future.*

Triplett, George, David Cohen, Wilbert Reimer, Sharon Rinaldi, Curtis Hill, Si-min Roshdieh, Elizabeth M. Stanczak, Karen Siscoe, and I. Donald Templer. 1995. "Death Discomfort Differential." *Omega: Journal of Death and Dying* 31: 295–304.

Trombetti, I. A. 2006. "Meanings in the Lives of Older Adults: In Their Own Voices." *Dissertation Abstracts International: Section B: The Sciences and Engineering* 66(9-B): 5130.

van Loon, R.A. 1999. "Desire to Die in Terminally Ill People: A Framework for Assessment and Intervention." *Health and Social Work* 24, no. 4: 260–268.

Varghese, F. T., and B. Kelly. 2001. "Counter Transference and Assisted Suicide." *Issues in Law and Medicine* 16, no. 3: 235–258.

Vaughn, M., and K. Swanson. 2006. "Any Life Can Be Fascinating: Using Spiritual Autobiography as an Adjunct to Therapy." In: K. B. Helmeke and C. F. Sori, eds., *The Therapist's Notebook for Integrating Spirituality in Counseling: Homework, Handouts and Activities for Use in Psychotherapy*, pp. 211–219. New York: Haworth.

Waldrop, D. P. 2008. "Evidence-Based Psychosocial Treatment at End of Life. *Journal of Gerontological Social Work* 50, no. S1: 267–292.

Walsh, K., and S. Hedlund. 2011. "Mental Health Risk in Palliative Care: The Social Work Role." In Terry Altilio and Shirley Otis-Green, eds., *Oxford Textbook of Palliative Social Work*, pp. 181–190. New York: Oxford University Press.

Walsh-Burke, K. 2004. "Assessing Mental Health Risk in End-of-Life Care." In Joan Berzoff and Phyllis R. Silverman, eds., *Living with Dying: A Handbook for End-of-Life Healthcare Practitioners*, pp. 360–379. New York: Columbia University Press.

Weisenfluh, S. 2011. "Social Work and Palliative Care in Hospice." In Terry Altilio and Shirley Otis-Green, eds., *Oxford Textbook of Palliative Social Work*. New York: Oxford University Press.

Wilber, K. 1993. 2d ed. *The Spectrum of Consciousness*. Wheaton, IL: Quest.

Worthington, E. and F. DiBlasio. 1990. "Promoting Mutual Forgiveness Within the Fractured Relationship." *Psychotherapy* 27:219–223.

Zigmond, A. S., and R. P. Snaith. 1983. "The Hospice Anxiety and Depression Scale." *Acta Psychiatrica Scandinavica* 67:261–70.

Zilberfein, F., and E. Hurwitz. 2004. "Clinical Social Work Practice at the End of Life." In Joan Berzoff and Phyllis R. Silverman, eds., *Living with Dying: A Handbook for End-of-Life Healthcare Practitioners*, pp. 297–317. New York: Columbia University Press.

5

MEZZO CONTEXT OF HOSPICE SOCIAL WORK

Work With Families, Groups, and Interdisciplinary Teams

This chapter explores hospice social work practice on the mezzo level. This includes work with families, groups, and interdisciplinary teams. Social workers have special skills in these areas that they can contribute to the hospice. A wonderful and unique aspect of hospice social work is that families and significant others are considered clients along with the patients. This allows the social work systems perspective to come fully into play for interventions that greatly benefit patients as well as their loved ones. Another area of special skill for social workers is group intervention, and group intervention has a place in hospice social work with families, patients, and staff. A great strength of hospice is its holistic approach to care; the last section of the chapter will review considerations when working with interdisciplinary hospice teams. First, we focus on families.

FAMILIES

ASSESSMENT WITH FAMILIES

Although the Social Work Assessment Tool provides guidance in assessment of the patient and primary caregiver, it is focused more on the micro level, and can be supplemented with a systems perspective in assessment of families. The developmental stage of a family should be taken into consideration—whether they have a history of past loss or medical conditions, whether they have young children to take care of, whether they are an aging couple. Assessment from a systems perspective also involves seeking information about the family's social environment and spiritual and cultural beliefs (Doka 2011). Areas on which to focus also include family structure and dynamics, history of coping and emotional responses, family strengths, and socioeconomic factors and resources (Blacker and Jordan 2004).

INTERVENTIONS WITH FAMILIES IN HOSPICE SOCIAL WORK

The health care system outside hospice still tends to be generally oriented toward patient care only (Foster and McLellan 2002). Visiting policies in inpatient health care facilities often restrict contact between patient and immediate family members, services are focused only on the individual patient, and the physical dimension of care is emphasized (Harris et al. 2009). A social worker or chaplain may be called in upon occasion, but psychosocial and spiritual services are seen as "ancillary" rather than an area for equal attention. Probably partly due to the social work background of hospice founder Dame Cicely Saunders, hospice philosophy incorporates the social work systems perspective and provides services to the social network of which the patient is a part.

We have evidence that social work intervention has a significant impact on individual hospice patient outcomes (Reese and Raymer 2004; Reese et al. 2006). We should be aware, though, that study of bereavement outcomes (Reese 2003) and primary caregiver outcomes (Reese et al. 2006) documented a lack of improvement through social work intervention. We don't know the reason why; perhaps improvement for caregivers and loved ones does not occur in the short period of time covered by the studies. But these study results serve as a reminder that we should review our efforts in family intervention and make sure we are providing the same level of care with loved ones that we are with patients.

We begin with a note that the term *family* may imply a traditional view that includes only blood relatives. We advocate for an alternative view described by the term *familiness* (Schriver 2010). This term recognizes that families are composed not only of nuclear families, blood relatives, or members documented by law. Gay and lesbian couples may not have equal rights to marriage, for example; and families in African American, Asian, Hispanic, Native American cultural groups, among many others, may include extended family members; African American and Native American families may be made up of a myriad of loved ones who are not connected through blood lines. The proverb "it takes a village to raise a child," attributed to both African and Native American cultures, reflects a difference in perspective from the dominant culture in our society. Thus, in this chapter, when we refer to work with the *family*, we are referring to the loved ones the patient considers family.

WORKING WITHIN THE FAMILY SYSTEM Chung (1993) outlines aspects of family dynamics to observe when several family members are present. It is helpful to understand which family members agree and which are in conflict, who puts up barriers and who speaks openly, who has decision-making power and what the rules are (Blacker and Jordan 2004). In this way the social worker can assist families in finding new ways of coping during crisis, handling the tasks of preparation for death such as saying good-byes, thank you, giving and asking for forgiveness, and making decisions about end-of-life care. Kramer and colleagues found that families were at risk for conflict if they had a history of conflict or experienced communication constraints (Kramer et al. 2010).

SHIFT IN FAMILY ROLES One of the first challenges that a family has to cope with when a family member becomes terminally ill is the change that occurs in family roles (Blacker and Jordan 2004; Hooyman and Kramer 2006). Wives and mothers tend to have a caregiving role in our society. When this changes and someone else takes over the care of a wife or mother, roles in the family must undergo a difficult change. This is also true when a husband or father who has been authoritative and taken care of a great deal of responsibility in the family becomes the patient. When responsibility is thrust on family members who have been dependent on the patient in various ways, family patterns and stability are disrupted. When family members assume a new role in asserting control over a patient, the family is at risk for conflict (Kramer et al. 2010). Healthy families with more flexible boundaries are better able to cope than those with rigid family roles who are not able to adjust. In families with rigid family roles, both patient and family members may attempt to cope through denial of the illness and prognosis, neglect the patient's physical needs, and continue to try to place the patient in a caregiving role. This seems especially to be the case when the patient is female and has a history of being thrust into a caregiver role because of parental neglect or previous difficult life experiences (Blacker and Jordan 2004).

A family systems approach is needed to address such a situation (Fineberg and Bauer 2011). Roberts, Baile, and Bassett (1999) make the following recommendations for social workers: 1. completing a family history that includes attention to past caregiving roles, 2. assessing the family's current functioning within a family systems and feminist framework, 3. communicating information about the family's functioning with other members of the health care team, and 4. arranging ongoing family counseling. The multivariate stress and coping model for caregivers (Kinsella, Cooper, Picton, and Murtagh 2000) expands the family systems approach to assess background and contextual factors, along with stressors and appraisals of strain, and garner all available psychosocial resources to enhance caregiving outcomes. Kramer and colleagues recommend development and testing of interventions to facilitate shared decision making and enhance open communication among at-risk families (Kramer et al. 2010).

A hospice patient, a young mother, was terminally ill with cancer. She was a single mother and had two small children. The mother was experiencing denial about her condition. Although bedridden, she still took sole responsibility for the care of her children. Staff was unable to identify family or friends to provide support. Perhaps the mother's desire to care for her children was heightened by awareness on some level that she would experience the loss of her children through her own death. For the children's safety, it was necessary for the social worker to counsel the mother to help her realize specific caregiving tasks she was unable to do and to obtain day care or an in-home caregiver for the children. At the same time, there were still things the mother could do, and the social worker encouraged her to do so—such as providing much affection from her bed, reading to the children, combing their hair, playing with toys in the bed, etc.

TAKING CARE OF OUR OWN: CULTURALLY COMPETENT WORK WITH FAMILIES

Working with families has everything to do with knowledge about and sensitivity to cultural perspectives. The subtitle of this section refers to the traditional perspective among African American families of self-reliance and communal support, rather than dependence on the health care system for support in death and dying. With sensitivity we can provide services that are relevant and acceptable to these families and that, after exposure to hospice care, they actually prefer over a nonhospice death (Reese et al. 2004). Families vary greatly of course in the importance they place on cultural traditions, but it is likely that in times of great stress, as in the death of a family member, that those who don't normally adhere to traditions may rely more greatly on them as a source of comfort and coping. Cultural traditions may overlap with religious beliefs and rituals; religion may also be a beneficial way of coping with anticipatory grief and bereavement. The social worker should become aware of the individual family's preferences in terms of preparation for death and after-death care and grieving rituals. There may be culture-relevant body-disposition wishes, and desires and needs of the family at the time of death. Orthodox Jewish families may not believe in autopsy; this author served in a case in which she had to advocate with the county coroner against laws about autopsy in sudden death so as to respect the family's beliefs. The coroner agreed not to conduct the autopsy since the patient had a history of heart disease and the death was expected. Cultural competence in hospice care will be discussed further in chapter 7.

SPIRITUALITY

Just as patients address unfinished business with loved ones during death and dying, reconciling, resolving conflicts, forgiving and asking for forgiveness, family members experience the same thing between themselves (Foster and McLellan 2002). From this author's perspective, these are spiritual issues; family members have spiritual needs similar to the patient, and addressing these issues leads to spiritual growth. Spirituality has been found to be a major way of coping for family members anticipating a loved one's death (Blacker and Jordan 2004). Family members need to find a sense of meaning in the death of their loved one and an acceptance of their loved one's life (Doka 2011), and Foster and McLellan (2002) argue that this is key in the ability to make end-of-life care decisions. Tools have been developed for helping families discuss such matters. Byock (1997) identifies five messages of relationship completion that patients need to say and their families need to say to them for them to have a peaceful death: "Forgive me," "I forgive you," "I love you," "Thank you," and "Good-bye."

Patients often have transpersonal experiences during the last months of life that seem to connect them to a spiritual dimension. Upbringing in our society generally doesn't provide an explanation for this type of experience, other than mental illness or drug side effects. Family members may need help, therefore, in coping with and understanding such experiences. The social worker should communicate with the family about such issues, normalizing them as near-death awareness. Sometimes the experiences may be seen as symbolic communication, for example, a patient who wanted to prepare for a train trip. Sometimes they may be seen as near-death experience, as in the case of a patient who said his recently deceased wife had appeared to him three times, saying, "Come on, I'm waiting, I can't go without you." Patients who have such experiences express relief at being listened to without judgment. The social worker should help families in listening without judgment, understanding, and realizing that these experiences are often normal parts of the dying process (Pflaum and Kelley 1986).

A client reported to the social worker that she had seen her deceased husband appear to her. It looked like he was opening a door and standing in it. When she got up to pass through the door, he closed it in her face. The social worker listened without judgment and asked, "What does this experience mean to you?" The client said, "It means it's not time for me to go yet."

SOCIAL SUPPORT

Social support is a key factor in the coping (Hooyman and Kramer 2006) and bereavement outcomes (Silverman 2004) of family members of hospice patients. In cohesive cultural groups that are more community-oriented than mainstream white culture, this is even more strongly a theme. Smith (1999) found the major coping strategies of bereaved African American daughters to be reciprocity, family continuity, and cognitive strategies framing an elderly mother's death as an important loss to the family and community.

Hospice social workers play an important role in providing encouragement and support to family members (Beresford, Adshead, and Croft 2007; Blacker and Jordan 2004; Glajchen 2011). This is especially so when caregivers are dissatisfied with the support they have from friends and family (Silverman 2004). Hospice support is also a major factor in these days of late referrals; family members may be exhausted with patient care when the patient is finally referred to hospice in the last month or weeks of life.

Social workers also have a role in helping patients maintain connections with supportive family members and friends, resolve conflicts, and seek and offer forgiveness. Support groups can be very helpful when informal supports are lacking (Glajchen 2011; Sutton and Liechty 2004). One issue in serious illness is the maintenance of intimacy between spouses or partners. Couples can grow closer during such an experience or can be driven apart because of their inability to meet each other's needs (Gallo-Silver 2011).

An elderly cancer patient was unable to engage in sexual intercourse, but was concerned about meeting his wife's sexual needs. He asked his social worker for advice on this matter; she was able to make suggestions about meeting his wife's sexual needs in alternative ways, for example by using a vibrator.

Another special issue is social support for partners of AIDS patients. Symptoms associated with AIDS have become more of a chronic than terminal disease, with advances in treatment, but in the end stages of disease patients may need hospice care. Partners of AIDS patients may have unique issues to address, including the residual social stigma as well as infection of the partner by the patient.

In a case in this author's experience, the caregiver never communicated to the social worker or any staff person whether he was the partner of the terminally ill AIDS patient he was caring for in his home. He was unwilling to discuss whether he might be infected himself. It was difficult for the social worker to provide support in a deeply meaningful way or to help with concerns when the clients preferred not to speak of sexual orientation. Fortunately, he was connected to an extremely supportive AIDS network, which provided emotional support and came out in great numbers for the patient's funeral. After the patient's death, he moved to another community. Kenneth Doka, in his book *Disenfranchised Grief* (2002), discusses the difficulty in bereavement when a relationship is not sanctioned by society (Gerbino and Raymer 2011).

Advocacy with the health care system may be necessary in work with gay and lesbian couples (Smolinski and Colon 2011). In a qualitative study with seven lesbian women who were former partners and caregivers of terminally ill patients (Reese and Melton 2003), participants said they would want their own end-of-life care decisions to be made by their partners. Most said the patient was not covered by the partner's health insurance.

Most thought they would have support from the lesbian community if they were ill, in the areas of household chores, help with bathing or dressing, loaning money, giving advice, and providing a place to stay for a few weeks. One participant did say the lesbian community was in denial of the patient's terminality, and no one came to see her. This caregiver was not familiar with hospice; her partner had received care from a hospital. If in the care of the hospice, one would hope that the social worker would have worked with their friends from the lesbian community, if wanted, to help them understand the prognosis and provide social support to the clients.

There were a number of good experiences with the health care system: support of the lesbian relationship by the doctor providing education for the staff and another doctor including the partner in all discussions. Others had a difficult experience with health care providers they characterized as homophobic: a doctor who refused to talk to the caregiver, even though she had a power of attorney, and staff that felt awkward when the partner stayed at the hospital with the patient. All the participants had told their doctors that they were in a lesbian partnership with patients, and one thought this revelation enhanced the quality of the health care because the staff knew the level of investment of the partner. All who had experienced hospice care thought that hospice staff lacks training in end-of-life care needs of lesbian women. They had experienced judgmental attitudes, and one participant quoted a hospice nurse as asking, "Is it just you two or is there a husband around?"

The participants made a number of recommendations for health care policy change that would better serve the needs and uphold the rights of lesbian partners. They felt that one partner's health insurance should cover the other, as it does in a marriage. They said that one partner should have the right to make end-of-life care decisions for the other. Some said they were denied the right to visit their partner in the hospital since they were not blood relatives or married. They said they should have the right to marriage and that lesbian partners should have the right to survivor benefits. One participant said that the terminal illness of her partner was a major crisis time, and it is isolating to be lesbian at this time. She said, "I would have killed myself if I did not have the support I did (from the lesbian community)."

DEATH ANXIETY, GRIEF, AND DEPRESSION

Family caregivers of dying cancer patients score higher on levels of anxiety and depression than the general population (Gough and Hudson 2009).

Clukey (2003) defines anticipatory mourning as a dynamic set of processes that involve emotional and cognitive transitions made in response to an expected loss. She identified five such processes: realization, caretaking, presence, fording meaning, and transitioning. Feelings that family members experienced during anticipatory mourning were sadness, anger, feeling overwhelmed, tired, trapped, guilty, frustrated, relieved, resolved, and feeling a sense of duty. She found that the attachment of the caregiver to the patient reflected the caregiver's personal development. Family caregivers experience isolation and financial vulnerability after sacrificing social activities and work duties and experience an increased mortality risk because of unrelieved emotional pain (Glajchen 2011). Springer (1999) found that major themes for caregivers were personal wishes and regrets, a change in perspective, being surprised by the illness, facing a difficult reality, transitioning out, and picking up the pieces. Caregiver coping strategies include support, social activities, roles outside the home, adaptive activities, spirituality, and avoidance (Glajchen 2011; Hooyman and Kramer 2006).

Disruption of family roles, the need to care for a family member who used to care for them, and financial hardship lead to feelings of frustration and anger, which may then lead to feelings of guilt and to attempts at repressing these feelings. Life plans and development of family members may have been disrupted by the patient's illness and should be explored by the social worker (Roberts, Baile, and Bassett 1999).

Unresolved grief may make it impossible for a family to let go of a patient. This has implications for a family's ability to make end-of-life decisions. Sanders (1989) said that "letting go represents the ultimate pain of grief." Foster and McLellan (2002) argue that it is not the loss of the person that is the most painful aspect, but the ability to come to a sense of meaning of the loss. Meaning is a spiritual issue; this means that spirituality has an impact on the resolution of grief.

Crisis intervention techniques may be helpful with families, especially since hospice social workers' contact with them may be limited to one or two sessions. Behavioral suggestions on ways of coping and a directive approach may be necessary, such as encouraging and giving family members permission to take a rest when they have been too long at the patient's bedside. Interventions that support communication skills, as well as skill training and providing information about the patient's condition may be very helpful. Research has documented emotional benefits for the caregiver with earlier referral to hospice (Glajchen 2011).

WORKING WITH FAMILIES IN END-OF-LIFE CARE
DECISION MAKING

In the U.S. the mainstream white cultural group's orientation is toward individual autonomy in making life choices, and the law is oriented in this same way. For example, the Patient Self-Determination Act gives the individual patient the right to make her own decisions about medical treatment. Family members are not formally included in this law. But for many or even most other cultural groups, the patient defers to elders of the family to make treatment decisions (Borgmeyer 2011), and this has, in reality, been found to be the case for most elderly individuals from the mainstream as well (Foster and McLellan 2002). Thus authors today recommend including the family in discussions about end-of-life care decisions for patients (Glajchen 2011). Inclusion of the family in the discussion is a challenge, though, for several reasons, and the help of a social worker can be very beneficial.

One challenge is that patients hesitate to talk openly and honestly to family members about the fact of their terminality. This is true for family members as well; they may be able to talk privately with the social worker about terminality but hesitate to mention it openly to the patient. Both sides are afraid of upsetting the other. In many cases, the patient or family members may be using denial as a way to cope with the situation. But in some cases the reality may be that an open discussion would help with coping, and that practical realities dictate decisions about end-of-life care preferences. Social workers in such a situation have to contend with ethics about confidentiality, disclosure and truth telling, value conflicts, and self-determination (Csikai 2004).

Conflicting priorities are a given when coming to a family consensus about end-of-life care decisions. Family members' first concern tends to be responsibility to care for the patient, which may mean a feeling of responsibility to prolong life. This author has seen complicated grieving in bereaved individuals that was based on a feeling of guilt for not calling 911 when a suffering, terminally ill loved one died. Family members may have difficulty coping with withholding of nutrition at the end of life, when food and hydration symbolize caring for the patient. If a patient is able to openly state a preference not to engage in life-sustaining measures, a family member is better able to allow the death to occur naturally. The situation becomes much more difficult when the patient is physically incompetent to make a decision and has no advance directives (Borgmeyer 2011; Csikai and Bass 2000).

Family members need emotional support in these and all matters and also need health care staff to be aware of their need for information and to demonstrate expertise in areas that will prepare them for the death and help them make end-of-life care decisions (Glajchen 2011). They need to know what to expect physically with the progression of the illness, what treatment options are realistically available, and the impact of these options on quality and length of life (Forbes, Bern-Klug, and Gessert 2000; Gerbino and Henderson 2004). One aspect of the patient's illness that should be assessed and addressed with caregivers is their beliefs and concerns about pain management (Parker Oliver et al. 2009).

Foster and McLellan (2002) point out that the social worker must help the family explore its personal ethical dilemmas connected to end-of-life care decisions within the perspective of the family system, since this will help to address the family's moral suffering—for example, questions about responsibility, guilt, and commitment. A family discussion allows exploration of ethical struggles at a collective level. Foster and McLellan stress that family dynamics such as scapegoating and triangulation have an impact on family decision making. Examples given are an adult child of a patient who is perceived as not helping enough with a patient's care may be blamed or scapegoated for the patient's worsening condition or an estranged spouse may claim the right to make end-of-life care decisions, but, because of unfulfilled family responsibilities, the family does not accept her in that role. Consideration of family dynamics can lead to a very different conclusion about the motivation behind end-of-life decisions—a primary caregiver who may normally be seen as being in denial for refusal to withdraw life support from his partner might actually be avoiding scapegoating and blame from family members for ending his partner's life. Social workers who address the moral dimension within the perspective of the family system can relate to their clients with less judgment and use of a label of denial. The family discussion can allow the family to reconcile end-of-life decisions with their family's moral perspective. Engaging in this family discussion creates the opportunity for family members to conduct some important end-of-life tasks. This author would identify these tasks as spiritual issues—including understand the meaning of their experiences, taking care of unfinished business, and reconnecting with family members.

For some family members, denial or avoidance of awareness of the terminal prognosis is a major coping mechanism (Parry 2001). When family members are in denial or hold different values than the patient or have unresolved grief that prevents them from letting go (Foster and McLellan 2002), it may become necessary for the social worker to advocate with the family to uphold patient wishes against their own for passive euthanasia. A study of primary caregivers in denial found that the caregivers were more likely to place patients in inpatient treatment, where the patients were likely to die, rather than at home as the patients had desired. This kind of action may feel necessary to loved ones grieving the terminality of the patient. But when it violates the clearly stated preferences of the patient, it may be time for the social worker to act as advocate. It will be necessary for the social worker to gently work with family members' denial and help them talk openly with the patient about preferences. Also it is often crucial to make sure that ambulance, emergency room, and hospital staff are knowledgeable about patient preferences. In some states health care professionals are legally and ethically bound to resuscitate a patient unless they have written confirmation of the patient's wish not to be resuscitated. The procedure under these circumstances is generally for the patient to carry a card detailing preferences. With no written directive, and when the patient is unable to express preferences at the time, the staff will look to immediate family members for a decision.

An opposite scenario may also occur. This author interviewed hospice patients who had a do not resuscitate order documented in their charts (Reese 1995) and asked whether they wanted to be resuscitated. A large number said yes! The reason for this was undocumented; patients may not have understood the original question when asked for their preference, or they may have just changed their minds over time. Patients tend to go in and out of denial as they can emotionally handle the pain of awareness of their terminal prognosis. But it may be that their original preference not to be resuscitated changed. In that case the social worker has a duty to advocate for this changed preference. It will be helpful to address the realities of the health care system's willingness to provide treatment when it is considered futile as well as the welfare of most patients who are resuscitated—many live their remaining time on life support rather than returning to a quality life.

Table 5.1 shows a list of issues addressed and interventions used by hospice social workers with families, based on unpublished data from the National Hospice Social Work Survey (Reese and Raymer 2004).

TABLE 5.1 Issues Addressed and Interventions Documented with
Families in National Hospice Social Work Survey

ASSESSMENT

ISSUES		ASSESSMENT TECHNIQUES
SOCIAL SUPPORT	Assessment of family's ability to care for patient at home	Review tensions
		Family members' risk of substance abuse
		Expressing love for patient through caregiving
	Assessment of needs	Evaluate how family is doing with transition from hospital to home
		Family dynamics/support system
		Needs of primary caregiver
		Risk assessment/referral for additional support for family members
	Family dynamics	Assess/explore family dynamics
END-OF-LIFE CARE DECISIONS	Physical environmen^t	Risk assessment of physical environment

Factors in model not reported as being assessed by social workers: Level of development, confrontation with mortality, cultural group, sense of control, spirituality, death anxiety, grief, depression, denial.

INTERVENTION

ISSUES		INTERVENTION TECHNIQUES
LEVEL OF DEVELOPMENT	Developmentally delayed family member	Ways to discuss death/funeral with developmentally delayed daughter
		Concern for developmentally delayed daughter's response to death
SENSE OF CONTROL	Support wish for control	Help family support patient's decision
		Support patient's/family's wish for control/limited hospice intervention

TABLE 5.1 Issues Addressed and Interventions Documented with Families in National Hospice Social Work Survey *(continued)*

SPIRITUALITY	Philosophy of life dimension	
	Meaning of life and suffering	Led caregiver/family in life review/positive value patient's life had for them
		Caregiver/family expressing feelings/thoughts/reminiscence to patient
		Explored family's anger
	Permission to die	Give patient permission to die
		Letting go/saying goodbye
	Belief system	Requested priest visit with family
		Validation of family's beliefs in a miracle
		Caregiver acknowledging death but praying for a miracle
SOCIAL SUPPORT	Self-care	Validating self-care for all
	Facilitating support for caregiver	Encouraging family support for caregiver after death of patient
		Exploring caregivers options after death
		Planning for future/caregiver needs
		Validated caregivers strategy for length of visitors' stay
		Caregiver needs at home for providing optimal patient care
		Caregiver/family emotional support
		Care-giver using family/friends for emotional support
		Encouraged caregiver to use support system
		Discussed with caregiver how to approach family for more support

	Staff providing support	Staff attend wake/funeral
		Supporting family through death and into bereavement
		Condolence call
		Time of death visits
		Assistance with phone calls at death
		Isolating patient so others won't see suffering
	Safety of patient	Contacted adult protective services
		Meeting to discuss issue of actively alcoholic son/daughter living with patient
	Family dynamics and communication	Education on communication
		Encourage assertiveness
		Patient verbally abusive to caregiver—provide education and support for alternatives
		Mediate between family members
		Discussion with spouse on family dynamics
		Support for positive aspects of family caregiving
		Family strengths identified
	Changing family roles	Allowing other family members to give care
		Discussion with patient to allow caregiver more decision making power
		Taught caregiver simple tasks to help her feel useful

TABLE 5.1 Issues Addressed and Interventions Documented with
Families in National Hospice Social Work Survey *(continued)*

DEATH ANXIETY	Caregiver fears	Caregiver afraid of being alone with patient
		Caregiver fear of patient dying at home
		Caregiver afraid of patient being alone at time of death
	Family fears	Forum for family to discuss fears, alleviate stress and anxiety
GRIEF	Education	Education on grief process
		Educate/validate significance of relationship between patient/ caregiver
	Ventilation for family	Family pain related to patients dying
		Forum for family to discuss earlier losses
DEPRESSION	Patient's depression	Helping family members deal with patient's depression
		Discussing risk of suicide
DENIAL	Education	Education to caregiver on death process
		Education on diagnosis
	Patient's need for openness	Work with patient & family regarding patient's need for openness about illness
		Facilitated discussion between patient/caregiver to share thoughts on prognosis
GENERAL COPING WITH EMOTIONAL DISTRESS	Substance abuse	Referred caregiver to chemical dependency counselor
	Education	Education of impact of stress on health
		Education on compartmental izing tasks

TABLE 5.1 Issues Addressed and Interventions Documented with Families in National Hospice Social Work Survey *(continued)*

	Advocating self-care	Self-care for caregiver/family
	Ventilation of feelings	Encouraged caregiver/family to express feelings
END-OF-LIFE CARE DECISIONS giving	Medical information	Education on need for care-
		Education on future care needs of patient
		Discussion with family of signs of impending death
		Caregiver education/ information on dealing with patient's confusion
		Education on in-home help/ resources
		Education regarding neglect
	Supporting decision-making	Facilitate family communication/discussion/ decision making
		Forum for family to discuss process of dying
		Validate family's concern regarding ability to care for patient
	Supporting planning	Assisted caregiver in devising a plan for family to be present twenty-four hours a day
		Family task of keeping vigil

Issues in model not reported as being addressed through social work intervention: cultural group.

Analysis of unpublished data, National Hospice Social Work Survey (Reese and Raymer 2004).

WORK WITH TERMINALLY ILL CHILDREN AND
THEIR FAMILIES

Psychosocial assessment in the case of a terminally ill child includes assessing the micro level as well as mezzo and macro level aspects. This would include all individual family members, the family as a unit, organizations and groups in the community the family is part of, including cultural and faith groups, and the larger community. Assessment would take a holistic approach as always in hospice, including the biopsychosocial and spiritual as well as history of the family (Orloff 2011).

A study about children's bereavement found that they experienced the same spiritual issues as adults except for an absence of concern about their relationship with God (Reese and Rosaasen 1999). They also reported many transpersonal experiences, consistent with Morse's description of children's near-death experiences in his book *Closer to the Light* (1991).

Social work intervention with child patients includes art and play therapy, through which children can express feelings and concerns as a way to cope. Other interventions are using children's literature on death and dying and support to grieving siblings, teachers, and classmates. Relationships between the child and family with health care providers are vital in coping with a child's death, and social workers are skilled in this aspect. Parents have a strong need for honest information from health care providers (Orloff 2011).

It is helpful to children's comfort and well-being for parents to nurture their natural instincts to play. Planning a fun experience for a child, such as buying a pet or taking a trip, provides a treasured family memory. Continuing normal activities and association with friends has been found to be important to children at the end of life (Jones 2006). If the child is physically unable to travel, simple experiences such as bringing snow, flowers, or butterflies indoors may help the family experience the joy of the moment (Cincotta 2004). Cincotta (2004) also reminds us that children continue to develop as long as they live and can learn and be exposed to new experiences as part of that development. A support group for terminally ill children can also be a great comfort for children, who naturally relate to their peers (Cincotta 2004).

The loss of one's child is one of the most painful events a human being can experience, and parents may experience post-traumatic stress disorder after the loss (Orloff 2011). The inability to protect one's child from dying is the ultimate failure for a parent and invokes an extreme feeling of vulnerability. Not surprisingly, a parent's sense of control over treatment decisions may be very important to her during the illness (Goldring and Solomon 2011) and predicts better coping during bereavement. A parent's knowledge that he attempted all possible treatment options may make him feel he better fulfilled his responsibilities as a parent. Signing a do not resuscitate order on behalf of one's child may be much more challenging than signing one for oneself. In this situation it is important for the social worker to "meet the client where he or she is" (Orloff 2011).

It may be very difficult for the parents, in the midst of their anticipatory grief, to provide the support the child needs. They may begin the process of emotionally separating from the child before the death occurs. Also, in an effort to protect the child, the parents may avoid discussing the prognosis, resulting in an "atmosphere of constricted communication" (Cincotta 2004:319). In reality, often children know what is happening to them and are able to discuss it openly and benefit from honest communication (Cincotta 2004; Jones 2006). Sometimes, though, the child may try to protect the parent by avoiding the subject and may speak more freely with the social worker. An important point made by Cincotta (2004) is that a child will model the parents' attitude about dying. If the parents can express acceptance of death as a natural process, approaching it openly, the child will be able to as well.

Alternatively, the child may speak symbolically—through art, a dream, play with toys. Artwork, photograph albums, and journals may be helpful to the child in expressing what is happening to them as well as a treasured gift for the parents. This process can help children with life review, which can provide comfort, as it does with adults. These mediums can be used as play therapy with the children as well (Cincotta 2004; Goldring and Solomon 2011). Cincotta suggests that life review can become "life preview" for a child, talking about "what would have been" if their life had been lived longer (2004:333).

Kempson (2000/2001) documents the effectiveness of touch therapy for grieving mothers. Also, Cincotta (2004) notes that while some parents' grieving interferes with their ability to care for the child, parents may have an overwhelming desire to focus on the child's needs—and this action may help them cope. It is helpful to validate their adequacy as parents and encourage them to continue their childcare activities. Over time, they develop expertise about handling the illness and health care resources, which increases their sense of adequacy. It is also useful to allow the parents to ventilate their strong emotions of love, anger, remorse, attachment, separation, grief, and fear. It may also be helpful to validate a parent's hope of communication with one's child after death (Cincotta 2004).

Social workers can encourage parents to accept help with their other responsibilities to enable them to spend more time with their child. It is important to try to adhere to routines the family normally observes. It may be important to make sure that all family members have access to the patient, even if the treatment is not local. A child's level of pain may also be underestimated and should be closely monitored (Cincotta 2004).

Dying children's siblings are vulnerable and need special support as well. Siblings may have feelings of guilt that they were not the one that became ill or guilt over past conflicts with the dying child. They may also feel neglected by the parents during the illness, which then may lead to further feelings of guilt. Cincotta points out (2004) that siblings may be forced to be more independent as a result of this experience, which can remain a strength for them in later life. Sibling bereavement groups may be very helpful in sorting out all these feelings.

Cincotta (2004) notes the positives that can come through such a painful experience, as in all experiences of terminal illness. Spiritual and emotional development can occur for both the parent and child, and "living with dying often engenders emotions that have not been experienced before and allows for emotional intimacy unparalleled at other stages in life" (Cincotta 2004:322).

Pediatric cases are especially difficult for hospice staff, who may need support from the social worker. Expression of feelings of grief and finding a sense of meaning for the child's death have been found to be helpful. Feeling valued by other staff is important, and training and staff support groups may be helpful (McCoyd and Walter 2007).

This section has reviewed hospice social work intervention with families on the mezzo level. We must remember to define the concept of familiness as one that includes nonblood relatives, extended family members, gay or lesbian partners, and unrelated loved ones who are considered family by the patient. The next section will discuss group intervention in hospice social work.

GROUP INTERVENTION IN HOSPICE SOCIAL WORK

Social workers have specific training in group intervention and are the appropriate team members to develop and lead groups for clients and staff. The following presents ideas for psychoeducational or therapy groups for families, patients, and hospice staff members.

PSYCHOEDUCATIONAL GROUPS FOR FAMILIES

Although it may be difficult to cajole a family member, especially a primary caregiver, into leaving the patient's side, self-care is important for loved ones experiencing anticipatory grief. A volunteer may be helpful in sitting with the patient while the family member attends a group. A brief intervention format is practical in this situation and has been found to be effective with family caregivers of patients with psychosis (So et al. 2006). Knowledge, coping, and the caregiving burden can be addressed in a psychoeducational format (Glajchen 2011).

Such groups provide social support to caregivers and reduce isolation. Being with others going through a similar experience helps to normalize feelings. The group can be assembled in person, but can also take shape by telephone or through the Internet. Coping can be enhanced for caregivers and family members with access to this type of support (Sutton and Liechty 2004).

PATIENT SUPPORT GROUPS

Little literature was found on support groups for terminally ill patients. Breitbart and colleagues (2010) tested a meaning-centered therapy group for terminally ill cancer patients and found significant benefits in spiritual well-being, sense of meaning, anxiety, and desire for death. It may be difficult to bring hospice patients together in a group because of physical symptoms. This author personally knows of a successful online group in which laptops were provided to patients so that they could communicate with each other from their beds. Research testing the effectiveness of online groups for terminally ill patients, however, was not found.

Benefits of online groups to patients with chronic illness have been well-documented and will be discussed here. Such a group can be a self-help group without a moderator, but a social worker can act as the group leader to provide desired interventions. Moderating the group is important at times in keeping the group active, but has been found to be very time consuming (van Ulden-Kraan et al. 2008).

Rada (2007) has found that the more restrictive the group is in terms of allowing membership only of people in similar situations, the more openly members express themselves within the group. This expression is beneficial — when patients are able to verbalize their anticipatory grief process, including anger and emotional pain, they experience reduced physical suffering, depression, and other aspects of complicated grief (Zerbe and Steinberg 2000).

Research on benefits of online groups has found that group participants felt better informed, more accepting of their disease, more confident and experienced enhanced self-esteem, increased optimism, and a sense of control (van Ulden-Kraan et al. 2008). They benefited from the opportunity to exchange stories and felt understood by other patients (Hess, Weinland, and Beebe 2010). This was the case regardless of whether they actively participated in the group or mainly read posts by other members (van Ulden-Kraan et al. 2008). A different view has been expressed by Barker (2008), though, who discusses the problem of patients developing their own medical perspectives in contradiction to widely accepted professional knowledge and supporting each other in finding physicians with perspectives consistent with their own.

STAFF SUPPORT GROUPS

Stress, burnout, compassion fatigue, secondary trauma, and utter emotional exhaustion that can become a problem for staff working in the difficult area of end-of-life care. Staff members must face their own mortality and also must experience grief along with the patient's loved ones. Signs of this can include preoccupation with a patient, restless sleep, anxiety, and sadness. Loss of a client may trigger grief over past personal losses. Staff members may find themselves crying along with their clients; or it's possible that they may cope with feelings through having less client interaction than usual when a case particularly affects them. Irritation and frustration may serve as a way to defend themselves against responses of vulnerability and sadness. Working through this grief process requires an opportunity to process and mourn the loss (Renzenbrink 2004).

And in addition to the inherently grief-provoking nature of accompanying patients and families through the dying process, patients and family members may become difficult to work with. One of Kubler-Ross's (1970) classic stages of grief is anger; and it may be hard to identify exactly who to blame and upon whom to focus one's anger. The first question may be "Why would God do this to me?" but often it seems that the anger is projected onto healthcare staff (Zerbe and Steinberg 2000).

Staff may cope by talking informally among themselves about serving difficult patients, venting their emotional responses. However, this type of peer support may reinforce a negative perspective about clients, or offer emotional support and praise to a staff person whose handling of a case is questionable, without gaining an understanding of reasons for the client's behavior and new ways of handling a difficult case (Pullen 2002). Supervision of social workers by a social worker has been found to be important for hospice outcomes (Reese and Raymer 2004); it's likely that guidance on handling such cases is one reason why. But another important way to handle staff emotional needs in handling this difficult work is through a staff support group.

Members of such a group feel reduced stress through the support of their peers as well as the support of the administration in providing such a group (Nally 2006). Social workers are the appropriate staff to lead such a group because of their specific training in this area.

Negative affectivity is a significant factor in job satisfaction among hospice staff. Administrative support, in fact, has been found to be a significant factor in job satisfaction among hospice staff (Renzenbrink 2004). Support groups should also educate participants about compassion fatigue (Nally 2006). Facing their own mortality and resolving grief over the loss of patients may bring up spiritual needs that should be addressed. Members should be able to express their feelings and mourn their loss. The feelings may include regret, anger, and often grief includes feelings of guilt about things that one may have done better. Participants should be reminded that these feelings are normal. Recommendations for self care and ways to cope with grief should be made, including the benefits of exercise, diet, rest, social support, and recreation (Renzenbrink 2004). Memorial services, often held by hospices once a year, are an important way to recognize, allow, and cope with the grieving process that staff members experience, and staff should be encouraged to attend.

Despite the emotional challenge of work with hospice clients, the benefits received are greater than anything given. Research documents the spiritual growth of hospice staff along with patients and loved ones (Seccareccia and Brown 2009). This author's view is that I have learned more from my patients than I ever taught them. The experience of being a hospice social worker was one of awe and wonder and a definite time of personal growth.

Table 5.2 presents issues and interventions with hospice staff, found to be addressed by hospice social workers (unpublished data, Reese and Raymer 1994).

This section has reviewed hospice social work intervention with groups. Groups can be helpful for patients, their loved ones, and staff members as well. The social worker is the team member to intervene on the mezzo level, because of specific training in a systems perspective. This systems perspective also prepares them for work within the interdisciplinary team, which will be discussed in the next section.

TABLE 5.2 Issues Addressed and Interventions Documented with
Staff in National Hospice Social Work Survey

ASSESSMENT	
Assess staff grief needs	Evaluate need for bereavement services for staff

INTERVENTION	
Support for staff grief	Emotional support
	Education, normalization, and validation of staff grief process
	Encourage verbalization
	Provide individual counseling for staff

Analysis of unpublished data, National Hospice Social Work Survey (Reese and Raymer 2004).

WORKING WITH INTERDISCIPLINARY TEAMS

Social workers have a crucial role on the interdisciplinary team in hospice. In a national survey of hospices Reese and Raymer (2004) found that higher levels of social work services predicted better team functioning.[1] Furthermore, team functioning is very important to hospice outcomes—the same survey found that higher levels of team functioning predicted fewer average hospitalizations per patient, lower home health costs, lower nursing costs, lower labor costs, and lower overall hospice costs. This section discusses the history of interdisciplinary teams in hospice, difficulties that can arise on the team and solutions to address them, characteristics of high-functioning teams, the contribution of social workers to high-functioning teams, and the role of the social worker on the team.

LACK OF FULL UTILIZATION OF SOCIAL WORKERS ON THE INTERDISCIPLINARY TEAM

The founder of hospice in England, Dame Cicely Saunders, was trained as a social worker, nurse, and physician. Because of this background, she

---

1. The author would like to acknowledge the work of coauthors Stephen Connor, Kathy Egan, Donna Kwilosz, Dale Larson, and Mary-Ann Sontag. The work of these authors contributed greatly to the development of this section.

was able to understand the contributions of each of these professions, along with spiritual care, developing the concept of holistic care provided by an interdisciplinary team.

Development of hospice in the United States was based on the English interdisciplinary model, but it was led by physicians and nurses. Elisabeth Kubler-Ross, the foremost advocate for hospice in the U.S., was a physician; and the first U.S. hospice was established in Connecticut by a team from Yale University consisting of a nurse, two pediatricians, and a chaplain. The U.S. hospice movement has always espoused the holistic hospice philosophy developed by Dame Saunders, but psychosocial care was provided by the medical staff until the Medicare requirement for social work services in 1983. A comment made to the author by a longtime hospice nurse, "I was doing social work before there was social work," highlights the early resistance to the inclusion of social workers on the hospice team, a resistance that continues today on many teams despite decades of interdisciplinary experience.

Since 1983 all Medicare-certified hospices include social work services, but the social work role is somewhat limited. Medicare requires that a social worker be present on the team and conduct a timely psychosocial assessment for each patient. Social workers are not required to participate in the intake interview, however, and social work services are not required after the initial assessment. Social workers in hospices must either hold a BSW or MSW from an accredited social work program or a bachelor's in a related field, which limits the social work role to referrals and basic interviewing techniques. Nurses (Ben-Sira and Szyf 1992) and physicians (Abramson and Mizrahi 1996) have tended to view the social work role as provision of concrete services, and attempts to add social work interventions outside this view may result in conflict (Dawes and Dawes 2004). Social workers are normally supervised by nurses, who most often are the administrators of the hospice. This also contributes to a lack of understanding of the social work role and limits the effectiveness of social workers on the team (Raymer and Reese 2004; Reese and Raymer 2004).

This lack of understanding about the social work role in hospice exists both on the part of the other disciplines on the team and on the part of some social workers, who often report a lack of training in issues of death and dying. In a survey by Reese (2011), even hospice administrators who were social workers did not consider all the roles listed to be social work roles. A survey by Kadushin and Egan (1997) found that only 51 percent of health courses in their sample addressed the social worker's role, and a number of other authors have also found that social workers did not have adequate professional knowledge and training (Clark 2004; Kovacs and Bronstein 1999).

COMPETITION BETWEEN PROFESSIONS ON THE TEAM

The demand by health care administrators, health insurance companies, and the Medicare program to reduce health care costs has resulted in competition between health care providers. A profession that can present itself as the most competent in providing a service may survive budget cuts. Nursing has been most successful in this effort, with a more developed body of outcomes research. The response of administrators has been to add more and more responsibilities to the nursing job description, which has resulted in a shift of traditional social work duties to nurses (Reese and Sontag 2001).

In 1987 Kulys and Davis found that hospice directors, as well as nurses, believed that nurses were at least as qualified to perform traditional social work duties as social workers. They found that nurses provided all but two items on a list of social work functions and concluded that social workers did not have a unique role in hospice. This has changed quite a bit since then, with social workers' progress in documenting outcomes and their efforts to improve practice in the hospice field, but some duties social workers consider their own are still assigned to nurses. For example, in a national study of hospice directors, Reese (2011) found that nurses provided more

civil and legal assistance
on-call responsibilities
counseling patient/family about safety issues
supervising hospice workers
serving as hospice director
discharge planning
upholding preferences about environment
advocacy

These are generally roles that social workers believe should be ascribed at least equally to them. This has resulted in frustration on the part of social workers because of a perceived takeover of the social work role by nurses, and it has backfired, since overburdened nurses have experienced burnout and left the field. Nurses have felt particularly overwhelmed by the traditional social work responsibility for patients' psychosocial care, for which they have little training. This has resulted in a nursing shortage nationally (Reese and Sontag 2001).

At the same time, social workers have been encroaching on the traditional domain of spiritual caregivers in addressing spiritual issues with patients. The increasing emphasis on spirituality in social work (Canda and Furman 2010) brings health care social workers into what many consider the domain of chaplains. Just as social workers may compete with nurses for provision of psychosocial services, chaplains may view social workers as encroaching on their professional turf (Soltura and Piotrowski 2011). Moreover, chaplains provide psychosocial care, which may be viewed by social workers as better left to social work (Furman and Bushfield 2000; Reith and Payne 2009).

The reality of the social work role may be quite different from these perceptions held by the other disciplines on the team. A chart review in one hospice of the most recent home visits from nursing, social work, and clergy to thirty-seven home hospice patients indicated that although spiritual caregivers addressed more spiritual issues than the other two professions, social workers addressed spirituality more frequently than nurses. In addition, social workers addressed more psychosocial issues than the other two professions (Reese and Brown 1997). The National Hospice Social Work Survey (Reese and Raymer 2004) found that better team functioning was predicted by the social worker holding an MSW rather than a BSW degree, with no additional duties outside the social work responsibilities and a higher social worker to patient ratio. Better team functioning was quite important in hospice outcomes, predicting fewer hospitalizations of patients and lower home health aide, nursing, labor, and overall costs for the hospice. Poor team communication, on the other hand, has been linked to poor symptom control and more aggressive treatment than desired by the patient (Childress 2001).

BARRIERS THAT PREVENT TEAMS FROM FUNCTIONING AT THE HIGHEST LEVEL

LACK OF KNOWLEDGE OF THE EXPERTISE OF OTHER PROFESSIONS   Health care professionals are usually trained in isolation from each other (Reese and Sontag 2001), resulting in a lack of knowledge of the other disciplines' expertise, skills, training, values, and theory base. As discussed in the previous section, other disciplines on the team have a lack of understanding of the social work role (Reith and Payne 2009). At the same time, social workers have a lack of understanding of the role, training, and expertise of the other disciplines (Kovacs and Bronstein 1999), and cultural differences between professions may be interpreted by social workers as personal deficits on the part of other team members (Soltura and Piotrowski 2011).

This situation can lead to resistance to the inclusion of all team members on cases. Each profession may want to handle the case on its own, without fully involving the other members, based on a lack of understanding of what the other professions can contribute. Team members who distrust the other disciplines or who are defending their own turf may hesitate to share professional knowledge with the rest of the team. This further alienates team members, results in lower-quality services to clients, and undermines the holistic approach of hospice (Reese and Sontag 2001). An example of this is a team meeting in which a nurse reports that a patient got upset when the social worker initiated discussion of family conflicts. Team members may blame it on the social worker's lack of expertise, rather than a process to be expected to occur during psychosocial intervention. They may avoid future social work involvement for this reason. Unfortunately, successful team functioning requires recognition of colleagues' expertise (Soltura and Piotrowski 2011).

Proposed Solutions Interdisciplinary education is needed that allows each discipline to become aware of the expertise of the others (Corless and Nicholas 2004; Parry 2001). In the absence of such preparation, team leaders should establish clear team norms that include respecting the knowledge of the other professions and sharing professional knowledge with team members. Orientation to the role of each profession should be included in the training of new staff members and continuing education programs. Joint home visits help team members understand what each profession contributes, and it is instructive for a social worker to spend a day with a physician (Kovacs and Bronstein 1999). Sontag (1995a) has created a role clarification exercise in which disciplines take turns sharing their expertise and training with the rest of the team. Social workers should take an active part in educating the team on the social work role, and social work supervisors should communicate this expectation (Reese and Sontag 2001).

ROLE BLURRING Egan (1998) has developed a patient-family value-based end-of-life care model.that emphasizes shared roles between team members.

This is an ideal model in which team members give up defending their turf and address all issues — biopsychosocial and spiritual — in a common commitment to the well-being of their clients. The drawback to this model is that, until the time that all disciplines are fully accepted on the team, it can be used as an excuse for nurses to provide most of the care. In a field in which hospices employ three times the number of nurses as social workers, and an even greater difference in the ratio of nurses to spiritual caregivers (who are often employed part-time and may serve as volunteers rather than paid staff members), teams are not able to use this model in any other way.

Until the time equal services are provided by all team members, the overlap of roles on the interdisciplinary team will remain a barrier to full utilization of disciplines. Role blurring may lead to competition between professions and decreased quality of services (Raymer and Reese 2004). A hospice chaplain related an example of this to the author, a case in which he spent an hour counseling a patient about her feelings of guilt. He learned later that the social worker had left a few minutes earlier, and she had also spent an hour counseling the patient over guilt feelings. The chaplain and the social worker were using conflicting approaches, however, with the patient left exhausted and confused. One reason for role blurring is a lack of appreciation for the limits of one's own knowledge (Reese and Sontag 2001).

Proposed Solutions Administrative procedures should be developed by the team calling for automatic referrals to specific team members in certain case situations (Reese and Sontag 2001). A screening instrument can be developed as part of an assessment form indicating when the case is appropriate for a referral to a certain team member. For example, research has demonstrated that social worker/physician teams are effective in increasing the establishment of advance directives (Schonwetter, Walker, and Robinson 1995); thus a need for discussion of these issues should result in an automatic referral to the social worker. Other research (Reese and Brown 1997) has indicated that social workers are more likely than other professions to work on issues of death anxiety and social support with patients. Thus, although all team members may respond briefly to any issue that arises, they should subsequently ask for a social work referral on these topics. Finally, a treatment plan should be developed during the team meeting that clearly assigns tasks to each team member, utilizing each one's unique strengths (Reese and Sontag 2001).

CONFLICTS ARISING FROM DIFFERENCES BETWEEN PROFESSIONS IN VALUES
Every discipline on the team is trained in a starkly contrasting professional culture that promotes differing values and theoretical perspectives (Soltura and Piotrowski 2011). Members are usually unaware of these cultural differences; each member may see the difference, rather, in terms of a character flaw or cognitive limitation in the other member. This perspective can lead to open conflict on the team or, in contrast, a defensive "smoothing over" or avoidance of conflict when there are low levels of trust between members (Reese and Sontag 2001).

Social work values contrast with the traditional values of the medical profession, which advocate saving life rather than quality of life and physician setting of treatment goals rather than patient autonomy in setting treatment goals. The relationship between physician and patient is traditionally authoritarian, in contrast with the social work value of patient self-determination; thus the well-known phrase "doctor's orders." Physicians may value action and outcomes and have a lack of training regarding the professional-client relationship, while social workers place more importance on relationships. Social workers may be more oriented toward teamwork, and physicians toward automony (Reese and Sontag 2001; Soltura and Piotrowski 2011). A comparison of medical and social work students (Reese et al. 2005) found a number of significant differences in cultural and religious beliefs. Social workers were more likely to identify themselves as "spiritual but not religious" but, at the same time, were more likely to adhere to a number of traditional cultural and religious beliefs (surprisingly, this included traditional Chinese, Israeli, and U.S. beliefs).

In practice as a hospice social worker, the author has observed some nurses and chaplains to be oriented toward an authoritarian stance. Despite the hospice value of patient self-determination, other team members may freely advise the client on a course of action.

Also team members may have different orientations toward confidentiality. For example, spiritual caregivers may have different values regarding confidentiality. A time-honored tradition of confession to the clergy has established a value of keeping some information confidential even from other team members. In other cases, some chaplains may find it appropriate to reveal information that appears confidential to the social worker outside the team. In contrast, a social worker will feel a responsibility to reveal all case information to the team, but not to parties outside the team. The exception is in cases of child abuse or neglect—social workers are mandated reporters and trained to report suspected child maltreatment to protective services. This may also be the case with elder abuse. Chaplains, on the other hand, may not be mandated reporters because of the tradition of confession confidentiality and may keep child maltreatment incidents confidential from authorities unless they become extreme.

Again, according to practice experience, values about maintaining professional boundaries may vary between nurses and social workers, with nurses less concerned than social workers about developing personal relationships with clients. Social workers may be more trained and oriented toward work with disadvantaged populations and with clients from diverse cultural backgrounds. In contrast, other professions may have a lack of training in cultural competence and experience difficulty in relating to diverse clients (Reese and Sontag 2001).

Proposed Solutions Despite many differences between disciplines on the team, it is helpful to focus on areas of convergence. All professions are dedicated to the welfare of the patient (Corless and Nicholas 2004), and all adhere to the hospice philosophy. Nardi and colleagues found common underlying views shared by clergy and social workers including honest communication, death as natural, active counseling, and right to information (Nardi et al. 2001). These are higher values that transcend the differences between team members. A high-functioning team is able to focus on these values rather than personal agendas or turf battles. Moreover, all hospice professionals adhere to the hospice philosophy. This is a higher set of values that will usually supersede value differences between professions. Early in the development of a team, it is helpful to schedule time to discuss team values and shared meanings. As the group progresses through its development, it is natural to expect mistakes and conflicts and helpful to examine and discuss them (Reese and Sontag 2001).

When perspectives differ, views should be openly shared in an atmosphere of mutual respect, recognizing each profession's successes and strengths—i.e., nurses' dedication to patients and chaplain's respect for patient confidentiality. If members are able to trust each other, they will be more willing to share openly. The social work supervisor should promote understanding of the values of the other professions and orient the social worker toward commitment not only to the social work department, but to the organization as a whole and its transcendent goals, which take priority over individual professions' perspectives. Finally, Abramson (1984) suggests that teams should spend time clarifying individual and team values and learn a common moral language, establishing shared meanings of ethical concepts.

THEORETICAL DIFFERENCES AMONG MEMBERS OF THE TEAM Social work education focuses on evidence-based practice, in which psychosocial interventions are based on treatment models drawn from theory, which whenever possible have been tested for effectiveness. The social work theoretical perspective is also oriented toward systems theory where the source of the problem, and thus the solution, is not located solely within the client. Rather, interactions of the larger social system with the client are considered when assessing the problem and planning interventions. In addition, an important focus of social work training is the relationship with the client.

These theoretical perspectives may stand in contrast with the orientations of other members of the team (Corless and Nicholas 2004). Nurses, physicians, and chaplains may not use psychosocial theory as a basis for interventions. In fact, according to the author's practice experience, some nurses and chaplains may speak out in opposition to the use of theory. Some nurses may feel that theory-based assessment amounts to "pigeonholing" clients into theories. They may also object to a deficit approach that finds pathology in what they may view as a normal grief process. Spiritual caregivers may hold a perspective incompatible with the social work problem-solving approach. For example, the author has heard a chaplain advocate for "standing in the mystery" rather than encouraging the client to find an answer to the typical question, "Why is God doing this to me?" The other professions may be oriented more toward a medical model than the systems approach that is more natural to social work and may be more likely to locate the cause and solution of the problem within the individual. Relationships with clients may develop more genuinely and not be a focus of deliberate intervention. Finally, physicians may be more oriented toward physical care than psychosocial issues (Reese and Sontag 2001).

Proposed Solutions Social workers can benefit from considering all these perspectives, which have some merit and can temper our own views. Team members should become aware of and acknowledge sources of conflict. Respectful discussion of differing perspectives, as in any exposure to diversity, may result in growth and development and a richer understanding of issues.

Differences should be accepted without judgment, and social work skills should be drawn upon to help the team develop ways to relate competently across the differing cultures of the professions. Professions may quickly come to value the strength of the others in certain areas; for example, nurses may welcome handing over the burden of psychosocial care and community outreach to social workers (Reese and Sontag 2001).

NEGATIVE TEAM NORMS Part of the development of any group is the establishment of norms that guide members' behavior. As in any group, an interdisciplinary team may develop negative group norms that work against provision of quality care. The following discussion outlines some of these negative group norms.

Lack of Commitment to the Team Process Team members can easily be distracted by personal agendas that undermine the success of the team in caring for its clients. For example, one may promote one's own profession and attempt to exclude others, as illustrated by the following comments the author has heard in team meetings: "They don't want a social worker." "I don't think they could handle discussing psychosocial issues." "She's not religious—she wouldn't want a chaplain visit." Some team members may exhibit a lack of genuine personal interest in each other, without concern for the effect on the cohesion of the team.

Lack of Willingness to Share Equally in the Work of the Team While in practice as a hospice social worker, the author sometimes observed a lack of assertiveness on the part of social workers with regard to being routinely included in all cases or in on-call duties. Perhaps social workers gradually accept their ancillary role in hospice (nice but not necessary) rather than asserting what they can contribute. Or perhaps the large social work caseloads discourage them from taking on additional work (Reese and Raymer 2004). This lack of assertiveness may be understandable, but allows the ancillary role to continue unchallenged. In these days of downsizing due to cost-saving efforts, the perception of social work as ancillary can work to the detriment of the profession.

Effective interdisciplinary work incorporates the goals and opinions of all professions in the treatment plan, and each profession shares responsibility for carrying out the treatment. Full participation of all members is necessary to realize the original hospice perspective of holistic care.

Proposed Solutions One method for teaching positive group norms is the rules exercise developed by Sontag (1995a). In this exercise, each member writes down proposed rules for the team. The team leader creates a list of all the rules; the team then goes through the list and arrives at a consensus. When conflict occurs, the team leader should discuss behavioral expectations according to the established team rules.

Another solution is for the leader to guide the team in establishing a plan of action in which all members of the team share responsibility (Sands, Stafford, and McClelland 1990). In such a plan, clear assignments are made and accepted utilizing the abilities of each member fully. The leader reminds the team of the holistic hospice philosophy and the importance of including all members in the treatment plan. It is important in this approach for the team leader to consistently recognize success. When failure occurs, it is important to respond by revising the plan of action rather than blaming an individual member (Health Resources and Services Administration 1993).

In the author's practice experience, another important strategy is for each team member to participate fully in discussions. The social worker should advocate for psychosocial issues that need to be addressed and explain specifically how social work services can assist the client. The social worker is more likely to be active on the team if he is supervised by a fellow social worker (Reese and Raymer 2004). Another helpful approach is to create small teams that feature one member of each profession, so as to allow more opportunity of involvement for each one.

DYSFUNCTIONAL TEAM DYNAMICS

Scapegoating Team members may demonstrate a lack of responsibility for their own actions and decisions made by the group and blame it on the individual professional who carried out the treatment plan (Health Resources and Services Administration 1993).

Dysfunctional Communication An example of dysfunctional communication includes the development of subsystems that compete with each other within the team. Also individual members can develop conflict with others on the team. Team members or leaders can seek to dominate the others or a member can become isolated. Or one member can enter into conflict with the rest of the team.

Another type of dysfunctional communication is an implicit pattern in which group members avoid conflict through agreement. Dissenting members are ignored.

Power Differentials on the Team The culture of the health care system is largely hierarchical, with physicians directing the care and focusing mainly on the biological aspects of care (Connor et al. 2002). Differences in status between professions may be a source of conflict, and higher-status professions' perspectives may sway the treatment plan (Corless and Nicholas 2004). Salaries may be inconsistent with levels of education—in hospice, nurses are paid more than social workers with the same level of education. Members of a certain profession may far outnumber members of other professions; for example, hospices hire three times as many nurses as social workers (Reese and Raymer 2004).

Leadership may always fall under certain professions. For instance, Medicare mandates that physicians direct the hospice team. Physicians may oppose the full utilization of other professionals on the team, however. Both nursing and social work have been fighting for independent status from medicine and have found themselves in competition with each other for leadership, providing the same services (Corless and Nicholas 2004).

So far, nurses are winning, with 67 percent of respondents in a recent survey of hospice directors identifying themselves as nurses, as opposed to 12 percent identifying themselves as social workers (Reese 2011). Directors in this study believed that nurses were most qualified to supervise staff. This domination of the field by nurses may be a source of conflict. Equal status, authority, and autonomy may be lacking for social workers, despite the argument that they are necessary for the provision of competent services to clients (Reese and Sontag 2001).

Proposed Solutions Upon occasion, it is important for the team to examine how it is performing in order to address dysfunctional team dynamics (Parker Oliver and Peck 2006). Sontag (1995a) has developed two exercises to accomplish this task. In the observer exercise one person is appointed as observer for one team meeting. The observer records observations regarding interaction and content of the discussion. The observer then provides feedback to the team, and the team discusses it. In the assessments exercise anonymous questionnaires are filled out by team members about the process and content of the team meetings. Feedback is then given to the team for discussion.

A strategy for addressing power differentials on the team is to establish equality between team members through a collaborative or consensus model of team functioning, emphasizing egalitarianism, cohesion, and group problem solving. Power struggles should be avoided, leadership of the team should be rotated between all disciplines (Kovacs and Bronstein 1999), and social work administrators should lobby for support from hospital administrators in resolving inequities in salary and numbers of professionals on the team. Social workers and nurses, rather than seeing each other as competitors, should become allies in working to establish equality with physicians. As the balance of power in the health care system shifts from physicians to management, this may become more realistic (Corless and Nicholas 2004).

One strategy is for social work administrators to devise programs to address specific problems important to the hospital management. Addressing goals of the institution as a whole will lead to support and an expanded role for social work. An example of such a strategy is the National Hospice Social Work Survey, conducted by the Social Work Section of the National Hospice Organization (Reese and Raymer 2004). This study had the goal of illustrating the importance of social work to hospice administrators by addressing the administration's own agenda. Toward that end, the study demonstrated a beneficial effect of social work services on hospice costs and other important outcomes.

Until we can achieve equality of status, a fully holistic approach to patient care is impossible, reducing the quality of service to clients (Corless and Nicholas 2004; Reese and Raymer 2004). Some realities of differences in status will remain for the time being, however, because of the view of social work as an ancillary profession in health care (Corless and Nicholas 2004). Thus social workers should possess a variety of collaborative approaches that address these differences in status when necessary, but also focus more on sharing responsibility when other team members are interacting in an egalitarian manner (Soltura and Piotrowski 2011).

STEREOTYPING BY CLIENTS In the author's practice experience, failure to fully utilize all members of the team sometimes stems from the unwillingness of clients to agree to sessions with certain team members—often social work or the chaplain. This may be based on stereotypes or misperceptions held by clients about these professions. For example, clients may think social workers only visit to qualify them for welfare payments or to conduct a protective services investigation. They may think chaplains will proselytize rather than approaching spiritual questions from the client's own point of view.

Proposed Solutions Intake interviews should use an interdisciplinary approach and be conducted by a team that includes social work. Besides promoting a holistic view of the program, inclusion of a social worker during the intake interview has been found to result in many beneficial outcomes to the hospice including more issues being addressed by the social worker on the team and lower home health aide, labor, and overall hospice costs (Reese and Raymer 2004).

If it is not possible to set up an interdisciplinary team for the intake interview, the intake worker (usually a nurse) should present a holistic view of the program, presenting social work and chaplain visits as an established part of services. The team leader should encourage members to discuss concerns with regard to seeing a social worker or chaplain with clients in an effort to help resolve misconceptions and dispel stereotypes.

ADMINISTRATIVE BARRIERS The advent of managed care has meant that health care administrators are focused on cost-effectiveness. Although in many ways an admirable goal, this means services that are not seen as vital are being downsized. One result of a lack of social work outcomes research is a lack of awareness of the importance of social work services; this partially explains the 3:1 ratio of nurses to social workers in hospice.

Proposed Solutions The most convincing argument the social work profession can use for holistic care is to demonstrate that social work reduces costs for the provider. Social workers promote access to health insurance, increasing payments. Social workers help resolve psychosocial and spiritual issues that could lead to more frequent hospitalizations, greater need for pain medication, and other negative hospice outcomes that mean added expenses for the hospice (Reese and Raymer 2004).

Along with providing such interventions, it is important to document the cost savings through collecting and analyzing program data, perhaps in cooperation with local university social work researchers. In fact, the National Hospice Social Work Survey (Reese and Raymer 2004) found many reductions in hospice costs associated with increased social work services—including participation in the intake interview, hiring more social workers and more experienced social workers resulting in a higher social worker to patient ratio, furnishing higher social worker starting salaries, assigning no duties outside the social worker role, and providing a higher budget for social work services overall. Other studies have found similar cost-savings resulting from increase in social work services (Sherin 1997) or providing an interdisciplinary approach as opposed to a medically focused approach (Abrahm et al. 1996). A more systemic solution, which may be possible after demonstrating the cost-effectiveness of high-functioning teams, is the creation of payment structures that support the interdisciplinary team model (Connor et al. 2002).

CHARACTERISTICS OF HIGH-FUNCTIONING TEAMS

Effective intervention with terminally ill patients and their families requires a full range of interventions, holistic in nature, including the biopsychosocial and spiritual dimensions. Important contributions are made by all disciplines (Hodgson et al. 2004). High-functioning hospice teams possess excellent communication skills and group dynamics that further their purposes. They have values that support hospice philosophy and the well-being of clients and are able to honor differences in values. Their theoretical perspectives are also consistent with hospice philosophy, yet honor differences among the team members. These characteristics afford them a high quality of life as team members. The following discussion of these attributes is an integration of work by the author and others (Byock 1997; Connor et al. 2002; Corless and Nicholas 2004; Egan 1998; Reese and Sontag 2001; Reese and Raymer 2004; Soltura and Piotrowski 2011).

COMMUNICATION SKILLS AND GROUP DYNAMICS High-functioning teams have effective communication. They are able to work collaboratively to develop clear shared goals, coordinated evaluations, and a common treatment plan aimed at solving common problems.

Leadership functions are shared, as is responsibility for treatment. All disciplines are valued and fully utilized. Members share equally in the work of the team, and opinions of all team members are incorporated into treatment plans. This works against role blurring because all members have agreed to each individual's responsibilities. Team roles are clearly understood, disciplines are aware of the special expertise of each of the professions. Team members engage with each other, learn from each other, and share information. Scapegoating is not necessary, as treatment plans are agreed upon, and members take responsibility for them. Team members engage with each other and learn from each other. There are no alliances or subsystems that compete for power. Gossip and innuendo are minimal.

Relationships are positive among members of such a team. Members frequently exchange technical as well as emotional support. They trust each other, and an atmosphere of goodwill prevails.

High-functioning teams also have effective conflict resolution strategies. They acknowledge sources of conflict and challenge each other openly, in an atmosphere of mutual respect. Because of the atmosphere of trust, no secrecy or pretense of agreement is necessary. Thus conflicts are addressed and worked through. At the same time, high-functioning teams study themselves and learn from their own mistakes.

VALUES High-functioning hospice teams hold several shared values. Patient self-determination is a key perspective that influences the approach of the team. The patient and significant others are considered members of the team and govern the care they receive from the team. The team members have an overarching focus on serving the patient, are skilled in communicating with clients, and seek feedback from clients to measure client outcomes. Patient and family needs are communicated at team meetings, and the treatment plan is designed around these needs. This allows for culturally competent care, since patient and family values and perspectives dictate the approaches used. This focus on client perspectives also helps to prevent turf battles between professions, since team members are not so much focused on their own needs to govern and dictate the intervention plan; they identify more as a cohesive team than as individual professionals. They are able to focus on areas of shared values, but also have an awareness of the differences in values between team members and are able to honor these differences in an atmosphere of mutual respect.

THEORETICAL PERSPECTIVES High-functioning hospice teams share several theoretical perspectives that are consistent with hospice philosophy. They recognize the potential for growth and development at the end of life and view dying as a life stage with its own spiritual tasks. All dimensions of human experience are the focus of assessment and treatment—the biopsychosocial and spiritual; thus they believe that all disciplines are necessary to promote the comfort of the patient. Accordingly, they advocate with new clients to accept services from all team members. Along with this shared perspective, team members are aware of differences in theoretical perspectives and honor these differences.

QUALITY OF LIFE Because of their possession of the attributes previously described, high-functioning teams enjoy a high quality of work life. Research has found that team functioning, clarity of roles on the team, positive affectivity, and lack of role conflict predict job satisfaction between hospice team members (DeLoach 2002). Members of a high-functioning team also have a sense of efficacy, confident they can meet the challenges facing them. Staff morale is high, helping to reduce anxiety and prevent compassion fatigue.

IMPORTANCE OF TEAM FUNCTIONING TO HOSPICE OUTCOMES

Team functioning is not just an idealistic goal with no practical importance in the daily operation of a hospice. Better team functioning was found to be associated with fewer hospitalizations of hospice patients and lower costs to the hospice, including lower home health aide, nursing, and labor costs and lower overall hospice costs (Reese and Raymer 2004). These hospitalization and cost effects indicate the critical impact that teams have on client well-being.

CONTRIBUTION OF SOCIAL WORKERS TO HIGH FUNCTIONING TEAMS

The National Hospice Social Work Survey (Reese and Raymer 2004) found that hospices with a higher level of social work services had better team functioning. Specifically, higher-functioning teams were seen in hospices that had a higher social worker to patient ratio, had more MSW-prepared social workers, and did not assign additional duties to their social workers outside the social worker role. Team functioning was measured by the Team Functioning Scale by Sontag (1995b, see appendix C).

What is the cause of this effect, that greater social worker involvement predicts better team functioning? This relationship is not surprising when one thinks about the content of social work education. Social work education focuses on almost all the skills and characteristics of high-functioning teams discussed earlier. Social workers have extensive training in communication skills and group dynamics, enabling them to work collaboratively, observing and learning from dysfunctional group dynamics. Their skills are vital in furthering communication between team members and clients, one of the areas in which clients are least satisfied. They are also key advocates with the team in communicating client needs (Galambos 1998).

Some say that Dame Cicely Saunders drew hospice philosophy from her social work training, basing it on the values of client self-determination, advocacy for patients making them equal partners, human dignity, and the systems perspective that attends to biopsychosocial and spiritual dimensions. Social workers are trained to respect differences in worldviews, helping them to honor perspectives of team members and making them experts in cultural competence. They are oriented toward a consensus model of management in which leadership functions are shared. They are trained in conflict resolution skills, and the social work profession has incorporated spirituality into the literature and curriculum. Social workers are trained in group intervention and have the skills to assist a group in developing into a high-functioning team. Thus full participation by social workers on the team can be a vital strength that can impact the entire hospice along with the well-being of clients.

Weaknesses that social workers must be vigilant about are a lack of advocacy for themselves, including taking responsibility for full participation on the team. They must be able to effectively articulate their role and special expertise on the team, which will come only with improved end-of-life care training for social workers.

NECESSARY CONDITIONS FOR THE DEVELOPMENT OF HIGH-FUNCTIONING TEAMS

Such team functioning is possible only with strong leadership and support by an administrator who is knowledgeable about and values an interdisciplinary team approach. Awareness of the finding that high functioning teams save money (Reese and Raymer 2004) should promote this perspective in budget-conscious administrators. Time must be budgeted for an effective team process and interdisciplinary team training program. All professions must be trained to value interdisciplinary care (Corless and Nicholas 2004). Finally, internships should be offered in which the team process is taught to interdisciplinary groups of students (Connor et al. 2002).

EVALUATION OF TEAM FUNCTIONING

It is helpful to periodically evaluate team effectiveness in order to identify and work on any needed changes (Parker Oliver and Peck 2006). A suggested approach for evaluation is to use Sontag's (1995b) Team Functioning Scale to measure the team's progress (see appendix C). This scale has excellent reliability (Cronbach's alpha = .86) and is very short and easy to use. It measures staff morale, communication, support, equal valuing and utilization of disciplines, trust, and effectiveness of conflict resolution strategies. Higher scores on this scale predict better hospice and client outcomes (Reese and Raymer 2004).

ROLE OF THE SOCIAL WORKER ON THE TEAM

The National Association of Social Workers (2011) has developed the Standards for Palliative and End-of-Life Care (see appendix B). The following is a discussion of these standards as they pertain to the role of the social worker on the interdisciplinary team.

WORK COLLABORATIVELY AS A TEAM MEMBER The social worker should be able to communicate effectively and work collaboratively as a team member. This includes using the input of team members and their initial assessments in guiding commonly agreed upon care plans for clients.

ADVOCATE FOR CLIENTS WITH THE TEAM   At the same time, social workers work to empower clients and are advocates for clients' needs with the team. This means upholding client-client system self-determination, including honoring choices, preferences, decisions, rights, values, and beliefs. Social workers are responsible for arranging team conferencing on these issues. This will also promote cultural competence on the team. This advocacy should always be carried out with objectivity and respect.

FACILITATE COMMUNICATION BETWEEN CLIENTS AND TEAM Social workers should also facilitate communication between clients, family members, and the team. They should arrange for family-team conferencing when needed and encourage and assist clients in communicating with team members, resolving conflicts, and problem solving with the team. They should work to build trust between members.

ADVOCATE FOR PROFESSION WITH TEAM Social workers represent the profession and should interact with confidence and display competence in their professional roles. They should work to empower the profession of social work and advocate for its role in palliative and end-of-life care. They should organize trainings on the role of each discipline and their treatment philosophies.

LEND EXPERTISE ON PSYCHOSOCIAL ASPECTS OF CARE The social worker should assume the role of expert on psychosocial issues, helping the team to understand these issues and develop appropriate treatment plans.

ADDITIONAL ROLES OF THE SOCIAL WORKER ON THE TEAM This author has some additional functions to add, in which the social worker plays a vital role on the team.

Lend Expertise on Spiritual Aspects of Care The social worker should be familiar with the social work literature on spirituality in end-of-life care and should lend expertise on intervention with spiritual issues.

Provide Staff Support The social worker should provide staff support to team members, running staff support groups, providing individual support and in-service training on self-care and addressing staff grief over client death. At the same time, the social worker needs to be engaged in self-care for her own needs (Alkema, Linton, and Davies 2008).

Provide Leadership in Developing Culturally Competent Services Lack of cultural competence on the team is a major barrier to hospice access for diverse cultural groups. Although a number of models for culturally competent hospice services have been developed, they have in general not been implemented. Cultural and religious beliefs are major factors predicting hospice outcomes (Reese 1995–96; Reese et al. 1999), and social work intervention with these issues predicts better patient outcomes (Reese et al. 2006). Social workers are the experts on cultural competence on the team by virtue of their in-depth training in this area. Hospice directors in a national survey recognize this expertise (Reese 2011). Social workers have a responsibility to use this expertise to increase the quality of services.

Provide Leadership in Development of a High-Functioning Team Social workers have knowledge about group dynamics and the development of a high-functioning team. They should use this knowledge to assist team members in acquiring the characteristics of a high-functioning team.

Social workers have in the past been unclear about their role in hospice, due to the lack of professional education in this area. Social work education is beginning to address deficits in end-of-life care, and the profession is becoming clearer about its role. Social workers need to be sure that they understand the social work role in hospice through continuing education and individual efforts to become familiar with the social work end-of-life care literature. Once becoming clear themselves, they must educate the other disciplines on the team about the social work role in hospice.

This chapter has focused on hospice social work practice on the mezzo level, with families, groups, and interdisciplinary teams. The following chapter will review the social work role in macro practice in hospice — including assessment and intervention with organizations and communities.

REFERENCES

Abrahm, J. L., J. Callahan, K. Rossetti, and L. Pierre. 1996. "The Impact of a Hospice Consultation Team on the Care of Veterans with Advanced Cancer." *Journal of Pain and Symptom Management* 12:23–31.

Abramson, J. 1984. "Collective Responsibility in Interdisciplinary Collaboration: An Ethical Perspective for Social Workers." *Social Work in Health Care* 10, no. 1: 35–43.

Abramson, J., and T. Mizrahi. 1996. "When Social Workers and Physicians Collaborate: Positive and Negative Interdisciplinary Experiences." *Social Work* 41, no. 3: 241–336.

Alkema, K., J. M. Linton, and R. Davies. 2008. "A Study of the Relationship Between Self-care, Compassion Satisfaction, Compassion Fatigue, and Burnout Among Hospice Professionals." *Journal of Social Work in End-of-Life and Palliative Care* 4, no. 2: 101–119.

Barker, K. K. 2008. "Electronic Support Groups, Patient-Consumers, and Medicalization: The Case of Contested Illness." *Journal of Health and Social Behavior*, 49, no. 1: 20–36.

Ben-Sira, Z., and M. Szyf. 1992. "Status Inequality in the Social Worker-Nurse Collaboration in Hospitals." *Social Science and Medicine*, 34, no. 4: 365–374.

Beresford, P., L. Adshead, and S. Croft. 2007. *Palliative Care, Social Work, and Service Users: Making Life Possible*. Philadelphia: Jessica Kingsley.

Blacker, S., and A. R. Jordan. 2004. "Working with Families Facing Life-Threatening Illness in the Medical Setting." In Joan Berzoff and Phyllis Silverman, eds., *Living with Dying: A Handbook for End-of-Life Healthcare Practitioners*, pp. 548–570. New York: Columbia University Press.

Borgmeyer, T. 2011. "The Social Work Role in Decision Making: Ethical, Psychosocial, and Cultural Perspectives." In Terry Altilio and Shirley Otis-Green, eds., *Oxford Textbook of Palliative Social Work*, pp. 615–624. New York: Oxford University Press.

Breitbart, W., B. Rosenfeld, C. Gibson, H. Pessin, S. Poppito, C. Nelson, A. Tomarken, A. K. Timm, A. Berg, C. Jacobson, B. Sorger, J. Abbey, and M. Olden. 2010. "Meaning-Centered Group Psychotherapy for Patients with Advanced Cancer: A Pilot Randomized Controlled Trial." *Psycho-Oncology* 19, no. 1: 21–28.

Byock, I. 1997. *Dying Well: Peace and Possibilities at the End of Life*. New York: Riverhead.

Canda, E., and L. Furman. 2010. *Spiritual Diversity in Social Work Practice: The Heart of Helping*. New York: Oxford University Press.

Childress, S. B. 2001. "Enhanced End of Life Care." *Nursing Management* 32, no. 10: 32–35.

Chung, K. 1993. "Brief Social Work Intervention in the Hospice Setting: Person-Centered Work and Crisis Intervention Synthesized and Distilled." *Palliative Medicine* 7, no. 1: 59–62.

Cincotta, N. 2004. "The End of Life at the Beginning of Life: Working with Dying Children and Their Families." In Joan Berzoff and Phyllis R. Silverman, eds., *Living with Dying: A Handbook for End-of-Life Healthcare Practitioners*, pp. 318–347. New York: Columbia University Press.

Clark, E. J. 2004. In Joan Berzoff and Phyllis R. Silverman, eds., *Living with Dying: A Handbook for End-of-Life Healthcare Practitioners*, pp. 838–847. New York: Columbia University Press.

Clukey, L. 2003. "Anticipatory Mourning: Transitional Processes of Expected Loss." *Dissertation Abstracts International: Section B: The Sciences and Engineering* 63(7-B): 3467.

Connor, S., K. Egan, D. Kwilosz, D. Larson, and D. Reese. 2002. "Interdisciplinary Approaches to Assisting with End-of-Life Care and Decision-Making." *American Behavioral Scientist* 46, no. 3: 340–356.

Corless, I. B., and P. K. Nicholas. 2004. "The Interdisciplinary Team: An Oxymoron?" In Joan Berzoff and Phyllis R. Silverman, eds., *Living with Dying: A Handbook for End-of-Life Healthcare Practitioners*, pp. 161–170. New York: Columbia University Press.

Csikai, E. L. 2004. "Social Workers' Participation in the Resolution of Ethical Dilemmas in Hospice Care." *Health and Social Work* 29, no. 1: 67–76.

Csikai, E., and K. Bass. 2000. "Health Care Social Workers' Views of Ethical Issues, Practice, and Policy in End-of-Life Care." *Social Work in Health Care* 32, no. 2: 1–22.

Dawes, J., and J. Dawes. 2004. "End-of-Life Care in Prisons." In Joan Berzoff and Phyllis R. Silverman, eds., *Living with Dying: A Handbook for End-of-Life Healthcare Practitioners*, pp. 778–791. New York: Columbia University Press.

DeLoach, R. J. 2002. "Factors Influencing Job Satisfaction Among Interdisciplinary Team Members Working in Hospice Settings in Central Ohio." Ph.D. diss., Ohio State University. *Dissertation Abstracts International, A: The Humanities and Social Sciences* 63, no. 4 (October): 1556-A.

Doka, K. J. 2002. *Disenfranchised Grief*. Champaign, IL: Research.

——. 2011. "Religion and Spirituality: Assessment and Intervention." *Journal of Social Work in End-of-Life and Palliative Care* 7, no. 1: 99–109.

Egan, K. 1998. *Patient-Family Value Based End-of-Life Care Model*. Largo: Hospice Institute of the Florida Suncoast.

Fineberg, I. C., and A. Bauer. 2011. "Families and Family Conferencing." In Terry Altilio and Shirley Otis-Green, eds., *Oxford Textbook of Palliative Social Work*, pp. 235–249. New York: Oxford University Press.

Forbes, S., M. Bern-Klug, and C. Gessert. 2000. "End-of-Life Decision Making on Behalf of Nursing Home Residents with Dementia." *Image: Journal of Nursing Scholarship* 20:251–258.

Foster, L., and L. McLellan. 2002. "Translating Psychosocial Insight Into Ethical Discussions Supportive of Families in End-of-Life Decision-Making." *Social Work in Health Care* 35, no. 3: 37–51.

Furman, L., and S. Bushfield (formerly S. Fry). 2000. "Clerics and Social Workers: Collaborators or Competitors?" *ARETE, Journal of University of South Carolina School of Social Work* 24, no. 1: 30–39.

Galambos, C. 1998. "Preserving End-of-Life Autonomy: The Patient Self-Determination Act and the Uniform Health Care Decisions Act." *Health and Social Work* 23, no. 4: 275–281.

Gallo-Silver, L. 2011. "Sexuality, Sensuality, and Intimacy in Palliative Care." In Terry Altilio and Shirley Otis-Green, eds., *Oxford Textbook of Palliative Social Work*, pp. 397–411. New York: Oxford University Press.

Gerbino, S., and S. Henderson. 2004. "End-of-Life Bioethics in Clinical Social Work Practice." In Joan Berzoff and Phyllis R. Silverman, eds., *Living with Dying: A Handbook for End-of-Life Healthcare Practitioners*, pp. 593–608. New York: Columbia University Press.

Gerbino, S., and M. Raymer. 2011. "Holding On and Letting Go: The Red Thread of Adult Bereavement." In Terry Altilio and Shirley Otis-Green, eds., *Oxford Textbook of Palliative Social Work*, pp. 319–327. New York: Oxford University Press.

Glajchen, M. 2011. In Terry Altilio and Shirley Otis-Green, eds., *Oxford Textbook of Palliative Social Work*, pp. 223–233. New York: Oxford University Press.

Goldring, E., and J. Solomon. 2011. "Social Work and Child Life: A Family's Journey with Childhood Cancer." In Terry Altilio and Shirley Otis-Green, *Oxford Textbook of Palliative Social Work*, pp. 453–458. New York: Oxford University Press.

Gough, K., and P. Hudson. 2009. "Psychometric Properties of the Hospital Anxiety and Depression Scale in Family Caregivers of Palliative Care Patients." *Journal of Pain and Symptom Management* 37, no. 5: 797–806.

Harris, J., D. Bowen, H. Badr, P. Hannon, J. Hay, and K. Regan Sterba. 2009. "Family Communication During the Cancer Experience." *Journal of Health Communication* 14:76–84.

Health Resources and Services Administration. 1993. *Interdisciplinary Development of Health Professionals to Maximize Health Provider Resources in Rural Areas.* Washington, DC: Author.

Hess, R. F., J. A. Weinland, and K. Beebe. 2010. "'I Am Not Alone': A Survey of Women with Peripartum Cardiomyopathy and Their Participation in an Online Support Group." *Computers, Informatice, Nursing: CIN* 28, no. 4: 215–221.

Hodgson, H., S. Segal, M. Weidinger, and M. B. Linde. 2004. "Being There: Contributions of the Nurse, Social Worker, and Chaplain During and After a Death." *Generations* 28, no. 2: 47–52.

Hooyman, N. R., and B. J. Kramer. 2006. *Living Through Loss: Interventions Across the Life Span.* New York: Columbia University Press.

Jones, B. 2006. "Companionship, Control, and Compassion: A Social Work Perspective on the Needs of Children with Cancer and Their Families at the End of Life." *Journal of Palliative Medicine* 9, no. 3: 774–788.

Kadushin, G., and Egan, M. 1997. "Educating Students for a Changing Health Care Environment: An Examination of Health Care Practice Course Content." *Health and Social Work* 22, no. 3: 211–223.

Kempson, D. 2000/2001. "Effects of Intentional Touch on Complicated Grief of Bereaved Mothers." *Omega* 42, no. 4: 341–353.

Kinsella, G., B. Cooper, Picton, C., and D. Murtagh. 2000. "Factors Influencing Outcomes for Family Caregivers of Persons Receiving Palliative Care: Toward an Integrated Model." *Journal of Palliative Care* 16, no. 3: 46–54.

Kovacs, P., and L. Bronstein. 1999. "Preparation for Oncology Settings: What Hospice Workers Say They Need." *Health and Social Work* 24, no. 1: 57–64.

Kramer, B. T., M. Kavanaugh, A. Trentham-Dietz, M. Walsh, and J. A. Yonker. 2010. "Predictors of Family Conflict at the End of Life: The Experiences of Spouses and Adult Children of Persons with Lung Cancer." *Gerontologist* 50, no. 2: 215–225.

Kubler-Ross, E. 1970. *On Death and Dying.* New York: Macmillan.

Kulys, R., and M. Davis. 1987. "Nurses and Social Workers: Rivals in the Provision of Social Services?" *Health and Social Work* 12, no. 1: 101–112.

McCoyd, J. L. M., and C. Walter. 2007. "A Different Kind of Holding Environment: A Case Study of Group Work with Pediatric Staff." *Journal of Social Work in End-of-Life and Palliative Care* 3, no. 3: 5–22.

Morse, M. 1991. *Closer to the Light: Learning from Near Death Experiences of Children.* New York: Random House.

Nally, J. 2006. "Spirituality in Social Work: Spiritual Self-care and Its Effects on Compassion Fatigue." Master's thesis, University of Arkansas.

Nardi, D. A., F. Ornelas, M. Wright, and R. Crispell. 2001. "Clergy and Social Workers' Attitudes Towards Death and Palliative Care in an Acute Care Setting." *International Journal of Palliative Nursing* 7, no. 1: 30–36.

National Association of Social Workers. 2011. NASW *Standards for Social Work Practice in Palliative and End of Life Care.* Washington, DC: NASW.

Orloff, S. F. 2011. "Pediatric Hospice and Palliative Care: The Invaluable Role of Social Work." In Terry Altilio and Shirley Otis-Green, eds., *Oxford Textbook of Palliative Social Work,* pp. 79–86. New York: Oxford University Press.

Parker Oliver, D., and M. Peck. 2006. "Inside the Interdisciplinary Team Experiences of Hospice Social Workers." *Journal of Social Work in End-of-Life and Palliative Care* 2, no. 3: 7–21.

Parker Oliver, D., E. Wittenberg-Lyles, K. T. Washington, and S. Sehrawat. 2009. "Social Work Role in Hospice Pain Management: A National Survey." *Journal of Social Work in End-of-Life and Palliative Care* 5:61–74.

Parry, J. K. 2001. *Social Work Theory and Practice with the Terminally Ill.* 2d ed. New York: Haworth Social Work Practice Press.

Pflaum, M., and P. Kelley. 1986. "Understanding the Final Messages of the Dying." *Nursing86* 16, no. 60 26–29.

Pullen, M. L. 2002. "Joe's Story: Reflections on a Difficult Interaction Between a Nurse and a Patient's Wife." *International Journal of Palliative Nursing* 8, no. 10: 481–488.

Rada, R. 2007. "Entry Requirements and Membership Homogeneity in Online Patient Groups." *Medical Informatics and the Internet in Medicine* 32, no. 3: 215–223.

Raymer, M., and D. Reese. 2004. "The History of Social Work in Hospice." In Joan Berzoff and Phyllis R. Silverman, eds., *Living with Dying: A Handbook for End-of-Life Healthcare Practitioners*, pp. 150–160. New York: Columbia University Press.

Reese, D. 1995 (formerly D. Ita). "Physician Failure to Predict Terminality in Home Health Care Patients." Unpublished MS.

——. 1995–96. "Testing of a Causal Model: Acceptance of Death in Hospice Patients." *Omega: Journal of Death and Dying* 32, no. 2: 81–92.

——. 2003. "National Hospice Social Work Survey Results: Impact of Services on Hospice Outcomes." Paper presented at the Council on Social Work Education, Annual Program Meeting, February, Atlanta.

——. 2011. "Interdisciplinary Perceptions of the Social Work Role in Hospice: Building Upon the Classic Kulys and Davis Study." *Journal of Social Work in End-of-Life and Palliative Care* 7, no. 4: 383–406. Reese, D., R. Ahern, S. Nair, J. O'Faire, and C. Warren. 1999. "Hospice Access and Utilization by African Americans: Addressing Cultural and Institutional Barriers Through Participatory Action Research." *Social Work* 44, no. 6: 549–559.

Reese, D., L. Braden, C. Butler, and M. Smith. 2004. "African American Access to Hospice: An Interdisciplinary Participatory Action Research Project." Paper presented at the Clinical Team Conference, National Hospice and Palliative Care Organization, March, Las Vegas, Nevada.

Reese, D., and D. Brown. 1997. "Psychosocial and Spiritual Care in Hospice: Differences Between Nursing, Social Work, and Clergy." *Hospice Journal* 12, no. 1: 29–41.

Reese, D., C. L. W. Chan, D. Perry, D. Wiersgalla, and J. Schlinger. 2005. "Beliefs, Death Anxiety, Denial, and Treatment Preferences in End-of-Life Care: A Comparison of Social Work Students, Community Residents, and Medical Students." *Journal of Social Work in End-of-Life and Palliative Care* 1, no. 1: 23–47.

Reese, D., and E. Melton. 2003. "Needs of Lesbian Women in End-of-Life Care." Unpublished MS.

Reese, D., and M. Raymer. 1994. "Issues and Interventions with Hospice Staff Addressed by Social Workers." Unpublished MS. ——. 2004. "Relationships Between Social Work Services and Hospice Outcomes: Results of the National Hospice Social Work Survey." *Social Work* 49, no. 3: 415–422.

Reese, D., M. Raymer, S. Orloff, S. Gerbino, R. Valade, S. Dawson, C. Butler, M. Wise-Wright, and R. Huber. 2006. "The Social Work Assessment Tool (SWAT): Developed by the Social Worker Section of the National Council of Hospice and Palliative Professionals, National Hospice and Palliative Care Organization." *Journal of Social Work in End-of-Life and Palliative Care* 2, no. 2: 65–95.

Reese, D., and C. Rosaasen. 1999. "Spiritual Needs of Bereaved Children." Paper presented at Society for Spirituality and Social Work National Conference, June, St. Louis.

Reese, D., and M-A. Sontag. 2001. "Barriers and Solutions for Successful Inter-professional Collaboration on the Hospice Team." *Health and Social Work* 26, no. 3: 167–175.

Reith, M., and M. Payne. 2009. *Social Work in End-of-Life and Palliative Care.* Chicago: Lyceum.

Renzenbrink, I. 2004. "Relentless Self-care." In J. Berzoff and J. Silverman, eds.. *Living with Dying: A Comprehensive Resource for End-of-Life Care*, pp. 848–867. New York: Columbia University Press.

Roberts, C. S., W. F. Baile, and J. D. Bassett. 1999. "When the Care Giver Needs Care." *Social Work in Health Care* 30, no. 2: 65–80.

Sanders, C. M. 1989. "Grief, the Morning After: Dealing with Adult Bereavement." Hoboken, NJ: Wiley-Interscience.

Sands, R., J. Stafford, and M. McClelland. 1990. "'I Beg to Differ': Conflict in the Interdisciplinary Team." *Social Work in Health Care* 14, no. 3: 55–72.

Schonwetter, R., R. Walker, and B. Robinson. 1995. "The Lack of Advance Directives Among Hospice Patients." *Hospice Journal* 10, no. 3: 1–11.

Schriver, J. M. 2010. *Human Behavior and the Social Environment: Shifting Paradigms in Essential Knowledge for Social Work Practice.* 5th ed. Needham Heights, MA: Allyn and Bacon.

Seccareccia, D., and J. B. Brown. 2009. "Impact of Spirituality on Palliative Care Physicians: Personally and Professionally." *Journal of Palliative Medicine* 12, no. 9: 805–809.

Sherin, D. 1997. "Saving Services: Redefining End-Stage Home Care for HIV/ AIDS." *Innovations* (Winter): 26–27.

Silverman, P. R. 2004. "Dying and Bereavement in Historical Perspective." In J. Berzoff and P. Silverman, eds. *Living with Dying: A Handbook for End-of-Life Healthcare Practitioners*, pp. 128–149. New York: Columbia University Press.

Smith, S. H. 1999. "'Now That Mom Is in the Lord's Arms, I Just Have to Live the Way She Taught Me': Reflections on an Elderly, African American Mother's Death." *Journal of Gerontological Social Work* 32, no. 2: 41–51.

Smolinski, K. M., and Y. Colon. 2011. "Palliative Care with Lesbian, Gay, Bisexual, and Transgender Persons." In Terry Altilio and Shirley Otis-Green, eds., *Oxford Textbook of Palliative Social Work*, pp. 379–386. New York: Oxford University Press.

So, H. W., E. Y. H. Chen, C. W. Wong, S. F. Hung, D. W. S. Chung, S. M. Ng, and C. L. W. Chan. 2006. "Efficacy of Brief Intervention for Carers of People with

First-Episode Psychosis: A Waiting List Controlled Study." *Hong Kong Journal of Psychiatry* 16, no. 3: 92–100.

Soltura, D. L., and L. F. Piotrowski. 2011. In Terry Altilio and Shirley Otis-Green, eds., *Oxford Textbook of Palliative Social Work*, pp. 495–501. New York: Oxford University Press.

Sontag, M. 1995a. "Making It Happen: Interdisciplinary Collaboration in Hospices." Paper presented at the meeting of the National Hospice Organization, San Francisco.

——. 1995b. "Team Functioning Scale." Unpublished MS.

Springer, N. P. 1999. "Preparing for the Untimely Death of a Family Member: A Qualitative Study of the Role of Hospice Service in Partner-Caregiver Bereavement." *Dissertation Abstracts International, Section A: Humanities and Social Sciences* 60(4-A): 1349.

Sutton, A. L., and D. Liechty. 2004. "Clinical Practice with Groups in End-of-Life Care." In Joan Berzoff and Phyllis Silverman, eds., *Living with Dying: A Handbook for End-of-Life Healthcare Practitioners*, pp. 508–533. New York: Columbia University Press.

van Ulden-Kraan, C. F., C. H. C. Drossaert, E. Taal, E. R. Seydel, and M. A. F. J. van de Laar. 2008. Self-reported Differences in Empowerment Between Lurkers and Posters in Online Patient Support Groups." *Journal of Medical Internet Research* 10, no. 2: 101–109.

Zerbe, K., and D. Steinberg. 2000. "Coming to Terms with Grief and Loss: Can Skills for Dealing with Bereavement Be Learned?" *Postgraduate Medicine* 108, no. 6: 97–107.

6

MACRO CONTEXT OF HOSPICE SOCIAL WORK

Organization, Community, and Larger Society

In this chapter we consider hospice social workers' contributions and responsibilities on the macro level. The social work perspective is geared toward a systems perspective, which can be used to intervene in the organization, community, and larger society. Raymer and Gardia (2011:683) remind us of our "responsibility and obligation to practice advocacy on a broader basis." We will apply deep ecology theory as a framework for intervention at all of these levels, which includes social work responsibility for social action.

DEEP ECOLOGY

Shallow ecology concerns itself with the problems in the natural environment because of their effect on humans. Deep ecology goes beyond this perspective to see humans as inseparable from each other and nature, similar to the concept of "unity consciousness" (Maslow 1971, one of the dimensions of spirituality according to our definition) and consistent with perspectives of the highest level of spiritual development according to transpersonal theory (Robbins, Chatterjee, and Canda 1998). Humans develop when they grow beyond a self-concept of an isolated ego and identify with the whole—from family and friends and pets and houseplants to the whole of humanity and the earth. An "ecological consciousness" entails not a view of person-in-environment but one of the person existing within the environment as part of a complex system of interconnected relationships. These relationships become our actual identity (Besthorn 2001), and the interests of those with whom we identify, nature included, may be seen as one's own interests as well.

From this perspective, the oppression of humans toward nature is associated with social oppression, all emanating from the same sense of disconnectedness, a lack of this transpersonal awareness of unity consciousness. So the rape of women is the same as the rape of nature. From this perspective there is respect and honor for all ways and forms of life.

Fred Besthorn has applied deep ecology to social work education and practice (Besthorn 2001; Besthorn and McMillen 2002). He explains that deep ecology does not stop at the description of the interconnectedness of all beings, but also integrates a responsibility for social action. It seeks to transform our way of life, and aims to heal alienation from one's transpersonal self, one's community, and the earth. The deep ecological perspective, and our identity as part of an interconnected web of existence, leads us to question social norms that further stratification and privilege among humans and of humans over the natural world. All peoples and all beings, whether human or environmental, have equal inherent worth in this perspective, and action is required to promote equal quality of life for all humans and nonhuman beings.

Social action from the deep ecological perspective addresses the root causes of our culture's degradation of nature and peoples, seen as consumerism based on human hedonism and self-centeredness, and is committed to restoring the richness and diversity of ecosystems and human communities. Social workers with a deep ecological perspective have a responsibility to be active in organizational and social policy and work toward development that reshapes the basic economic, technological, and ideological structures of society, focusing on quality of life, social justice, ecojustice, and the rights and dignity of all humans and nonhumans rather than consumption and consumerism.

Deep ecology is relevant to hospice philosophy in its focus on quality of life and connection with what is natural and beneficial to all. It is a holistic perspective that relates to hospice's all-inclusive focus on the physical, psychological, social, and spiritual realms. It is consistent with the social activism roots of hospice, which began as a grassroots movement advocating for social justice in terms of patient self-determination. It is relevant to social work's commitment to advocacy and underlies our responsibility for community outreach and policy practice. We can use deep ecology as a framework to inform our practice on the organizational, community, societal, and global levels. The next section will discuss the organizational framework.

HOSPICE SOCIAL WORK INTERVENTION AT
THE ORGANIZATIONAL LEVEL

A national survey (Reese 2011) found that hospice directors' views of the role of social workers has greatly improved since the classic Kulys and Davis study of 1986. Directors consider social workers most qualified to address twelve of twenty-four interventions considered by social workers to define their role, as compared to three in the classic study. According to the great majority of these hospice directors, however, nurses are still most qualified to supervise hospice workers (71 percent) and direct the hospice (71 percent). It should be kept in mind when considering this opinion that 80 percent of the directors were nurses by profession and only 10 percent were social workers. Directors who were social workers by profession held similar views, though—only one-third thought that social workers were best qualified to supervise workers or direct the hospice.

The National Hospice Social Work Survey (Reese and Raymer 2004) found some evidence that conflicts with this view, however. This study showed benefits when social workers in a hospice were supervised by a social worker. Social workers with this quality of supervision addressed significantly more patient issues with the hospice team, and, subsequently, fewer visits were needed to patients by other members of the team. In addition, Dyeson and Hebert (2004) found that social service needs are often not accurately identified by nurses, Parker Oliver and Peck (2006) found that social workers feel a lack of support from administrators, and Sontag (1996) found evidence that the professional discipline of the hospice director impacted on the level and type of services provided. This author's study, just mentioned (Reese 2011), found that 70 percent of directors who were nurses held bachelor's or associate degrees, while 100 percent of the directors who were social workers were master's prepared. Furthermore, the shortage of bachelor's-prepared nurses in this country makes it an ever more common necessity to hire nurses with associate degrees and develop ways of training them in the skills they lack (Chaya et al. 2008).

Social work contributions in the roles of supervisor and director are valuable and will naturally have a different emphasis than that of other disciplines. For example, a MSW hospice director known to this author has budgeted for a community outreach position to increase hospice access for diverse cultural groups. Providing such a position is rare; directors say they can't afford it; but experts in the audience at a presentation made by this

224 MACRO CONTEXT OF HOSPICE SOCIAL WORK

author at the NHPCO Access and Diversity conference in 2005 said that the decision not to budget for such efforts is just a matter of priorities and values (Reese and Beckwith 2005).

Social workers should be prepared to function in the role of supervisor and administrator in the hospice setting. Supervision of social workers by social workers is key to hospice outcomes (Reese and Raymer 2004) and is a responsibility included in the National Association of Social Workers (2011) NASW *Standards for Palliative and End-of-Life Care.* They should provide leadership in the development of organizational cultural and linguistic competence, including increasing the diversity of staff and providing cultural competence training (Reese and Beckwith 2005).

The fact that directors who are social workers by discipline do not claim these roles as their own (Reese 2011) shows that social work research has not informed social work education, and that this content has not filtered down to the practice world. It is beyond the scope of this book to provide comprehensive content on this topic, but a social work perspective on hospice administration will be discussed in the following section.

SPIRITUALITY OF WORK

MEANING OF WORK AND THE CONSENSUS MODEL OF MANAGEMENT   Just as we acknowledge all dimensions of human experiences with our patients—the biopsychosocial and spiritual, a spiritual perspective in the workplace also acknowledges employees as whole persons (Karakas 2010). Again, we are not referring here to religion or prosyletizing in the hospice but to our two-dimensional definition of spirituality: transcendence in terms of philosophy of life and unity consciousness.

Since the industrial age, corporations in the U.S. have become increasingly centered on creating profit—putting economic goals before all others, including quality of product or service, and social and environmental impact of corporate actions (Walsh, Weber, and Margolis 2003). This is seen even in hospice, the last possible place one would think profit would take priority—in the managed care perspective of providing services that lead to profit and minimizing those that do not, regardless of quality of care and realization of the original holistic mission of hospice. The irony of this view is that, in reality, those activities that promote the well-being of all are the very ones that create profitability.

The philosophy of life dimension of spirituality centers on the purpose of life and what makes life meaningful. Employees who find meaning in their work—even seeing it as a calling, a sacred duty, or a service opportunity—are more engaged, productive, and committed to their work, performing better and leading to improved results for the organization as a whole, including profits (Karakas 2010).

The way to accomplish this is by incorporating the employee's own life purpose into the mission of the corporation. This can be furthered through the use of a consensus model of management, which is an alternative feminist approach to administration, contrasting with the paternalistic hierarchical model traditionally used. In this approach decisions are made by consensus rather than through authority, and staff have input into the mission of the organization. In this way, realization of the mission of the organization *is* the life purpose of the employee—creating the ultimate employee commitment. Deep ecology theory informs this approach to management in its inclusion of the spirituality dimension of philosophy of life.

This approach fosters a socially responsible corporation, one with a social mission and dedicated to the welfare of all. This does not seem like much of a stretch for a hospice organization; most people would agree that the work of hospice is a sacred calling. Those with intimate knowledge of hospice will realize though, that improvements need to be made—in truly holistic rather than mainly physical care—and true efforts to provide hospice access for all people regardless of cultural heritage. A deep ecological perspective brings with it a responsibility for social action; this will be discussed further on in this chapter in the section on intervention with the community.

SENSE OF COMMUNITY A second aspect of organizational life that affects employee productivity is a sense of interconnectedness and community. This aspect is considered part of the spirituality of work, and is relevant to the unity consciousness dimension of spirituality. Deep ecology informs this aspect of organizational life as well, in its emphasis on the interconnectedness of all.

Contemporary U.S. society has seen a decline in a sense of connectedness in local communities, social and religious groups, and families. This results in a society filled with isolation, connected mainly through Facebook and e-mail. The Protestant work ethic and pressure to perform that is part of our mainstream culture has brought profits and accomplishment, but at the sacrifice of human relationships. In fact, contemporary writers on the spirituality of work acknowledge the workplace as the primary source of relationships in our society today and encourage administrators to enhance this factor as an aspect of spirituality of work. Employees who have a sense of community and connectedness at work also have a sense of attachment, loyalty, and belonging to the organization (Karakas 2010).

Organizations with this point of view "are not just machines for producing goods" (Karakas 2010:97), but foster satisfying and meaningful life experiences for employees. High-quality relationships at the workplace are what create a sense of community and connectedness. High-quality relationships at work have been found to predict group performance and efficiency. Aspects of such relationships include intimacy, wholeness, authenticity, altruism, integrity, consideration toward others, and showing concern. Unfortunately, this type of community is often not realized because of team dysfunction. The philosophy of life dimension of spirituality may play a part in creating this community through shared values and sense of purpose. Thus a consensus model of management may foster these relationships as it fosters integration of life purpose with organizational mission (Karakas 2010).

ECOFEMINISM VERSUS TRADITIONAL ORGANIZATIONAL MANAGEMENT Since organizations are communities—in fact, the primary communities that contemporary individuals are a part of—they produce significant social values and impacts on society (Lupo and Bailey 2011). These impacts may be for good or for ill; for example, organizations that value profits above all may have negative effects on democracy and human rights, environmental health, psychological health, and the well-being of animals. Crittenden (2000) describes elements of this harmful worldview, including *domination* (in which those considered superior have the right to subordinate the well-being of others to their own), *objectification* (those with whom one is unable to empathize are seen as lacking in emotions or thoughts or other bases for respect and connection), and *dissociation* (a perspective of separateness— from nature, the other gender, other cultural groups, etc.). She credits this value system, promoted by corporations, as responsible for the oppression of workers in international corporations, the destruction of the environment, a psychological state that is disconnected with emotion or empathy, and the use of animals for human consumption and profit.

In contrast, an organization that has a worldview consistent with ecofeminism or deep ecology promotes a set of alternate values, as identified by Crittenden (2000):

1. *Anti-oppression*—engaging in activism against any form of social domination
2. *Inclusiveness*—giving an equal voice and full representation to oppressed persons and nature
3. *Relational sense of self*—identifying with the network of all
4. *Anti-objective*—lack of belief in the existence of an objective point of view
5. *Pluralism*—respecting multiple sets of moral values
6. *Ecocentrism*—engaging in protecting diversity in ecosystems

Organizations with this point of view promote democracy and human rights by insisting that the voices of the oppressed be fully represented—for example, as members of the board of directors. They promote environmental health by ecofriendly practices regardless of profit implications, such as arranging for recycling and using recycled products. They advocate for rights of animals, for example, within the medical research system. They promote psychological health through encouraging empathic connection, incorporating morality into politics and business, and focus on bringing harmony and psychological and moral health into the entire interconnected system. Profit is seen not just in terms of money, but in consumption of services in a way that the well-being of the whole is promoted. Monetary costs as well as environmental and psychological, including income distribution, are taken into consideration and included in calculation of productivity.

IMPLICATIONS FOR SOCIAL WORK Social workers in a position of management can work to realign the organizational mission away from an overemphasis on economic factors and toward a consensus model of management in which the organizational mission is a composite of a shared employee vision, and profit and productivity are seen in terms of the resulting well-being of all. Such an administrator can promote high-quality employee relationships between employees, leading to greater commitment to the organization. Research shows that team functioning is improved when members have strong communication and trust, feel equally respected as a member of the team, and feel supported by the administrator (Parker Oliver and Peck 2006; Reith and Payne 2009). Delightfully, this approach also brings in a greater economic gain; this evidence can be used to persuade upper administrators of the value of such a management approach.

Social workers not in a position of management also have much work to do in intervention with the organization. Always a part of the social worker's personal job description (if not the official employee job description), advocacy for organizational practices that reflect spirituality of work as well as for quality services for individual clients and the community can lead to improvements with far-reaching effects. In addition, social workers supervising other social workers should directly observe social work interventions and seek patient feedback about client satisfaction (Doherty and DeWeaver 2004). The following discusses additional important considerations within hospice organizational management.

ACCREDITATION

The federal agency Centers for Medicare and Medicaid Services has set standards that hospices must meet in order to become "Medicare certified." Upon receiving this certification, hospices are eligible to be reimbursed by Medicare when they serve eligible patients. Since most hospice patients are covered by Medicare (National Hospice and Palliative Care Organization 2009), most hospices want to be Medicare certified. Centers for Medicare and Medicaid Services has given authority to several organizations to accredit hospices based on CMS standards as well as the standards of the organization. These organizations include the Joint Commission, the Community Health Accreditation Program, and the Accreditation Commission for Health Care. The hospice administrator is responsible for overseeing the accreditation process for the hospice (National Association of Social Workers, Social Work Policy Institute 2010).

STANDARDS FOR HOSPICE CARE

The National Hospice and Palliative Care Organization has developed standards for practice that include responding to client needs and exceeding client expectations; ethical conduct and advocacy for client rights; ensuring excellence of care and promoting safety; ensuring access for all; building an organizational culture of quality and accountability that values collaboration, communication and ethics; promoting workforce excellence through a collaborative culture, accountability, training, and support; adopting professional standards; compliance with laws and regulations; being fiscally responsible; and measuring performance in order to foster quality and performance improvement (National Hospice and Palliative Care Organization, Quality Partners 2011). The hospice administrator is responsible for overseeing organizational compliance with these standards.

PROGRAM EVALUATION

As part of its conditions of participation, CMS requires that hospices assess their performance using its Quality Assessment and Performance Improvement (QAPI) program. The program includes procedures for assessing both patient and hospice organization outcomes. Hospice outcomes assessed include aggregate data on patient outcomes, client satisfaction, administration, marketing, outreach to the community, profitability, and fundraising. Assessment factorss the processes of care, effectiveness, safety, quality, and outcomes of care. The hospice is required to track adverse events, analyze causes, and develop processes and training to prevent them. Data is used to demonstrate areas that have improved, identify additional areas for improvement and decision making by the hospice. Performance improvement projects must be implemented and improvement must be measured. Licensed professionals conduct the QAPI assessments. The hospice administrator's responsibility in CMS-required evaluation is to define, implement, and maintain the QAPI program, identify and address quality of care and patient safety priorities, and designate the individuals who are responsible for operating the QAPI program (National Association for Social Workers, Social Work Policy Institute 2010).

RECOMMENDATIONS FOR ACTION

The National Association of Social Workers, Social Work Policy Institute (2010:18, 21) along with Reith and Payne (2009) have made recommendations for action by hospice agencies to enhance the quality of services provided by social workers. These are actions that social workers can take as administrators or can advocate for within their agencies:

- Decrease social work caseloads
- Offer competitive salaries that reward social workers for educational achievements and acquired licenses and credentials

- Offer incentives for social workers that seek training opportunities and continually incorporate research into practice
- Provide quality and consistent supervision and consultation of social workers by social workers to help build practice skills and efficacy; document outcomes; and evaluate performance to increase effectiveness and efficiency of service delivery
- Help define and support the social worker's roles and responsibilities on the interdisciplinary care team
- Ensure electronic case notes have sections designed for capturing elements of social work service delivery
- Increase accessibility for practitioners to research journals

This section has discussed the social work role and intervention approaches at the organizational level. The next section will turn to intervention with the community.

HOSPICE SOCIAL WORK INTERVENTION AT THE COMMUNITY LEVEL

Raymer and Gardia (2011) remind us that social workers must "be at the decision-making tables . . . instead of just responding to changes as they occur" (p. 685). Social workers should be prepared for outreach to the community, through skills in general public education, collaboration and advocacy within the broader health care system, and in developing relationships with leaders of diverse cultural groups in order to increase access for these communities. They should develop skills in needs assessment and participatory action research studies in order to identify populations that are not being served by hospice or unmet needs for services. They must become involved in leadership of professional organizations at the state and national levels in order to influence policy about end-of-life care. Deep ecology theory continues to inform our practice in the wider world as we work toward quality of life at the end of life for all.

DISSEMINATION OF PUBLIC INFORMATION

Although most Americans are in favor of palliative care in terminal illness and say they want to die at home, most are not familiar with hospice. The reality is that the majority are being cared for in hospitals with acute or curative care, and half die there (National Hospice and Palliative Care Organization 2001).

In addition, most patients are referred to hospice by their physician—this creates barriers to access since most physicians do not refer appropriate patients to a hospice and since oppressed cultural groups do not have access to health care, thus do not get referred by a doctor. Many terminally ill patients, whether receiving nursing home, home health, or palliative care, or assisted living services, are not referred to hospice when appropriate. Many patients do not receive any medical care at all, but are being cared for at home by significant others with no professional support.

A hospice team may provide care to terminally ill patients in the nursing home setting, but may face challenges in this environment. Hospice services may not be provided when appropriate, advance directives may not be established, and hospice referrals and palliative care treatment may delayed until shortly before death (Bern-Klug and Ellis 2004; Chapin et al. 2007). In one study, although terminally ill nursing home patients who were enrolled in hospice had better pain management than those who were not, the pain management for all patients was inadequate (Miller et al. 2002). Family members of patients who died in long-term care said staff were not knowledgeable about end-of-life issues, but patients who were referred to hospice had better quality care because of the increased attention the patient received (Munn and Zimmerman 2006).

Thus, it is clear that general connection with the community and various forms of integration and public information are needed; and, in order to create hospice access for all, these are a social worker's ethical responsibility. The NASW Standards for Palliative and End-of-Life Care (2011) challenge social workers to engage in social action for equal access to palliative and end-of-life care resources and to lead educational, supervisory, administrative, and research efforts in this field.

If this is not part of the social worker's job description, and time is not provided for this, a social worker can take several routes—volunteering time outside the workday, advocating for this work to be included in one's own or another's job description, or collaborating with a local university to provide this work through faculty presentations or students in a field placement. This author argues that social work is the discipline on the team with the skills and training for community intervention.

Such intervention includes developing relationships with and providing training for local physicians and health care staff within all aspects of the health care system, along with staff of assisted living communities, and with community leaders including leaders of diverse cultural groups. It also includes public education aimed at community members through talks at meetings of local groups or through the media. Problems that can be addressed through this type of community intervention include lack of referrals to hospice or late referrals shortly before death, lack of pain control in terminal illness, and lack of coordination among health care providers.

Hospice staff routinely visit patients in a variety of health care settings. They do intake interviews and provide services in nursing homes and hospitals. Efforts can be made to increase staff awareness in such settings, as well as in emergency rooms, palliative care services, home health care agencies, and assisted living and longterm care facilities. A good strategy for connecting with other agencies and health care providers is to partner with their social workers to promote hospice as a valuable option in end-of-life care (National Association of Social Workers 2011).

Advocacy for advance directives and consideration of end-of-life care decisions through public education also brings these issues into community consciousness and promotes the option of hospice. We should involve the community as a whole, including young, healthy individuals, in this discussion rather than focusing only on elderly patients with terminal prognoses. African Americans (Reese et al. 1999) and Latino/as (Reese 2002) have suggested that hospice "make friends with us," rather than waiting to make contact until the time of death. Content should include how to communicate with health care professionals and significant others about advance directives (Galambos 1998). Further discussion of outreach to diverse communities will be included in the chapter on cultural competence. The following discusses an important improvement that is needed in the field of end-of-life care—continuity between different approaches to care as a patient moves toward the end of life.

CONTINUITY OF CARE

Families and patients need transition care that addresses the dichotomy between curative and palliative care in America (Finn 2002). Family members need to find a sense of meaning in the death of their loved one and an acceptance of their loved one's life, and Foster and McLellan (2002) argue that this is key in the ability to make an end-of-life care decision for palliative care. Access to interventions to prepare them for palliative care and ability to face their mortality could be provided in transition care, would allow them to accomplish these tasks. For example, social work intervention around meaning of the patient's death and addressing denial could make it possible for patients and families to accept hospice care.

Another important consideration is that lack of continuity of care is a known factor in the desire for suicide among terminally ill patients (Chibnall et al. 2002). Patients can feel abandoned by their physicians if their case is closed and transferred elsewhere when it is decided that their illness is terminal; stable relationships with health care providers can reduce suicidality in terminally ill patients. Lack of continuity of care can prevent health care professionals from recognizing risk of suicide and providing appropriate interventions.

Another argument is that certain diagnoses have uncertain prognoses, such as chronic obstructive lung disease and congestive heart failure. It is very difficult to predict how long a patient with such a diagnosis might survive. There is not a predictable decline toward death as in cancer. It is possible that these patients might experience a sudden death. Thus, early in the course of the disease, it is helpful to make end-of-life decisions as well as address patients' biopsychosocial and spiritual needs. Such cases provide an example in which there is a need for preparation for death, but at the same time reason to hope for recovery and continued survival (Chibnall et al. 2002).

The National Hospice and Palliative Care Organization has advocated for continuity of care, which involves the hospice team from the first diagnosis of a life-threatening illness. The World Health Organization (2003) states that palliative care is appropriate early in the course of a life-threatening illness, even in combination with curative care. It advocates for extending the principles of hospice care in this way to a broader population.

An innovative approach to providing this continuity of care has been implemented in a number of settings across the country through hospice-hospital partnerships. The partnership could be through a contractual relationship, a hospital-based hospice, or an informal connection with a free-standing hospice. The goal of these programs is to integrate hospice into palliative care within the hospital, to provide end-of-life care earlier in the illness, and to increase patient satisfaction in hospitals. The National Hospice and Palliative Care Organization has published a report (National Hospice and Palliative Care Organization 2001) outlining this approach. Its main points are summarized here.

Current barriers to the quality and success of this continuity of care approach include a lack of insurance coverage and lack of regulations and standards for such programs. Medicare has restrictive eligibility for hospice that creates barriers to care, including the required prognosis of death within six months and a requirement that the patient give up access to curative measures. Palliative care programs have developed ways to provide services that are palatable to such patients and families and can obtain Medicare reimbursement, but they are not necessarily holistic or delivered by a comprehensive team that includes medical, social work, and spiritual disciplines.

These innovative programs have potential for further development, though, and promise for high-quality services to clients. Approaches used may include a contract between a hospital and hospice that includes procedures for referring clients between services, a hospice liaison nurse position at the hospital, a hospice inpatient unit, an acute palliative care unit that may include hospice beds, a "comfort suite" for dying patients, inpatient and outpatient palliative care consultation services that serve the hospital, clinics, patients in the home, nursing homes, etc., independent palliative care physician practices, and palliative home care. Such a program may formally provide the community interventions recommended in this chapter, including professional education and programs targeting specialized patient populations. It can also include bioethics committees, palliative care coordinating committees, life transition counseling and case management, grief support and counseling, and provide services within a managed care project.

Goals of such programs include a coordinated continuum of palliative care that provides wider access to such care and improved quality of care for patients and families confronting life-threatening illness. A problem that remains to be resolved is the lack of health insurance coverage — current health care insurance covers acute/curative care or end-of-life care, with a gap in services for chronic illness. This lack could result in legal concerns if care is provided to those who are not seen as falling into these two categories. Finally, the same relationship and power issues may arise as we find in interdisciplinary teams. Effort is needed to develop respectful relationships and identify mutual goals and mutual recognition of experience and skills (National Hospice and Palliative Care Organization 2001). The next section reviews considerations in international social work focused on hospice care.

EMERGING GLOBAL ISSUES IN END-OF-LIFE CARE

The hospice movement, originating in England, has extended across the globe. For example, hospice leaders work to further the movement and hold regional meetings through the Asia Pacific Hospice Conference, and U.S. hospices partner with and help to financially support African hospices through the Foundation for Hospices in Sub-Saharan Africa. The AIDS pandemic and other international health concerns result in a need for quality end-of-life care. The hospice field is not as accepted in some eastern or southern countries and may not be as relevant to some cultural traditions as others.

In global efforts it is important to engage in an empowerment model for international practice, consistent with the principles of deep ecology. End-of-life care must be harmonious with the local culture; Western models should not be applied when inappropriate, but should be tailored to the beliefs and needs of the people. Leaders of that culture should be involved in the local effort. Implications of poverty must be addressed, as local governments may be unable to provide such services. Cultural considerations will be further addressed in the following chapter, on cultural competence. We now turn to general policy practice issues in the field of hospice social work.

POLICY PRACTICE

Part of the social work orientation is policy practice—working to influence public policy that affects the rights and well-being of their clients. Social workers should encourage their colleagues to pursue hospice social work credentials and work for any changes needed in organizations, programs, policies, and legislation. A wide range of policies affect hospice patients—from their very access to health care, to Medicare regulations about who can receive hospice care, to the lack of requirements for culturally competent services, to the requirements for who can provide social work services in a hospice.

HEALTH CARE REFORM

Social work input is needed in attempts to reform the provision of health care in the U.S. This includes general provisions for health care for all as well as funding for continuity of care between curative and palliative care (National Association of Social Workers, Social Work Policy Institute 2010).

CULTURALLY COMPETENT SERVICES

The most recent Conditions of Participation of the CMS included a groundbreaking, first-of-its-kind stipulation that hospices demonstrate attempts toward cultural competence in order to qualify for Medicare reimbursement. This is not enough though—hospices should be required to demonstrate cultural competence, not attempts toward it! This requires social work advocacy with CMS for a stronger regulation in this area.

QUALIFICATIONS FOR HOSPICE SOCIAL WORK

The last CMS Conditions of Participation also weakened the required qualifications for a hospice social worker. Although they still ask that hospices include a social worker on the interdisciplinary team, they no longer demand that the social worker hold a degree from an accredited school of social work, as in the past. With the new conditions of participation a "social worker" in hospice can hold a degree from a related field as long as she is supervised by an MSW.

This violates state licensing requirements for holding the title of a social worker and must be overturned. As their reason for making this change, the CMS declared there to be no strong evidence that the degree of social work makes a difference in social work outcomes in hospice. In addition, rural hospices argued that they do not have access to employees with social work degrees. This author has personally long argued with rural hospice directors that if they pay the social workers will come. They don't argue that anyone can provide nursing care, even in a rural environment; and they pay nurses a great deal more than social workers, even though nurses are bachelor's or associate degree prepared and social workers overwhelmingly have master's degrees. I am making a clarion call for social work research on this topic.

POLICY PRACTICE STRATEGIES

Ways to help effect policy change include becoming active with professional organizations in this area of practice, both state chapters and national, including the National Hospice and Palliative Care Organization, National Association of Social Workers, and Social Work in Hospice and Palliative Care Network, among others. These organizations have advocacy efforts with federal research and funding agencies as well as government bodies that social workers can help to promote.

Finally, a way to develop evidence of the need for change is through participatory action research (PAR). This author has developed a PAR model (Reese 2010) that includes eight strategies: integration with social work education, policy analysis, literature review, collaboration between practitioners and researchers, collaboration with the target population through qualitative research, quantitative study, ongoing social action efforts, and evaluation. This approach develops a partnership between social work practitioners, students, and faculty and the people to be served. Any one of these partners can initiate such a project. Students can help conduct a policy analysis and literature review, and collect and analyze data, under the supervision of faculty. Part of the data collected is through qualitative interviews with people in need, in their own words, in order to gain evidence of the urgency for policy change. At the conclusion of the project, partners can be asked for feedback on its effectiveness, providing a method for evaluation of macro practice efforts.

The evidence collected can be used for efforts toward policy change, through approaching policy makers at all levels. Evidence, as opposed to opinions, holds a lot of weight and makes a difference. An example is the citation of results from the National Hospice Social Work Survey (Reese and Raymer 2004) by the Centers for Medicare and Medicaid Services in one of their proposed Conditions of Participation, which they used to advocate for higher quality social work services in hospice.

This chapter has presented areas of importance for hospice social work intervention in organizations, communities, and the broader society. Much work remains to be done; this is what keeps our field alive, growing, and changing as the world changes. The next chapter will focus in more closely on cultural competence within the hospice organization and hospice social work efforts within the community to increase access and utilization of hospice for diverse cultural groups.

REFERENCES

Bern-Klug, M., and K. Ellis. 2004. "End-of-Life Care in Nursing Homes." In Joan Berzoff and Phyllis R. Silverman, eds., *Living with Dying: A Handbook for End-*

of-Life Healthcare Practitioners, pp. 628–641. New York: Columbia University Press.

Besthorn, F. H. 2001. "Transpersonal Psychology and Deep Ecological Philosophy: Exploring Linkages and Applications for Social Work." *Social Thought* 20, nos. 1/2: 23–44.

Besthorn, F. H., and D. P. McMillen. 2002. "The Oppression of Women and Nature: Ecofeminism as a Framework for an Expanded Ecological Social Work." *Families in Society* 83, no. 3: 221–232.

Chapin, R., T. Gordon, S. Landry, and R. Rachlin. 2007. "Hospice Use by Older Adults Knocking on the Door of the Nursing Facility: Implications for Social Work." *Journal of Social Work in End-of-Life and Palliative Care* 3, no. 2: 19–38.

Chaya, J., M. Reilly, D. Davin, M. Moriarty, V. Nero-Reid, and P. Rosenfeld. 2008. "Preparing Newly Licensed Associate Degree Nurses to Work in Home Health Care." *Home Health Care Management and Practice* 21, no. 1: 44–53.

Chibnall, J. T., S. D. Videen, P. N. Duckro, and D. K. Miller. 2002. "Psychosocial-Spiritual Correlates of Death Distress in Patients with Life-Threatening Medical Conditions." *Palliative Medicine* 16:331–338.

Crittenden, C. 2000. "Ecofeminism Meets Business: A Comparison of Ecofeminist, Corporate, and Free Market Ideologies." *Journal of Business Ethics* 24:51–63.

Doherty, J. B., and K. L. DeWeaver. 2004. "A Survey of Evaluation Practices for Hospice Social Workers." *Home Health Care Services Quarterly* 23, no. 4: 1–13.

Dyeson, T., and C. Hebert. 2004. "Discrepant Perceptions of Home Health Care Professionals Regarding Psychosocial Issues of Older Patients." *Gerontologist* 44, no. 1: 409.

Finn, W. 2002. "The Evolution of the Hospice Movement in America." *Revija za Socijalnu Politiku* 9, nos. 3–4: 271–279.

Foster, L., and L. McLellan. 2002. "Translating Psychosocial Insight Into Ethical Discussions Supportive of Families in End-of-Life Decision-Making." *Social Work in Health Care* 35, no. 3: 37–51.

Galambos, C. 1998. "Preserving End-of-Life Autonomy: The Patient Self-Determination Act and the Uniform Health Care Decisions Act." *Health and Social Work* 23, no. 4: 275–281.

Karakas, F. 2010. "Spirituality and Performance in Organizations: A Literature Review." *Journal of Business Ethics* 94, no. 1: 89–106.

Kulys, R., and M. Davis. 1986. "An Analysis of Social Services in Hospice." *Social Work* 11, no. 6: 448–454.

Lupo, C., and C. Bailey. 2011. "Corporate Structure and Community Size: Factors Affecting Occupational Community Within the Pulp and Paper Industry." *Society and Natural Resources* 24, no. 5: 425–438.

Maslow, A. 1971. *The Farther Reaches of Human Nature.* New York: McGraw-Hill.

Miller, S. C., V. Mor, N. Wu, and P. Gozalo. 2002. "Does Receipt of Hospice Care in Nursing Homes Improve the Management of Pain at the End of Life?" *Hospice Care and Nursing Home Pain Management* 50, no. 3: 507–515.

Munn, J., and S. Zimmerman. 2006. "A Good Death for Residents of Long-Term Care: Family Members Speak." *Journal of Social Work in End-of-Life and Palliative Care* 2:45–59.

National Association of Social Workers. 2011. NASW *Standards for Social Work Practice in Palliative and End-of-Life Care.* Washington, DC: NASW. Retrieved from: http://www.socialworkers.org/practice/bereavement/standards/default.asp.

——. Social Work Policy Institute. 2010. *Hospice Social Work, Linking Policy, Practice, and Research: A Report from the March 25, 2010 Symposium.* Washington, DC: NASW.

National Hospice and Palliative Care Organization. 2001. *Hospital-Hospice Partnerships in Palliative Care: Creating a Continuum of Service.* Alexandria, VA: NHPCO.

——. 2009. "NHPCO Facts and Figures: Hospice Care in America." Retrieved from www.nhpco.org/files/public/Statistics_Research/NHPCO_facts_and_figures.pdf.

——. Quality Partners. 2011. Retrieved from www. nhpco.org/i4a/pages/Index. cfm?page ID=4900.

Parker Oliver, D., and M. Peck. 2006. "Inside the Interdisciplinary Team Experiences of Hospice Social Workers." *Journal of Social Work in End-of-Life and Palliative Care* 2, no. 3: 7–21.

Raymer, M., and G. Gardia. 2011. "Enhancing Professionalism, Leadership, and Advocacy: A Call to Arms." In Terry Altilio and Shirley Otis-Green, eds., *Oxford Textbook of Palliative Social Work,* pp. 683–687. New York: Oxford University Press.

Reese, D. 2002. "Hospice Access for Latino/Latinas." Unpublished MS.

——. 2011. "Proposal for a University-Community-Hospice Partnership to Address Organizational Barriers to Cultural Competence." *American Journal of Hospice and Palliative Medicine* 28, no. 1: 22–26. ——. 2011. "Interdisciplinary Perceptions of the Social Work Role in Hospice: Building Upon the Classic Kulys and Davis Study." *Journal of Social Work in End-of-Life and Palliative Care* 7, no. 4: 383–406.

Reese, D., R. Ahern, S. Nair, J. O'Faire, and C. Warren. 1999. "Hospice Access and Utilization by African Americans: Addressing Cultural and Institutional Barriers Through Participatory Action Research." *Social Work* 44, no. 6: 549–559.

Reese, D., and S. Beckwith. 2005. "Organizational Barriers to Cultural Competence in Hospice." Paper presented at the National Hospice and Palliative Care Association, Opening Doors, Building Bridges: Access and Diversity Conference, August, St. Louis, MO.

Reese, D., and M. Raymer. 2004. "Relationships Between Social Work Services and Hospice Outcomes: Results of the National Hospice Social Work Survey." *Social Work* 49, no. 3.

Reith, M., and M. Payne. 2009. *Social Work in End-of-Life and Palliative Care*. Chicago: Lyceum.

Robbins, S. P., E. R. Canda, and P. Chatterjee. 1998. *Contemporary Human Behavior Theory: A Critical Perspective for Social Work*. Boston: Allyn and Bacon.

Sontag, M. 1996. "Hospices as Providers of Total Care in One Western State." *Hospice Journal* 11, no. 3: 71–94.

Walsh, J. P., K. Weber, and J. D. Margolis. 2003. *Social Issues and Management: Our Lost Cause Found*. Ann Arbor: University of Michigan Business School.

World Health Organization. 2003. *WHO Definition of Palliative Care*. Retrieved from http://www.who.int/cancer/palliative/definition/en/.

7

CULTURAL COMPETENCE IN HOSPICE

A large number of studies have indicated that patients from diverse cultural groups are not receiving the same quality and quantity of health care as those from the dominant culture (Haas et al. 2007). The hospice field mirrors the disparities in the health care system as a whole. Cultural differences between diverse patients and the hospice staff, who are almost entirely of the mainstream Caucasian cultural group (Reese and Beckwith 2005; Galambos 2003), act as barriers to hospice care (Bullock 2011). Although models of culturally competent hospice services have been developed (National Hospice and Palliative Care Organization, Access and Diversity Advisory Council 2007), in general hospices are not using these models (Reese and Beckwith 2005). The author's previous research discovered barriers within hospices that prevent them from providing culturally competent care. In this chapter we prefer terms such as *diverse cultural group* rather than *race*, since *race* is a social construct and not based on biological fact (Werth et al. 2002). This chapter will review the barriers to culturally competent care in hospice and the social work role in addressing these barriers.

Today the general American public is in favor of palliative care (Weiss and Lupkin 2009). For patients with a mainstream U.S. cultural heritage, maintaining a sense of control, including involvement in treatment decisions and having preferences honored about arrangements in their environment, may be a vital aspect of psychological well-being. Orientations of diverse populations, however, may differ from the mainstream population (Bullock 2011).

Traditional African American beliefs, for example, are oriented toward praying for a miracle. Beliefs in myths about hospice, along with a history of mistreatment within the health care system predominantly staffed by Caucasians, may lead African Americans to prefer curative care regardless of access to care (Gerbino and Henderson 2004; Reith and Payne 2009; Washington, Bickel-Swenson, and Stephens 2008). Spiritual beliefs about ghosts inhabiting the place of death may lead them to prefer dying in the hospital. And for Chinese clients, the family may make the treatment decisions, following the advice of their elders, rather than the individual patient. Patient self-determination is a cultural concept inherent in mainstream U.S. culture and may not be relevant to other cultural groups (Anngela-Cole, Ka'opua, and Yim 2011; Reese et al. 2010). For Latino/a people, friends and family may be the main resources when sick, rather than formal medical care, and there may be a preference for traditional medicine (Curry et al. 2000). Those among white mainstream Americans who adhere more strongly to a traditional Christian belief system also are more in favor of curative care at the end of life rather than palliative care (Reese et al. 2010). Hodge (2003) has noted a tendency on the part of social workers to discriminate against these more conservative clients; we must also keep that in mind when honoring diversity.

Early literature explained health care disparities in the hospice field by identifying differences within diverse cultures that explained patients' reluctance to opt for hospice care (Burrs 1995; Gordon 1995). Our challenge is not to change our clients' cultures, however, but to change hospice so that it is culturally relevant to the people we serve. This chapter will discuss the end-of-life beliefs of several diverse cultural groups, identifying how they contrast with hospice philosophy. This is important for hospice staff to understand in order to provide culturally sensitive care. But we will also discuss organizational barriers posed by the hospice itself as well as barriers within the health care system that must be addressed to develop culturally competent ways of serving diverse groups.

HOSPICE PHILOSOPHY AND DIVERSE CULTURAL BELIEFS—MANY DIFFERING WORLD VIEWS

This section will describe traditional beliefs relevant to death and dying among several cultural groups: African American, Chinese, and Latino(a) communities. It is beyond the scope of this book to provide a comprehensive discussion of these perspectives or of other cultural groups. It is hoped that a brief overview of differing perspectives will provide an awareness of the great diversity of worldviews.

Most cultures incorporate belief elements that may influence end-of-life care decisions (Bullock 2011; Lin 2003; Reith and Payne 2009). We may not assume that any cultural group is homogeneous, though, since there is wide variability between members in terms of income, education, employment, geographic region, and country of origin. Each individual and family within any diverse group is unique and subscribes to cultural standards to varying degrees. Cultural groups and traditional beliefs change over time, and great diversity exists within a country and even within cultural groups within that country. As media, commerce, and communication are increasingly global in scope, cultures influence each other as well as retaining some traditional differences. As social workers learn about diverse cultural beliefs, it is also important for them to prepare to ask questions rather than to assume to know a client's views. Within this diversity, however, a cultural unity may be detected that has traditionally characterized families in a certain group (Bullock 2011). In addition, nontraditional clients who have not subscribed to traditional ethnic cultural traditions may, nevertheless, fall back on traditional behavior in times of great stress such as terminal illness (Bonura et al. 2001).

TRADITIONAL AFRICAN AMERICAN BELIEFS IN END OF LIFE

Research has found that African American traditional cultural and religious beliefs contrast in some ways with hospice philosophy regarding treatment preferences (Bullock 2011; Reese et al. 2004). It should be noted, though, that, with diversity within the African American population, there are also areas of convergence with hospice philosophy.

Spirituality is a major way of coping in many populations and is very pronounced among African Americans with traditional belief systems. Although spirituality is found to reduce depression in serious illness for the general population, its effects are significantly greater among African Americans (Battle and Idler 2003). Its importance can be traced back to the experience of slavery, when African slaves were stripped of their social heritage. They were captured, shipped, and sold without any regard for family or tribal affiliation. Attempts to preserve or use native languages or

TABLE 7.1 Differences Between Traditional African American
Cultural and Religious Beliefs and Hospice Philosophy

HOSPICE PHILOSOPHY	TRADITIONAL AFRICAN AMERICAN PERSPECTIVES
Acceptance of death	God will perform a miracle
	God determines whether you live or die, not choice of care
	Opting for all available curative care to give God time
	Acceptance of death means a lack of faith
Speaking openly about terminality	Taboo about discussing death
Preparing for death	Prefer not to prepare for death
Dying at home surrounded by loved ones	Prefer not to die in the home
Accessing all palliative care	Prefer not to take strong pain medication
	Prefer access to all curative care
	Nobility of suffering

religious traditions was discouraged or prohibited. Christianity was forced on the slaves and used to justify slavery. But these new Christian religious beliefs, practices, and traditions formed a new basis of social cohesion, creating solidarity and a sense of union among strangers from a variety of African nationalities.

Slaves were not allowed to congregate without the presence of Caucasians, but an invisible institution took root. They held secret church meetings in the woods, and the church became the most important social institution in African American culture. It was a source of social stability, and the pastor, as leader of this institution, has played a significant leadership role in African American culture. Traditional African American beliefs have changed over time, especially among middle- and upper-class and northern urban African American communities. But most African Americans still consider themselves religious, seek health care advice from their pastors, and use religion as a coping strategy. The U.S. Religious Landscape Survey (Pew Research Center, Forum on Religion and Public Life 2007), found that, compared to other racial and ethnic groups, African Americans are most likely to report a formal religious affiliation:

59 percent	Historically black Protestant
15 percent	Evangelical Protestant
5 percent	Catholic
12 percent	Unaffiliated
5 percent	Other

Caucasian Americans have failed to honor and respect traditional African American beliefs; mainstream America's attitude has been characterized as condescending amusement (Frazier 1974). Clearly it is of key importance to understand and honor this aspect of African American culture in order to adequately serve these clients in hospice. Traditional African American beliefs are shown in comparison with hospice philosophy in table 7.1.

GOD WILL PERFORM A MIRACLE Reese and colleagues' (1999) participants stated that many African Americans would rather pray for a miracle than accept terminality. They further explained that acceptance of terminality, while everyone around the patient is praying for a miracle, would be seen as a lack of faith (Washington, Bickel-Swenson, and Stephens 2008). Participants believed in opting for all curative care so as to give God time to perform the miracle. They believed that God determines whether you live or die, not the choice of curative or palliative care (Hooyman and Kramer 2006; Reese et al. 1999).

These beliefs contrast with the hospice perspective of consenting to palliative care because of an acceptance of terminality. It should be noted that this perspective may be misinterpreted by hospice social workers as denial of terminality. Belief in recovery after a miracle is different from a psychological coping mechanism, when it represents a belief system. If God does not perform a miracle, the traditional African American perspective would be to accept God's will in taking the loved one to be with him in heaven. At a funeral this author attended of an African American patient, the pastor said, "We loved you, but God loved you more," explaining God's decision to take the loved one "home." The funeral was called a "homecoming celebration," and indeed had the air of a celebration. The acceptance of suffering and acceptance of God's will is discussed further in the sections to follow.

TABOO REGARDING DISCUSSING DEATH A traditional norm within African American culture is a taboo about discussion of death. This value may also partially explain Reese and colleagues' (1999) findings that participants preferred not to plan for death — i.e., legal wills, living wills, funeral plans, do not resuscitate orders, power of attorney, plans for dependents, etc., all of which are discussed with clients by hospice staff.

DYING IN THE HOSPITAL Research indicates that African Americans traditionally prefer to die in the hospital rather than at home, which is promoted by hospice philosophy in the U.S. This is consistent with the desire for access to all curative care. This is also explained by a belief among some that the ghost of the deceased will continue to inhabit the place of death (Reese et al. 1999). Another aspect may be that African Americans do not want to burden their families with end-of-life care decisions and financial hardship (Washington, Bickel-Swenson, and Stephens 2008).

ACCEPTANCE OF STRUGGLE AS PART OF LIFE What may appear to those outside the community as unnecessary suffering during the dying process might be perceived within the community as an expected part of life's continual struggle. In the African American community such personal struggle takes on an air of dignity and nobility, which resonates with broader social and political struggles to ensure equality or correct injustice. Suffering may be connected with spiritual beliefs and seen as part of religious commitment (Washington, Bickel-Swenson, and Stephens 2008). This acceptance of suffering, when it represents patience and lack of action in illness, is also consistent with the belief that God will perform a miracle if given the time. It is also the case that African Americans are ready to accept God's will even if it means dying (Werth et al. 2002). This African American perspective of patience and acceptance in sickness may be misinterpreted as apathy, fatalism, and pessimism.

The importance placed on struggle may partially explain a reluctance to take strong pain medication. Acceptance of suffering is to some extent an area of convergence with hospice philosophy; but it is not necessarily compatible with the goals of palliative care, which are to relieve physical, psychological, and spiritual suffering.

THEY NEED IT ANYWAY A logical reaction to these perspectives may be that when a patient and family do not agree with hospice philosophy and don't want palliative care they should not enroll in hospice. However, the reality may be that hospice is the best care available to terminally ill patients and families. Health insurance companies today restrict "futile care" as a waste of money, and nonhospice options may be limited to dying in a nursing home or at home with no palliative care and little professional support.

Research backs this up—interviews with family members of African American patients who died with or without hospice care found that those who received hospice care were more satisfied. Most nonhospice participants said they would prefer hospice for themselves or another loved one after learning about it through the study (Reese et al. 2004). Those without hospice had little access to pain control, or any medical care, and cared for their patient at home alone without support. Alternatively, since family members worked full time, some had to place the patient in a nursing home against their beliefs. African Americans believe in caring for their own and do not believe in nursing home placement for a loved one—but that is often or even usually the place of death in reality (Reese et al. 1999). Nonhospice patients also suffered from a lack of information provided by the health care system about the diagnosis and prognosis of the patient and experienced a lack of self-determination. Some experienced inadequate care, with a lack of psychosocial services and failures to bathe patients (Reese et al. 2004).

It is important, therefore, to design hospices services to adequately serve these patients in a way that honors their own perspectives and needs (Bullock 2011). We must avoid "tactical socialization" (Mesler 1995), in which we influence clients to conform with hospice philosophy against their wishes but find areas of convergence and develop policies that allow for transition care, continuity of care (discussed further in this chapter), and programs that address the needs of hospice patients whose family members work and cannot care for them in the home.

AREAS OF CONVERGENCE An area of convergence between traditional African American views and hospice philosophy includes the desire to be at home with family members when ill and a holistic approach to care that includes the spiritual dimension. Another area of convergence lies in the ability to accept God's will, even if it be to take the patient in death. Struggle is seen as a part of life for African Americans, a view that is reflected in traditional African American spiritual music. Consistent with this view, many within the African American community consider death to be a welcomed friend (Johnson 1992). This perspective recognizes the inevitability of death, which comes at the end of life. Those who have died may be referred to as having "gone home," a notion that views death as a transition rather than as a final state (Mbiti 1991). An African American funeral attended by this author was referred to as a "homecoming celebration." This perspective on death and its recognition through ritual can be traced back to African funeral customs.

TRADITIONAL CHINESE BELIEFS IN END OF LIFE

Evidence suggests that hospice in the U.S. is not effectively reaching Chinese American clients. Residents of China generally feel reluctant to use hospice care; the largest Hong Kong hospice was closed in 2003 because of a low utilization rate (Reese et al. 2010). The literature indicates that the Chinese hospice movement is having an influence and traditional views are changing (Chan and Pang 2007; Ming-Lin Chong and Shiu-Yeu 2009). A study with social work students in Hong Kong found that very few students affiliated with traditional Chinese religions—Buddhist, Taoist, or ancestor worship; many were Protestant and many said they had no religion (Reese et al. 2010). It was interesting to see evidence in this study of the transmission of cultures internationally—U.S. students agreed more than Hong Kong students with several traditional Chinese beliefs.

Still, traditional culture has an affect regardless of religious affiliation or colonization. Chinese people generally have not made end-of-life decisions and are not interested in receiving information about hospice (Chan and Pang 2007). Chinese students in the Hong Kong study disagreed more with hospice philosophy than U.S. students and were less likely to say that going to hospice care would be a comfort in terminal illness (Reese et al. 2010). In general, Hong Kong student beliefs reflected a traditional majority Chinese preference toward curative care.

We conclude that cultures influence each other throughout the world, and no assumptions can be made that an individual holds traditional beliefs. Nevertheless, traditional beliefs may wield a subtle influence, even in those who hold nontraditional beliefs, and color one's attitudes at the end of life. The following will outline several traditional Chinese perspectives in end-of-life.

DISCUSSION OF DEATH IS TABOO Those with traditional Chinese perspectives may avoid discussion of death (Leung and Chan 2011; Walsh-Burke 2004). Family members may subtly communicate the terminal prognosis to the patient by performing traditional rituals rather than speaking about it openly. As noted above, however, this perspective may be changing (Chan and Pang 2007).

DENIAL OF TERMINALITY The traditional preference not to acknowledge death and terminality may lead to denial (Reese et al. 2010). An early or painful death may be considered a result of past wrongdoing (Woo 1999), thus making it difficult to accept a terminal prognosis.

STRESS CONCEPTUALIZED AS DEATH When compared to Western cultures, dominant Asian conceptions of stress are more centered around death (Tan 1994).

PREFER NOT TO DIE IN THE HOME Traditional Chinese beliefs oppose dying in the home. It is thought that the spirit of the deceased may remain in the home and cause harm to the inhabitants. Contact with a bereaved family or seeing a dead body or coffin may be considered bad luck. In the cross-cultural comparison study of social work students, Chinese students were more oriented than U.S. students toward dying in a hospital (Leung and Chan 2011; Reese et al. 2010). This trend was even more pronounced when expressing preference for place of death for a family member.

END-OF-LIFE CARE DECISIONS ARE MADE BY THE ELDERS IN THE FAMILY, NOT BY THE PATIENT The comparison of social work students found that Americans were more worried about "having other people make medical decisions for you" (Reese et al. 2010) and Chinese preferred decisions to be made by the elders of the family rather than the patient (Leung and Chan 2011). Alternatively, the patient may defer to the doctor to make such decisions (Chan and Pang 2007). This requires a different perspective on patient self-determination by hospice staff. Again, some recent studies have documented some evidence of changing views; a survey of Chinese residents found that the patient was thought of as the main decision maker in decisions about euthanasia (Ming-Lin Chong and Shiu-Yeu 2009).

A Value on Stoicism and Taboos Against the Use of Strong Drugs A value on stoicism and taboos against the use of strong drugs may influence the willingness to take pain medicine. There is a general cultural avoidance of the use of painkillers (Chan and Mak 2000). A history of struggle with an illegal drug market and strong legal penalties for drug offenses may influence this perspective.

A Value on Fighting to Survive A value on fighting to survive may color end-of-life decisions (Woo 1999).

Preference for Traditional Folk Medicine Preference for traditional folk medicine could influence treatment preferences in the end of life (Leung and Chan 2011).

THEY NEED IT ANYWAY Regardless of perspectives on end-of-life decisions, Chinese patients have a need for hospice care in terminal illness. They express psychosocial and spiritual issues that can be addressed by hospice staff, including unfinished business, death anxiety, lack of control and dependency, guilt because they cannot ease the patient's suffering, anticipatory grief, and isolation after bereavement (Fielding and Chan 2000; Kong, Kwok, and So 1997; Leung and Chan 2011). Hong Kong research comparing the experience of terminally ill patients who died in palliative care and nonpalliative care units has led to conclusions that palliative care improved the patients' quality of life through less curative care and more symptom control (Tse et al. 2007).

In addition, despite existing preferences for curative care in terminal illness, this is not a realistic possibility within the health care system in either China or the U.S. (Guillemin 1992). Increasingly, neither health care system is willing to provide care considered "futile" by the patient's physician or the health insurance company. Thus, over time, it may become more common for hospice to be the service provided for those who are terminally ill. As hospice more frequently comes to be the treatment of choice, it will grow more common for hospice social workers to serve patients and family members from many different cultural groups. Thus they must be prepared to engage effectively across cultures.

AREAS OF CONVERGENCE Despite the differences between traditional Chinese cultural beliefs and U.S. hospice philosophy, areas of convergence can be found; for example, in the Confucianist belief that death is not a personal loss but a reunion with heaven and earth and one's forefathers. The Chinese belief in the responsibility of the family to care for the patient, and the value placed on the sick and elderly, could be areas of convergence, but the family may feel responsible to prolong life because of these beliefs (Chan et al. 2008; Leung and Chan 2011).

Traditional values about acceptance of suffering and the realities of life, being able to learn nonattachment to the things of this world, a view of death as release from suffering (Woo 1999), and belief in reincarnation may also be consistent with acceptance of death. Discussing these perspectives might be a helpful focus, then, for public information efforts.

TRADITIONAL LATINO/A BELIEFS IN END OF LIFE

The language barrier has been noted in studies as the most difficult hurdle to overcome for Latino/a people (del Rio 2010). Most Latino/as who have come to the United States do so for better work opportunities, and often in these work settings it is not necessary to speak English. Speaking a language other than English is a major barrier to care (Contro et al. 2010). Entering into a medical situation where there is no one who can understand their explanation of symptoms and relate medical findings back to them causes additional lack of trust (Talavera, Elder, and Velasquez 1997). Frequently the only interpreter available is a family member, often a child (Kemp 2001). This results in invasion of privacy and embarrassment for the patient (Burgos-Ocasio 1996); medical care is often avoided by Latino/as due to this language barrier.

In addition, Latino/a people with traditional views may share some cultural beliefs that act as barriers to hospice utilization. Even though the term Latino/a covers many different cultural origins, there is a common thread of cultural beliefs shared by the majority. Some of these traditional beliefs will be discussed in the following.

FAMILISM Rather than formal medical care, friends and family are the main resources for Latino/a people during illness (del Rio 2010). Values involving familism keep some from choosing to participate in the health care system at all (Curry et al. 2000). Familism is a cultural value that involves an individual's strong identification with and attachment to a nuclear family as well as strong feelings of loyalty and solidarity among members of the same family. The decision-making process is based on the opinions of everyone in the family (Bullock 2011; del Rio 2010), often including theextended family: aunts, uncles, and cousins (Kemp 2001).

This value requires a different approach for hospice staff oriented toward patient self-determination.

PREFERENCE FOR TRADITIONAL MEDICINE Latino/a people may be more likely to seek out medical care that is traditional in their culture of origin because it seems more familiar (Kemp 2001). In addition, undocumented residents may not have access to local care at all. They may look for traditional healers or return temporarily to their country of origin for medical care.

FATALISM Due to strong religious convictions, Latino/as may feel that their fate is completely in God's hands, and that they cannot do anything to alter the outcome. This outlook could prevent Hispanics from seeking additional help when in crisis because they may feel that God will orchestrate the outcome and not allow them to suffer (Talavera, Elder, and Velasquez 1997).

STOICISM Many Latino/as do not want to trouble others with their pain and will therefore be less likely to show it (Gordon 1995). This has a result similar to fatalism—it is an accepting attitude that appears to the dominant U.S. culture as general passivity. Many U.S. medical practitioners have misinterpreted this to be a lack of caring or a naïveté about medical practices.

RESPECT Respect is important in the Hispanic family hierarchy and community relations (del Rio 2010). Typically, the father is the breadwinner and the mother is the keeper of the home and the one to pass on culture to the children. Cultural tradition requires that in addressing the family the head of the household be addressed first. A formal way of addressing the father, using Mr. instead of the first name, is an important way to demonstrate respect, and Latino/a clients may lose trust in hospice staff who fail to follow this custom (Talavera, Elder, and Velasquez 1997). This is a challenge for those with feminist perspectives and a controversial point. Some argue that human rights, such as equality for women, transcend cultural values (Reichert 2007). Social workers are committed to advocacy for the rights of the vulnerable. Perhaps there is a way to honor the principle of equality and respect for women while nevertheless following custom in addressing the males of the family.

In addition, Latino/a culture provides a special place and deference for other authority figures within the community such as spiritual leaders and physicians. This should not be inaccurately interpreted as passivity (Kemp 2001; Talavera, Elder, and Velasquez 1997).

THEY NEED IT ANYWAY Latino/a beliefs are not in opposition to hospice philosophy to the extent that African American and Chinese beliefs may be. There are some barriers that may keep them away from hospice, but many areas of convergence exist. Clearly, they do need hospice, for the same reason as anyone else does. It is the best form of care available in terminal illness.

AREAS OF CONVERGENCE Areas of convergence with hospice philosophy for Latino/a people may be an emphasis on symptom control, being with family and friends, and enjoying the time left as much as possible. Many have a preference for dying at home as well as desiring the presence of a spiritual adviser (Curry et al. 2000). Familism is very compatible with hospice philosophy, which encourages familial caretakers and involvement with the patient, as long as clients can accept strangers coming into the home. In a participatory action research study in one Southeastern community, Latino/a residents were asked, "What should hospice do to increase access to hospice for Latino/a people?" The response was, "Make friends with us" (Curry et al. 2000). This is a reminder that hospice needs to create a connection with diverse communities long before the end of life. A stranger from another culture, showing up at one's door when one is near death, is much less likely to be accepted than someone who has been there all along—who has connected with the community, made friends with them, and presents a caring service with which they are familiar.

We have looked at three traditional cultural perspectives; many more exist and we have just touched the surface of each. Although barriers exist that are based on differences between hospice philosophy and cultural and religious beliefs, areas of convergence can be seen in each case. Interestingly, all three cultures have similarities in the ability to accept suffering and the realities of life and death. African American and Latino/a perspectives are based in a Christian trust in God's will; traditional Chinese perspectives are based on Buddhism, which does not rely on a deity but on nonattachment and the ability to experience without judgment what is occurring in the moment. The outcome of all, though based on different worldviews, is an ability to accept death. As hospice social workers, we can work with that and find a way to provide culturally competent hospice care to those with differing worldviews. The next section will discuss institutional barriers—barriers within the hospice organization itself.

BARRIERS WITHIN THE HOSPICE ITSELF

I became involved in my first participatory action research study, without planning to, when I was invited by African American ministers during a Saturday presentation to appear on a radio show and speak in a church the next day. By Sunday I had gained the support of the African American community, with one elderly woman telling me after my church presentation, "I will help you any way I can." On Monday I thought I had better alert the two community hospices that I had been involved in a public recruitment effort over the weekend. When I called one of the hospice directors, though, she said, "I'm not sending my nurses to those people's houses."

This quote has had a stunning effect on my presentations ever since and serves as an introduction here to the fact that hospices themselves present barriers to hospice access for diverse populations. In the first section of this chapter we discussed cultural beliefs that may make diverse clients hesitant to accept hospice. Early literature focused mainly on these differences and on an effort to "educate" other cultural groups about hospice philosophy. In this section we will discuss organizational barriers to hospice access that need to be addressed within the hospice itself.

MAJOR ORGANIZATIONAL BARRIERS TO CULTURAL COMPETENCE IN HOSPICE

Organizational cultural competence in health care describes the ability of systems to provide care to patients with diverse values, beliefs, and behaviors, including tailoring delivery to meet patients' social, cultural, and linguistic needs (Hooyman and Kramer 2006). A number of models for developing culturally competent services have been developed (Ahmann 2002; Alexander 2002; del Rio 2004; Dhooper 2003). Models of organizational cultural competence include maximizing diversity of staff, providing cultural competence training, conducting community needs assessments and outreach, cultivating partnerships with diverse community leaders and inviting them to serve on the hospice board, developing mechanisms for community and patient feedback, implementing systems for patient preference data collection, constructing quality measures for diverse patient populations, and ensuring culturally and linguistically appropriate health education materials and health promotion and disease prevention interventions (del Rio 2004).

Capitman and colleagues' assessment handbook guides the exploration of six domains: mission; governance and administration; personnel practices and staffing patterns; service offerings and caregiving approaches; targeting; marketing and outreach (Capitman et al. 1991). Mendez-Russel, Widerson, and Tolbert (1994) developed *Exploring Differences in the Workplace*, which is used by organizations to assess their own cultural competency in four areas: knowledge, understanding, acceptance, and behavior. Brach and Fraser (2000) have identified components of organizational competency in health care organizations including interpreter services, appropriate recruitment and retention, training, coordinating with traditional healers, use of community health workers, culturally competent health promotion (including family and community members), immersion into another culture, and administration and organizational accommodations. Finally, the National Hospice and Palliative Care Organization developed the *Inclusion and Access Toolbox* in 2007, which includes the *Self-Assessment Checklist for Personnel Providing Primary Health Care Services*. The *Toolbox* can be obtained from the NHPCO—it is very helpful in assessing and developing cultural competence in hospice.

A national mixed methods study (Reese and Beckwith 2005) identified major organizational barriers to cultural competence in the opinion of hospice directors. Items in the questionnaire were formulated from this author's existing research. Results of the study indicated that hospice staff, volunteers, and patients were almost entirely Caucasian. Organizational barriers viewed as most problematic by hospice directors (n = 207) included 1. lack of funding for additional staff for community outreach, 2. lack of applications from diverse applicants, 3. lack of funding for additional staff for development of culturally competent services, 4. lack of knowledge about diverse cultures, and 5. lack of awareness of which cultural groups are not being served.

Qualitative results enriched our understanding of these relationships. Elements of an organizational culture that create barriers to access do not count cultural competence as a priority, rather the funding priority is on direct patient care. Staff members in such a culture do not believe that awareness of cultural differences is important, are uncomfortable with diversity, and stereotype diverse individuals.

Qualitative results also identified problems that occur when there is no funding for community outreach—lack of a relationship with diverse communities, lack of referrals of diverse patients, lack of awareness of what cultural groups are not being served, and a lack of applications from diverse and bilingual professionals. In addition, diverse individuals in communities served by these hospices do not understand hospice services.

Results showed that hospices without funding for culturally competent services are characterized by a lack of culturally appropriate materials, a lack of interpreters, and a lack of services to patients with no health insurance. Hospices that have a lack of funding for cultural competence training have a lack of knowledge about diverse cultures, a lack of awareness of organizational barriers, and a lack of knowledge about how to access resources for culturally competent care (Reese and Beckwith 2005). When I mentioned the phrase "lack of funding" at our presentation, an expert in the audience raised her hand and asked, "Lack of *funding* or lack of *budgeting* for culturally competent care?" There is a difference—the budget reflects the priorities of the organization.

Recent research has discovered that those African Americans who do receive end-of-life care have reported lower satisfaction than Caucasians with the care provided (Welch, Teno, and Mor 2005). We will further discuss these hospice organizational barriers to cultural competence below.

LACK OF FUNDING FOR ADDITIONAL STAFF FOR COMMUNITY OUTREACH Hospice organizations have been criticized for ineffectual or nonexistent efforts at outreach to diverse communities (del Rio 2004; Werth et al. 2002). Hospices are generally located in the wealthier areas of town (Haas et al. 2007), and a reluctance to send staff to poorer areas is not uncommon. An e-mail message on a popular listserv addressed this issue, asking whether colleagues had a "no night call" policy for certain patients and whether that would be considered discriminatory. As noted earlier, Latino/a participants' main response when asked what hospice should do to increase access was, "Make friends with us." It is a little difficult to make friends or to do community outreach if policies deliberately reduce home visits to oppressed populations.

Barriers for African Americans include a fear of white strangers coming into the home (Reese et al. 2004). It is clear that, for African Americans, having a white person show up at your door, for the first time, when you are dying, and recommending that you sign a do not resuscitate order, is not going to work.

Along with the general U.S. population, African Americans are broadly unaware of hospice services (Reith and Payne 2009; Washington, Bickel-Swenson, and Stephens 2008). African American pastors, on whom many people rely for advice if a family member is dying, are unaware of hospice (Reese et al. 1999). Because of the strong influence of the church, the role of the clergy and their degree of awareness of palliative care options similarly affects end-of-life care in the African American community.

Much misinformation abounds within the African American community, including a fear that the hospice staff will kill the patients "with all that medicine" or by denying food and water. There is a misconception that hospice care is the same as assisted suicide and confusion with the nursing home experience of losing one's property to pay the bill (Reese et al. 2011).

Another concern of African American people may be that the hospice is in competition with African American pastors for leadership and guidance at the end of life. Community outreach strategies will be discussed in the following section.

Intervention Techniques for Community Outreach The overall theme for community outreach is "make friends with us," including through socialization at diverse community events. Referrals will come in through word of mouth recommendations from friends and family members of patients well served. There is a strong need for empowerment, including treating clients with respect and reassuring them that the hospice staff will not come in and take over the patient's home and care. It is helpful in public information sessions to address these fears of the health care system and misconceptions and myths about hospice care. In addition, it is helpful to focus on areas of convergence between hospice philosophy and the community cultural beliefs. For example, most diverse cultural groups have a strong sense of family connection and support, and a sense of responsibility to care for loved ones. This is consistent with the home hospice approach of caring for the patient in the home. Also, African American people often agree with many aspects of hospice philosophy, an area of convergence between traditional African American religious beliefs and hospice philosophy includes an acceptance of terminality based on God's will. Latino(a) people have also agreed with aspects of hospice philosophy, such as symptom control, honoring the wishes of the patient, being with family and friends until the time of death, enjoying the time left as much as possible, dying in the home, and incorporating spiritual care into the treatment plan.

Community outreach efforts can be made at places where community members naturally go, such as their churches or multicultural service centers. It is important to collaborate with leaders in the community, notably spiritual leaders such as African American ministers, incorporating them into the staff and board of directors of the hospice and asking them to present hospice in a way that is consistent with the religious beliefs of the people. It will also be important in outreach to the Latino/a community to use materials in Spanish at all levels of literacy. It is most effective to arrange for members of the cultural group to be the ones to provide the information, including former caregivers and pastors. Television commercials are considered effective by African Americans (Reese et al. 2004).

Important information to stress includes an explanation of hospice philosophy: that hospice does not hasten death and that the doctor provides care to relieve suffering. Concerns about cost should be addressed, explaining the benefits available through hospice, whether the hospice will provide care for those without insurance, and that medication and all needed equipment is provided along with services in the home. Community members should be reassured that the hospice staff will really be there when they are needed and that family members can still care for the patient while in hospice.

The hospice should address the concern of competition with local leaders by developing a partnership with them. Many of these leaders in both the Hispanic and African American communities are priests and pastors. The NHPCO (2007) recommends working to establish relationships built on trust and including diverse community leaders in planning for services. Partnering with them includes inviting them to serve on the hospice board of directors and in decision-making positions in the organization (Talamantes, Lawler, and Espino 1995). These positions should be salaried. In one community project the hospice invited African American ministers to volunteer as members of the team. The ministers were offended by this, though, confronting them with the fact that the local hospital had never hired an African American chaplain. They could not understand why such a position would be on a volunteer basis (Reese et al. 1999). This is an example of the many subtle differences that will come as a surprise but that can be navigated when a trusting relationship has been established. When such a partnership is developed, it will pave the way for hiring diverse staff and attracting diverse patients (Reese et al. 2011; Reese et al. 2004).

LACK OF APPLICATIONS FROM DIVERSE APPLICANTS Community outreach is necessary to attract diverse applicants (Reese and Beckwith 2005). Current hospice utilization is predominantly by Protestant Caucasians and is staffed by persons with a similar background. African Americans who cared for a terminally ill patient, with or without hospice care, shared with us openly intimate reasons for the importance of diverse staff within hospice having to do with the history of African American marginalization in society. Participants expressed a sense of shame in asking white authorities for help. Difficult experiences with Caucasian-led programs left them with an expectation that white professionals would disrespect one's beliefs and an unwillingness to participate in government programs. African American people have responded to a lack of care by society with an ethic of "taking care of our own." The church has played a major role in caring for the African American people and keeping them safe. Participants expressed a fear of actual harm by health care staff. Participants believed, based on past experience with the health care system, that if you complain about the services the patient will be punished (Reese et al. 2004). Given these negative experiences and the resulting fear of the white health care system, it is understandable that a diverse staff would seem more approachable and safe to clients from oppressed minority groups.

In addition, hospice staff needs to be more religiously diverse and have training in spiritually sensitive work with religiously diverse clients. A largely Protestant staff may experience challenges working competently with Jewish and Catholic clients, for example, who may have views that differ in ways from hospice philosophy and Protestant perspectives. Jewish hospice organizations have been created to address this need; it seems consistent with social work values, though, to develop a diverse staff that is prepared to adequately serve religiously diverse clients.

A recent national study of 207 hospices found that 94 percent of staff and 96 percent of volunteers were Caucasian and non-Latino/a. Only 2 percent of the staff and 1 percent of volunteers (and 4 percent of the patients) were African American and even fewer were Latino/a (Reese and Beckwith 2005). Changing these statistics is not easy—diverse applicants may not be equally considered in the hiring process and when hired may feel unwelcome and uncomfortable in the all-white/non-Latino/a agency and resign fairly quickly. A study of African American social work students (McGaughey 2006) found that the students had no desire to practice in the hospice social work field for the same reasons that African American community members are unreceptive to receiving hospice services.

Strategies for Recruiting Diverse Applicants A social work student field placement may be helpful in recruiting staff, as students can be hired after graduation. This strategy would be particularly successful if scholarship assistance was included (Kepner 2009). A project including such a field placement will be described later in this chapter.

During the field placement, and after staff are successfully hired as well, it will be necessary to show them the support needed to keep them in the hospice. An example from this author's practice experience is a Caucasian client who complained about having an African American staff member sent to his home. The hospice responded that if he wanted hospice services he would accept whomever they sent. The patient went through a transformation during his experience with this African American staff person, who was able to remain compassionate toward him. In his last days he saw her as an angel of mercy, there at his time of greatest need.

LACK OF FUNDING FOR ADDITIONAL STAFF FOR DEVELOPMENT OF CULTURALLY COMPETENT SERVICES Lack of funding for culturally competent services results in a dearth of culturally and linguistically appropriate materials and interpreters (Reese and Beckwith 2005). This adds to the major barrier for Latino/a clients, that of language (del Rio 2010).

Interventions for Increasing Culturally Competent Services As mentioned previously in this chapter, an expert audience member in a presentation by this author made the distinction between lack of funding and lack of budgeting for culturally competent services. An idea to address the understaffing can be addressed, nevertheless, by providing culturally competent services through a social work student field placement. A model field placement program will be discussed further on in this chapter. Cultural competence training provided by social work students in this program (Reese et al. 2011) and another (Curry et al. 2000) produced significant differences in cultural competence scores of hospice staff. At the post-test in both projects, staff members reported higher levels of concern about the problem, lower assessment of success by programs in meeting needs, and greater interest in cultural diversity training and community outreach.

LACK OF KNOWLEDGE ABOUT DIVERSE CULTURES Hispanics have felt alienated from hospice due to providers' lack of understanding about their culture (Contro et al. 2010). Sue and Sue (1999) have argued that underutilization of services is often related to culturally insensitive and inappropriate formalized services to culturally diverse groups and that lack of cultural competence on the part of health care professionals may also serve to further oppress culturally diverse clients that have already faced biased behavior within the larger society.

Addressing Lack of Knowledge Cultural competence training should be required at least once a year for all staff and volunteers.

LACK OF AWARENESS OF WHICH CULTURAL GROUPS ARE NOT BEING SERVED Some hospice directors in a study in one Southeastern state claimed that there was no need for their staff to be culturally competent, since their communities were not diverse (Reese, Melton, and Ciaravino 2004). This reflects a failure to assess the population being served and come to an understanding of the needs of the community. Few communities have no diversity at all, especially when considering the surrounding rural areas. Some rural African Americans have never in their lives come into town to seek medical help, feeling safer to rely on their own families for support in illness. In the rare case that a community actually has no racial or ethnic diversity, there is still the presence of religious diversity as well as gay, lesbian, bisexual, and perhaps transgendered individuals. There is always a necessity for staff to be trained in cultural competence in order to be prepared to serve all clients with sensitivity and awareness.

Addressing Lack of Awareness of Which Cultural Groups Are Not Being Served A needs assessment should be conducted annually to compare U.S. Census Bureau reports of the diverse cultural groups within the catchment area of the hospice with 1. the percentage of patients served from each cultural group and 2. the percentage of staff and volunteers from each cultural group.

AN ORGANIZATIONAL CULTURE THAT CREATES BARRIERS This term describes an organization that is in denial of racism, discrimination, and oppression — or worse, one that actually promotes it. Cultural competence is not considered important and is not a priority. Staff members are uncomfortable with diversity, stereotype diverse cultural groups, serve their own kind, and hire their own kind.

White racial identity development theory (Helms 1995) can shed some light on this problem. Whites are in a process of development as far as ownership of privilege and responsibility for oppression. As they develop through stages of racial consciousness, they develop an understanding that their racial group membership influences psychological, emotional, and physical functions relevant to race—referring to what they think, what they feel, and what their behaviors are in terms of race (Pack-Brown 1999). As an individual becomes more developed, she will become consciously aware of her own stereotypes and socialization into racist attitudes (del Rio 2004). With this awareness the individual can then confront these attitudes and begin to change them. In lower levels of racial identity development, individuals from the dominant culture do not even acknowledge the oppression that other cultural groups experience.

Some authors point out that the general Caucasian culture in the U.S. does not acknowledge the obvious prejudice and discrimination that go on all around us (Morin 2001). Despite tangible evidence of continuing disparities, European Americans often discount individual and institutional racism. Ignoring the structural dimensions of racial advantage and disadvantage, many believe that racial inequality has little to do with racism, but more to do with bad individual choices and inappropriate cultural values (Conley 1999). European Americans continue to express support for negative stereotypes of minority groups even though few would identify themselves as bigoted or racist.

This may explain the tendency of the health care disparities literature to identify cultural differences within the African American population as barriers to utilization of health care services, the focus on public "education" for this population to orient them to hospice philosophy, and the contrasting lack of information about barriers inherent within the health care provider organization itself and recommendations for hospice policy change.

Addressing the Organizational Culture The way to address this is again through cultural competence training. In addition, as diverse community leaders are included within the hospice board of directors and administration of the hospice, the culture will naturally begin to change.

The next sections discuss the role of the hospice director in achieving hospice cultural competence, approaches to hospice self-assessment for cultural competence, and a model for addressing organizational barriers involving a social work student field placement.

ROLE OF THE HOSPICE DIRECTOR

A mixed methods study of hospices (n = 22) in one southeastern state by this author and colleagues (Reese, Melton, and Ciaravino 2004) found the role of the hospice director to be of key importance in increasing the percentage of culturally diverse patients served by the hospice. The directors' knowledge of disparities in access and utilization predicted the diversity of the volunteers in their programs, which in turn predicted the diversity of their patient populations. The results of this study demonstrated that directors should provide leadership in welcoming diversity.

HOSPICE SELF-ASSESSMENT

Hospices should periodically conduct self-assessment to develop awareness of strengths and areas for growth in the cultural competence of their staff and organization. An excellent resource is the Self-Assessment Checklist for Personnel Providing Primary Health Care Services. This is provided in the *Inclusion and Access Toolbox* (National Hospice and Palliative Care Organization 2007) available from NHPCO.

A SOCIAL WORK STUDENT FIELD PLACEMENT PROJECT TO ADDRESS ORGANIZATIONAL BARRIERS

The author and colleagues developed, implemented, and evaluated a social work field placement project to address the organizational barriers to hospice cultural competence (Reese et al. 2011). The major barriers and student interventions to address them are outlined in table 7.2. These interventions will be discussed in the sections that follow.

LACK OF FUNDING FOR CULTURALLY COMPETENT SERVICES Students in a field placement can provide services at no cost to the hospice other than supervision. They can provide important elements of culturally competent services such as cultural competence training for the staff, community outreach activities, and direct services to African American clients. Part of their work can also be to seek additional funding resources for the hospice, including free cultural competence training.

LACK OF APPLICATIONS FROM AFRICAN AMERICAN APPLICANTS
African American students can specifically be recruited for the hospice field placement, along with other cultural groups. Hopefully some of the African American students can be hired in a hospice after graduation.

TABLE 7.2 Major Organizational Barriers to Cultural Competence in Hospice and Ways to Address Them Through a Social Work Student Field Placement

BARRIER	STUDENT INTERVENTIONS
Lack of funding for culturally competent services	Provide services at no cost to the hospice other than supervision. Seek additional funding resources for the hospice, the hospice, provide community outreach activities, and provide social work services to African American clients.
Lack of applications from African American	It is likely that some of the students will obtain employment in a hospice after graduation. Some of the students will be African American applicants and thus will increase the diversity of the staff of the hospice by which they are employed.
An organizational culture that creates barriers to access	Provide some cultural competence training and facilitate staff access to additional free NHPCO training. Conduct a policy analysis and make recommendations for culturally sensitive hospice policies.
A lack of awareness of which cultural groups are not being served	Conduct a needs assessment of the community to identify the groups not being served by hospice.

AN ORGANIZATIONAL CULTURE THAT CREATES BARRIERS TO ACCESS Along with cultural competence training, students can conduct a policy analysis and make recommendations for culturally competent hospice policies.

A LACK OF AWARENESS OF WHICH CULTURAL GROUPS ARE NOT BEING SERVED Students can conduct a needs assessment of the community to identify groups not being served by the hospice.

EVALUATION OF THE PROJECT Analysis revealed significant differences (p < .05) between pretests and post-tests in organizational barriers, staff cultural competence, and knowledge and attitudes toward hospice of community members. Qualitative results documented successes as well as lessons learned through the project. In addition, the number of African American patients and volunteers increased in the hospice from the beginning of the project to the end.

The project provided evidence that a social work student field placement can address organizational barriers to culturally competent services in hospice. This is a practical strategy that could improve practice in the field, including in rural areas, and assist hospices in compliance with the new CMS requirement to demonstrate attempts toward cultural competence. This study is limited by its small sample and intervention in just one hospice; further research is needed to document the role of social workers in development of cultural competence in hospice.

This section has focused on barriers to cultural competence within the hospice itself and some approaches to addressing these barriers. The next section will discuss barriers within the broader health care system.

BARRIERS WITHIN THE HEALTH CARE SYSTEM

Hospice began as a grassroots social movement to address inadequacies within the health care system. It has been successful in changing the face of end-of-life care and reorienting the majority of Americans toward palliative care. It unfortunately still reflects many of the shortcomings of U.S. health care, as discussed. Additional general barriers exist within the health care system as a whole that affect access to hospice care for diverse cultural groups. The Institute of Medicine (1999) recommendations for reducing racial and ethnic disparities in health care include increasing awareness about disparities among the general public, health care providers, insurance companies, and policy makers. Additional recommendations will be discussed in the following sections.

FEAR OF THE WHITE HEALTH CARE SYSTEM

General racism in our society results in fearfulness of oppressed patients to seek health care from Caucasian-staffed health care providers. The more disturbing fact is that oppressed groups relate a history of negative health care experiences based on their own experience or stories they have heard about oppression, which may lead them to avoid health care in general and hospice specifically (Reese et al. 2004; Washington, Bickel-Swenson, and Stephens 2008).

The African American community is aware of the infamous Tuskegee study in which African American men with syphilis were observed through the course of their illness without being offered treatment and afraid of "ending up being a guinea pig in one of their experiments" (Reese et al. 1999). The Tuskegee incident was one in a history of medical experiments performed both on African American slaves and citizens in the southern United States in the early twentieth century (Kepner 2009; Werth et al. 2002).

In addition, African American family members of terminally ill patients related in qualitative interviews a personal history of negative health care experiences including inadequate care and racism (Reese et al. 2004). They expressed a suspicion of doctors, feeling that doctors were not doing enough to save the patient's life. Nonhospice clients particularly expressed dissatisfaction at communication with doctors and nurses, feeling intimidated, saying that doctors and nurses don't talk to them or look at them. They explained this lack of communication as a result of racism. They expressed a need for empowerment, that doctors should seek their input about the condition of the patient.

Participants stated that many African Americans have never gone to a doctor for these reasons. Many African Americans would rather care for themselves at home with traditional alternative remedies or pray for a miracle than seek health care from the health care system. They have described a preference for life-sustaining treatment (chemotherapy, resuscitation, life support, artificial nutrition, and hydration) as opposed to the palliative care that is received in hospice.

African Americans have developed the value of "taking care of our own" in response to the lack of care provided by the health care system—a cultural value that one's own people—church and family—should provide care in terminal illness rather than strangers. They may especially be hesitant to allow strangers of the dominant cultural group into their homes, fearing that they will take charge of the care of the patient rather than honor the traditional value of taking care of one's own. Home visits may be experienced as an intrusion and violation of privacy for these reasons (Reese et al. 2004). Lack of diversity among health care staff is cited as part of this problem (Reese et al. 1999; Washington, Bickel-Swenson, and Stephens 2008). Similar fears are also expressed by Latino/a residents (Contro et al. 2010).

ADDRESSING FEARS OF THE WHITE HEALTH CARE SYSTEM Key strategies in addressing these fears include increasing the diversity of health care staff, requiring culture competence training, and ending discriminatory practices. Cultural groups that experience discrimination within the U.S. are underrepresented among health care professionals, and their numbers have been declining further since erosion of affirmative action practices during the George W. Bush presidency. Efforts to increase these numbers, and to specifically increase awareness of diverse physicians, could have important effects on referrals and utilization of hospice. Such physicians have an understanding of diverse patient perspectives and can address fears and myths about hospice (Komaromy et al. 1996). In addition, diverse patients who seek medical attention are more likely to seek it from diverse physicians, so the impact of these physicians' knowledge will affect end-of-life care in these patients' communities. The ideal would be to attract and train diverse physicians for practice specifically in end-of-life care. Another important point in increasing diversity of staff is the importance of hiring bilingual staff. Interpreters for a variety of languages should be available in clinics and hospitals to overcome language barriers that may affect the quality of care.

Negative biases, whether conscious or unconscious, exist within physicians and other health care staff as they do within all members of the dominant cultural group. This issue needs to be addressed through required cultural competence training. Another point to include in professional education is addressing fears of the health care system. A trusted doctor's personal recommendation for hospice staff, empowerment of a caregiver with the promise that hospice staff would not do anything without her permission, and personally bringing the hospice staff to the patient's home to introduce them was key in one African American caregiver's decision to opt for hospice (Reese et al. 2004). These actions on the part of a physician sound unbelievable in the current profit-oriented health care environment. Still, we must make efforts to retain and promote this type of dedication to excellence in patient care.

There are also indications that African American patients are specifically not advised of their prognosis or options and are disproportionately referred to high-deficiency nursing homes (Grabowski 2004; Reese et al. 2004). This is especially a concern since African American people generally do not believe in nursing home care; it conflicts with the value of "caring for our own." Efforts must be made to identify and eliminate these discriminatory practices by physicians themselves and by health care administrators.

LACK OF HEALTH INSURANCE

The United States stands alone among developed countries in its failure to provide health care for all its citizens. The only exception is South Africa, which has a similar history of racism. Due to their lack of health insurance coverage and lack of awareness that many hospices provide care free of charge, many African Americans believe they cannot afford hospice (Washington, Bickel-Swenson, and Stephens 2008). The reality remains that many hospices are for-profit and refer patients who do not have insurance coverage elsewhere. Barriers created by a lack of insurance have been documented for Latino/a people as well (Contro et al. 2010), with undocumented residents having limited resources for care.

ADDRESSING LACK OF HEALTH INSURANCE Don Schumacher, president and CEO of the National Hospice and Palliative Care Organization (2003), argues for economic resources that free programs from overreliance on government funding that limits care to a certain model that may be inappropriate for diverse cultural groups. The general lack of access of the American people to health care will need to be addressed in the near future through major health care financing reform. As our population ages, there will be no choice but to provide care, and this has major implications for the provision of end-of-life care and hospice.

LACK OF REFERRALS

Most hospice referrals are made by physicians, and hospice access is limited in general by the failure of physicians to refer their terminally ill patients. As previously mentioned, this is especially true for African American patients, who are disproportionately referred to nursing homes (Grabowski 2004; Reese et al. 2004). There may be a number of reasons for the failure to refer African Americans to hospice. One may be African American hesitancy to accept hospice and the lack of culturally competent hospice programs to address this hesitancy. Another may be the continuing lack of physician knowledge about hospice and perhaps lack of minority physician orientation toward hospice (Burrs 1995).

Another factor is employed family members who cannot care for the patient in the home, making a home hospice program unrealistic (Reese et al. 2004). Other barriers include the lack of health insurance on the part of oppressed minorities and a failure of physicians to inform the patient of the terminal prognosis (Reese et al. 2004).

Another issue is that African Americans, for a number of reasons, have a lack of access to regular physicians for a number of reasons including preference for emergency room care over a regular physician regardless of other demographic factors such as income or insurance coverage (Reese et al. 2004). Medicare regulations require certification of terminality by a physician. In this author's practice experience, emergency room physicians are not oriented toward palliative care—they spend their days attempting to save lives. Also lacking a comprehensive medical record on an emergency room patient to provide information on terminality, it would be unlikely for an emergency room physician to refer an African American to hospice (Kepner 2009).

ADDRESSING LACK OF REFERRALS There is still a relative scarcity of physicians trained to deliver culturally competent end-of-life care (Reese et al. 2004); efforts to educate physicans about end-of-life care options must continue. African Americans may be more likely to seek out minority physicians if they engage in the health care system at all; thus education of minority physicians about hospice is especially important. In addition, a variety of health care professionals are key in referring diverse patients to hospice—so it is important for this training to be provided to all (Reese et al. 2004). A point to address in this professional education includes the patient's right to informed consent. A patient is unable to provide "informed" consent unless he has been provided with all information about his condition, including the prognosis. Social workers should advocate for providing complete and accurate information to clients and should ensure that clients have received information about and understood all treatment options (Washington, Bickel-Swenson, and Stephens 2008). Another strategy to increase appropriate referrals (Institute of Medicine 1999) is the use of "evidence-based" guidelines to help providers and health plans make decisions about which procedures to order or pay for based on the best available science.

CENTERS FOR MEDICARE AND MEDICAID SERVICES REGULATIONS

CULTURAL COMPETENCE TRAINING Centers for Medicare and Medicaid Services has recently added a requirement that hospices demonstrate efforts toward cultural competence. This is not enough—hospices should be required to demonstrate not just efforts, but mastery of cultural competence (Kepner 2009).

ASSUMPTION THAT THE PATIENT HAS A STAY-AT-HOME CAREGIVER Hospice in the U.S. is oriented toward home hospice care, which assumes that the patient will have a primary caregiver who can provide care in the home. Constraints in the Medicare Hospice Benefit program mandating in-home care particularly affect African American patients where family members work full-time and cannot provide care in the home (Reese et al. 2004). This reality implies an increased need for inpatient hospices, day hospices, or benefits to provide caregivers in the home.

CONTINUUM OF CARE Recommendations for a continuum of care have been made by NHPCO and leaders in the field (Jennings et al. 2003) and are discussed in chapter 1. They focus on the integration of hospice and palliative care, and would better meet patient needs and increase access and utilization for all, but particularly address the needs of diverse populations. The Harlem Palliative Care Network is an example of a community-based, collaborative effort between the Memorial Sloan-Kettering Cancer Center, North General Hospital, a community hospital in Harlem, and the Visiting Nurse Service of New York. The HPCN is also comprised of a large network of Harlem doctors, pharmacies, churches, and community organizations. This project provides culturally competent, holistic care, including preventive, curative, palliative, and end-of-life care to African Americans and other diverse populations that have historically had difficulty accessing medical services. Such community-based interventions, ones that have their origins *within* the community and reflect these larger concerns, are more likely to flourish. An objective is to enhance the quality of health care services through a continuum of care.

UNDOCUMENTED RESIDENTS AND ACCESS TO HEALTH CARE Finally, undocumented immigration status may affect a patient's ability to receive health care (Kemp 2001). Immigration reform policy must address this need.

ATTEMPTS TO ADDRESS HEALTH CARE SYSTEM BARRIERS

A number of attempts have been made by professional organizations and government agencies to address cultural competence and access to hospice by diverse communities. Some of these efforts will be outlined in the following section.

NATIONAL HOSPICE AND PALLIATIVE CARE ORGANIZATION

In 1987 the NHPCO established the Task Force on Access to Hospice Care by Minorities, which conducted research and made policy recommendations to the end-of-life care field for improved services to culturally diverse groups. The organization passed the Resolution on Access to Hospice Care in May 1992, supporting the principle of universal access to hospice care for all terminally ill individuals regardless of nationality or creed. In 1994 the task force published its report (National Hospice and Palliative Care Organization 1994), which included guidelines on outreach activities and staff diversity training. The NHPCO also established the Access and Diversity Advisory Council in 2004; it published the *Inclusion and Access Toolbox* in 2007 and currently makes suggestions for inclusion and access through its Quality Partners program.

ROBERT WOOD JOHNSON FOUNDATION

The Robert Wood Johnson Foundation has a national program, Last Acts (http://www.lastacts.org), that is specifically aimed at promoting awareness and finding solutions in end-of-life care. Grants are provided to interview volunteers in the field, disseminate information for public awareness, increase knowledge of palliative care in the medical setting, and host conferences on diversity issues, among other aspects related to end-of-life care.

FEDERAL EFFORTS

The U.S. Department of Health and Human Services has funded a project of the American Medical Student Association in conjunction with the Promoting, Reinforcing, and Improving Medical Education (PRIME) project. This effort establishes cultural competency training for students during medical training and provides specific cultural information pertinent to their location (http:// www.woundcare.org/newsvol6n1/ed1.htm). The U.S. Department of Health and Human Services also established the elimination of racial and ethnic disparities in health as one of four overarching goals in *Healthy People 2020*. The Bureau of Primary Health Care mandates that health centers should engage in practices that respect and respond to the cultural diversity of the communities and clients served, should develop systems that ensure participation of the diverse cultures in their community, and should hire culturally and linguistically appropriate staff.

The CMS recently added a requirement, in order for hospices to demonstrate attempts toward cultural competence in order to qualify for Medicare reimbursement; CMS also endorsed the National Quality Forum domains of quality care, which included cultural aspects of care. These and other recommendations are not required, unfortunately, but are only recommended. They, as summarized by Kepner (2009), include the following:

- Develop and document a plan based on an assessment of religious, spiritual, and existential concerns using a structured instrument and integrate the information obtained from the assessment into the palliative care plan.
- Provide information about the availability of spiritual care services and make spiritual care available either through organizational spiritual care counseling or through the patient's own clergy relationships.
- Specialized palliative and hospice spiritual care professionals should build partnerships with community clergy and provide education and counseling related to end-of-life care
- Incorporate cultural assessment as a component of comprehensive palliative and hospice care assessment, including but not limited to locus of decision making, preferences regarding disclosure of information, truth telling and decision making, dietary preferences, language, family communication, desire for support measures such as palliative therapies and complementary and alternate medicine, perspectives on death, suffering, and grieving, and funeral/burial rituals.
- Provide professional interpreter services and culturally sensitive materials in the patient's and family's preferred language
- Treat the body after death with respect according to the cultural and religious practices of the family and in accordance with local law

NATIONAL ASSOCIATION OF SOCIAL WORKERS,
SOCIAL WORK POLICY INSTITUTE

The Social Work Policy Institute, affiliated with the National Association of
Social Workers, developed the following recommendations for enhancing
diversity in hospice:

- Advocate for the expansion of services and outreach to more ethnically
  and culturally diverse populations by engaging with members of the local community and other health care professionals to educate them on
  the value of hospice
- Incorporate patient's and family's involvement in developing a plan of
  care, which includes the patient's and family's cultural considerations
  of care
- Partner with other hospice organizations to develop awareness campaigns
- Encourage hospice agencies to increase access of services
- Encourage hospice agencies to seek out employees from diverse backgrounds
- Help recruit qualified social workers from diverse backgrounds to explore
  careers in EOL (National Association of Social Workers, Social Work
  Policy Institute 2010:19)

This section has outlined professional organizations' attempts to address
cultural barriers to hospice care access. The next section will provide
guidance for the social worker's own personal preparation for culturally
competent practice.

PERSONAL PREPARATION FOR CULTURALLY
COMPETENT PRACTICE

One of the most honored principles in hospice philosophy is patient self-determination. Advocates within the U.S. hospice movement in the 1970s promoted respect for patient wishes as a way to protect the rights of patients and
improve quality of life during terminal illness. Originally a grass-roots, social action based movement, hospice professionals maintain the zeal of the
movement even today, in their commitment to promoting hospice philosophy. Perspectives of diverse clients that depart from the hospice philosophy

pose a challenge to that zeal, that is based on client rights and wellbeing, but that must be tailored to fit diverse cultural perspectives. Our job is not to orient clients toward the hospice philosophy, but to adjust our approach so that hospice serves them in a culturally competent manner.

Schriver (2010) discusses the predominance of the traditional paradigm in professional services. This perspective may become part of a worldview that is not fully conscious, that is thought of as "normal", and as a worldview that should be held by all. In this case, hospice policies, practice methods, recommendations to patients, and communication styles will unintentionally reflect one's own worldview (Galambos 2003; Schriver 2010). Recommendations by hospice professionals to clients may not include all options or may not honor client values (del Rio 2004). When confronted with a different world view, one may react with surprise and a negative response. Staff communication in this case can cause offense. This is a fertile breeding ground, then, for an organizational culture that creates barriers to access and utilization (Reese and Beckwith 2005).

Racism may also exist unconsciously. Discomfort with diversity translates itself into a negative bias with hesitance to serve diverse patients or hire diverse staff. This underscores the importance of personal preparation for culturally competent practice that includes examination of one's own world views. This preparation can occur in social work education and in cultural competence training for hospice staff. Self-awareness, of one's own world view, as well as one's own socialization into racist and discriminatory views, is what enables a social worker to develop cultural respect and value diversity. Aspects of cultural competence training will be discussed next.

CULTURAL COMPETENCE TRAINING

A visiting scholar from Norway once attended a presentation I made about cultural competence in hospice, and she expressed surprise, saying that in her country communication with culturally diverse groups centers on acculturating them to the dominant society. The many hospices that do provide cultural competence training deserve credit, therefore, for attempts toward a multicultural society that may be groundbreaking in terms of a world view. Clearly we have far to go, though. Excellent formats for cultural competence training have been developed (National Hospice and Palliative Care Organization 2007) and will not be repeated here. Some general points will be considered below.

Cultural competence is a life-long process, in which an individual learns new information, discards old perspectives, and becomes more self-aware and personally accountable for achieving identified goals. This process occurs through lecture as well as open discussion and self-exploration. Through this process staff as well as the hospice agency finds health care delivery strategies that are meaningful and useful to diverse people (Sloam, Groves, and Brager 2004). Some aspects of cultural competence that should be addressed in cultural competence training include developing knowledge about diverse world views, celebration of diversity, developing cultural communication skills, addressing the history of oppression, and advocacy within the organization.

KNOWLEDGE ABOUT WORLDVIEWS

As discussed above, cultures influence each other globally, and clients will hold non-traditional beliefs. Stereotyping clients after learning about traditional beliefs will be seen as very offensive. At the same time, traditional beliefs may be playing an underlying role which is important to understand. We must acquire knowledge about the cultural heritage, beliefs, attitudes, values, and the language of those for whom we provide care. We should consult with all possible sources within the community, including religious leaders and language interpreters.

It is also helpful to come to an understanding of areas of convergence between hospice philosophy and diverse cultural world views. The extended family networks and strong social support evident in African American, Chinese, and Latino(a) cultures, for example, are consistent with the hospice focus on families as clients and the promotion of home care. The hospice team itself can become part of this supportive social network. Other areas of convergence with the hospice philosophy acceptance of death are the traditional Chinese belief in respect for nature and letting go of control, and the African American belief in acceptance of God's will. It is helpful to discuss such areas of convergence with individual clients and in public information sessions.

CELEBRATION OF DIVERSITY

After learning about differences in world views, the challenge is to move to a position of acceptance of these views, then ultimately of celebration of diversity. This does not mean agreement or change in one's own world view, but respect of the fact that many perspectives coexist. A caveat is that we do not accept or honor traditions that violate human rights (Reichert 2007). But this is difficult terrain to travel; the judgment that a tradition violates human rights can be made in error, based on a lack of full understanding of the other perspective or a sense of superiority of world view.

CULTURAL COMMUNICATION SKILLS

In a participatory action research project conducted by this author with an African American community, the Caucasian hospice partners unknowingly created offense by failure to follow the expected protocol of greeting the pastor's wife when arriving at the church building for a presentation. The pastor trusted that this was unintentional, based on the positive relationship we had developed. But he recommended that hospice staff be trained by members of his community in proper communication approaches that were culturally appropriate.

Nonverbal as well as verbal communication is important; and the subtlety of these issues makes them quite difficult to master. It is also important to be aware of the history of dominance and oppression when relating to some cultural groups, and make sure that no communication resembles that history. We should also learn about how patients and family express themselves verbally when discussing illness and death (Koenig and Davies 2003) and try to make our communication relevant to those patterns. Effective communication also requires hiring bilingual staff, using interpreters for non-English speaking patients, and learning common words or phases of the language used by the patient population.

ADDRESSING THE HISTORY OF OPPRESSION

Hospice programs should openly discuss the history of oppression and its resulting fear of the white health care system with staff, and be prepared to talk about such concerns with patients. While it is important to identify barriers that influence access to and utilization of palliative care services for oppressed populations, it is equally important to understand how those barriers were constructed in the first place and what forces maintain them. Honest discussions about the role that racism and discrimination play in the lives of African

Americans and Latino(a)s, and many other cultural groups, daily is also need-ed within the infrastructure of hospice programs. Understanding this history will provide insight to staff when patients and family members resist the hos-pice notion of a "good death" when prior access to basic preventive services and treatment was limited due to institutional racism (Reese et al. 2004).

ADVOCACY WITHIN THE HOSPICE ORGANIZATION

Finally, we should learn how to integrate the information learned into hos-pice treatment plans in order to improve the quality of care. Cultural knowl-edge should be reflected in service delivery. The hospice should connect with diverse communities and seek their guidance on the design of services that meet cultural needs. The following will focus in on cultural compe-tence on the micro level.

CULTURALLY COMPETENT MICRO-LEVEL PRACTICE IN HOSPICE

DEVELOPING A RELATIONSHIP

As always, the relationship between a social worker and a client is the most important aspect of intervention. Faux pas in relating across cultures will be forgiven if trust is established. This is especially difficult when a Cauca-sian health care professional approaches a member of an oppressed cultural group. While working to understand and honor traditional cultural perspec-tives, it is important not to stereotype clients and assume that all adhere to these traditional perspectives. Assessment of client preferences should be conducted, using one's knowledge about traditional cultural beliefs as preparation for demonstrating respect and honor for such perspectives, but never for making assumptions about the client's personal views.

INTAKE PROCESS

In the intake process fears of the health care system need to be addressed through client empowerment, reassuring them that they are in charge of the care of the patient, including medicine, food, and water intake and place of death. A requirement for a do not resuscitate order, in order to be admitted to hospice, is a barrier that should be removed.

Personal contact has been found to be important in promoting utilization of hospice. A doctor who made the effort to introduce the hospice staff to an African American caregiver in a home visit, empowering her through reassurance that hospice staff would not take control of the patient's care, enabled her to accept hospice (Reese et al. 2004). For this same reason, trusted spiritual leaders from the cultural group can be powerful allies in the admissions process (Kepner 2009). They should be included as members of the team as well as in the spiritual care plan.

EMPOWERMENT

Patient self-determination is probably the ultimate value in hospice philosophy and is called into play in the empowerment of culturally diverse clients. With diverse cultures, though, the value may be more on family self-determination than on the patient alone. As previously mentioned, an African American caregiver must know that she is in charge of the care of the patient, and hospice workers should only do what she allows them to do. Patient self-determination includes dying in the place of choice, even if not in the home.

We should avoid socialization of clients to the hospice point of view, in which hospice workers try to teach clients hospice philosophy. An example is the probably common practice of socializing them not to call 911 in the event of the patient's death. As always, we must honor our clients' wishes, and this is especially important in relating across cultural boundaries. One approach that may help is inviting clients to express their wishes and explain the underlying beliefs and feelings that lead to these wishes. For example, the preference of an African American or Chinese client to die in the hospital may be founded on traditional beliefs about the presence of spirits if death occurs in the home. Violating this preference may be quite upsetting for reasons not understood by hospice social workers who don't ask.

Another approach that may help the social worker respect client views is finding areas of convergence between hospice philosophy and cultural traditions. For example, it is not difficult to respect the desire to pray for a miracle. One perspective is that when medical doctors can no longer provide a cure the patient is in God's hands. It is also quite possible to respect the desire to die in the hospital, while wanting to have the family provide care up to that point. It is possible to opt for palliative care, but retaining the option to switch to curative care at some future point. If clients express a preference for curative care, social workers should respect this decision and provide support in referring them for the care they prefer (Washington, Bickel-Swenson, and Stephens 2008).

LITERACY

As always, social workers should not assume that their clients can read and write. This may be especially true for impoverished and oppressed populations—and especially for the elders of these populations (Gordon 1995, 1996). If written materials are provided, they should be at the appropriate level of literacy and in the appropriate language.

CLINICAL APPROACHES

A cross-cultural comparison study of death and dying perspectives among Hong Kong and U.S. social work students (Reese et al. 2010) revealed that effective practice models may vary between cultural groups. Our Hong Kong sample recommended the use of cognitive therapy, while U.S. students recommended providing an opportunity for the client to share/ventilate feelings. This may reflect differences in the practice models taught in their respective social work courses. Alternatively, it might reflect cultural differences in emotional expressiveness: U.S. culture is considered to be generally more expressive and Hong Kong culture generally less emotionally expressive. This would be consistent with the greater emphasis found by Hong Kong participants on a stoic acceptance of death. Hong Kong students valued cognitive approaches to coping in which they used rationales for why death itself is not fearful. A participant said, "Death is a neutral thing, a process that humans must experience."

SOCIAL SUPPORT

The cultural group may also predict the level of social support, with diverse cultural groups experiencing more or less social support than mainstream America. An African American research participant once reported that "hospice is all white people have. We don't need hospice, we have each other"

(Reese et al. 1999). We still think they need hospice! But it is important to realize the nature of the cohesive social group of which many clients are a part.

In the African American community, the "kinship" network includes a web of blood relatives as well as nonblood-related individuals who provide continual support to families in crisis throughout their lives (Mills, Usher, and McFadden 1999). In general, African American participatory action research project participants experienced a great deal of support from friends and an extended family that participated in patient care and helped financially. They also described their church as fulfilling the functions of a family (Reese et al. 2004). For hospice to seem relevant, staff should collaborate with this support group and become part of it. Otherwise hospice will be providing an ancillary service, not really part of the primary, vital care being furnished by those who "take care of our own." Hospice social workers should assess the authority and cohesiveness of the family as well as the preferred role of family members.

Another practice implication with diverse groups is in the authority and involvement of the family. In the U.S. dominant culture, social workers focus on the individual patient's rights, and patients are informed directly of their terminality. With other cultures, notably within Chinese culture, the family would expect to be the ones informed and may not necessarily want the patient to know the prognosis (Leung and Chan 2011). Patient rights laws about informed consent in the U.S. require that the patient be given information about the prognosis, but social workers can make a point to include the family as well. And, again, although it is important for social workers to understand traditional perspectives on the authority and involvement of the family in Chinese culture, professionals must be observant of changing views and the preference of some Chinese clients for the patient to make a decision about palliative care (Reese et al. 2010).

Finally, the importance of family for many culturally diverse clients has some additional practice implications. Although these are the case with most clients, they may have special importance to diverse clients. Chinese patients may be concerned that others be with them at death ("If there is somebody [to] accompany you to die, it is not so fearful") and about the welfare of loved ones after their death (Reese et al. 2010).

DENIAL

A point to remember is that we should not misinterpret differing views as psychosocial/spiritual problems. The traditional African American belief that God will perform a miracle in terminal illness could be seen as denial to those unfamiliar with the culture and working out of another paradigm. Also, spiritual tasks having to do with finding meaning in a loved one's life and death may have to be completed before family members can resign themselves to make end-of-life care decisions for palliative rather than curative care (Foster and McLellan 2002).

END-OF-LIFE CARE DECISIONS

A participatory action research study conducted by this author and colleagues (Reese et al. 2004) explored end-of-life care preferences among African American caregivers of terminally ill patients who were either served or not served by hospice. Interestingly, although some preferences were not in agreement with hospice philosophy, both groups held a number of preferences that *were* consistent with hospice philosophy. This may be partially explained by the fact that many of the participants who did not receive hospice were unaware of the option.

WANTING TO UPHOLD THE PATIENT'S WISHES A family characteristic that predicted choice of hospice was the desire to uphold the patient's wishes.

PATIENT DID NOT WANT FUTILE CARE An individual reason for choosing hospice was that the patient did not want futile care.

PAIN CONTROL Views went both ways here—there was hesitation about pain control, preferring not to use drugs unless absolutely necessary. Some, however, wanted to ease the patient's suffering through pain control and ending painful curative treatment.

WANTING TO CARE FOR PATIENT AT HOME Family characteristics that promoted choice of hospice included a desire for patient to be at home.

DESIRE FOR HELP FOR CAREGIVER Hospice clients expressed a need for help for the caregiver.

HOSPICE PROVIDES MEDICINE One important reason for using hospice was that it provides medicine.

ACCEPTANCE OF DEATH There was an acceptance of death based on religious beliefs pertaining to God's will.

WANTING QUALITY OF LIFE WHILE DYING Participants expressed this preference, consistent with hospice philosophy. Similarly, Torke and colleagues found that a majority of African American respondents said they would want a peaceful death if all treatment options had been exhausted. They still hoped for a cure, but did not want intrusive life-sustaining medical interventions (Torke et al. 2005).

PREFERENCE TO DIE IN THE HOSPITAL Most participants in both groups preferred to die in the hospital.

Other studies have found differing results—Owen and colleagues found that African American family caregivers of Alzheimer's patients were less likely to make a decision to withhold treatment at the time of death, less likely to have their relative die in a nursing home, and reported less acceptance of death and greater perceived loss than did Caucasians (Owen, Goode, and Haley 2001). Further research is needed.

Meanwhile, social workers should be flexible about the place of death, recognizing that patients may prefer to die in the hospital. Arrangements should be made to transfer the patient to the hospice room in the hospital, if available, when the time comes. Moreover, there are some families who are unable to care for the patient in the home or feel too strongly that hospice is an intrusion in the home. In these cases hospice care should be provided in other settings such as inpatient units, assisted living facilities, and nursing homes. Finally, it is important to be flexible about treatment choices— some clients want curative care; hospice staff should honor this and transfer out of hospice if and when it is necessary.

In previous times those who opted out of hospice could continue futile care during their terminal illness; this is becoming less of an option today with health insurance companies aiming toward cost-effectiveness in the care for which they will pay. The reality for many culturally diverse Americans who do not receive hospice care is no care, or nursing home care—disproportionately in high-deficiency nursing homes—that may not address end-of-life issues. For historically oppressed groups, this means "perpetuating a sin that cannot be forgiven, that final insult of unmitigated suffering" (Kepner 2009).

This chapter has reviewed barriers to cultural competence in hospice and suggested approaches for resolving these barriers. The next chapter will focus more in-depth on personal preparation for work in hospice.

REFERENCES

Ahmann, E. 2002. "Developing Cultural Competence in Health Care Settings." *Pediatric Nursing* 28, no. 2: 133–138.

Alexander, G. R. 2002. "A Mind for Multicultural Management." *Nursing Management* 33, no. 10: 30–35.

Anngela-Cole, L., L. S. Ka'opua, and Y. Yim. 2011. "Palliative Care, Culture, and the Pacific Basin." In Terry Altilio and Shirley Otis-Green, eds., *Oxford Textbook of Palliative Social Work*, pp. 527–530. New York: Oxford University Press.

Battle, V. D. and E. L. Idler. 2003. "Meaning and Effects of Congregational Religious Participation." In M. A. Kimble and S. H. McFadden, eds., *Aging, Spirituality, and Religion: A Handbook*, 2:121–33. Minneapolis: Fortress.

Betancourt, J., A. Green, and J. E. Carrillo. 2002. *Cultural Competence in Health Care: Emerging Frameworks and Practical Approaches.* New York: Commonwealth Fund. Retrieved from: http://www.commonwealthfund.org/Publications/ Fund-Reports/2002/Oct/Cultural-Competence-in-Health-Care--Emerging- Frameworks-and-Practical-Approaches.aspx.

Bonura, D., M. Fender, M. Roesler, and D. Pacquiao. 2001. "Culturally Congruent End-of-Life Care for Jewish Patients and Their Families." *Journal of Transcultural Nursing* 12, no. 3: 211–220.

Brach, C., and I. Fraser. 2000. "Can Cultural Competency Reduce Racial and Ethnic Disparities? A Review and Conceptual Model." *Medical Care Research and Review* 57, 1:181–217.

Bullock, K. 2011. "The Influence of Culture on End-of-Life Decision Making." *Journal of Social Work in End-of-Life and Palliative Care* 7, no. 1: 83–98.

Burgos-Ocasio, H. 1996. "Understanding the Hispanic Community." In M. C. Julia, *Multicultural Awareness in the Health Care Professions*, pp. 111–130. Boston: Allyn and Bacon.

Burrs, F. A. 1995. "The African American Experience: Breaking the Barriers to Hospices." *Hospice Journal* 10, no. 2: 15–18.

Capitman, J., G. Hernandez-Gallegos, D. Yee, and W. Madzimoyo. 1991. *Diversity and the Aging Network: An Assessment Handbook.* Waltham, MA: National Aging Resource Center: Long-Term Care, Heller School, Brandeis University.

Chan, W. C. H., I. Epstein, D. Reese, and C. L. W. Chan. 2008. "Family Predictors of Psychosocial Outcomes Among Hong Kong Chinese Cancer Patients in Palliative Care: Living and Dying with the "Support Paradox." *Social Work in Health Care* 48, no. 5: 519–532.

Chan, C. L. W., and J. M. H. Mak. 2000. "Benefits and Drawbacks of Chinese Rituals Surrounding Care for the Dying." In R. Fielding and C. L. W. Chan, eds., *Psychosocial Oncology and Palliative Care in Hong Kong: The First Decade*, pp. 255–270. Hong Kong: Hong Kong University Press.

Chan, H., and S. Pang. 2007. "Quality of Life Concerns and End-of-Life Care Preferences of Aged Persons in Long-term Care Facilities." *Journal of Clinical Nursing* 16, no. 11: 2158–2166.

Conley, D. 1999. *Being Black, Living in the Red: Race, Wealth, and Social Policy in America*. Berkeley: University of California Press.

Contro, N., B. Davies, J. Larson, and B. Sourkes. 2010. "Away from Home: Experiences of Mexican American Families in Pediatric Palliative Care." *Journal of Social Work in End-of-Life and Palliative Care* 6, nos. 3–4: 185–204.

Curry, S. M., J. E. Watkins, N. Davis, R. Hall, J. Keeling, A. Millerd-Johnson, A. Whiteley, and T. R. Graham. 2000. "An Undergraduate Participatory Action Research Study of Hispanic Access to End-of-Life Care: Implications for Social Work Education." Unpublished MS.

del Rio, N. 2004. "A Framework for Multicultural End-of-Life Care: Enhancing Social Work Practice." In Joan Berzoff and Phyllis R. Silverman, eds., *Living with Dying: A Handbook for End-of-Life Healthcare Practitioners*, pp. 439–461. New York: Columbia University Press.

——. 2010. "The Influence of Latino Ethnocultural Factors on Decision Making at the End of Life: Withholding and Withdrawing Artificial Nutrition and Hydration." *Journal of Social Work in End-of-Life and Palliative Care* 6, nos. 3–4: 125–149.

Department of Health and Human Services. 2010. "Healthy People 2020." Retrieved from http://www.healthypeople.gov/2020/about/default.aspx.

Dhooper, S. S. 2003. "Health Care Needs of Foreign-Born Asian Americans: An Overview." *Health and Social Work* 28, no. 1: 63–74.

Fielding, R., and C. L. W. Chan, eds. 2000. *Psychosocial Oncology and Palliative Care in Hong Kong: The First Decade*. Hong Kong: Hong Kong University Press.

Foster, L., and L. McLellan. 2002. "Translating Psychosocial Insight Into Ethical Discussions Supportive of Families in End-of-Life Decision-Making." *Social Work in Health Care* 35, no .3: 37–51.

Frazier, E. F., and C. E. Lincoln. 1974. *The Negro Church in America: The Black Church Since Frazier*. New York: Schocken.

Galambos, C. M. 2003. "Moving Cultural Diversity Toward Cultural Competence in Health Care." *Health and Social Work* 28, no. 1: 3.

Gerbino, S., and S. Henderson. 2004. "End-of-Life Bioethics in Clinical Social Work Practice." In Joan Berzoff and Phyllis R. Silverman, eds., *Living with Dying: A Handbook for End-of-Life Healthcare Practitioners,* pp. 593–608. New York: Columbia University Press.

Gordon, A. K. 1995. "Deterrents to Access and Service for Blacks and Hispanics: The Medicare Hospice Benefit, Healthcare Utilization, and Cultural Barriers." *Hospice Journal* 10, no. 2: 65–83.

——. 1996. "Hospice and Minorities: A National Study of Organizational Access and Practice." *Hospice Journal* 11, no. 1: 49–70.

Grabowski, D. C. 2004. "The Admission of Blacks to High-Deficiency Nursing Homes." *Medical Care* 42, no. 5: 456–64.

Guillemin, J. 1992. "Planning to Die." *Society* 29, no. 5: 29–33.

Haas, J. S., C. C. Earle, J. E. Orav, P. Brawarsky, B. Neville, D. Acevedo-Garcia, and D. R. Williams. 2007. "Lower Use of Hospice by Cancer Patients Who Live in Minority Versus White Areas." *Journal of General Internal Medicine* 22, no. 3: 396–399.

Helms, J. E. 1995. "An Update of White and People of Color Racial Identity Model." In J. G. Ponterotto, J. M. Casa, L. A. Suzuki, and C. M. Alexander, eds., *Handbook of Multicultural Counseling,* pp. 181–198. Thousand Oaks, CA: Sage.

Hodge, D. 2003. "Value Differences Between Social Workers and Members of the Working and Middle Classes." *Social Work* 48, no. 1: 107–119.

Hooyman, N. R., and B. J. Kramer. 2006. *Living Through Loss: Interventions Across the Life Span.* New York: Columbia University Press.

Institute of Medicine. 1999. *Measuring the Quality of Health Care.* Washington, DC: National Academy.

Jennings, B., T. Ryndes, C. D'Onofrio, and M. A. Baily. 2003. "Access to Hospice Care: Expanding Boundaries, Overcoming Barriers." *Hastings Center Report Special Supplement* 33, no. 2: S3–S59.

Johnson, J. W. 1992. "Go Down Death." In M. G . Secundy, ed., *Trials, Tribulations, and Celebrations: African American Perspectives on Health, Illness, Aging and Loss,* pp. 171–173. Yarmouth, ME: Intercultural.

Kemp, C. 2001. "Culture and the End of Life." *Journal of Hospice and Palliative Nursing* 3, no. 1: 29–33.

Kepner, E. 2009. *Policy Analysis of Barriers to African American Access to Hospice.* Unpublished MS.

Koenig, B., and E. Davies. 2003. "Cultural Dimension of Care at Life's End for Children and Their Family." In National Academy of Science, *When Children*

Die: Improving Palliative and End of Life Care for Children and Their Families, pp. 363–403. Washington, DC: National Academy of Science.

Komaromy, M., K. Grumbach, M. Drake, K. Vranizan, N. Lurie, D. Keane, and A. B. Bindman. 1996. "The Role of Black and Hispanic Physicians in Providing Health Care for Underserved Populations." *New England Journal of Medicine* 334, no. 20: 1305–1310.

Kong, T. W., M. C. Kwok, and D. So. 1997. *Make Your Boat of Death* (in Chinese). Hong Kong: Breakthrough.

Leung, P. P. Y., and C. L. W. Chan. 2011. In Terry Altilio and Shirley Otis-Green, eds., *Oxford Textbook of Palliative Social Work*, pp. 573–578. New York: Oxford University Press.

Lin, A. H.-M. H. 2003. "Factors Related to Attitudes Toward Death Among American and Chinese Older Adults. *Omega: Journal of Death and Dying* 47, no. 1: 3–23.

McGaughey, A. B. 2006. "Barriers to Employment of African American Social Workers in Hospice." Master's thesis, University of Arkansas, Fayetteville.

Mbiti, J. S. 1991. *Introduction to African Religion*. Portsmouth, NH: Heinemann Educational.

Mendez-Russel, A., E. Widerson, and A-S. Tolbert. 1994. *Exploring Differences in the Workplace*. Carlson Learning.

Mesler, M. 1995. "Negotiating Life for the Dying: Hospice and the Strategy of Tactical Socialization." *Death Studies* 19:235–255.

Mills, C. S., D. Usher, and J. McFadden. 1999. "Kinship in the African American Community." *Michigan Sociological Review* 13 (Fall): 28–45.

Ming-Lin Chong, A., and F. Shiu-Yeu. 2009. "Attitudes Toward Euthanasia: Implications for Social Work Practice." *Social Work in Health Care* 48, no. 2: 119–133.

Morin, Richard. 2001. "A Different Kind of Tax Break." *Washington Post*, September 16.

National Association of Social Workers, Social Work Policy Institute. 2010. *Hospice Social Work, Linking Policy, Practice, and Research: A Report from the March 25, 2010 Symposium*. Washington, DC: NASW.

National Hospice and Palliative Care Organization (formerly National Hospice Organization). 1994. *Caring for Our Own with Respect, Dignity and Love the Hospice Way*. Alexandria, VA: NHPCO.

— —, Access and Diversity Advisory Council (ADAC). 2007. *Inclusion and Access Toolbox*. Alexandria, VA: NHPCO.

Owen, J. E., K. T. Goode, and W. E. Haley. 2001. "End of Life Care and Reactions to Death in African-American and White Family Caregivers of Relatives with Alzheimer's Disease." *Omega* 43, no. 4: 349–361.

Pack-Brown, S. 1999. "Racism and White Counselor Training: Influence of White Racial Identity Theory and Research." *Journal of Counseling and Development* 77, no. 1: 87–92.

Pew Research Center, Forum on Religion and Public Life. 2007. *U.S. Religious Landscape Survey.* Retrieved from http://www.pewforum.org/A-Religious-Portrait-of-African-Americans.aspx.

Reese, D., R. Ahern, S. Nair, J. O'Faire, and C. Warren. 1999. "Hospice Access and Utilization by African Americans: Addressing Cultural and Institutional Barriers Through Participatory Action Research." *Social Work* 44, no. 6: 549–559.

Reese, D., C. Baker, S. Buila, E. Jurkowski, J. McFadden, S. Cox, J. Davis, and E. Kepner. 2011. "University-Community-Hospice Partnership to Address Organizational Barriers to Cultural Competence in Hospice." Paper presented at the Annual Program Meeting of the Council on Social Work Education, October 30, Atlanta.

Reese, D., and S. Beckwith. 2005. "Organizational Barriers to Cultural Competence in Hospice." Paper presented at the National Hospice and Palliative Care Association, Opening Doors, Building Bridges: Access and Diversity Conference, August, St. Louis, MO.

Reese, D., C. L. W. Chan, W. C. H. Chan, and D. Wiersgalla. 2010. "A Cross-national Comparison of Hong Kong and U.S. Student Beliefs and Preferences in End-of-Life Care: Implications for Social Work Education and Hospice Practice." *Journal of Social Work in End-of-Life and Palliative Care* 6, nos. 3–4: 1–31.

Reese, D., E. Melton, and K. Ciaravino. 2004. "Programmatic Barriers to Providing Culturally Competent End of Life Care." *American Journal of Hospice and Palliative Medicine* 21, no. 5: 357–364.

Reese, D., M. Smith, L. Braden, and C. Butler. 2004. "Creating an Interface Between Hospice and the African American Community: An Interdisciplinary Participatory Action Research Project." Paper presented by Larry Braden and Michelle Smith at the Clinical Team Conference, National Hospice and Palliative Care Organization, March, Las Vegas, Nevada.

Reichert, E., ed. 2007. *Challenges in Human Rights: A Social Work Perspective.* New York: Columbia University Press.

Reith, M., and M. Payne. 2009. *Social Work in End-of-Life and Palliative Care.* Chicago: Lyceum.

Schriver, J. M. 2010. *Human Behavior and the Social Environment: Shifting Paradigms in Essential Knowledge for Social Work Practice.* 5th ed. Needham Heights, MA: Allyn and Bacon.

Schumacher, J. D. 2003. "The Future of Hospice Leadership—How Do We Go from Good to Great?" Opening Plenary of the Eighteenth Management and

Leadership Conference, National Hospice and Palliative Care Organization, Phoenix.

Sloam, E., S. Groves, and R. Brager. 2004. "Cultural Competency Education in American Nursing Programs and the Approach of One School of Nursing." *International Journal of Nursing Education Scholarship* 1, no. 1.

Sue, D., and D. Sue. 1999. *Counseling the Culturally Different.* 3d ed. New York: Wiley.

Talamantes, M., W. Lawler, and D. Espino. 1995. "Hispanic American eEders: Caregiving Norms Surrounding Dying and the Use of Hospice Services." *Hospice Journal* 10, no. 2: 35–49.

Talavera, G., J. Elder, and R. Velasquez. 1997. "Latino Health Beliefs and Locus of Control: Implications for Primary Care and Public Health Care." *American Journal of Preventive Medicine* 13, no. 6: 408–410.

Tan, A. G. 1994. "Investigating People's Conceptions of Stress in Multicultural and Cross-cultural Frameworks: Germans, Japanese, and Malaysians." *Tohoku Psychologica Folia* 53:64–75.

Torke, A.M., N. S. Garas, W. Sexson, and W. T. Branch, 2005. "Medical Care at the End of Life: Views of African American Patients in an Urban Hospital." *Journal of Palliative Medicine* 8:593–602.

Tse, D., K. Chan, W. Lam, K. Lau, and P. Lam. 2007. "The Impact of Palliative Care on Cancer Deaths in Hong Kong: A Retrospective Study of 494 Cancer Deaths." *Palliative Medicine* 21, no. 5: 425–433.

Walsh-Burke, K. 2004. "Assessing Mental Health Risk in End-of-Life Care." In Joan Berzoff and Phyllis R. Silverman, eds., *Living with Dying: A Handbook for End-of-Life Healthcare Practitioners*, pp. 360–379. New York: Columbia University Press.

Washington, K. T., D. Bickel-Swenson, and N. Stephens. 2008. "Barriers to Hospice Use Among African Americans: A Systematic Review." *Health and Social Work* 33, no. 4: 267–274.

Weiss, G. L., and L. N. Lupkin. 2009. "First-Year College Students' Attitudes About End-of-Life Decision-Making." *Omega: Journal of Death and Dying* 60, no. 2: 143–163.

Welch, L., J. Teno, and V. Mor. 2005. "End-of-Life Care in Black and White: Race Matters for Medical Care of Dying Patients and Their Families." *Journal of American Geriatric Society* 53:1145–1153.

Werth, J. L., D. Blevins, K. L. Toussaint, and M. R. Durham. 2002. "The Influence of Cultural Diversity on End-of-Life Care and Decisions." *American Behavioral Scientist* 46, no. 2: 204–219.

Woo, K. Y. 1999. "Care for Chinese Palliative Patients." *Journal of Palliative Care* 15, no. 4: 70–74.

8

PERSONAL PREPARATION AND SOCIAL WORKER SELF-CARE

As in all areas of social work practice, work with dying patients can be difficult emotionally, and hospice social workers may experience some or all of the psychosocial and spiritual issues affecting their clients. Social workers must face their own mortality, in fact, in preparation for effective work with terminally ill clients and families (Zilberfein and Hurwitz 2004). This vicarious confrontation with mortality can result in spiritual growth for those who work with dying patients (Callahan 2009; Jacobs 2004; Derezotes and Evans 1995). But, at the same time, hospice social workers must engage in personal preparation to cope with the emotional reactions that may be brought on by their work. In addition, once engaged in this work, social worker self-care is an important consideration to prevent or reduce compassion fatigue (Alkema, Linton, and Davies 2008; Clark 2011; Zilberfein and Hurwitz 2004). This chapter discusses these issues and how to address them.1

NEED FOR PERSONAL PREPARATION

Understanding one's own perspectives and emotional reactions to issues of death and dying is important for several reasons. Social work students often feel unprepared and struggle to cope with these feelings when working with grieving or dying clients (Christ and Sormanti 1999; Kovacs and Bronstein 1999). This may be particularly true for young students. According to psychosocial theory (Erikson 1950), young individuals who are in the process

---

1. The author would like to acknowledge the work of Jolanda Nally, and also my coauthors Cecilia Chan, David Perry, Diane Wiersgalla, and Jennifer Schlinger. The work of these authors contributed greatly to the development of this chapter.

of establishing identity and intimacy may experience heightened death anxiety when thinking about the loss of identity and loved ones inherent in death. Thus, not surprisingly, death anxiety tends to be higher in younger people (Simons and Park-Lee 2009).

In addition, female students have been found to have higher death anxiety than males (Noppe 2004). This may possibly be based on a greater willingness to express emotion or a lower level of denial that allows awareness of anxiety about death. Awareness of gender differences is helpful since a majority of social workers are female. A study of social work students in a Midwestern university (Reese et al. 2005) found that students had a moderate level of death anxiety, specifically worrying about the possibility of pain when dying and worrying about what it will be like after death.

Social workers who are unaware of their own beliefs and feelings are more susceptible to countertransference, which may lead to professional recommendations about end-of-life care that do not include all available options (Gerbino and Raymer 2011; Peck 2009; Simons and Park-Lee 2009) and do not honor client values. Complicating this is the fact that client cultural and religious beliefs are likely to differ from social worker perspectives (Canda and Furman 2010; Hodge 2003). In the study of social work students mentioned previously (Reese et al. 2005), social work students were more likely than community residents to describe themselves as "spiritual but not religious" and less likely to agree with a list of cultural and religious beliefs about end-of-life care. They had lower denial of terminality and more positive views about talking about their own death, were less likely to place a dying family member in the hospital, and were more positive than community members toward bereavement counseling and organ donation. Professional education should prepare students for the use of practice techniques and policies that are sensitive to clients' potential higher levels of denial. At the same time, many students must work to replace denial with acceptance of death (Altschuler and Katz 2001).

Differences in beliefs may be particularly likely when professionals and clients represent different cultural groups (del Rio 2004). An important principle for quality end-of-life care is to base services on the values of the patient and family (Egan and Labyak 2001), but the hospice field has been developed around hospice philosophy. This in itself may act as a barrier to access to the extent it differs from client beliefs and values (Reese et al. 1999). Most Americans prefer palliative care, although they may be uninformed of hospice (Gallup 1997; Reese et al. 2005). Professionals should be aware, though, of a subgroup that prefers hospital placement when dying—particularly among African Americans, Asians, and other diverse cultural groups. Schriver (2010) explains the importance of understanding one's own paradigm before one is able to honor the alternative paradigms of clients. This underscores the importance of personal preparation for hospice social work practice.

Kramer (1998) points out that social workers must also deal with losses in their own lives before they are prepared to help clients with loss. One's own bereavement does not necessarily lead to countertransference, though, but may be a strength in providing end-of-life care (Browning 2003).

Another issue is that unaware social workers experiencing strong emotions may find it difficult to maintain a professional boundary. In addition to the risks posed to the client, lack of a professional boundary can lead to burnout or compassion fatigue for the social worker.

Just how do we proceed with personal preparation? The next section will discuss ways to address these issues.

APPROACH TO PERSONAL PREPARATION

Harper (1977) describes stages similar to the Kubler-Ross (1970) stages of grief that hospice social workers progress through in their ability to handle the emotions associated with working with the dying: the stages of intellectualization, emotional survival and depression, and finally emotional arrival and compassion. Progress through these stages explains the personal growth that hospice workers experience. This process can be aided through support during social work education, continuing education, or through hospice orientation for new workers.

Preparation should also address awareness of one's own cultural and religious beliefs and how they might influence one's practice (Clark 2011). It should include personal work on death anxiety and denial in order to increase professionals' ability to make referrals in the best interests of their clients.

Social workers should become aware of possible differences between themselves and their clients, including beliefs about death and dying and end-of-life care preferences. They should be aware of the likelihood of client preference for home or hospice death, but also be able to honor the preferences of a subgroup that prefers hospital placement when dying.

Social workers should also learn practice techniques that are sensitive to clients' potential higher levels of denial.

In addition, social workers should be aware of differences in religious preferences and beliefs between professions and let this guide their interactions on the interdisciplinary team. They should be aware of gender differences because of their possible influence on beliefs and death anxiety; including the potentially higher level of death anxiety among females. Finally, students should be aware of possible differences in end-of-life care treatment preferences between professions, including preference for bereavement counseling and organ donation.

SOCIAL WORKER SELF-CARE

COMPASSION FATIGUE

Research with hospice social workers has found they had low levels of death anxiety, were very comfortable working with dying patients, and had a high sense of personal accomplishment. In addition, they have a strong sense of gratification, or compassion satisfaction, from helping to ease the suffering of dying clients and their significant others (Radley and Figley 2007).

At the same time, workers reported stress and burnout (Alkema, Linton, and Davies 2008), with symptoms including distress, anxiety, depression, loss and grief, and emotional exhaustion (Clark 2011; Reith and Payne 2009), hopelessness, irritability, anger, lowered ability to feel joy, and low self-esteem (Hooyman and Kramer 2006). Physical symptoms have been reported, such as gastrointestinal disturbances, chronic pain, and fatigue (Davis 2003).

As already mentioned, Harper (1977) proposed that hospice social workers progress through stages in their ability to handle these emotional reactions to working with the dying, including intellectualization, emotional survival and depression, and finally emotional arrival and compassion. But even after developing this capacity for compassion, the difficulty of work with the dying and their loved ones can lead to compassion fatigue (Alkema, Linton, and Davies 2008).

Compassion fatigue develops from the social worker's experience of *empathy*, which is an accurate understanding of the client's feelings. As a result of ongoing and cumulative exposure to clients' suffering, one may lose the ability to maintain this empathy (Alkema, Linton, and Davies 2008; Clark 2011; Renzenbrink 2004). A deep physical, emotional, and spiritual exhaustion may set in, accompanied by acute emotional pain (Reith and Payne 2009). Characteristics of compassion fatigue are similar to post-traumatic stress disorder and may include reexperiencing the traumatic events, avoidance/numbing of reminders of the event, or persistent arousal (Renzenbrink 2004). Actual physiological changes may occur as a result of secondary exposure to trauma, including physiological alterations in neuroendocrine and hormonal systems and psychological alterations in cognitive functioning (Adams, Boscarino, and Figley 2006; Renzenbrink 2004).

Social workers may attempt to alleviate these feelings through substance abuse, eating disorders, workaholism, or blaming others for one's feelings. They may develop chronic lateness or experience a diminished sense of personal accomplishment. The social worker's own feelings about previous losses and traumatic experiences may resurface, even if they were not problematic in the past. Social workers may become overwhelmed and need assistance to cope with the effects of experiencing the dying process along with their clients.

In addition, compassion fatigue may reduce the quality of clinical work with clients. The social worker may have difficulty maintaining a professional boundary or, on the other hand, have difficulty establishing a relationship. The social worker may feel hostile toward clients or develop conflict with colleagues regarding treatment plans, avoid emotional awareness of client experiences, develop distrust or safety issues, have a decreased capacity for empathy, make mistakes and errors in judgment (Alkema, Linton, and Davies 2008).

Some social workers are more at risk than others for developing compassion fatigue. Those who lack a sense of competency, have difficulty maintaining a professional boundary, have not resolved personal trauma (Gerbino and Raymer 2011), and those who do not engage in self-care techniques (Alkema, Linton, and Davies 2008) are at higher risk. Participants in Nally's (2006) study reported that when they don't take care of themselves it is impossible to take care of others—"I call it the 'empty tank syndrome'" (p. 29).

In addition, those who do not have buffering personal beliefs via their worldview are more at risk (Bell 2003). Social workers vicariously experiencing the suffering of their clients can experience some of the same spiritual questioning that arises for their clients—which may include disruptions in one's sense of meaning, worldview, and belief system (Berzoff and Silverman 2004; Bride 2004). Self-care techniques to address these issues will be discussed in the following section.

SELF-CARE TECHNIQUES

PHYSICAL AND PSYCHOSOCIAL APPROACHES Various authors have suggested self-care strategies that are successful in addressing compassion fatigue. These include regular exercise, a balanced life including a spiritual life, interests outside of work, time with family and friends, relaxed and nutritious meals, humor, and rest (Alkema, Linton, and Davies 2008; Clark 2011; Gerbino and Raymer 2011; Hooyman and Kramer 2006; Renzenbrink 2004). Clark (2011) suggests taking time to deal with your emotions, keeping a journal of psychosocial successes, continuing education on self-care, and seeking counseling if needed. Social workers may be able to cope through a sense of competence, control, and pleasure from one's work (Vachon 2002).

Social support from colleagues is also important, and it is recommended that hospices provide employee support groups to address the needs of staff (Alkema, Linton, and Davies 2008; Clark 2011). Anecdotal evidence exists for the positive impact of such a support group, where participants felt a reduction in stress based on the recognition of their needs by the administration as well as through the support of peers. Support groups should also educate participants about compassion fatigue (Hooyman and Kramer 2006; Nally 2006). Supervisors may also offer empathy, support, and the opportunity for ventilation (Gerbino and Raymer 2011; Simons and Park-Lee 2009). Suggestions for self-care strategies that may be provided by supervisors include awareness of physical and fatigue symptoms and promoting separation between work and personal life (Inbar and Ganor 2003).

Other recommended strategies include continuing education programs (Hooyman and Kramer 2006; Simons and Park-Lee 2009), "caring distancing" techniques, and prevention and promotion of coping skills with the incorporation of humor in workshops and e-mail (Inbar and Ganor 2003). Inbar and Ganor (2003) describe cognitive-behavioral techniques that can change irrational ways of interpreting events, stress-innoculation training, and interventions that promote development of self-control, improvement of problem-solving abilities, teamwork coordination, and psychological resilience. They also make suggestions for intervention on an organizational level, including crisis management strategies and creating an organizational culture that prevents burnout conditions. They argue for consensus-based leadership styles that promote support systems, including a buddy system in which staff members share concerns and experiences with each other. Gentry (2002) has found that eye movement desensitization and reprocessing has been effective for treatment of secondary trauma.

SPIRITUAL APPROACHES Spiritual self-care has also been found to prevent or reduce compassion fatigue (Alkema, Linton, and Davies 2008). Among these practices are prayer, meditation (Renzenbrink 2004), identifying what is important through self-reflection, and living according to such principles in life as well as at work (Gerbino and Raymer 2011; Hooyman and Kramer 2006). A study of social workers that implemented a meditation group found a significant decrease in compassion fatigue after a few sessions of meditation (Nally 2006).

Several rationales exist for why spiritual practice may be helpful in addressing compassion fatigue. Many social workers enter the field for spiritual reasons; some even articulate their choice of profession as a "spiritual calling" (Bell 2003). Others may not explain it this way, but their reasons may fit within the author's definition of spirituality. A desire to help vulnerable people, a concern for the welfare of all, fits within one of the author's dimensions of spirituality—the dimension of transcendence in terms of philosophy of life. A social worker's desire to help others is transcendent in its focus on the welfare of all rather than the welfare only of oneself. A philosophy of life that focuses on helping others, then, gives life a transcendent meaning for the social worker.

Spiritual practice may allow social workers to keep this transcendent perspective, helping social workers maintain a sense of meaning beyond self-interest, which then serves as a source of psychological well-being, sustaining the capacity for caring, hope, and emotional well-being, thereby preventing compassion fatigue.

Transpersonal theory (Wilber 1993) explains the effects of transcendence on mental health. As outlined in chapter 3, transpersonal theory proposes several stages of development—the pre-egoic, egoic, and transegoic. Wilber assigns various types of psychopathology to the lower levels of development, while the highest level is characterized by a sense of the sacred. Heightened empathy and compassion naturally arise as the individual experiences a profound connection with others (Canda and Furman 2010).

Development into this stage does not automatically occur, but must be achieved through spiritual practice in which individuals make deliberate efforts toward functioning at a transegoic level of consciousness. According to this point of view, it makes sense that spiritual practice could help a social worker to maintain a transcendent perspective, which would enable continued compassion and empathy despite ongoing exposure to client suffering. In fact, Levenson and colleagues (Levenson et al. 2005) found that meditation practice was positively related to self-transcendence. Nally (2006) explains that a social worker with a transcendent perspective views the client from "a place of unconditional love wherein the clinician can provide a loving presence and can allow a space wherein very deep work can occur. When this kind of work is being done between the client and clinician it can be very rewarding and assist the clinician in preventing compassion fatigue. In fact, this type of work may be extremely replenishing" (p. 9).

As mentioned earlier, Nally (2006) conducted a nonexperimental study in which social workers participated in a meditation group for several weeks. The group used a modified Trechod method, which is similar to the Buddhist practice of Vipassana meditation. In this practice the participant simply observes the mind without judgment or analysis. The Trechod method, however, varies from Vipassana in that it is divided into three periods: a period of arriving, a period of focusing, and a period of rest. In Nally's program, "during the first five minutes of the meditation, the subject simply sat and was still, eyes, closed, with no agenda. Then, during the next fifteen minutes of the meditation, the subject was to focus on their breath and maintain a conscious and alert awareness of their breath without judging any thoughts that may arise. During the last five minutes, the subjects were to simply rest with no focused awareness on the breath. After the twenty minute meditation was finished, participants were asked to process the experience." (Nally 2006:23). Participants were also exposed to various other forms of meditation and asked to practice the meditation on their own every day. Periods of discussion followed the various forms of meditation. The program included an overnight retreat, two additional meditative sessions during the next ten days, and a focus group to gather qualitative data.

Results (Nally 2006) showed that levels of compassion fatigue were significantly reduced from pretest to post-test. Qualitative results helped to explain the quantitative results, with participants reporting spiritual effects. They related that their spiritual worldview had been expanded by participating in the study and that "the practice has shown me how much compassion

I really have." Participants also reported that they experienced benefits physically (releasing tensions from the body, promoting sleep), psychologically
(feeling calm and relaxed, less irritable, happier dealing with the client's
trauma), and maintaining a professional boundary (I can address my home
life issues; I leave my job at the office).

Although social work students are encouraged to engage in self-assessment
and share personal experiences that are relevant to course content, personal
preparation and methods of self-care are not major elements of the social
work curricula. Adding to this deficit is the fact that end-of-life care holds
a very insignificant place in social work education. The result is that hospice social workers are personally unprepared for work with clients and lack
knowledge about methods of self-care. Personal preparation and self-care
are vital in maintaining well-being and quality of practice for the sake of
clients. These skills will sustain us as we go on providing hospice social work
services. Chapter 9 will discuss the challenges we need to address for the
future of hospice social work.

REFERENCES

Adams, R. E., J. A. Boscarino, and C. R. Figley. 2006. "Compassion Fatigue and
Psychological Distress Among Social Workers: A Validation Study." *American
Journal of Orthopsychiatry* 76:103–108.

Alkema, K., J. M. Linton, and R. Davies. 2008. "A Study of the Relationship Between Self-care, Compassion Satisfaction, Compassion Fatigue, and Burnout
Among Hospice Professionals." *Journal of Social Work in End-of-Life and Palliative Care* 4, no. 2: 101–119.

Altschuler, J., and A. D. Katz. 2001. "Countertransference Reactions Toward Older
Adults Facing HIV and AIDS." *Clinical Gerontologist* 23, no. 1–2: 99–114.

Bell, H. 2003. "Strengths and Secondary Trauma in Family Violence Work." *Social
Work* 48, no. 4 (October): 513–522.

Berzoff, J., and P. R. Silverman, eds. 2004. "Introduction: Clinical Practice." In
Joan Berzoff and Phyllis R. Silverman, eds., *Living with Dying: A Handbook for
End-of-Life Healthcare Practitioners*, pp. 265–272. New York: Columbia Uni-
versity Press.

Bride, B. E. 2004. "The Impact of Providing Psychosocial Services to Traumatized
Populations." *Stress, Trauma, and Crisis* 7, no. 1: 29–46.

Browning, D. 2003. "Pathos, Paradox, and Poetics: Grounded Theory and the Experience of Bereavement." *Smith College Studies in Social Work* 73, no. 3: 325–336.

Callahan, A. M. 2009. "Spiritually-Sensitive Care in Hospice Social Work." *Journal of Social Work in End-of-Life and Palliative Care* 5, nos. 3–4: 169–185.

Canda, E., and L. Furman. 2010. *Spiritual Diversity in Social Work Practice: The Heart of Helping.* New York: Oxford University Press.

Christ, G., and M. Sormanti. 1999. "Advancing Social Work Practice in End-of-Life Care." *Social Work in Health Care* 30, no. 2: 81–99.

Clark, E. 2011. "Self-care as Best Practice in Palliative Care." In Terry Altilio and Shirley Otis-Green, eds., *Oxford Textbook of Palliative Social Work*, pp. 771–777. New York: Oxford University Press.

Davis, S. 2003. "Can Caregivers Care Too Much?" *DVM: The Newsmagazine of Veterinary Medicine* 34, no. 8: 58–59.

del Rio, N. 2004. "A Framework for Multicultural End-of-Life Care: Enhancing Social Work Practice." In Joan Berzoff and Phyllis R. Silverman, eds., *Living with Dying: A Handbook for End-of-Life Healthcare Practitioners*, pp. 439–461. New York: Columbia University Press.

Derezotes, D., and K. Evans. 1995. "Spirituality and Religiosity in Practice: In-depth Interviews of Social Work Practitioners." *Social Thought* 18, no. 1: 39–56.

Egan, K. A., and M. J. Labyak. 2001. "Hospice Care: A Model for Quality End-of-Life Care." In B. R. Ferrell and N. Coyle, eds., *Textbook of Palliative Nursing*, pp. 7–26. New York: Oxford University Press.

Erikson, E. H. 1950. *Childhood and Society.* Philadelphia: Norton.

Gallup International Institute. 1997. *Spiritual Beliefs and the Dying Process.* Princeton: Nathan Cummings Foundation.

Gentry, J. E. 2002. "Compassion Fatigue: A Crucible of Transformation." *Journal of Trauma Practice* 1, nos. 3/4: 37–61.

Gerbino, S., and M. Raymer. 2011. "Holding On and Letting Go: The Red Thread of Adult Bereavement." In Terry Altilio and Shirley Otis-Green, eds., *Oxford Textbook of Palliative Social Work*, pp. 319–327. New York: Oxford University Press.

Harper, B. C. 1977. *Death: The Coping Mechanism of the Health Professional.* Greenville, SC: Southeastern University Press.

Hodge, D. 2003. "Value Differences Between Social Workers and Members of the Working and Middle Classes." *Social Work* 48, no. 1: 107–119.

Hooyman, N. R., and B. J. Kramer. 2006. *Living Through Loss: Interventions Across the Life Span.* New York: Columbia University Press.

Inbar, J., and M. Ganor. 2003. "Trauma and Compassion Fatigue: Helping the Helpers." *Journal of Jewish Communal Service* 79, nos. 2/3: 109–111.

Jacobs, C. 2004. "Spirituality and End-of-Life Care Practice for Social Workers." In Joan Berzoff and Phyllis R. Silverman, eds., *Living with Dying: A Handbook for End-of-Life Healthcare Practitioners*, pp. 188–205. New York: Columbia University Press.

Kovacs, P., and L. Bronstein. 1999. "Preparation for Oncology Settings: What Hospice Workers Say They Need." *Health and Social Work* 24, no. 1: 57–64.

Kramer, B. 1998. "Preparing Social Workers for the Inevitable: A Preliminary Investigation of a Course on Grief, Death, and Loss." *Journal of Social Work Education* 34, no. 2: 1–17.

Kubler-Ross, E. 1970. *On Death and Dying*. New York: Macmillan.

Levenson, M., P. Jennings, C. Aldwin, and R. Shiraishi. 2005. "Self-transcendence: Conceptualization and Measurement." *International Journal Aging and Human Development* 60, no. 2: 127–143.

Nally, J. 2006. "Spirituality in Social Work: Spiritual Self-Care and Its Effects on Compassion Fatigue." Unpublished master's thesis, University of Arkansas.

Noppe, I. C. 2004. "Gender and Death: Parallel and Intersecting Pathways." In Joan Berzoff and Phyllis R. Silverman, eds., *Living with Dying: A Handbook for End-of-Life Healthcare Practitioners*, pp. 206–225. New York: Columbia University Press.

Peck, M. R. 2009. "Personal Death Anxiety and Communication About Advance Directives Among Oncology Social Workers." *Journal of Social Work in End-of-Life and Palliative Care* 4, no. 1–2: 49–60.

Radley, M., and C. Figley. 2007. "The Social Psychology of Compassion." *Clinical Social Work Journal* 35:207–214.

Reese, D., R. Ahern, S. Nair, J. O'Faire, and C. Warren. 1999. "Hospice Access and Utilization by African Americans: Addressing Cultural and Institutional Barriers Through Participatory Action Research." *Social Work* 44, no. 6: 549–559.

Reese, D., C. L. W. Chan, D. Perry, D. Wiersgalla, and J. Schlinger. 2005. "Beliefs, Death Anxiety, Denial, and Treatment Preferences in End-of-Life Care: A Comparison of Social Work Students, Community Residents, and Medical Students." *Journal of Social Work in End-of-Life and Palliative Care* 1, no. 1: 23–47.

Reith, M., and M. Payne. 2009. *Social Work in End-of-Life and Palliative Care*. Chicago: Lyceum.

Renzenbrink, I. 2004. "Relentless Self-Care." In J. Berzoff and P. Silverman, eds., *Living with Dying: A Comprehensive Resource for End-of-Life Care*, pp. 848–867. New York: Columbia University Press.

Schriver, J. M. 2010. *Human Behavior and the Social Environment: Shifting Paradigms in Essential Knowledge for Social Work Practice.* 5th ed. Needham Heights, MA: Allyn and Bacon.

Simons, K., and E. Park-Lee. 2009. "Social Work Students' Comfort with End-of-Life Care." *Journal of Social Work in End-of-Life and Palliative Care* 5, no. 1–2: 34–48.

Vachon, M. L. S., and M. Muller. 2009. "Burnout and Symptoms of Stress in Staff Working in Palliative Care." In Harvey M. Chochinov and William Breitbart, eds., *Handbook of Psychiatry in Palliative Medicine,* pp. 236–266. New York: Oxford University Press.

Wilber, K. 1993. 2d ed. *The Spectrum of Consciousness.* Wheaton, IL: Quest.

Zilberfein, F., and E. Hurwitz. 2004. "Clinical Social Work Practice at the End of Life." In Joan Berzoff and Phyllis R. Silverman, eds., *Living with Dying: A Handbook for End-of-Life Healthcare Practitioners,* pp. 297–317. New York: Columbia University Press.

9

FUTURE CHALLENGES IN THE FIELD OF HOSPICE SOCIAL WORK

Looking Ahead

This book has reviewed the history of the experience of dying in the United States—from dying at home surrounded by family to dying in the hospital surrounded by technology—and the movement toward patient rights and self-determination in decisions about end-of-life care. New approaches that have developed include passive euthanasia or palliative care. A form of palliative care is hospice care, which recognizes the terminal prognosis and helps the patient and family prepare for death. Another approach that has developed in recent years is active euthanasia or physician-assisted suicide. Although most Americans are still not aware of the option of hospice care, most at this point prefer palliative care in terminal illness.

The hospice philosophy advocates for holistic care provided by an interdisciplinary team that includes social workers. Our profession has made impressive strides toward developing the field of hospice social work, including establishing standards for care, evaluation methods for documenting effectiveness, providing training and working toward certification, and developing new professional organizations that provide information, training, and advocacy.

Research indicates that these efforts have had a notable effect—utilization of social workers on the team has expanded considerably, and social workers are now considered by hospice directors to be the most qualified to perform many more of the roles that hospice social workers consider their own (Reese 2011). Models for social work intervention in hospice have been developed for use on the micro, mezzo, and macro levels. Much work still remains, though. This chapter will discuss future challenges that we will together address in the field of hospice social work.

FURTHER NEEDS FOR RESEARCH

A long-existing reason for the lack of recognition of the importance of the social worker on the hospice team has been a lack of research showing the effectiveness of social work intervention. We need to use evidence-based practice — using models of intervention that have been found to be effective through evaluation research — and hospice social workers need to evaluate their practice (Ivanko 2011; Oliver and Washington 2011). Part of advocacy for the profession itself and its role in hospice care includes writing and participating in research.

The National Association of Social Workers (National Association of Social Workers, Social Work Policy Institute 2010) has reported that social workers do not always record case notes after seeing a client! Sometimes the reason for this is a lack of space on an electronic form for social work intervention. Social workers need to advocate with directors for ways to document their case notes if this is not available.

The Second Summit on End-of-Life and Palliative Care, held in 2005, emphasized the importance of using standard outcome measures in documenting the effectiveness of social work intervention in palliative and end-of-life care (Palos 2011). Many social workers nationally are using the Social Work Assessment Tool (SWAT, Reese et al. 2006) as part of the electronic documentation package. Often they had to advocate to get it added to the package. Use of the SWAT at every session is an easy way to end up with a pretest and a post-test that can show improvement in client scores after social work intervention. Social workers should also be helpful in participating in research conducted by others.

PRACTITIONER-RESEARCHER DISCONNECT

One problem we are faced with is a lack of recognition of existing research on the part of hospice social workers. Social workers need to use techniques that have been developed and shown to be helpful through research. They should be aware of the new information and problems documented in the field as well as the challenges they are called upon to address by the leaders in the field.

One reason for this may be that the research itself often does not address practice problems — it can be helpful for practitioners to provide input to help drive the agenda for research (National Association of Social Workers

2010). Perhaps having this input would encourage hospice social workers to value research in practice.

Practitioners often don't have access to journals or conferences. Hospices should provide these for their social workers; social workers can advocate with the director for such access. Alternatively, with membership in the Social Work in Hospice and Palliative Care Network, one is subscribed to the *Journal of Social Work in End-of-Life and Palliative Care*, which is the leading journal in the field of hospice social work and the only one solely dedicated to the field. This organization also provides online information and training; they have an excellent ask the expert series that is free to members and can be accessed online. This resource provides hospice social workers with the latest information in the field.

RESEARCH AGENDA FOR THE FUTURE

The latest CMS Conditions for Participation for hospices requires evaluation of effectiveness. We still need clear evidence of the effectiveness of hospice social workers. We have a few studies (see Reese and Raymer 2004), but we need a body of research that can be analyzed and summarized. We need documentation of the effectiveness of existing interventions and to test new interventions (Csikai 2005, first issue of the *Journal of Social Work in End-of-Life and Palliative Care*).

Another gap in research is in the area of pediatric hospice social work. Research also needs to identify gaps and challenges in care as well as strategies for cost effectiveness and efficacy of social work practice models. Interdisciplinary research has also been recommended (National Association of Social Workers 2010).

The National Association of Social Workers (2010) recommends mixed methods studies. Qualitative methods provide more detailed and in-depth information, while quantitative results provide statistical evidence of the effectiveness of intervention models.

RESEARCH INFRASTRUCTURE

We also need to develop a research infrastructure. We need to find ways to develop hospice social work research, including educating and mentoring new researchers, and we need to build a commitment to funding hospice social work research. We should promote our research agenda through inter- and intradisciplinary practice-oriented collaborations and representation on national research advisory boards (Palos 2011).

DISSEMINATION OF RESEARCH

Our research results face barriers in reaching social work practitioners as well as other hospice disciplines. Clark (2004) recommends that we publish our research findings in interdisciplinary journals—we need to increase the knowledge of other members of the interdisciplinary team about the role of social work in hospice.

FURTHER CLARIFICATION OF SOCIAL WORK ROLES

Although research documents significant improvements in the importance of social work in the eyes of hospice directors (Reese 2011), the role of social work on the hospice team is still not entirely clear to hospice administrators, policy makers, and other hospice disciplines. High caseloads continue to be a problem, along with limited access to training and lack of supervision by a social worker, despite documentation of most of this in 2004 (Reese and Raymer 2004). Documentation and recognition of services provided by telephone also remains an issue. Social workers receive the lowest salaries among end-of-life care professionals (National Association of Social Workers 2010). An avenue for advocacy in terms of salary may be social workers billing for services (Clark 2004; Goldberg and Scharlin 2011; National Association of Social Workers 2010).

A current challenge is the qualifications of hospice social workers required by the CMS. Reese and Raymer (2004) found better hospice and client outcomes when social work services were provided by an MSW and when the social worker was supervised by a social worker. The CMS failed to require an MSW for hospice social workers in the last hospice conditions of participation. They require *either* an MSW from a school of social work accredited by the Council on Social Work Education and one year of experience *or* a BSW from an accredited school of social work and one year of experience *or* a bachelor's degree in psychology, sociology, or a related field and one year of experience. With a bachelor's degree, they require MSW supervision. The supervision does not have to be provided on-site but can be by phone or e-mail. But social workers prepared with a bachelor's degree already employed at the time of the new regulation are exempt from this supervision; therefore all hospices should be exempt from this new regulation (Centers for Medicare and Medicaid Services 2008).

The reasoning of the CMS was that licensing requirements for social workers are inconsistent between states and rural hospices claim limited access to MSW-qualified social workers (National Association of Social Workers 2010). This author has made the argument to rural hospice directors that they don't seek to undermine the qualifications for hospice nurses due to their rural location. If they pay an adequate salary, hospice social workers will come. This continues to be an issue, therefore, that needs to be addressed.

Clark (2004) recommends that we communicate the standards that have been developed to educational programs, professional associations, and legislative and regulatory bodies. Also, the following hospice social workers acquiring credentials launched by NASW may be helpful in establishing our expertise in the field:

Advanced Certified Hospice and Palliative Social Worker (ACHP-SW—MSW level)
Certified Hospice and Palliative Social Worker (CHP-SW—BSW level)

National Association of Social Workers (2010) also advocates for full participation of social workers on the team. They recommend that social workers provide training about effective team collaboration and orient team members about the training and perspectives of social work (National Association of Social Workers 2010; Reese and Sontag 2001). They also suggest providing a framework for resolving disagreements about client assessment and intervention (National Association of Social Workers 2010).

In order to claim our role in end-of-life care, social workers must take leadership within the field of hospice (Chachkes and Foster 2004). We must assume a highly visible leadership role through activities at all levels of social work: education, practice, research, professional associations, administration, and policy (Clark 2004).

This remains difficult, as social workers are still seen as ancillary professionals within medical settings (Clark 2004), and other disciplines claim the expertise that social workers view as their own role (Chachkes and Foster 2004; Reese 2011). Other times, social workers in leadership roles identify more with their institutions than as advocates of their profession (Chachkes and Foster 2004). This was seen in a recent study of hospice administrators' views of social work roles in hospice (Reese 2011). Even administrators who were social workers by profession did not recognize all the roles that social workers should be playing in their organization. This is also seen among spokespersons in the media, and in public and policy development forums, or psychotherapists or PhDs who fail to identify themselves as social workers (Chachkes and Foster 2004). We must engage in leadership by

> presenting innovative programs nationally;
> encouraging professional organizations to promote the profession with policy makers and the media;
> taking leadership positions outside the social work field while identifying ourselves as social workers;
> taking seminars on leadership in end-of-life care (e.g., at the Smith College School of Social Work Post-Master's Program in End of Life Care);
> ensuring that social work researchers are included on national panels that review and award research grants (Clark 2004).

To summarize, we need to be at the decision-making table. We need to strengthen the connection between social work and policy makers such as the CMS and the NIH and we need to include the voice of social work in health care reform efforts (National Association Social Workers 2010).

RESPONSIBILITY FOR MACRO ADVOCACY

Raymer and Gardia state that "advocacy is not optional; it is one of our profession's ethical obligations and a cornerstone of social work practice" (2011:683). We must identify opportunities to effect change. Some current issues needing advocacy from social workers include client access to quality care, disparities in hospice care, and honoring advance directives.

CLIENT ACCESS TO QUALITY CARE

Although most people prefer palliative care in terminal illness, knowledge about hospice as an option is limited. Still less than one-third of people die with hospice services (Simmons 2004). We need to address the barriers to care, which include physicians' values and lack of education about making a terminal prognosis as well as the difficulty or impossibility of making an accurate prediction about this. In addition, we need to address physician difficulty in having such a conversation with a patient, which is required by law, since the patient must sign a statement relinquishing access to curative care in order to be eligible for hospice. Due to these barriers, patients who are referred to hospice are referred too close to death for the program to offer full services (Simmons 2004). We should advocate for social workers to be called in to help conduct that conversation with the patient and family. We should engage in public education, actually beginning in elementary and middle schools (Clark 2004).

DISPARITIES IN HOSPICE CARE

Cultural competence in hospices and access to care for diverse populations is still a problem (Clark 2004; National Association of Social Workers 2010). Almost all the patients and staff in hospice are European American whites (Reese and Raymer 2004). We need to engage with leaders of diverse communities, invite them to serve on hospice boards, engage in outreach to the community, and explore mechanisms to reach underserved populations (Raymer and Gardia 2011).

We need to educate health care professionals and engage with universities educating disciplines on the hospice team. We need to hire diverse employees. We need to develop cultural competence training tools for continuing education and for our staff (Clark 2004).

HONORING ADVANCE DIRECTIVES

Most people are still not preparing advance directives, and evidence exists that, when they do, the advance directives are often not being honored (Arons 2004). The focus on informing patients of their right to an advance directive should switch to a focus on a "developmental discussion process" (Peres 2011:764). Social workers can be very helpful in that discussion.

SOCIAL WORK EDUCATION NEEDS

FORMAL SOCIAL WORK EDUCATION

As baby boomers age, there will be a great shortage in end-of-life care professionals (Clark 2004). There is a lack of interest and a lack of education now among social work programs; we must greatly increase our participation in this field in order to prepare for future client needs. Social work education programs at both the BSW and MSW levels must offer specialized hospice social work curricula as well as infusing the curriculum with end-of-life care content (Clark 2004; National Association of Social Workers 2010). Also NASW recommends field placements and collaboration with community programs. Browning and Gerbino (2011) assert that education should be tied to practice realities and should be a growth process grounded in the relationship between the teacher and student. Social work education is key to continuing our progress in advancing the field of hospice social work. The following will discuss recommended content for hospice social work education.

Social work education should use a holistic approach, including biopsychosocial and spiritual aspects of end-of-life care, and address micro/mezzo/ and macro levels of practice. It should use theoretical frameworks that incorporate all these. It should incorporate current literature and current standards for practice in end-of-life care.

We can prepare social work students to advocate for changes needed in the field. First, we need to prepare them to articulate the social work role. Second, we need to prepare students to document social work outcomes by teaching them research skills and a value orientation toward gathering evidence of the effectiveness of social work practice on the hospice team.

Social work education should include personal preparation of social workers, addressing their own experience of death anxiety as they are exposed to end-of-life content and field placement experiences. They should develop awareness of their own beliefs about end-of-life care and consider how they may differ from clients served.

Micro level content should include interventions with spirituality, suicide and assisted suicide, denial of terminality and distinguishing it from genuine hope or religious belief in a miracle. It should include crisis intervention and the importance of social work participation in on-call responsibilities. It should include content about advance directives, intervention models, and any existing evidence of their effectiveness.

Mezzo level content should address practice with families. Research with the Social Work Assessment Tool (SWAT, Reese et al. 2006) indicated less success with caregivers than with patients. Social workers need to address denial with families if it is causing problems such as the safety of the patient or children in the home. Bereavement issues also should be addressed—social workers play an important role in the hospice field as bereavement coordinators.

An important area for consideration is interdisciplinary team collaboration. It is quite effective if the course itself can be interdisciplinary in order to demonstrate negative team issues and learn to address them. An area of concern continues to be finding ways to articulate the social work role to other disciplines. Content should be included about how to promote high-functioning interdisciplinary teams, how to provide staff support, and how to advocate with the team for client self-determination.

Macro level content should include intervention with the organization, focusing on administration of the organization, development of organizational cultural and linguistic competence, community outreach, increasing the diversity of staff, providing cultural competence training, and conducting a needs assessment for the hospice. Much of this content can be taught in a hospice field placement. Macro level content should also include community intervention: collaboration with health providers, public education about end-of-life care options (Clark 2004), and outreach to diverse communities.

CONTINUING EDUCATION

In addition, practicing social workers should provide as well as participate in continuing education opportunities (Clark 2004; Csikai and Jones 2011; National Association of Social Workers 2010). Many opportunities exist, including courses in end-of-life care offered by Schools of Social Work, and end-of-life care certificate programs including the Zelda Foster Studies in Palliative and End-of-Life Care at the Silver School of Social Work at New York University as well as the Smith College/Bay State Medical Center End-of-Life Certificate Program. There is a postgraduate social work fellowship in palliative and end-of-life care at the Beth Israel Medical Center, Department of Pain Medicine and Palliative Care. There are also conferences sponsored by national organizations, including the NHPCO, the American

Academy of Hospice and Palliative Medicine, the Association of Pediatric Oncology Social Work, and the Association of Oncology Social Work. There is a two-day workshop traditionally provided as a preconference at the annual NHPCO Clinical Team Conference, the Social Work End-of-Life Education Project, presented by Mary Raymer and Theresa Altilio.

In addition, the first doctoral program in palliative care has been developed at the School of Health and Medicine at Lancaster University in the United Kingdom. Continuing education is also available online through various professional organizations including NASW, the Social Work Hospice and Palliative Care Network, and the Association for Death Education and Counseling (Clark 2004).

Csikai (2011) emphasizes the importance of joining professional organizations so as to have access to the latest information in the field. The National Association of Social Workers has developed the NASW *Standards for Social Work Practice in Palliative and End-of-Life Care* and recommends that we use them as a guide (www.socialworkers.org/practice/bereavement/standards/default.asp.

FUTURE VISION FOR THE ROLE OF HOSPICE WITHIN PALLIATIVE CARE

"It is becoming clear that there is not a boundary between when life-prolonging therapy ends and palliative care begins and that both can be provided concurrently" (Peres 2011:756), and Simmons (2004) argues that it is artificial to draw an abrupt line at six months between curative and palliative care. To enter hospice one must give up traditional Medicare benefits and enter the Medicare hospice benefit, which has great advantages because it pays for everything. But clients have to give up their current caregivers and enter a new program at a stressful time for which they may be emotionally and spiritually unprepared.

One response to this has been the development of palliative care units in hospitals. They are not labeled terminal care like hospice, so they may be less threatening to patients who have not faced these issues, but they don't have access to the same financing. Goals for treatment for patients with the same conditions may vary widely; a possible criticism of palliative care with terminally ill patients is collusion with denial and thereby not providing needed biopsychosocial and spiritual end-of-life services such as hospice provides. This was true in a study this author conducted in a home health care agency. In this study I interviewed the physicians of home health care patients whose nurse had told me they were terminally ill. Their doctors said they were not terminal. Of this group of patients, most were referred to hospice or died within a few months of my study, thus being deprived of the benefits of patient and family care geared toward terminal illness (Reese, 1998).

For over a decade, in the hope of addressing these problems, hospice professionals have been advocating for a coordinated continuum of care between different forms of care in a life-threatening illness, beginning from the first diagnosis (Clark 2004; National Hospice and Palliative Care Organization 2001). Hospitals and hospice programs should be brought together to partner in improved end-of-life care. Hospices should participate in palliative care program development in hospitals. Patients and families need wider access to such care and improved quality of care. Health insurance reimbursement for such programs needs to be a focus. Aspects of such programs should be professional education about hospice, hospice inpatient units, encouraging admission to hospice, a hospice liaison nurse position at the hospital, a hospice team at the hospital to facilitate admissions, and palliative care coordinating committees. Positioning hospice in partnerships within a broader continuum of palliative care services that can respond to patients' needs from the point of diagnosis is seen as beneficial for patients and families as well as for hospice programs. We need to encourage earlier conversations about end-of-life treatment preferences and familiarize clients and professionals with hospice care. With these efforts in place, patients and families may be more open to a hospice referral when that becomes appropriate.

This chapter has summarized current needs for further development of the hospice field, including research priorities, continued advocacy for the social work role, needs for advocacy on the macro level, further development of social work education in end-of-life care, and continued advocacy on behalf of a continuum of care for patients with life-threatening diagnoses. The development of this relatively new field already underway is tremendous and has been a result of hospice social work advocates working together, with their final goal the well-being of the patients and families they serve.

I would like to end this chapter and this book with a saying I heard often as a hospice social worker: "I have learned more from my patients than they ever learned from me." Serving in a hospice is a life-changing experience. These pages have attempted to convey that; a person who has the privilege of joining a client on this life journey will never be the same. We must exert our utmost efforts to provide the best care and work tirelessly toward further improvement in our field, all the while knowing that the highest benefit, and sometimes the only benefit, will come from "just offering one's presence." Thank you for accompanying me on the adventure of writing this book; I hope it has provided some helpful insights for your work in the sacred space that is hospice social work.

REFERENCES

Arons, S. 2004. "Current Legal Issues in End-of-Life Care." In J. Berzoff and P. Silverman, eds., *Living with Dying: A Handbook for End-of-Life Practitioners*, pp. 730–760. New York: Columbia University Press.

Browning, D. M., and S. Gerbino. 2011. "Navigating in Swampy Lowlands: A Relational Approach to Practice-Based Learning in Palliative Care." In Terry Altilio and Shirley Otis-Green, eds., *Oxford Textbook of Palliative Social Work*, pp. 673–681. New York: Oxford University Press.

Centers for Medicare and Medicaid Services. 2008. *Conditions of Participations*. Retrieved from https://www.cms.gov/CFCsAndCoPs/05_Hospice.asp#TopOfPage.

Chachkes, E., and Z. Foster. 2004. In Joan Berzoff and Phyllis R. Silverman, eds., *Living with Dying: A Handbook for End-of-Life Healthcare Practitioners*, pp. 823–837. New York: Columbia University Press.

Clark, E. J. 2004. "The Future of Social Work in End-of-Life Care." In Joan Berzoff and Phyllis R. Silverman, eds., *Living with Dying: A Handbook for End-of-Life Healthcare Practitioners*, pp. 838–847. New York: Columbia University Press.

Csikai, E. L. 2005. "In this Issue." *Journal of Social Work in End-of-Life and Palliative Care* 1, no. 1: 1–2.

———. 2011. "Professional Connections for Palliative Social Workers." In Terry Altilio and Shirley Otis-Green, eds., *Oxford Textbook of Palliative Social Work*, pp. 703–707. New York: Oxford University Press.

Csikai, E. L., and B. L. Jones. 2011. "Professional Development: Educational Opportunities and Resources." In Terry Altilio and Shirley Otis-Green, eds., *Oxford Textbook of Palliative Social Work*, pp. 695–701. New York: Oxford University Press.

Goldberg, J., and M. Scharlin. 2011. "Financial Considerations for the Palliative Social Worker." In Terry Altilio and Shirley Otis-Green, eds., *Oxford Textbook of Palliative Social Work*, pp. 709–718. New York: Oxford University Press.

Ivanko, B. 2011. "Quality Improvement and Organizational Change." In Terry Altilio and Shirley Otis-Green, eds., *Oxford Textbook of Palliative Social Work*, pp. 745–752. New York: Oxford University Press.

National Association of Social Workers, Social Work Policy Institute. 2010. *Hospice Social Work, Linking Policy, Practice, and Research: A Report from the March 25, 2010 Symposium*. Washington, DC: NASW.

National Hospice and Palliative Care Organization. 2001. *Hospital-Hospice Partnerships in Palliative Care: Creating a Continuum of Service*. Alexandria, VA: NHPCO.

Oliver, D. P., and K. T. Washington. 2011. "Merging Research and Clinical Practice." In Terry Altilio and Shirley Otis-Green, eds., *Oxford Textbook of Palliative Social Work*, pp. 735–743. New York: Oxford University Press.

Palos, G. R. 2011. "Social Work Research Agenda in Palliative and End-of-Life Care." In Terry Altilio and Shirley Otis-Green, eds., *Oxford Textbook of Palliative Social Work*, pp. 719–733. New York: Oxford University Press.

Peres, J. R. 2011. "Public Policy in Palliative and End-of-life Care." In Terry Altilio and Shirley Otis-Green, eds., *Oxford Textbook of Palliative Social Work*, pp. 753–769. New York: Oxford University Press.

Raymer, M., and G. Gardia. 2011. "Enhancing Professionalism, Leadership, and Advocacy: A Call to Arms." In Terry Altilio and Shirley Otis-Green, eds., *Oxford Textbook of Palliative Social Work*, pp. 683–687. New York: Oxford University Press.

Reese, D. 1998. "Patient Self-Determination Study." Unpublished data.

Reese, D. 2011. "Interdisciplinary Perceptions of the Social Work Role in Hospice: A Replication of the Classic Kulys and Davis Study." *Journal of Social Work in End-of-Life and Palliative Care* 7, no. 4: 383–406.

Reese, D., and M. Raymer. 2004. "Relationships Between Social Work Services and Hospice Outcomes: Results of the National Hospice Social Work Survey." *Social Work* 49, no. 3: 415–422.

Reese, D., M. Raymer, S. Orloff, S. Gerbino, R. Valade, S. Dawson, C. Butler, M. Wise-Wright, and R. Huber. 2006. "The Social Work Assessment Tool (SWAT): Developed by the Social Worker Section of the National Council of Hospice and Palliative Professionals, National Hospice and Palliative Care Organization." *Journal of Social Work in End-of-Life and Palliative Care* 2, no. 2: 65–95.

Reese, D., and M-A. Sontag. 2001. "Barriers and Solutions for Successful Inter-professional Collaboration on the Hospice Team." *Health and Social Work* 26, no. 3: 167–175.

Simmons, J. 2004. "Financing End-of-Life Care." In J. Berzoff and P. Silverman, eds., *Living with Dying: A Comprehensive Resource for End-of-Life Care*, pp. 813–824. New York: Columbia University Press.

Social Work Assessment Tool (SWAT) Handbook

The Social Work Assessment Tool was developed by the Social Work Outcomes Task Force of the Social Worker Section, National Hospice and Palliative Care Organization, National Council of Hospice and Palliative Professionals. Members of the task force included Mary Raymer, ACSW, Ruth Huber, Ph.D., MSW, Dona Reese, Ph.D., MSW, Stacy Orloff, Ed.D., LCSW, and Susan Gerbino, Ph.D., MSW. Charlotte Butler, Ph.D., had major responsibility for writing this handbook.

INTRODUCTION

The purpose of this booklet is to provide practical information on the development and use of the Social Work Assessment Tool (SWAT). Hopefully you will find the booklet informative and a valuable guide when using the SWAT. If you have any additional questions or need more help please contact:

Social Worker Section
National Council of Hospice and Palliative Professionals
National Hospice and Palliative Care Organization
1700 Diagonal Road, Suite 625
Alexandria, VA 22314
(703) 837–1500

SOCIAL WORK SERVICES IN HOSPICE AND PALLIATIVE CARE: IMPORTANCE AND IMPACT IN THE TREATMENT PROCESS

There is no doubt that social work services are important in effective end of life care. Research has demonstrated that increased social work involvement is significantly associated with:

- Lower hospice costs
- Lower pain costs
- Fewer on-call visits by staff
- Fewer hospitalizations of patients
- Fewer nights of continuous care
- Better team functioning
- Fewer visits by home health aides, nurses, and the agency
- Decreased staff turnover
- Increased job satisfaction for MDs, nurses, and social workers.
- Higher client satisfaction and quality of life for patients
- Lower severity of problems in the case

(Combined results from Cherin 1997; Mahar, Eickman, and Bushfield 1997; Paquette 1997; and Reese and Raymer 2004)

We also know that certain psychosocial and spiritual issues are associated with client outcomes (see table A.1). We know that social workers are addressing these issues, but without documentation there is no way to demonstrate social work effectiveness in routine agency quality assurance efforts.

CREATING THE SWAT

In response to requests from all over the nation for a tool to document social work effectiveness, the Social Worker Section of the National Hospice and Palliative Care Organization's National Council of Hospice and Palliative Professionals has developed the SWAT. Our hope is that the SWAT will be used as part of the routine quality assurance activities of hospices and palliative care programs nationally as well as contributing to a national database on hospice and palliative care social work outcomes. Calculating national averages will allow development of benchmarks for social work outcomes. Examining service approaches in programs with higher scores can then identify best practices. National dissemination of this information will eventually contribute to improved social work practice in end of life care.

SWAT CONTENT

There are eleven individual psychosocial and spiritual issues that make up the SWAT. These issues were selected based on research results and practice wisdom about areas of major influence on end of life care outcomes. Table A1 lists the issues, a description of each issue, and related tasks to be accomplished with each issue. Following the table is a sample of the SWAT form and brief instructions on how to use the form.

ISSUE	DESCRIPTION	TASKS TO BE ACCOMPLISHED
1. End of life decisions consistent with their religious and cultural norms	Patient self-determination is a key aspect of hospice philosophy and so important social work value. The ability to make one's own choice promotes self-determination. Legal and ethical questions may be involved, as well as cultural and religious beliefs and preferences regarding end of life care.	Social worker discusses end-of-life preferences with clients, advocates for patient self-determination with team. Helps clarify values, assesses whether there are concerns. Refers to religious leaders for specific religious questions. Provides resources if needed. Develops practice approaches and policies that make room for differing beliefs and preferences, leads the way in developing cultural competence.
2. Patient thoughts of suicide or wanting to hasten death	Practice wisdom suggests that suicidal ideation, request for assisted suicide, or a suicide attempt may be an issue for a patient. Often unmet needs, death anxiety, a need to control the circumstances of death, or other emotional distress create a desire to hasten death.	Meeting the needs leading to suicidal ideation may address the issue: counseling regarding complicated anticipatory grief, pain, and symptom control, obtaining resources to support the family in caregiving, addressing financial needs, advocating for patient self-determination.
3. Anxiety about death	Elements of death anxiety are fear of loneliness, fear of personal extinction, fear of suffering, and fear of the unknown.* Much of this entails questions about the afterlife; thus death anxiety may overlap with spiritual issues. Death anxiety leads to lack of awareness of prognosis or denial.	Allow patient to openly discuss spiritual issues, clarify own beliefs. Spirituality and social support reduce death anxiety. Coming to a sense that one's own life has been valuable as it is and a sense of oneness with all may decrease death anxiety.
4. Preferences about environment (e.g., pets, own bed, etc.)	Patient self-determination regarding preferences about the environment is an important part of hospice philosophy. Preferences may include where the bed is located, the desire for pets in the room, preferences about who visits and when, having treasured objects close by, music, books, etc.	Preferences should be elicited and explored. Social workers act as advocates for patient preferences with family members and the hospice and palliative care team.
5. Social support	Informal and formal support, patient's environment, family, significant others, friends, and resources. Better social support predicts a preference for home hospice care. Spirituality increases social support.	Help promote open discussions, remove barriers to intimacy and help maintain intimacy. Provide insight into family strength, needs, and adjustment to terminality.
6. Financial resources	A major concern is the adequacy of health insurance to cover end-of-life care expenses, medications, medical equipment. Other issues may be a need for caregivers in the home and a loss of income due to the illness.	Assessing how well clients' financial resources meet their needs; referring to formal supports when needed.
7. Safety issues	Client safety becomes an issue when activities of daily living become more difficult. Clients who live alone or with family members in denial about the patient's condition may be in danger of injury in the home.	Social worker assesses client safety and obtains informal and formal supports as needed. Provides counseling if family denial is leading to an unsafe situation.

ISSUE	DESCRIPTION	TASKS TO BE ACCOMPLISHED
8. Comfort issues	Patient's physical comfort is influenced by the psychosocial and spiritual dimensions. Increased social work services is associated with decreased pain control costs.	Social workers are becoming knowledgeable about nonphysical pain control interventions, including relaxation and meditation techniques.
9. Complicated anticipatory grief (e.g., guilt, depression, etc.)	Some factors interfere with resolution of anticipatory grief. These include guilt about one's past actions, anger and depression in response to the terminal illness, spiritual questions. Patient cannot die in peace.	Assess patient's beliefs and concerns, provide counseling, opportunities to resolve conflicts or ask for forgiveness, refer to religious leaders for specifically religious questions.
10. Awareness of prognosis	Lack of awareness of terminality although being informed of it. Denial is a way of coping with death anxiety, but one cannot accomplish tasks of dying while in denial. Denial compromises patient self-determination. Denial of patient's terminality by primary caregiver can lead to unsafe home conditions or lack of support for patient end of life decisions.	Avoid confronting the patient and stripping them of their denial. A little bit of denial is considered positive. Intervene when harmful situations develop. Patients go in and out of denial, and will bring up questions about their terminality during periods when they are ready to address it. Death anxiety leads to denial; reducing death anxiety by addressing spirituality will reduce denial.
11. Spirituality (e.g., higher purpose in life, sense of connection with all)	Different concept from religion. Religion has to do with a certain belief system, affiliating with an organized religion. Spirituality applies to everyone, regardless of religious or nonreligious path. Finding meaning and purpose in life, sense of connection with all (nature, others, God, ultimate reality, according to one's own belief system). Spirituality was the most frequently addressed issue in home visits to clients in a study of a Midwestern hospice. Addressed by all team members; refer to appropriate chaplain for specifically religious issues.	Help patient discover a higher purpose in life and a sense of connection or oneness with all. Encourage patient to resolve spiritual issues connected with the meaning of life and suffering, unfinished business, clarifying his/her belief system, relationship with the Ultimate, isolation, and transpersonal experiences. These may include reconciling with someone, praying for forgiveness, or forgiving oneself and asking for forgiveness from another.

H. Conte, M. Weiner, and R. Plutchik. 1982. "Measuring Death Anxiety: Conceptual, Psychometric, and Factor-Analytic Aspects." Journal of Personality and Social Psychology 43, no. 4: 775–785.

USING THE SWAT

This section provides a case scenario of a hospice patient and family and details the clinical interventions utilized by the social worker in providing care in this case. Following the case study are instructions on using the SWAT to document client outcomes. Then a completed SWAT is provided, with the scores we would have given these clients. Finally, another case example is provided with a practice SWAT to be completed for training purposes.

CASE EXAMPLE

Mary, seventy-year-old terminally ill patient
  David, fifty-year-old son, lives with mother, travels a lot
  Michael, forty-five years old, lives with mother much of time
  Susan, forty-year-old daughter, lives in Florida
  Dorothy, thirty-five-year-old daughter, lives locally, has been designated as the primary caregiver

The patient, a Caucasian protestant widow, is diagnosed with end-stage chronic obstructive pulmonary disease and has a history of asthma. She has shortness of breath with minimal exertion and uses oxygen most of the time. She was on a ventilator in 1994 after respiratory arrest, but now has a living will that states her wish for comfort care only—she doesn't want any death-delaying procedures. She also has a do not resuscitate order, and has designated her son David as power of attorney for health care decisions and finances. Her physician predicts she has six months or less to live, according to concrete guidelines developed for determining prognosis.

Mary lives with her son David, who travels a lot and isn't home much. Her other son Michael also lives with her much of the time. The patient feels that she lives in an unsafe neighborhood and keeps a gun in the house for that reason. The Department of Aging has provided an aide to do housework two hours per week. She has two daughters; one is Susan, in Florida, whom she doesn't see very often. The other daughter, Dorothy, lives close by, but works and visits on Mondays. Dorothy is the primary caregiver and has slowly been taking over her mother's care and responsibilities. Mary's husband died many years ago when he was in his twenties, and she appears to have coped well with this loss. She was divorced due to her alcoholism. She raised four children alone, and now enjoys her grandchildren. She was an LPN, but became disabled and retired on Social Security Disability at age sixty-two. She has Medicare and the Medicare Hospice Benefit.

Her children say that, due to her alcoholism, she was not there for them as children. The patient complains that her son David insults her, but Dorothy reported that the patient has always insulted David. Dorothy is resentful about her mother's abuse toward her children and their father. Dorothy also complains of a lack of support from her siblings, who leave the care of their mother to her. She is glad, though, that her sister Susan has been looking into hospices in Florida.

Mary states that she wants to stay at home and die in her own bed, but has been afraid she will panic when she gets short of breath. She has had difficulty with the idea of calling hospice instead of 911 at times like this. She has expected that she would want to go to the hospital and would be afraid to be home alone during respiratory arrest. Her family also is not used to the hospice philosophy of dying at home. Dorothy was able to make an agreement with hospice staff, though, that she would call the hospice nurse first before calling 911. If the nurse is not able to be there immediately, and she is really afraid her mother will choke to death, she will call 911.

Mary has portable oxygen tanks, a wheelchair, bedside commode, and a home alert system. She states that her home is arranged the way she wants it. She is obese and has diabetes. She takes medications for shortness of breath and anxiety. She says she has been shaky on her feet lately, feeling "hyper" from all the meds, and has difficulty breathing. Staff is concerned that she smokes. She is concerned about finances. She has many unpaid medical bills and wants to be able to keep her house so that her children can sell it to pay for her funeral.

Mary needs help with bathing, dressing, feeding, transfers from bed to wheelchair, and ambulation to the commode. She complains that her children will assume no responsibility for her. She wants to be able to get out of the house for outings. She went to a nursing home temporarily in 2/96, and did well there according to staff, but did not consider it good quality of life and would not stay. She does not want to return to the nursing home. Mary is fearful of thinking about death, but is capable of open discussion of thoughts and feelings. She discussed dying a peaceful death in bed. Discussed funeral plans—patient knows funeral home, wants cremation, wants memorial service only, private service only.

She copes through focusing on the positives, and staying involved with her children's lives. She does worry about leaving her children behind. Although she takes medication for anxiety, she has coped fairly well and denies any thoughts of ending her life.

She felt close to God the last time she was sick. She says she is not religious, though, and has no belief in life after death. Her philosophy of life has been to have fun all her life. Her life has been carefree, she has partied, drunk alcohol, she says she has basically done whatever she wanted in her life. Her one regret is that she wishes she could have been a better mother. But recognizes that she did the best she could—has forgiven herself.

When Dorothy was asked about her beliefs, she stated that she no longer believes in God. If there was a God, He wouldn't have let her be abused, let her father die so young, and let her mother die in this painful way.

INSTRUCTIONS

The Social Work Assessment Tool (SWAT) was designed for use by social workers to document outcomes achieved by the patient and/or caregivers. The case example presents the history of a patient who can typically be seen in any hospice environment. The instructions provided in this section will detail how to effectively document and assess the patient's outcome.

Following these instructions, a sample SWAT that has been completed based on the case example of Mary is provided.

GENERAL INSTRUCTIONS

1. Complete the SWAT immediately after each patient and/or primary caregiver visit. Do not complete it after phone calls or other kinds of interventions in the case. Rate the patient and primary caregiver on how well they are doing on each issue listed on the SWAT. Each of these issues is an important factor in hospice outcomes and

should be assessed on every visit. Assessment on each visit will allow documentation of progress in the case and ensure that clients are not having difficulty in these areas.

2. Questions should not necessarily be read to the client, because it is possible clients are not ready to face issues that openly. The social worker should use assessment skills with the patient and/or family members to come to an understanding of the clients' progress on these issues and then complete the SWAT after the session based on the social worker's own judgment.

3. Fill in the date of the contact—note the month, day, and year.

4. Rate the patient on how well s/he is doing on concerns related to each issue, and rate the primary caregiver on how well s/he is doing on his/her own related to the issue (or on how well s/he is coping with the concerns of the patient regarding the issue, whichever seems to apply). Circle 1 if, in comparison to most cases in your experience, the client is having far more difficulty than usual. Circle 2 if the client is having some difficulty, but not to a severe level. Circle 3 if the client is not having difficulty with the issue, but is not doing well either. Circle 4 if the client is doing reasonably well compared to most clients, but not as well as some clients. If there are no concerns at all regarding the issue, circle 5 for "extremely well." There should be no responses of "not applicable." It is not possible to use the SWAT with unresponsive patients. In that case the social worker could still use the SWAT with the primary caregiver.

5. There is no one correct rating in a case. Social workers will vary somewhat in their ratings, but there will be a trend toward general agreement overall.

6. After rating the clients, calculate a total score for the patient by adding the individual item scores in the patient column. Calculate a total score for the primary caregiver by adding the individual item scores in the primary caregiver column.

7. If there is more than one social work visit in a case, there will be a SWAT completed on the first visit (pretest) and one completed on the last visit (post-test). When the case is closed, compare the pretest scores with the post-test scores to determine whether the clients experienced progress on the issues included in the SWAT. The hospice or palliative care program may want to record these scores in an additional file as a part of their quality assurance efforts. The total scores can be compared for an overall summary of social work outcomes. Individual item scores can be compared as well. Usually total scores will show general improvement on the part of clients, even if clients did not experience resolution of certain individual issues.

8. Scores can just be compared for differences between the pretest and post-test without using data analysis. If preferred, the scores of all patients can be entered into a Microsoft Office Excel file (or any other data analysis program), then a t-test can be used to compare all pretest scores to all post-test scores. A t-test will indicate whether the difference between pretest and post-test scores is statistically significant.

OUR SWAT RATINGS BASED ON THE CASE EXAMPLE

   1. *End-of-life decisions consistent with their religious and cultural norms*

Mary and her primary caregiver have been struggling with end-of-life decisions. Mary does not want to be placed on a respirator and wants to die peacefully in her bed. On the other hand, she is afraid of the process of dying of respiratory distress and is more used to the idea of dying in the hospital. Dorothy, the primary caregiver, has made an agreement with the hospice nurse. She will call the nurse before calling 911, but if Dorothy is fearful about Mary's symptoms and feels she needs help immediately, she will call 911. There do not appear to be cultural or religious concerns about the ethics involved in the decision. Since Mary has worked on this issue and is making progress toward a decision, we did not give her a rating of 1. She has not made a decision, however, and still feels quite anxious and confused about these issues. Thus, we gave her a rating of 2.

Dorothy has been able to make a decision despite expressing some discomfort with the possibility of not calling 911, so we did not give her a negative rating of 1 or 2. On the other hand, Mary was not involved in this decision and thus it is not clear that the plan will uphold Mary's wishes. Thus we do not consider this issue resolved and did not give Dorothy a positive rating. We gave her a rating of 3, Neutral, indicating neither a negative nor a positive rating.

   2. *Patient thoughts of suicide or wanting to hasten death*

Although the patient keeps a gun in the house, she has denied any suicidal ideation. Since no concerns have been noted about this issue in this case, we have given Dorothy a rating of 5. Mary's history of alcohol abuse is a risk factor, however. Thus we gave her a rating of 4.

   3. *Anxiety about death*

Mary is afraid she will panic when she becomes short of breath. She is fearful of thinking about death and takes medication for anxiety, but is capable of open discussion of thoughts and feelings and has coped fairly well by focusing on the positives and staying active in her children's lives. Death anxiety is difficult to rate; a client may appear to be calm when in reality s/he is too anxious to acknowledge his/her feelings and copes through denial. Since Mary is experiencing a significant amount of anxiety and needs medication as a result, we would not give her a positive rating of 4 or 5. However, she is handling her anxiety well enough that she is able to discuss issues openly rather than resorting to a significant degree of denial. Thus, we gave her a rating of 3 for this issue.

Dorothy does not exhibit any signs of death anxiety or significant concern about her mother's anxiety. She is somewhat concerned about end-of-life decisions, though, so we gave her a rating of 4.

4. *Preferences about environment (e.g., pets, own bed, etc.)*

Mary states that her home is arranged the way she wants it. She has some concerns about her environment, however, since she feels that her neighborhood is unsafe and she is afraid of dying alone. Thus, we gave her neither a positive nor a negative rating. We gave her a 3.

Dorothy does not appear to have any concerns regarding her mother's environment or her mother's coping with this issue. Thus we gave her a 5.

5. *Social support*

Both the patient and primary caregiver have some forms of support and are lacking others. Mary has resources provided for her by the Department of Aging and has a home alert system. She feels that she is involved in her children's lives and states that she enjoys her grandchildren. Her daughter Dorothy has shown support in agreeing to serve as the primary caregiver and has been providing some care and taking over responsibilities. Her son David has been supportive in allowing Mary to live with him and has agreed to serve as power of attorney. On the other hand, David isn't home much, and Mary is afraid to be home alone during respiratory arrest. She feels that her neighborhood is unsafe. Her relationships with her children seem strained, and she feels that her children are not assuming responsibility for her. She has lived for many years without the support of a husband. It is unclear whether she has supportive friendships. Since Mary has some supports, both formal and informal, we did not give her a rating of 1 or 2. Since her physical needs are great and she is spending much of her time alone, however, we also did not give her a positive rating of 4 or 5. Since the pros and cons seem to weigh equally for Mary, we gave her a rating of 3.

Since Dorothy feels some support from her sister Susan, who is looking into hospices in Florida, we did not give her a rating of 1. She feels, however, that most of the care of her mother has been left to her and has felt a lack of support from her mother due to alcoholism and abuse. We gave her a rating of 2, since she seems to lack the support she needs.

6. *Financial resources*

Mary has resources from the Social Security Administration and has the medical equipment and medications she needs. She has her financial affairs in order, as she has designated David as power of attorney for financial decisions. Thus we did not give her a rating of 1 or 2. She is concerned about unpaid bills, however, and concerned about being able to keep her house in order to pay for her funeral. Thus we did not give her a positive rating of 4 or 5. We gave her a 3. Dorothy does not express concerns about finances; thus we gave her a rating of 5.

7. Safety issues

There seem to be some safety concerns in this case. Mary states that the neighborhood is unsafe. Although she needs quite a bit of help with activities of daily living, her primary caregiver works. Mary uses oxygen and smokes. We gave her a rating of 2 for safety issues. Dorothy is not adequately addressing these concerns, thus we also gave her a 2. We have seen more unsafe situations, for example, extremely unsanitary conditions or abuse or patients without primary caregivers. Thus we did not give them a rating of 1.

8. Comfort issues

Mary appears to be fairly uncomfortable and fairly anxious about her symptoms—she has shortness of breath with minimal exertion, is afraid she will panic when she gets short of breath, is afraid to be home alone during respiratory arrest. She is shaky on her feet lately and feeling "hyper." Since we have seen patients in more severe discomfort, we would not give her a rating of 1, but since she seems to need work in this area, we gave her a 2.

Dorothy is also anxious about her mother's symptoms, stating she is afraid her mother will choke to death. Thus, she is not exhibiting a sense of peace and comfort with her mother's dying process. Still, we have seen other primary caregivers with far more anxiety about their loved one's symptoms. Based on this reasoning, we also gave her a rating of 2.

9. Complicated anticipatory grief (e.g., guilt, depression, etc.)

Mary and Dorothy have both expressed elements of complicated anticipatory grief. Mary's one regret is wishing she had been a better mother, and she worries about leaving her children behind. She states though that she did the best she could and forgives herself. Since she has come to peace about this issue, we have given her a rating of 4. We did not give her a rating of 5 because she has not resolved this issue directly with her children.

Dorothy expresses resentment toward her mother about not being there for them as children, being abusive toward them and their father. She has not shown a resolution of these issues. Thus we gave her a rating of 2. We did not give her a rating of 1 since we have seen much worse cases.

10. *Awareness of prognosis*

Both Mary and Dorothy have a realistic awareness of Dorothy's prognosis, and are able to openly discuss it. Mary has made funeral plans, designated a power of attorney, has openly discussed end-of-life decisions. Dorothy also has openly discussed her mother's terminality and plans for end-of-life treatment decisions. We rated both of them as 5 for this issue.

11. *Spirituality (e.g., higher purpose in life, sense of connection with all)*

Mary's philosophy of life has been to have fun, drink, do what she wants. She is not religious and does not believe in life after death. She regrets that she was not a better mother, but she has forgiven herself for this. Based on this, we would say that Mary's purpose in life was focused more on her own pleasure than on a higher purpose that included the welfare of others. She regrets that now, implying that she is now concerned about a higher purpose; however, she has come to a sense of peace about it. In the sense-of-connection dimension, Mary does not appear to feel close to her children, saying they will take no responsibility for her and that David insults her, but she does feel close to God. We have seen cases in which the patient seems to have a deep sense of meaning and purpose in life or is taking action at the end of life that will promote a sense of purpose in life or in the process of dying. Also, we have seen patients with a deep connection to others, humankind, and the universe, or taking steps to reconcile and reconnect with those whom they have hurt. Thus we would not give Mary a 5 on this issue at this point in the case. Since she has some positive resolution in both dimensions of spirituality, however, we would give her a rating of 4.

When Dorothy was asked about her beliefs, she stated that she no longer believes in God. If there was a God, He wouldn't have let her be abused, let her father die so young, and let her mother die in this painful way. Dorothy has lost her belief system, and we don't have an indication that she has developed a new philosophy of life that represents a higher purpose. She does not express signs of strong connection with others or with a spiritual dimension. She is expressing spiritual concerns that need to be addressed. Thus we would give her a rating of 2 for this issue. We would not give her a 1 since we have seen clients with more intensity of emotion about these concerns.

SWAT COMPLETED FOR CASE EXAMPLE

Complete after each social work visit. Rate the patient on how well s(h)e is doing on concerns regarding each issue. Rate the primary caregiver on how well s(h)e is doing on each issue, OR on how well s/he is coping with patient concerns regarding the issue. If there are no concerns in an area, circle 5 ("extremely well"). Each issue should be assessed during each client contact.

Date of social work visit: _____

HOW WELL ARE PATIENT AND PRIMARY CAREGIVER DOING?

ISSUE:	PATIENT					PRIMARY CAREGIVER				
	1 Not well at all	2 Not too well	3 Neutral	4 Reasonably well	5 Extremely well	1 Not well at all	2 Not too well	3 Neutral	4 Reasonably well	5 Extremely well
1. End-of-life decisions consistent with their religious and cultural norms	1	(2)	3	4	5	1	2	(3)	4	5
2. Patient thoughts of suicide or wanting to hasten death	1	2	3	(4)	5	1	2	3	4	(5)
3. Anxiety about death	1	2	(3)	4	5	1	2	3	(4)	5
4. Preferences about environment (e.g., pets, own bed, etc. hasten death	1	2	(3)	4	5	1	2	3	4	(5)
5. Social support	1	2	(3)	4	5	1	(2)	3	4	5
6. Financial resources	1	2	(3)	4	5	1	2	3	4	(5)
7. Safety issues	1	(2)	3	4	5	1	(2)	3	4	5
8. Comfort issues	1	(2)	3	4	5	1	(2)	3	4	5
9. Complicated anticipatory grief (e.g., guilt, depression, etc.	1	2	3	(4)	5	1	(2)	3	4	5
10. Awareness of prognosis	1	2	3	4	(5)	1	2	3	4	(5)
11. Spirituality (e.g., higher purpose in life, sense of connection with all)	1	2	3	(4)	5	1	(2)	3	4	5

TOTAL Patient Score:_____ TOTAL PCG Score:_____

NOTE: To calculate total scores: add the score for each item in the patient column to get a total patient score. Add the score for each item in the primary caregiver column to get a total primary caregiver score.

The Social Work Assessment Tool was developed by the Social Work Outcomes Task Force of the Social Work Section, National Hospice and Palliative Care Organization, National Council of Hospice and Palliative Professionals. Members of the Task Force included Mary Raymer, ACSW, Dona Reese, Ph.D., MSW, Ruth Huber, Ph.D., MSW, Stacy Orloff, Ed. D., LCSW, and Susan Gerbino, Ph.D., MSW. Further information can be obtained from the Social Worker Section, National Council of Hospice and Palliative Professionals, National Hospice and Palliative Care Organization, (703) 837–1500.

PRACTICE EXAMPLE

INSTRUCTIONS: Complete the practice SWAT for this case.

THE CASE OF FRANCES

Frances, a fifty-year-old African American woman with breast cancer, lived with her thirty-year-old son David, who was designated as her primary caregiver. She was a widow, her husband having died under hospice care three years earlier. David was very close to his mother and a lay minister at their church. He was married with two children and was designated as the primary caregiver. Frances stated she preferred to die at home in her own bed and not go to the hospital if she could avoid it. Based on this treatment preference as well as the prognosis that this patient would most likely die within six months, Frances's primary care physician referred her to hospice.

Frances's sister Annie had taken a leave of absence from her job and was able to stay with Frances during the day; the nurse was confident that Annie was attentive to the patient's needs. Frances preferred to stay in her private bedroom with her favorite belongings by her bedside and did not choose to lay in the living room with the family. Annie made sure to let her little dog into the bedroom in accordance with Frances's wishes. The nurse suggested that the volunteer could sit with Frances occasionally and give Annie a break. Annie welcomed this idea, although she said that since church members sat with Frances quite often she would only need this occasionally.

Frances said that although she did not want to be put on a ventilator and wanted to die at home, she felt uncomfortable with a do not resuscitate (DNR) order and didn't want a living will. The patient and family said their financial needs were taken care of with the help of their Southern Baptist Church.

At first Frances and David had said they didn't need spiritual care from the hospice; that they would rather talk with their own pastor. After gaining an understanding of the hospice philosophy and team approach and having the role of their own pastor respected, however, the family agreed to chaplain visits as part of the hospice approach.

After the family agreed to work with the chaplain, she privately assessed the spiritual dimension with David. David said his mother had given up on life and wanted to die in order to be with her husband in the afterlife. He thought his mother's acceptance of her terminality was a sign of a lack of faith. He believed that if she just had enough faith, God would perform a miracle and cure her. He had urged his aunt to call 911 if his mother had respiratory arrest. The chaplain then spoke privately with Frances and found that she felt guilty about her lack of faith and that her son was so upset with her. Despite David's concerns, the chaplain did not see any evidence of suicidal ideation in Frances. His view was that Frances was in agreement with hospice philosophy; she had after all served as the primary caregiver when her husband was a hospice patient. She was not interested in hastening death, but she was accepting of it occurring naturally.

The home health aide, an African American woman, visited the next day. She was able to assess more of the social dimension since Frances confided in her that she had a general mistrust of the health care system. She had heard stories of mistreatment of African Americans by doctors. Despite this fear, however, she was even more afraid she might panic and ask her sister to call 911. She said she had not signed a DNR order because she was frightened about the idea of white doctors wanting to let her die.

SOCIAL WORK ASSESSMENT TOOL (SWAT)

Complete after each social work visit. Rate the patient on how well s(h)e is doing on concerns regarding each issue. Rate the primary caregiver on how well s(h)e is doing on each issue, OR on how well s(h)e is coping with patient concerns regarding the issue. If there are no concerns in an area, circle 5 ("extremely well"). Each issue should be assessed during each client contact.

NOTE: To calculate total scores: add the score for each item in the patient column to get a total patient score. Add the score for each item in the primary caregiver column to get a total primary caregiver score.

The Social Work Assessment Tool was developed by the Social Work Outcomes Task Force of the Social Work Section, National Hospice and Palliative Care Organization, National Council of Hospice and Palliative Professionals. Members of the Task Force included Mary Raymer, ACSW, Dona Reese, Ph.D., MSW, Ruth Huber, Ph.D., MSW, Stacy Orloff, Ed. D., LCSW, and Susan Gerbino, Ph.D., MSW. Further information can be obtained from the Social Worker Section, National Council of Hospice and Palliative Professionals, National Hospice and Palliative Care Organization, (703) 837–1500.

Patient I.D.# _____ Date of social work visit: _____

HOW WELL ARE PATIENT AND PRIMARY CAREGIVER DOING?

ISSUE:	PATIENT					PRIMARY CAREGIVER				
	1 Not well at all	2 Not too well	3 Neutral	4 Reasonably well	5 Extremely well	1 Not well at all	2 Not too well	3 Neutral	4 Reasonably well	5 Extremely well
1. End-of-life decisions consistent with their religious and cultural norms	1	2	3	4	5	1	2	3	4	5
2. Patient thoughts of suicide or wanting to hasten death	1	2	3	4	5	1	2	3	4	5
3. Anxiety about death	1	2	3	4	5	1	2	3	4	5
4. Preferences about environment (e.g., pets, own bed, etc. hasten death	1	2	3	4	5	1	2	3	4	5
5. Social support	1	2	3	4	5	1	2	3	4	5
6. Financial resources	1	2	3	4	5	1	2	3	4	5
7. Safety issues	1	2	3	4	5	1	2	3	4	5
8. Comfort issues	1	2	3	4	5	1	2	3	4	5
9. Complicated anticipatory grief (e.g., guilt, depression, etc.	1	2	3	4	5	1	2	3	4	5
10. Awareness of prognosis	1	2	3	4	5	1	2	3	4	5
11. Spirituality (e.g., higher purpose in life, sense of connection with all)	1	2	3	4	5	1	2	3	4	5

TOTAL Patient Score:_____ TOTAL PCG Score:_____

JOURNAL

Journal of Social Work in End-of-Life and Palliative Care. Haworth. Editor: Ellen
L. Csikai, BASW, MSW, MPH, PhD. Available at http://www.haworthpressinc.
com/store/product.asp?sku=J457

READINGS

Berzoff, J. and P. Silverman, eds. 2004. *Living with Dying: A Comprehensive Re-*
source for End-of-Life Care. New York: Columbia University Press.

National Hospice and Palliative Care Organization. *Guidelines for Social Work in*
Hospice. Alexandria, VA: NHPCO.

Canda, E., and L. Furman. 1999. *Spiritual Diversity in Social Work Practice: The*
Heart of Helping. New York: Free Press.

Cherin, D. 1997. "Saving Services: Redefining End-Stage Home Care for HIV/
AIDS." *Innovations* (Winter), pp. 26–27.

Connor, S. 1993. "Denial in Terminal Illness: To Intervene or Not to Intervene."
Hospice Journal 8, no. 4: 1–15.

Csikai, E. L., and M. Raymer. 2005. "Social Workers' Educational Needs in End-of-
Life Care." *Social Work in Health Care* 41, no. 1: 53.

Early, B. 1998. "Between Two Worlds: The Psychospiritual Crisis of a Dying Adolescent." *Social Thought: Journal of Religion in the Social Services* 18, no. 2: 67–80.

Huber, R., and J. Bryant. 1996. "The 10-Mile Mourning Bridge and Brief Symptom
Inventory: Close Relatives?" *Hospice Journal* 11, no. 2: 31–46.

Huber, R., V. M. Cox, and W. B. Edelen. 1989. "Right-to-Die Responses from a
Random Sample of 200." *Hospice Journal* 8, no. 3: 1–19. This article was reviewed
by the *Palliative Care Letter* 4, no. 6, in 1992, a publication of Roxane Laborato-
ries, Inc.

Huber, R., and J. W. Gibson. 1990. "New Evidence for Anticipatory Grief." *Hospice*
Journal 6, no. 1: 49–67.

Mahar, T., L. Eickman, and S. Bushfield. 1997. "Efficacy of Early Social Work Intervention." Paper presented at the National Hospice and Palliative Care Organization's Eleventh Management and Leadership Conference.

National Association of Social Workers. 2007. NASW Standards for Social Work
Practice in Palliative and End of Life Care. Available at http://www.socialwork-
ers.org/practice/bereavement/standards/default.asp.

Pearlman, R. A., C. Hsu, H. Starks, and A. L. Back. 2005. "Motivations for Physician-Assisted Suicide; Patient and Family Voices." *Journal of General Internal*
Medicine 20, no. 3: 234.

Reese, D. (formerly Ita, D.) 1995–96. "Testing of a Causal Model: Acceptance of Death in Hospice Patients." *Omega: Journal of Death and Dying* 32, no. 2: 81–92.

——. 2000. "The Role of Primary Caregiver Denial in Inpatient placement during Home Hospice Care." *Hospice Journal* 15, no. 1: 15–33.

——. 2001. "Addressing Spirituality in Hospice: Current Practices and a Proposed Role for Transpersonal Social Work." *Social Thought: Journal of Religion in the Social Services* 20, nos. 1–2: 135–161.

Reese, D., R. Ahern, S. Nair, J. O'Faire, and C. Warren. 1999. "Hospice Access and Utilization by African Americans: Addressing Cultural and Institutional Barriers Through Participatory Action Research." *Social Work* 44, no. 6: 549–559.

Reese, D., and M. Raymer. 2004. "Relationships Between Social Work Services and Hospice Outcomes: Results of the National Hospice Social Work Survey." *Social Work* 49, no. 3: 415–422.

Reese, D., M. Raymer, S. Orloff, S. Gerbino, R. Valade, S. Dawson, C. Butler, M. Wise-Wright, and R. Huber. 2006. "The Social Work Assessment Tool (SWAT): Developed by the Social Worker Section of the National Council of Hospice and Palliative Professionals, National Hospice and Palliative Care Organization." *Journal of Social Work in End-of-Life and Palliative Care* 2, no .2: 65–95.

Smith, E. 1995. "Addressing the Psychospiritual Distress of Death as Reality: A Transpersonal Approach." *Social Work* 40, no. 3: 402–412.

Stein, G. and K. Bonuck. 2001. "Attitudes on End-of-Life Care and Advance Care Planning in the Lesbian and Gay Community." *Journal of Palliative Medicine* 4, no. 2: 173–190.

Van Loon, R. A. 1999. "Desire to Die in Terminally Ill People: A Framework for Assessment and Intervention. *Health and Social Work* 24, no. 4: 260–268.

WEB SITES

American Board of Hospice and Palliative Medicine
www.abhpm.org
American Hospice Association
www.americanhospice.org
Association of Oncology Social Workers
www.aosw.org
Hospice Foundation of America
www.hospicefoundation.org
Hospice Net
www.hospicenet.org

Hospice Service-Medicaid
www.hcfa.gov/medicaid/itc2.htm
Hospice Service-Medicare
www.medicare.gov
National Association of Black Social Workers
www.nabsw.org
National Association of Puerto Rican and Hispanic Social Workers
www.naprhsw.org
International Association of Hospice and Palliative Care
www.hospicecare.com
National Hospice and Palliative Care Organization
www.nhpco.org
National Association of Social Workers
www.naswdc.org
Social Work in Hospice and Palliative Care Network
www.swhpn.org

Standards for Palliative and End-of-Life Care

National Association of Social Workers

STANDARD 1. ETHICS AND VALUES

The values, ethics, and standards of both the profession and contemporary bioethics shall guide social workers practicing in palliative and end of life care. The NASW Code of Ethics (NASW 2000) is one of several essential guides to ethical decision making and practice.

STANDARD 2. KNOWLEDGE

Social workers in palliative and end of life care shall demonstrate a working knowledge of the theoretical and biopsychosocial factors essential to effectively practice with clients and professionals.

STANDARD 3. ASSESSMENT

Social workers shall assess clients and include comprehensive information to develop interventions and treatment planning.

STANDARD 4. INTERVENTION/TREATMENT PLANNING

Social workers shall incorporate assessments in developing and implementing intervention plans that enhance the clients' abilities and decisions in palliative and end of life care.

STANDARD 5. ATTITUDE/SELF-AWARENESS

Social workers in palliative and end of life care shall demonstrate an attitude of compassion and sensitivity to clients, respecting clients' rights to self-determination and dignity. Social workers shall be aware of their own beliefs, values, and feelings and how their personal self may influence their practice.

STANDARD 6. EMPOWERMENT AND ADVOCACY

The social worker shall advocate for the needs, decisions, and rights of clients in palliative and end of life care. The social worker shall engage in social and political action that seeks to ensure that people have equal access to resources to meet their biopsychosocial needs in palliative and end of life care.

STANDARD 7. DOCUMENTATION

Social workers shall document all practice with clients in either the client record or in the medical chart. These may be written or electronic records.

STANDARD 8. INTERDISCIPLINARY TEAMWORK

Social workers should be part of an interdisciplinary effort for the comprehensive delivery of palliative and end of life services. Social workers shall strive to collaborate with team members and advocate for clients' needs with objectivity and respect to reinforce relationships with providers who have cared for the patient along the continuum of illness.

STANDARD 9. CULTURAL COMPETENCE

Social workers shall have, and shall continue to develop, specialized knowledge and understanding about history, traditions, values, and family systems as they relate to palliative and end of life care within different groups. Social workers shall be knowledgeable about, and act in accordance with, the NASW Standards for Cultural Competence in Social Work Practice (NASW 2001).

STANDARD 10. CONTINUING EDUCATION

Social workers shall assume personal responsibility for their continued professional development in accordance with the NASW Standards for Continuing Professional Education (NASW 2002) and state requirements.

STANDARD 11. SUPERVISION, LEADERSHIP, AND TRAINING

Social workers with expertise in palliative and end of life care should lead educational, supervisory, administrative, and research efforts with individuals, groups, and organizations.

This document was accessed from the National Association of Social Workers Web site. For an in-depth discussion of these standards, see http://www.socialworkers .org/practice/bereavement/standards/standards0504New.pdf.

Team Functioning Scale

Mary-Ann Sontag, Ph.D.
1997

INSTRUCTIONS: PLEASE ANSWER THE FOLLOWING REGARDING YOUR HOSPICE TEAM. Please indicate whether you Strongly agree, Agree, Agree more than disagree, Disagree more than agree, Disagree, or Strongly disagree with the following statements regarding this case:

SA = Strongly agree
A = Agree
AM = Agree more than disagree
DM = Disagree more than agree
D = Disagree
SD = Strongly disagree

	SA	A	AM	DM	D	SD
1. Staff morale is good at my hospice program	6	5	4	3	2	1
2. Our hospice team members communicate effectively with one another.	6	5	4	3	2	1
3. Our hospice team members are supportive of one another.	6	5	4	3	2	1
4. All disciplines on the hospice team are valued.	6	5	4	3	2	1
5. There is trust among members of our hospice team.	6	5	4	3	2	1
6. The expertise of all hospice team members is utilized in the care of patients and families.	6	5	4	3	2	1
7. All hospice team members have input into the care of patients and families.	6	5	4	3	2	1
8. Our hospice team has effective conflict resolution strategies.	6	5	4	3	2	1

NOTE: To score, add up the numbers circled for each item. The higher the score, the better the team functioning.

FROM: D. Reese, M.-A. Sontag, M. Raymer, and J. Richardson. 1998. "National Hospice Social Work Survey: Plan and Preliminary Results." Paper presentation at the National Hospice Organization, Annual Symposium and Exhibition, November, Dallas, Texas.

INDEX

Abortion, 126, 136

Abuse, 131, 199–200, 325

Access, *see* Barrier

Accreditation: CMS standards for, 228, 236, 304–5; in definition of social worker, 32–33; Medicare requirement for, 194; *see also* Qualifications

Accreditation Commission for Health Care, 228

ACHP-SW, *see* Advanced certified hospice and palliative social worker

Active euthanasia, 9–10, 24–25, 107–9

Active listening, 78

Addiction, 94

Adolescent, 96–97, 103, 154

Advanced Certified Hospice and Palliative Social Worker (ACHP-SW), 43, 305

Advance directive, 116; advocacy for, 232; barriers to establishing, 13–14; barriers to implementing, 12–13, 14–15, 307; education about, 12, 13–14; LGBT patients and, 99–100; self-determination through, 24–25; social work and, 13–14, 15; value conflicts and, 14–15

Advocacy: for advance directives, 232; cultural knowledge and, 277; deep ecology theory and, 221; empowerment through, 211, 212; ethics and, 306; for family, 78; in job description, 227–28, 231; for LGBT patients, 176–77; with Medicare, 104; in *NASW Standards*, 211, 334; in NHPCO standards, 228–29; by nurses, 195; for patient care preferences, 4, 78; preparation for, 230; for salary, 304; for SWAT, 302

Affectivity, 192

Affirmative action, 266–67

Afterlife: in history, 1; homosexuality and, 62; hope and, 64–65; in spiritual intervention, 105; in transpersonal mission, 152–53

Age, 96–97, 106–7, 153–54, 289–90

AIDS: pandemic, 235; religion and, 59–60; *see also* HIV

Alcohol: grief and, 87; as suicide risk, 322

Alternative care, 94, 266

Alzheimer's, 282

American Academy of Hospice and Palliative Medicine, 309–10

American Hospital Association, 5

American Medical Student Association, 271–72

Ancillary staff, 22–23, 306

Animal rights, 227

Anticipatory grief: definition of, 63; perceived social support and, 103; in stage theory, 107; in SWAT, 318, 324; transegoic model and, 149

Anticipatory mourning, 177–78

Anti-objective, 227

Anxiety, *see* Death anxiety

Areas of convergence: with African American beliefs, 247–48; with Chinese beliefs, 250–51; finding, 278–79; with Latino/a beliefs, 253; understanding, 275

Ashcroft, John, 10

Asia Pacific Hospice Conference, 235

Assagioli, R., 138, 151

Assisted living, 231–32

Assisted suicide, *see* Euthanasia

Association of Oncology Social Work, 42–43, 309–10

Association of Pediatric Oncology Social
Work, 309–10
Autonomy, *see* Self-determination
Autopsy, 173–74

Baby boomer, 308
Barrier: to administrative care, 196–207;
from administrator, 206–7; DNR order
as, 277–78; to establishing advance
directive, 13–14; in hospice, 254–65;
hospice philosophy as, 290–91; to hospice
use, 16–21, 123; to implementing advance
directive, 12–13, 14–15, 307; language as,
251; *see also* Cultural competence
Beck Depression Inventory Short Form,
109–10
Belief: of children, 155; of client, 129–30, 138,
155; cultural, 275, 280–81, 308; personal,
126–27, 293–94; rituals in, 129–30; *see also*
Afterlife; Areas of convergence; End-of-
life belief
Benedict, Joleen, 128
Bereavement, 5, 8; child, 153–54, 156, 187;
social work and, 31, 91; in social work
education, 41, 309; spirituality and, 156
Berzoff, Joan, 43–44
Besthorn, Fred, 222
Biopsychosocial intervention, *see* Psychosocial
theory
Blame, 64–65
Breathing exercise: appropriateness of, 132–33;
intentional breathing, 148; as transpersonal
intervention, 146; in Trechod method, 296
Bronstein, Laura, 42
Budgeting, 256, 260; *see also* Funding
Bureau of Primary Health Care, 271–72
Burnout: in nurses, 195–96; preventing,
294–95; professional boundary and, 291;
self-care and, 292–95; staff support group
for, 191
Bush, George W., 19, 266–67

Calling, 295
Cancer: family caregivers and, 177–78; family
roles and, 173, 178; prognosis, 17–18,
233; in social work education, 41, 42–43;
suicide risk and, 68–69
Canda, Edward: *Domains of Spirituality*,
128–29; on ethics, 147; on prayer activities,
145

Care: advances in, 1–2, 301; alternative, 94,
266; continuity of, 23, 232–34, 310–11;
continuum of, 20, 23–25, 270, 310–11;
curative, 4, 232–34, 242; evidence-based,
201, 269; in home, 7–8, 281; as obligation,
2, 6–7; options for, 2–3; reform, 235–36;
system, 265–70; traditional, 250, 252,
266; *see also* Futile care; Holistic care;
Interdisciplinary care; Palliative care
Care decision: denial and, 67–68, 112–13;
ethics and, 115–18; perceived social support
and, 68, 103; spirituality and, 67–69;
surrogate, 14
Caregiver: cancer and, 177–78; continuity of
care and, 310–11; satisfaction, 34; *see also*
Primary caregiver
Care preference: ability to communicate,
117; advocacy for, 4, 78; conflicting, 14,
15; cultural group and, 68, 102; data
collection, 254; documenting, 12–13;
patient-physician communication and,
14; sense of control and, 100–1; Social
Work Survey on, 83; in SWAT, 81; *see
also* Advance directive; Environment
preference; Informed consent; Self-
determination
Caring Conversations, 117
Caring distance, 294–95
Caseload, 79, 91–92, 304
Census Bureau, 261
Center for Practical Bioethics, 117
Centers for Medicare and Medicaid Services
(CMS): accreditation standards, 228, 236,
304–5; Conditions of Participation, 236,
237, 303; on cultural competence, 236,
264–65, 269–70; degrading qualifications,
94, 304–5; hospice certification and,
18, 229; on length of hospice stay, 16;
Medicare reimbursement and, 23;
psychosocial assessment and, 80; on
quality of care, 272; *see also* Qualifications
Certification, *see* Accreditation; Qualifications
Certified Hospice and Palliative Social
Worker (CHP-SW), 43, 305
Child: abuse, 131, 199–200; belief system
of, 155; bereavement, 153–54, 156, 187;
communication, 188; DNR order for,
187–88; ego of, 153; family and, 187–89;
Joseph on, 139, 153–54; of LGBT couples,
99; philosophy of life in, 154–55; research

on, 303; social work with, 97; spirituality and, 139–40, 153–57, 187; support group for, 187; transpersonal experiences of, 156; unfinished business and, 154; unity consciousness in, 155–56

CHP-SW, *see* Certified hospice and palliative social worker

Christ, Grace, 41–42

Chronic disease, 176

Chung, K., 92–93

Clark, Elizabeth, 43

Client empowerment, 277–78

Clinical Team Conference, NHPCO, 309–10

Closer to the Light (Morse), 187

CMS, *see* Centers for Medicare and Medicaid Services

Code of Ethics, NASW, 11, 128, 333

Cognitive-behavioral technique, 294–95

Comfort: suite, 234; in SWAT, 318, 324

Communication: ability, 117; child, 188; cultural, 276; developmental discussion process, 307; dysfunctional, 203–4; in interdisciplinary team, 207; in *NASW Standards*, 211; in NHPCO standards, 228–29; Non-Violent Communication, 137–38; patient-physician, 11, 14, 17; racism and, 266, 276–77; through ritual, 248–49; of standards, 305; symbolic, 188; in Team Functioning Scale, 335; *see also* Family-patient communication

Community Conversations on Compassionate Care Program, 13–14

Community Health Accreditation Program, 228

Community outreach, 223–24, 254–62

Compassion fatigue, 191, 291, 292–95; *see also* Burnout

Compassion satisfaction, 292

Competition: between hospice and church, 257; between professions, 195–96

Complicated grief: 911 call and, 179; in stage theory, 107; in SWAT, 318, 324; unfinished business and, 63

Conditions of Participation, CMS, 236, 237, 303

Confidentiality, 179, 199–200, 251

Conflict, *see* Value conflict

Connor, Stephen, 66

Consensus model, 225, 227

Continuity of care, 23, 232–34, 310–11

Continuum of care, 20, 23–25, 270, 310–11

Control, *see* Sense of control

Convergence, *see* Areas of convergence

Coping: perceived social support in, 175; religion as, 244; in SWAT, 325; with transpersonal experiences, 174–75; *see also* Denial as coping

Costs: of futile care, 3; life-sustaining treatment and, 1, 3; pain, 77; in research, 303; as social problem, 24; social work and, 316; in SWAT, 317, 323–24

Council on Social Work Education, 32–33, 42–43, 121

Countertransference, 290–91

Crisis intervention, 91–92, 178

Cruzan, Nancy, 9

Csikai, Ellen, 33, 42

Cultural competence: barriers to, 254–65, 264; CMS on, 236, 264–65, 269–70; education for, 260–61, 274–77; in hospice practice, 277–82; in *NASW Standards*, 334; need for, 261; NHPCO on, 271; organizational, 254–56, 262; personal preparation for, 273–74; PRIME project, 271–72; self-determination and, 273–74, 278; Social Work Policy Institute on, 273; training for, 274–77

Cultural group, 98–99; awareness of, 261–62; care preferences and, 68, 102; communication and, 276; cultural beliefs, 275, 280–81, 308; dissociation and, 226; emotional expressiveness and, 279; euthanasia and, 107–8; familiness and, 171–72; family and, 173–74; home care and, 281; hospice philosophy and, 68, 235; informed consent and, 18, 24, 269, 280; insurance and, 267–68; knowledge about, 260–61, 275; life-sustaining treatment and, 68, 282; pain control and, 281; perceived social support and, 102–4, 106–7, 279–80; practice model and, 279; quality of care and, 241; quality of life and, 282; "race" and, 241; referrals and, 268–69; sense of control and, 101–2; spirituality and, 59–60; trust between, 277

Curative treatment, 4, 232–34, 242

Data collection, *see* Outcomes measurement

Davis, M., 30–31, 46

Death: depression, 109–10; at home, 1, 23–24, 249; in hospice, 2; in hospital, 16, 246; imagery, 143; as life stage, 55, 58–59, 97–98; meaning in, 151; normalization of,

149–50; respectful, 7; taboo on discussing, 130, 245–46, 248–49

Death anxiety, 106–7; age and, 289–90; denial and, 65–66, 105; education and, 44; gender and, 290, 292; HADS and, 105, 109–10; pain and, 105; perceived social support and, 62–63, 102–3; predictors of, 55, 61–63; sense of control and, 106–7; sexual orientation and, 62; spiritual experiences and, 141–42, 143–44; spirituality and, 57, 61–62, 105–6; in SWAT, 317, 322–23; transegoic model and, 149; unity consciousness and, 106–7

Death with Dignity Act, 10

Decision, *see* Care decision

Deep ecology theory, 130–31, 135, 221–22

Democracy, 227

Denial: care decisions and, 67–68, 112–13; cultural beliefs and, 280–81, 308; death anxiety and, 65–66, 105; degrees of, 66; dysfunctional, 112–13; family-patient communication and, 112–13; informed consent and, 20; life-sustaining treatment and, 69; palliative care and, 310–11; pathological, 131; in placement, 15, 16–17, 44–45, 181–82; spirituality and, 113, 131; in stage theory, 112; SWAT and, 37, 44, 318, 325

Denial as coping: death anxiety and, 65–66, 105; for family, 180–81, 185; palliative care and, 21; in practice model, 55, 57; in stage theory, 112

Deontological principle, 11

Department of Health and Human Services, 271–72

Depression, 63–65, 103; Beck Depression Inventory Short Form, 109–10; death, 109–10; HADS and, 105, 109–10; intervention with, 110–11; perceived social support and, 110–11; spirituality and, 110–11; suicide and, 64, 107–9

Developmental discussion process, 307

Diagnostic and Statistical Manual of Mental Disorders (DSM-IV), 105, 110, 120

Differential diagnosis, 105

Dignity, 77, 134–35, 246

Director: perception of social work role, 46, 47–48, 48–49; role of, 262–63; social worker as, 223–24

Disclosure, 179, 199–200

Disenfranchised Grief (Doka), 176

Disidentification, 138

Dissociation, 226

DNR order, *see* Do not resuscitate order

Documentation: of care preferences, 12–13; death taboo and, 130; NASW on, 302; in *NASW Standards*, 334; in outcomes measurement, 32–40; Social Work Policy Institute on, 94; Social Work Survey on, 123

Doka, Kenneth, 176

Domains of Spirituality (Nelson-Becker, Nakashima, and Canda), 128–29

Domestic violence, 131

Domination, 226

Do not resuscitate (DNR) order: accuracy of, 117, 181; as barrier, 277–78; for child, 187–88; denial and, 112; family and, 15; in outcome prediction, 69; Patient Self-Determination Act and, 12

Dramaturgy, 134

Drug use, 59–60, 90, 249–50, 293

DSM-IV, *see* *Diagnostic and Statistical Manual of Mental Disorders*

Duke Summit, 43

Durable power of attorney, 116

Dysfunction: in communication, 203–4; in denial, 112–13; in interdisciplinary team, 203–5, 226

Dysfunctional use of religion, 131–32

Ecofeminism, 226–27

Ecology: deep ecology theory, 130–31, 221–22; transecological perspective, 135

Education: adequacy of, 40–41; about advance directives, 12, 13–14; continuing, 309–10, 334; for cultural competence, 260–61, 274–77; death anxiety and, 44; holistic, 308; about hospice, 17, 230–32, 307; interdisciplinary, 197, 210, 309; language, 309; macro level, 45–46, 118–19; about Medicare Hospice Benefit, 103; mentoring, 118–19; mezzo level, 44–45; micro level, 44; in *NASW Standards*, 334; psychoeducational group, 190; stage theory and, 291; standards and, 305

Ego: of child, 153; deep ecology theory and, 221; disattachment, 150, 151–52; experiential techniques and, 132–33; integrity, 57, 95, 133–34; mindfulness and, 144–45; Psychosocial Inventory of Ego Strength, 95–96; transegoic model, 138,

149–53; in transpersonal theory, 57–58, 97–98, 105–6, 151–52
Elder abuse, 199–200
Emergency room, 268–69
Emotional exhaustion, 191
Emotional expressiveness: cultural group and, 279; gender and, 290
Emotional support, 2, 8, 180
Empathy, 292–93
Empowerment: through advocacy, 211, 212; in community outreach, 257; cultural competence and, 267; deep ecology and, 235; in intake process, 277–78; in NASW Standards, 334; in quality of care, 266; self-determination and, 278–79; of social work, 212; Social Work Survey on, 88; through spirituality, 65; in stage theory, 151–52; suicide and, 101; in U.S. culture, 100
Empty-tank syndrome, 293
End-of-life belief, 242–43, 244; African American, 243–48; Chinese, 248–51; Latino/a, 251–53; in personal preparation, 291–92
End-of-life care, see Care
End-of-Life Care Researchers' Interest Group, 42–43
Environment preference: informed, 21; as social work role, 48; in SWAT, 37, 44
Erikson, Erik, 54–55, 95
Ethics, 6–7; in addressing spirituality, 122, 147–48; advocacy and, 306; care decisions and, 115–18; Code of Ethics, NASW, 11, 128, 333; of euthanasia, 11–12, 24–25, 108–9; experimental design and, 39–40; family and, 179–80; of futile care, 11–12; in NASW Standards, 333; in NHPCO standards, 228–29; policy, 115–16; prayer and, 147–48; value conflicts and, 11–12, 179
Euthanasia: active, 9–10, 24–25, 107–9; continuity of care and, 233; cultural group and, 107–8; ethics of, 11–12, 24–25, 108–9; in Oregon, 10, 64, 67, 100–101; passive, 9, 67; in social work education, 308; see also Suicide
Evidence-based practice, 201, 269
Experiential technique, 132–33
Exploring Differences in the Workplace (Mendez-Russel, Widerson, and Tolbert), 255

Family: advocacy for, 78; assessment, 170–71; child patients and, 187–89; cultural

group and, 173–74, 249; denial as coping for, 180–81, 185; doctor, 1–2; ethics and, 179–80; familiness, 171–72, 189; familism, 251–52; intervention, 171–73; kinship network, 60, 280; perceived social support and, 175–76, 182, 183–84; reconciliation, 136; role, 172–73, 178; sense of control in, 187–88; Social Work Survey on, 181, 182–86; social work with, 179–81, 182–86; spirituality and, 173–75; systems theory, 93, 170–71; value conflict with, 15
Family-patient communication: constricted, 188; denial and, 112–13; informed consent and, 14; in NASW Standards, 81; self-determination and, 179; in social work, 116–17; support groups and, 14
Fatalism, 252
Feminism, 172–73, 225; ecofeminism, 226–27
Field placement, 259–60, 263–65
Financial assistance, 104; see also Insurance
Folk medicine, 250, 252, 266
Forgiveness, 95–96, 137–38, 175–76, 325
For-profit hospice, 22, 267–68
Foundation for Hospices in Sub-Saharan Africa, 235
Framework for Spiritual Assessment, 129
Frankl, Viktor E., 150–51
Friendship, 232, 253, 256; see also Social support, perceived
Funding, 256–58, 260, 263
Futile care, 282; costs of, 3; ethics of, 11–12; hospice as, 281, 282; insurance for, 246–47, 282; willingness to provide, 181, 250

Gardia, Gary, 92
Gay patient, see LGBT patients
Gender: death anxiety and, 290, 292; dissociation and, 226; emotional expressiveness and, 290; family roles and, 172; of primary caregiver, 90; support groups and, 90; see also LGBT patients
Genogram, 129, 132, 133–34
Geriatric Social Work Faculty Scholars Program, 41–42
Goals, 135–36
Goelitz, A., 110
Gratification, 292
Grief: alcohol and, 87; perceived social support and, 103, 110–11; spirituality and, 64–65; of staff, 191; stage theory and,

63–64, 107; suicide and, 107–11; in SWAT, 318, 324; *see also* Anticipatory grief; Complicated grief; Depression
Group intervention, 189, 192; psychoeducational group, 190; support group, 190–92, 193
Guided imagery, 137, 149
Guilt, 118, 136–37, 179

HADS, *see* Hospice Anxiety and Depression Scale
Harlem Palliative Care Network (HPCN), 270
Hartford Foundation, 41–42
Health care, *see* Care
Health Care Financing Administration (HCFA), *see* Centers for Medicare and Medicaid Services
Health care reform, 235–36
Health care system, 265–70
Health insurance, *see* Insurance
Health Maintenance Organization (HMO), 22
Health Symposium, 42–43
Healthy People 2020, 271–72
Heart failure, 1–2
Hierarchical model, 225
High-functioning team, 207–10, 212–13
Hippocratic Oath, 11
HIV: anxiety and, 61; perceived social support and, 176; treatment options for, 19; *see also* AIDS
HMO, *see* Health Maintenance Organization
Holistic care: by high-functioning team, 207; hospice providing, 7–8; by HPCN, 270; Medicare Hospice Benefit and, 5; palliative and, 23; Saunders promoting, 3–4, 49
Holistic education, 308
Home: care in, 7–8, 281; death in, 1, 23–24, 249
Homosexuality, *see* LGBT patients
Hope, 113, 114–15
Hospice: barriers to use of, 16–21, 123, 307; barriers within, 254–65; competition with diverse religious leaders, 257; cultural competence in, 277–82; death in, 2; definition of, 5; education about, 17, 230–32, 307; for-profit, 22, 267–68; as futile care, 281, 282; home care, 7–8, 281; length of stay, 43; model of care, 7–8, 16–17; providing holistic care, 7–8; rural, 22, 236, 305; St. Christopher's, 3–4, 5; value conflicts and, 16

Hospice Anxiety and Depression Scale (HADS), 105, 109–10
Hospice philosophy: active euthanasia and, 108–9; as barrier, 290–91; cultural group and, 68, 235; deep ecology theory and, 222; development of, 1, 3–5, 193–94; Johnson and, 6–7; Medicare Hospice Benefit and, 5–6; perceived social support and, 103; self-determination in, 78; tactical socialization to, 247
Hospital, death in, 16, 246
Hovland-Scafe, C., 42
HPCN, *see* Harlem Palliative Care Network
Human rights, 276

Immigration, 270
Inclusion and Access Toolbox, NHPCO, 255, 263
Individual autonomy, *see* Self-determination
Informed consent: checking, 117; cultural group and, 18, 24, 269, 280; denial and, 20; Medicare Hospice Benefit and, 18; patient-physician communication and, 14; sanctity of life and, 11
Institute of Medicine, 6–7
Insurance: continuum of care and, 311; cultural group and, 267–68; for futile care, 246–47, 282; patients without, 21; policy and, 24, 31–32; in SWAT, 317
Intake process, 277–78
Intentional breathing, 148
Interdisciplinary care: administrative barriers in, 206–7; barriers to, 196–207; of children, 189; commitment to, 202; competition in, 195–96, 196; dysfunctional, 203–5, 226; education for, 197, 210, 309; evaluation of, 211; high-functioning, 207–10; lack of, 17, 20; Medicare Hospice Benefit and, 5; in NASW *Standards*, 334; power differential in, 204–5; role blurring in, 197–98, 207–8; salary and, 205–7; social workers in, 30–32, 79, 91, 193–94; spirituality in, 37–38, 54–55, 121, 124–25; training for, 42, 45; transdisciplinary team, 125; trust in, 335; understanding in, 196–97; value conflicts in, 199–201; *see also* High-functioning team; Holistic care
Interdisciplinary journal, 304
Interpreter, 81, 251, 260

Johnson, Robert Wood, 6–7

Joint Commission, 228
Joseph, M. Vincentia: on childhood, 139, 153–54, 155; on religion, 120
Journal: access to, 230, 303; child communicating through, 188; finding meaning through, 134–35; interdisciplinary, 304; in self-care, 230; as social work intervention, 90; spiritual, 138; as transpersonal intervention, 146
Journal of Social Work in End-of-Life and Palliative Care, 43–44, 303

Kinship network, 60, 280
Kovacs, Pamela J., 42
Kramer, Betty J., 42
Kubler-Ross, Elisabeth, 3–4, 5, 23–24, 194
Kubler-Ross stages of grief: confrontation with mortality in, 59; denial in, 112; grief and, 63–64, 107; in personal preparation, 291–92; projection of anger on staff, 191
Kulys, Regina, 30–31, 46

Language: as barrier to care, 251; in community outreach, 255–56, 257–58; education, 309; funding and, 260; literacy, 278–79; in *NASW Standards*, 81; quality of care and, 266–67; slavery and, 243–44
Last Acts, 271
Lesbian patient, *see* LGBT patients
Level of consciousness, 57–58
LGBT (lesbian, gay, bisexual, and transgendered) patients: advance directives and, 99–100; advocacy for, 176–77; as AIDS risk, 59–60; children of, 99; cultural competence and, 261; familiness and, 171–72; perceived social support and, 99–100; religion and, 59–60, 62
Liability, 13
Life review, 133–34, 188
Life stage: death as, 55, 58–59; in *NASW Standards* assessment, 81
Life-sustaining treatment: cultural group and, 68, 282; denial and, 69; medical advances and, 1–2; refusal of, 11, 77, 179; religion and, 18–19; in value conflicts, 199
Literacy, 279
Living will, 12, 116
Logotherapy, 150–51

Make-A-Wish Foundation, 135–36

Mandated reporter, 199–200
Maslow, Abraham, 93–94, 119–20, 151
Medicaid, 1, 16, 104; *see also* Centers for Medicare and Medicaid Services
Medical advances, 1–2, 301
Medical care, *see* Care
Medical power of attorney, 12
Medicare, 1; advocacy with, 104; certification, 228; continuum of care and, 20; eligibility, 234; limiting hospice use, 16–18; reimbursement, 23, 234, 311; social work requirement, 194; SWAT and, 79; *see also* Centers for Medicare and Medicaid Services
Medicare Hospice Benefit: continuity of care and, 310; education about, 103; hospice philosophy and, 5–6; informed consent and, 18; reimbursement rate, 22
Meditation: compassion fatigue and, 295, 296–97; finding meaning through, 134–35; guided imagery, 137, 149; for pain management, 94; relaxation in, 148; techniques, 148–49; transcendence and, 296; as transpersonal technique, 105–6, 146; Trechod method of, 296; Vipassana, 296
Mendez-Russel, A., 255
Mentoring, 118–19
Mindfulness, 144, 148
Miracle, 245, 266
Mission of organization, 255
Mixed methods study, 303
Morse, M., 187
Mother Teresa, 127

Nakashima, M., 128–29
NASW, *see* National Association of Social Workers
NASW Standards for Palliative and End-of-Life Care, 333–34; assessment, 80–81, 333; care access in, 231; Clark developing, 43; role of social worker in, 211–13; social work supervision in, 45, 224, 334
National Association of Social Workers (NASW): certification, 42–43; *Code of Ethics*, 11, 128, 333; credentials, 43, 305; definitions by, 4–5; on documentation, 302; in policy practice, 236–37; recommendations by, 229–30
National Council of Hospice and Palliative Professionals (NCHPP), 32–33, 36–37, 43

National Hospice and Palliative Care Organization (NHPCO): certification, 43; Clinical Team Conference, 309–10; on community outreach, 223–24, 255–56, 258; in continuing education, 309–10; on continuity of care, 233–34; on continuum of care, 23; on cultural competence, 271; guidelines, 35; on hospice movement growth, 6; *Inclusion and Access Toolbox*, 255, 263; Pathway Document, 77, 79; in policy practice, 236–37; *Self-Assessment Checklist for Personnel Providing Primary Health Care Services*, 255, 263; Spiritual Caregiver Section, 124–25; standards, 228–29; *see also* Social Worker Section

National Hospice Social Work Survey: bereavement in, 91; caseloads in, 79; documentation in, 123; family intervention in, 181, 182–86; pain cost in, 77; practice models in, 49–50; qualifications in, 35; social support intervention in, 103; social work impact in, 33, 34–36, 206–7; social work interventions in, 82, 83–89, 90; social work supervision in, 223; spirituality in, 82, 100, 121, 133; team functioning in, 196; transpersonal intervention in, 138

National Model Performance Improvement Project, 38–39

National Quality Forum, 272

National Social Work Summit on End-of-Life and Palliative Care, 41–42, 302

NCHPP, *see* National Council of Hospice and Palliative Professionals

Nelson-Becker, H., 128–29

NHPCO, *see* National Hospice and Palliative Care Organization

911 call: complicated grief and, 179; cultural competence and, 278; dysfunctional denial and, 112; value conflict and, 15

Non-Violent Communication, 137–38

Nurse: advocacy by, 195; burnout, 195–96; in hospice development, 193–94; hospice liaison, 311; on-call responsibilities of, 90–91, 195; outcomes measurement and, 195; in power differentials, 204; role, 46, 47–48, 48–49; social workers and, 46, 48, 195–96; utilization, 30–32

Nursing home, 7–8, 282

Objectification, 226

On-call responsibility, 90–91, 195

Oncology, *see* Cancer

On Death and Dying (Kubler-Ross), 5

Online support group, 190–91

Oppression, 222, 227, 265, 276–77

Oregon, 10, 64, 67, 100–1

Organ donation, 136, 290, 292

Organizational cultural competence, 254–56, 262

Otis-Green, Shirley, 80

Outcomes measurement, 8, 69–70; documentation in, 32–40; nursing and, 195; social work education and, 44

Outreach, 223–24, 254–62

Oxford Textbook of Palliative Social Work, 43–44

Oxytocin, 62–63

Pacourek, L., 42

Pain control: alternative, 77, 94; in children, 189; cost, 77; cultural group and, 281; death anxiety and, 105; patients without, 2; in quality of life, 77; refusal of, 246, 249–50; transcendence and, 93–94

Paired samples t-test, 80

Palliative care, 2; continuity of care and, 232–34; denial and, 310–11; guilt and, 118; holistic and, 23; informing public about, 230–32, 301; NASW on, 4–5; as separate field, 19–20; in value conflict, 15; *see also* Hospice

PAR, *see* Participatory action research

Parent, 99, 187–89; *see also* Child; Family

Participatory action research (PAR), 237, 281

Passive euthanasia, 9, 67

Path analysis, 55, 56, 69

Pathway Document, NHPCO, 77, 79–80

Patient Bill of Rights, 5, 11

Patient-family communication; *see* Family-patient communication

Patient-physician communication, 11, 14, 17

Patient Self-Determination Act, 11, 12–13, 100–1, 179

Pay, *see* Salary

PDIA, *see* Project on Death in America

Pediatrics, *see* Child

Perceived social support, *see* Social support, perceived

Perls, Fritz, 146

Personal preparation, 291; for cultural competence, 273–74; self-knowledge in, 289–91; stage theory in, 291–92

Philosophy of life, 57, 59, 133–38; in children, 154–55; death anxiety and, 61–62; end-of-life care and, 67; in psychosocial development, 95; in social work, 120–21, 225, 295

Physician-patient communication, 11, 14, 17

Pigeonholing, 201

Play therapy, 187

Pluralism, 227

Policy: ethics, 115–16; insurance and, 24, 31–32; public, 235, 236–37; visiting, 171

Porter, Theresa, 155

Post-traumatic stress disorder, 187

Power differential, 204–5

Power of attorney, 12, 116

Practice model, 55, 56, 57; cultural group and, 279; Social Work Survey on, 49–50

Prayer: activities, 145, 146; ethics and, 147–48; respecting, 278–79

Preference, see Care preference

Primary caregiver, 16, 18; gender of, 90; SWAT and, 321, 325

PRIME project, see Promoting, Reinforcing, and Improving Medical Education project

Privacy, 266; see also Confidentiality

Privilege: racial, 261–62; therapeutic, 11

Process evaluation, 39

Professional boundary, 291, 293, 296–97

Profit, 224, 226–27; for-profit hospice, 22, 267–68

Prognosis: cancer, 17–18, 233; informing patients of, 2–3, 248–49, 280; terminal, 2, 16–18, 24, 310–11; uncertain, 233

Project on Death in America (PDIA), 33, 41–42, 43

Promoting, Reinforcing, and Improving Medical Education (PRIME) project, 271–72

Proselytization, 122, 224

Psychoeducational group, 190

Psychosis, 133, 147

Psychosocial assessment, 79–80, 91–92, 187

Psychosocial Inventory of Ego Strength, 95–96

Psychosocial Pain Assessment Form, 80

Psychosocial theory: age in, 289–90; development systems, 54–55; evidence-based practice and, 201; knowledge of, 333;

Psychosocial Inventory of Ego Strength, 95–96; in self-care, 294–95; in social work education, 308; in SWAT, 316

Psychosynthesis, 138, 151

Public policy, 235, 236–37

QAPI, see Quality Assessment and Performance Improvement

Qualifications, 43; adequacy of, 40–41; CMS degrading, 94, 304–5; salary and, 236, 305; Social Work Survey on, 35; see also Accreditation

Quality Assessment and Performance Improvement (QAPI), 229

Quality of care: cultural group and, 241; improving, 234; language and, 266–67; National Quality Forum on, 272

Quality of life, 2–3, 76–77; cultural group and, 282; in high-functioning team, 209; indicators, 6–7; over length of life, 116; in value conflicts, 199

Quinlan, Karen Ann, 9

Race, 241; see also Cultural group

Rapid Response Program, 92

Raymer, Mary, 33, 42

Reconciliation, 136

Recycling, 227

Reese, Dona, 46, 47–48, 48–49

Relaxation: in meditation, 148; as pain control, 77, 94; as transpersonal technique, 105–6, 146

Religion, see Spirituality

Republican right, 18–19

Research, 302–4

Respect: in Latino/a culture, 252; respectful death, 7

Resuscitation, 1–2, 2–3, 11–15; see also Do not resuscitate order

Right to die, 19, 20–21

Rituals: authorization for, 147–48; in client beliefs, 129–30; communication through, 248–49; therapeutic, 135, 144; as transpersonal technique, 146

Robert Wood Johnson Foundation, 271

Rogers, Carl, 92–93

Roles: blurring, 197–98, 207–8; captivity, 149, 150; director, 223–24; family, 172–73, 178; of hospice director, 262–63; nurse, 46, 47–48, 48–49; see also Social work role

Rosenberg, Marshall, 137–38
Rules exercise, 203
Rural hospice, 22, 236, 305

Safety, 77, 317, 324
Salary: advocacy for, 304; in interdisciplinary team, 205–7; qualifications and, 236, 305
Saunders, Cicely: interdisciplinary background of, 49, 193–94; promoting holistic care, 3–4, 49; on spiritual work, 120
Scapegoating, 203, 207–8
Schiavo, Terri, 19
Schools of Social Work, 309–10
Schumacher, Don, 268
Self-Assessment Checklist for Personnel Providing Primary Health Care Services, NHPCO, 255, 263
Self-care, 292–97
Self-determination: through advance directive, 24–25; cultural competence and, 273–74, 278–79; family and, 179; in hospice philosophy, 78; in NASW *Standards*, 333
Self-knowledge, 127, 275; in personal preparation, 289–91; value conflict and, 290–91
Self-transcendence, *see* Transcendence
Sense of control, 7, 100–2; in adolescents, 96–97; death anxiety and, 106–7; in parents, 187–88; in self-care, 294; spirituality and, 65; *see also* Euthanasia
Sexuality, 175–76
Sexual orientation, *see* LGBT patients
Shallow ecology, 221
Shame, 258–59
Silverman, Phyllis, 43–44
Sin, 136–37
Singer, Peter A., 7
Slavery, 243–44, 265
Smith, Elizabeth, 98, 152–53; *see also* Transegoic model
Social action, 222, 273–74
Socialization: into racism, 261–62; tactical, 247
Social security, 104
Social support, perceived: care decisions and, 68, 103; in coping, 175; cultural group and, 102–4, 106–7, 279–80; death anxiety and, 62–63, 102–3; depression and, 110–11; family and, 175–76, 182, 183–84; grief

and, 103, 110–11; HIV and, 176; hospice philosophy and, 103; LGBT patients and, 99–100; in NASW *Standards* assessment, 81; oxytocin and, 62–63; in self-care, 294; by social workers, 82, 103; spirituality and, 60–61; in SWAT, 317, 323
Social work: advance directives and, 13–14, 15; assertiveness in, 202; bereavement counseling in, 31, 91; caseloads in, 79, 91–92, 304; commitment in, 202; countertransference in, 290; definition of, 32–33; determining need for, 31; directive, 92–93; in director role, 223–24; empowering, 212; evidence-based, 94; with family, 179–81, 182–86; family-patient communication in, 116–17; final goals and, 135–36; financial assistance and, 104; impact of, 33, 34–36, 315–16; in interdisciplinary care, 30–32, 79, 91, 193–94; Medicare requirement for, 194; on-call responsibilities in, 90–91; organization intervention in, 227–28; philosophy of life in, 120–21, 225, 295; social support as, 82, 103; as spiritual calling, 295; utilization of, 30–32, 39, 193–94, 301; *see also* Spirituality in social work
Social Work Acuity Scale for Hospice (SWASH), 35
Social Work Assessment Tool (SWAT): advocacy for, 302; care preferences in, 81; case example, 319–20; comfort issues in, 318, 324; complicated anticipatory grief in, 318, 324; coping in, 325; data analysis, 80, 321; death anxiety in, 317, 322–23; denial and, 37, 44, 318, 325; environment preference in, 37, 44; in family assessment, 170–71; financial issues in, 317, 323–24; Medicare and, 79; perceived social support in, 317, 323; practice example, 327–28; primary caregiver and, 321, 325; psychosocial issues in, 316; safety issues in, 317, 324; spiritual issues in, 316, 318, 322, 325; SWAT Handbook, 315–29; thoughts of suicide in, 317, 322
Social work education: bereavement in, 41, 309; cancer in, 41, 42–43; Council on Social Work Education, 32–33, 42–43, 121; outcomes measurement and, 44; psychosocial theory in, 308; spirituality in, 308; suicide in, 308

Social Worker Section, NHPCO, 36–37, 43, 124–25
Social Work in Hospice and Palliative Care Network, 303
Social Work Leadership Development Awards, 41–42
Social Work Outcomes Task Force, 33, 36–37, 315
Social Work Policy Institute, 82, 229–30; on cultural competence, 273; on documentation, 94
Social work role, 304–6; director perception of, 46, 47–48, 48–49; lack of understanding of social work role by team, 194–95; NASW Standards on, 211–13; nurses and, 46, 48, 195–96
Social work supervision: in NASW Standards, 45, 224, 334; qualifications and, 304–5; Social Work Survey on, 223; support group and, 191–92
Social Work Survey, see National Hospice Social Work Survey
Society for Social Work and Research, 42–43
Society for Social Work Leadership in Health Care, 43
Society for Spirituality and Social Work, 147–48
Solution focus, 78, 90
Sontag, M., 203
Spiritual Caregiver Section, NHPCO, 124–25
Spirituality: AIDS and, 59–60; as ancillary, 171; autopsy and, 173–74; bereavement and, 156; calling, 295; childhood and, 139–40, 153–57, 187; confidentiality and, 199–200; confrontation with mortality and, 58–59, 76, 97–98, 106–7; as coping, 244; cultural group and, 59–60; death anxiety and, 61–62, 106–7; denial and, 113; depression and, 110–11; empowerment through, 65; and end-of-life care decisions, 67–69; family and, 173–75, 183; forgiveness and, 95–96; functional and dysfunctional use of religion, 131–32; grief and, 64–65; guilt and, 136–37; hope and, 113, 114–15; in hospice care model, 7–8, 16–17; hospice competing with diverse religious leaders, 257; in interdisciplinary care, 37–38, 54–55, 121, 124–25; Joseph on, 120; journaling and, 138; life-sustaining treatment and, 18–19; medical advances

and, 2; in NASW Standards assessment, 81; perceived social support and, 60–61; predictors of, 57–60; religious diversity, 259; on sanctity of life, 11, 18–19, 68; in self-care, 295–97; sense of control and, 65; sexual orientation and, 59–60, 62; in social work education, 308; Social Work Survey on, 82, 100, 121, 133; spiritual experiences, 141–44; in SWAT, 316, 318, 322, 325; therapeutic use of, 144–45; transcendence and, 57; transpersonal theory and, 98; value conflicts and, 11, 15–16, 126–27; see also Afterlife; Belief; Prayer
Spirituality in social work, 119–20, 156–57; afterlife in, 105; assessment, 128–32; client beliefs and, 129–30, 138, 155; current practice with, 120–24; of employees, 224–28; ethics in, 122, 147–48; importance of, 48–49; interdisciplinary competition and, 196; issues in, 130–31, 132–33; personal beliefs and, 126–27, 293–94; referral, 125–26; responsibility for, 37–38; Saunders on, 120; training for, 82, 100, 121–23; unfinished business and, 135; way of being and, 127–28
Spiritual Shower, 140, 141
Spiritual system, 54–55
St. Christopher's Hospice, 3–4, 5
Staff: ancillary, 22–23, 306; applicant diversity, 258–60, 265; support groups, 191–92, 193
Standards for Palliative and End-of-Life Care, see NASW Standards for Palliative and End-of-Life Care
Statistical analysis, 80
Stereotype, 205–6, 260
Stoicism, 249–50, 252, 279
Struggle, 246
Substance abuse, 59–60, 90, 249–50, 293; see also Alcohol
Suicide: alcohol and, 322; cancer and, 68–69; depression and, 64, 107–9; empowerment and, 101; grief and, 107–11; intervention, 111; in SWAT, 317, 322; unity consciousness and, 67; see also Euthanasia
Support group, 175–76; for adolescents, 103; for children, 187; family-patient communication and, 14; gender and, 90; in group intervention, 190–92, 193; membership restrictions, 190; online, 190–91; in self-care, 294; staff, 191–92, 193

Supreme Court, 9, 10, 19
Surgery, 1–2, 2–3
Surrogate decision making, 14
SWASH, *see* Social Work Acuity Scale for Hospice
SWAT, *see* Social Work Assessment Tool
Swett, Laura, 137, 140, 141
Syphilis, 265
Systems theory, 93, 170–71, 201, 221

Tactical socialization, 247
Targeting, 255
Tax Equity and Fiscal Responsibility Act, 5
Team, *see* High-functioning team; Interdisciplinary care
Team Functioning Scale, 35, 209, 211, 335–36
Teenager, *see* Adolescent
Terminal prognosis, 2, 16–18, 24, 310–11
Theory: deep ecology theory, 130–31, 221–22; differences in, 201–2; systems theory, 93, 170–71, 201, 221; white racial identity development theory, 261–62; *see also* Kubler-Ross stages of grief; Psychosocial theory; Transpersonal theory
Therapeutic privilege, 11
Tibetan Book of the Dead, 144
Tolbert, A-S., 255
Toolbox, see Inclusion and Access Toolbox
Touch therapy, 188
Traditional medicine, 250, 252, 266
Transcendence, 57, 144–45, 152–53; Maslow on, 93–94, 119–20; meditation and, 296; in self-care, 295–96
Transdisciplinary team, 125
Transegoic model, 138, 149–53
Transegoic stage, *see* Transpersonal theory
Transition care, 232–34
Translation, 81, 251, 260
Transpersonal experience, 140–44, 174–75
Transpersonal intervention, 145, 146
Transpersonal mission, 133–34, 152–53
Transpersonal self, 152

Transpersonal technique, 105–6, 146
Transpersonal theory, 57–58; children and, 156; confrontation with mortality in, 97–98; ego in, 57–58, 97–98, 105–6, 151–52; meditation in, 105–6, 146; in self-care, 295–96
Treatment, *see* Care
Trechod meditation, 296
Trust: between cultural groups, 277; in interdisciplinary team, 335
Turf battle, *see* Interdisciplinary care
Tuskegee study, 265

Uncertain prognosis, 233
Unfinished business: children and, 154; complicated grief and, 63; death anxiety and, 57, 61–62; social work and, 135
Unity consciousness, 139–40; in children, 155–56; death anxiety and, 106–7; deep ecology theory and, 221; in disidentification, 152; Maslow on, 119–20; suicide and, 67; in transpersonal theory, 57–58
U.S. Religious Landscape Survey, 244
Utilitarian principle, 11–12

Value conflict: advance directives and, 14–15; ethics and, 11–12, 179; with family, 15; hospice use and, 16; in interdisciplinary team, 199–201; 911 call and, 15; religion and, 11, 15–16, 126–27; self-knowledge and, 290–91
Vipassana meditation, 296
Visiting policy, 171
Volunteer, 8, 18, 231

Way of being, 127–28
Weisman, 66, 111–12
White racial identity development theory, 261–62
Widerson, E., 255
World Health Organization, 63, 233

Young adult, 96

CPSIA information can be obtained
at www.ICGtesting.com
Printed in the USA
JSHW011650010523
41096JS00007B/681